The politics of British arms sales
since 1964

MANCHESTER
UNIVERSITY PRESS

For Jamie and Hayley

The politics
of British arms sales
since 1964

'To secure our rightful share'

Mark Phythian

Manchester University Press
Manchester and New York

distributed exclusively in the USA by St. Martin's Press

Published by Manchester University Press
Oxford Road, Manchester M13 9NR, UK
and Room 400, 175 Fifth Avenue, New York, NY 10010, USA
http://www.man.ac.uk/mup

Distributed exclusively in the USA by
St. Martin's Press, Inc., 175 Fifth Avenue, New York,
NY 10010, USA

Distributed exclusively in Canada by
UBC Press, University of British Columbia, 2029 West Mall,
Vancouver, BC, Canada V6T 1Z2

British Library Cataloguing-in-Publication Data
A catalogue record for this book is available from the British Library

Library of Congress Cataloging-in-Publication Data applied for

ISBN 0 7190 5196 7 *hardback*
     0 7190 5907 0 *paperback*

First published 2000

09 08 07 06 05 04 03 02 01 00   10 9 8 7 6 5 4 3 2 1

Typeset in Sabon with Gill Sans
by Action Publishing Technology Limited, Gloucester
Printed in Great Britain
by Biddles Ltd, Guildford and King's Lynn

Contents

Tables and figures

Tables

Figures

Preface

Today, by most measures, Britain is second only to the US among the world's leading arms suppliers. However, throughout the period since 1964, when the incoming Wilson government moved to commercialise the arms export drive, Britain's prominent role in the international arms trade has proved increasingly controversial. Measured in terms of orders won and jobs apparently secured, it has been a success story. Yet, as this study shows, this vision of success needs to be heavily qualified. British arms sales success has not been without cost.

In considering the politics of British arms sales during this period, a number of themes emerge: the role of arms sales in foreign policy – in cementing relationships and projecting British influence against a backdrop of gradual decline; the relationship between arms sales and human rights in policy formulation; the corrupting impact of the commission culture in arms sales; the 'Labour dilemma' – how the Labour Party on assuming office has dealt with the delicate arms sales cases it has faced (South Africa in 1964, Chile in 1974, and Indonesia in 1997); the related question of the degree to which party impacts on the course of British arms sales; the importance of the role of the US in facilitating British arms sales in the 1960s and aiding the British arms industry by default in the 1970s and 1980s owing to the immobilising effect of the pro-Israeli lobby in Congress. While this study resists the temptation to look into the future, it is clear that the absence of US competition or a US alternative (for whatever reason) has been perhaps the most significant factor in explaining the UK's arms export success. However, the changed conditions of the post-1990 international environment mean that the UK can no longer count on this, and the impact of unrestrained US competition is beginning to be felt. Outside the Middle East, however, the UK arms industry has continued to profit from congressional limitations on the US arms export drive.

It is clearly not possible in a study of this size to account for every UK arms sale made since 1964. The detailed cases included here have been selected because of their usefulness in highlighting one or more of the themes set out above. In doing so for the period up to 1969 I have drawn heavily on the files of the Public Record Office. Thereafter the specialist press increases in scope and sophistication, media reporting becomes more detailed, and Parliament shows increased interest, all of which produce valuable sources of information. Relatively few files on arms sales issues remain closed at the PRO beyond the thirty-year closure period, allowing a full picture to be constructed. However, more than once in writing this book it has occurred to me that the diligent researcher who goes to the PRO in the year 2025 to begin writing the definitive account of the arms sales politics of the 1980s and 1990s is not going to enjoy such good fortune. For the very reasons set out here, it is unlikely that all the relevant files on arms sales to Iran, Iraq, Jordan, Saudi Arabia, Oman, Indonesia, Malaysia and Chile, and so on, will be opened after just thirty years.

I would like to thank a number of people who have helped greatly in the writing of this book. Firstly, I would like to thank those who agreed to be interviewed or agreed to discuss their recollections with me, and who helped clarify the official record and my thinking. In this respect I would like to thank Frank Brenchley, Michael Brown, the late Lord Caldecote, John Christie, the late Alan Clark, MP, K. W. Cotterill, Donald Hamley, Ken Purchase, MP, Ted Rowlands, MP, A. W. Stephens and Sir Michael Weir.

In addition, in the course of following the subject I have incurred a number of debts, some specific to this book, others long-standing. In particular, I would like to thank everyone at CAAT, Kevin Cahill, John Callaghan, Peter Carey, Neil Cooper, Tam Dalyell, MP, Alan Doig, Stephen Dorril, Martin Durham, Gerald James, Walter Little, Davina Miller, Robin Robison, Paul Rogers, Mark Watts and Pieter Wezeman at SIPRI. None of the above is responsible for any errors of fact or interpretation. I would also like to thank Nicola Viinikka, Pippa Kenyon and everyone involved at MUP.

The book could not have been written without the generous financial assistance of the Leverhulme Trust, which is supporting a research project on British arms sales policy since 1945 of which this volume forms a part.

Special thanks are due to Jonathan Jardine, a first-rate research assistant destined for greater things still, for his diligent and hard work in a variety of libraries and archives.

Finally, I would like to thank Anne-Marie, Jamie and Hayley for making it worth while.

M.P.

Acronyms and abbreviations

ACDA	Arms Control and Disarmament Agency (US)
ADV	air defence variant
AEDC	Aerospace Engineering Design Corporation
AEI	Associated Electrical Industries
ASEAN	Association of South East Asian Nations
ATP	aid and trade provision
AWACS	airborne warning and control system
AWP	Arms Working Party
BA	British Airways
BAC	British Aircraft Corporation
BAe	British Aerospace
b/d	barrels per day
BAEE	British Army Equipment Exhibition
BCC	British Communications Corporation
BP	British Petroleum Company
CACSA	Committee Against Corruption in Saudi Arabia
C&AG	Comptroller and Auditor General
CBI	Confederation of British Industry
CENTO	Central Treaty Organisation
CIA	Central Intelligence Agency (US)
COCOM	Co-ordinating Committee for Multilateral Export Controls
DESO	Defence Export Services Organisation
DESS	Defence Export Services Secretariat
DFID	Department For International Development
DIS	Defence Intelligence Staff
DMA	Defence Manufacturers' Association
DSO	Defence Sales Organisation
DTI	Department of Trade and Industry
DUS (Pol.)	Deputy Under-Secretary (Political)
EC	European Community

ECGD	Export Credit Guarantee Department
ECO	Export Control Organisation
EEC	European Economic Organisation
EG(C)O	Export of Goods (Control) Order
ELA	Export Licence Application
ELU	Export Licensing Unit
EU	European Union
FAC	Foreign Affairs Committee
FCO	Foreign and Commonwealth Office
FMAE	Fabricas y Maestranzas del Ejercito
FO	Foreign Office
GCC	Gulf Co-operation Council
GCHQ	Government Communications Headquarters
GDP	gross domestic product
HDES	Head of Defence Export Services
HMG	His/Her Majesty's Government
IAEA	International Atomic Energy Authority
ICCPR	International Covenant on Civil and Political Rights
IDC	International Development Committee
IDS	interdict/strike version
ILN	International Logistics Negotiations (US)
INS	inertial navigation system
IMS	International Military Services
IT	information technology
J.D.W.	*Jane's Defence Weekly*
JIC	Joint Intelligence Committee
MAS	Malaysian Airlines System
MDAP	Mutual Defense Assistance Program (US)
MoA	Ministry of Aviation
ML	Military List
MoD	Ministry of Defence
MP	Member of Parliament
MTCR	Missile Technology Control Regime
MTS	Millbank Technical Services
NAO	National Audit Office
NATO	North Atlantic Treaty Organisation
NEACC	Near East Arms Co-ordinating Committee
NGO	non-governmental organisation
NPD	Non-proliferation Treaty
OBE	Order of the British Empire
ODA	Overseas Development Administration
OPEC	Organisation of Petroleum Exporting Countries
OPD	Overseas and Defence Policy Committee (of the Cabinet)
OSCE	Organisation for Security and Co-operation in Europe

PAC	Public Accounts Committee
P5	five permanent members of the UN Security Council
PKI	Partai Komunis Indonesia
PL	Political List
PLO	Palestine Liberation Organisation
PPS	Principal Private Secretary
RAF	Royal Air Force
REU	Restricted Enforcement Unit
RN	Royal Navy
RNEE	Royal Navy Equipment Exhibition
RO	Royal Ordnance
RSAF	Royal Saudi Air Force
SAS	Special Air Service
SBAC	Society of British Aerospace Constructors
SE(M)C	Strategic Exports (Ministerial) Committee
SE(O)C	Strategic Exports (Official) Committee
SFCN	Société Française des Constructions Navales
SIGINT	signals intelligence
SIPRI	Stockholm International Peace Research Institute
STU	Sensitive Technologies Unit
SXWP	Security Export Controls Working Party
Tapol	Indonesian human rights campaign
TISC	Trade and Industry Select Committee
UAE	United Arab Emirates
UAR	United Arab Republic
UK	United Kingdom of Great Britain and Northern Ireland
UN	United Nations
UNIKOM	UN Iraq–Kuwait Observer Mission
UNSCOM	UN Special Commission (on Iraq)
USSR	Union of Socialist Soviet Republics
VIP	very important person

1

British arms exports, 1964–99: an overview

In the post-1964 period, British arms sales policy has been influenced by international developments, US policy and preferences, the economic interests at stake, the evolution of military technology, the shifting importance of human rights issues, and developments in British politics. The tension at its heart was set out by Defence Secretary Denis Healey in 1966, at the outset of the government's commercialisation drive. 'While the Government attach the highest importance to making progress in the field of arms control and disarmament,' Healey explained, 'we must also take what practical steps we can to ensure that this country does not fail to secure its rightful share of this valuable commercial market.'[1] Just what constituted Britain's 'rightful' share was defined by Britain's imperial past, the influence it had once wielded, and the role based on this that it aspired to play, even at that stage of the Cold War.

Before the *débâcle* in Vietnam and the rise in Third World demand, sales issues (South Africa apart) were a relatively low-key matter. In the 1970s, in light of the South African and Chilean cases, they became much more charged, with the Labour left pushing harder for restraint and regulation. Although it was under Labour governments that some of the most significant steps in commercialising British arms sales occurred – for example, via the creation of the Defence Sales Organisation (DSO) in the 1960s and the establishment of the British Army and Royal Navy Equipment Exhibitions in the 1970s (BAEE/RNEE) – in the 1980s controls were relaxed under successive Conservative governments to an unprecedented degree, as the approach recommended in the Stokes Report found a new champion, with Mrs Thatcher herself openly touting for sales.

In his 1965 report, Donald Stokes had enjoined the Ministry of Defence (MoD) to ensure that its future requirements were compatible with export industry's needs. Although there were some notable successes in this regard – the outstanding example is the Hawk 'trainer' aircraft – it was an injunction which in 1980 Mrs Thatcher felt compelled to restate. Eric

Beverley of British Aerospace (BAe) interpreted it as the beginning of an era of close government–industry co-operation, noting that: 'regrettably in the past this has not always been so. But it is the hope of the British aerospace industry that at last we have a government which understands the important contribution that aerospace can make, not only to the economics and the employment of the country as a whole, but also to its foreign policy.'[2]

In the face of a contracting post-Cold War market, the Major government cemented this approach – with considerable success when measured in terms of the value of orders secured, but not without considerable cost. Under 'New' Labour, the situation has continued to evolve in a somewhat contradictory manner. On the one hand, Western states demand selective restrictions on the trade with the developing world, particularly in the Middle East, but, on the other, sell arms to those countries as and whenever possible, and in fierce competition with each other.

Although economic explanations of Britain's heavy involvement in the international arms trade have traditionally been considered persuasive, the politics of British arms sales need to be considered beyond the issue of employment, and take in more fully their contribution to UK foreign and security policies. In the post-1945 world, both US and UK approaches to these issues were defined by the need to maintain the existing beneficial configuration of power and influence in the international system. Arms sales played a key role in cementing influence and securing the continuation of the existing order. For states that aspired to play a world role and wield influence on the global stage, arms sales were an important mechanism. For post-war Britain, as much as for Cold War-era America and the Soviet Union, arms sales were, in Andrew J. Pierre's memorable phrase, 'foreign policy writ large', a gateway to the continued exercise of political influence.[3]

Britain and the international arms market since 1945

Phase one: 1945–65

Prior to World War II, Britain, the workshop of the world, met all its arms requirements from domestic production. However, the costs of re-equipping after the war were high because of the limited production runs involved. Export orders were sought to extend production and so reduce unit costs. At the same time, although Britain had emerged victorious from the war, economic trend indicators suggested that colonial possessions would soon become imperial burdens, with the military obligations of victory only adding to the strain. Politically, Britain still thought of itself as a 'great power' – undefeated in war, the empire still a reality, one of the 'Big Three' alongside the US and the USSR at the war's end. The reality was that Britain could no longer afford to maintain its pre-war commitments. Economically it was not one of the 'Big Three', despite its continuing 'great-power complex'.[4] However, its leading role in the post-war international arms market was one highly visible way in which it could still play a prominent global role, shape regional security configurations, retain a highly developed military industrial base, and at the same time earn valuable foreign currency to help finance the obligations that sustaining the great-power delusion entailed.

In terms of the market, the post-1945 decolonisation process had created a large number of new states amongst whom the acquisition of modern armaments was as much a symbol of national virility as a matter of security. The supply of arms was dominated by the US and UK, as it would be until the mid-1950s, when France re-emerged as an arms exporter and the USSR agreed to supply Soviet arms outside the Eastern bloc for the first time, heightening regional tensions and accelerating arms races as weapons became the leading currency of Cold War competition. The most important case was that of Egypt, where the USSR supplied around 150 MiG fighter aircraft during 1955 and 1956. Up to this point, Britain had supplied 95 per cent of all jet aircraft delivered to the Middle East, but in the following decade its market share fell to below 10 per cent.[5] The same pattern applied in South East Asia. Up to 1955 Britain supplied nearly all the jet aircraft sold to India, Pakistan, Australia and New Zealand. In the following decade, Britain was displaced by the US and USSR, while France made important inroads, for example, selling to India.

In the 1945–55 period, Britain also sold 51 per cent of all warships delivered (with the US selling 40 per cent). All but three of these 47 ships were ex-Royal Navy (RN). In the following decade it still sold 34 per cent (45) of a market also affected by Soviet entry (for example, in stimulating demand for submarines). In contrast to the previous decade, 22 of these British-built vessels were newly constructed. British naval sales to Latin America remained particularly strong during this period, and included the sale of an aircraft carrier to Brazil in 1958 and destroyers to Chile.

Britain also exported a large number of Centurion tanks, including 120 to Iraq, 30 to Egypt and 25 to Kuwait. Although these tanks were replaced in the British army by the Chieftain in the 1960s, they continued to be employed across the developing world – for example, by Israel in the 1967 and 1973 wars, and in the 1982 invasion of Lebanon.

During this period British arms exports were primarily motivated by political considerations, although they still produced economic benefits. As the 1955 White Paper, *Export of Surplus War Material*, stated, 'the general policy of H.M. Government on the sale of arms is primarily governed by political and strategic considerations: only when these have been satisfied are economic considerations – i.e. the contribution of arms sales to export earnings – taken into account.'[6] One expression of this priority was the attempt by the US and UK to control the nature of the Middle Eastern arms market, a task made more difficult with the involvement of the USSR. However, as the Foreign Office Planning Committee were told at the end of 1964, local attitudes had already made this tough: in the first instance, almost 'all the governments concerned' depended on arms 'for the control of their own subjects'; most were 'frightened of their neighbours'; while Iran had taken 'considerable exception in 1957 to the idea of the Great Powers taking decisions concerning the Middle East without the consent of the countries concerned'.[7]

The principal formal mechanism for exercising this control was the Near East Arms Co-ordinating Committee (NEACC), set up in 1952 in accordance with the May 1950 Tripartite Declaration, and whose members were the US, UK, France and, later, Italy. This sought to balance demand for arms with avoidance of arms races or, even worse, a switch to Soviet supply. As Bernard Braine, the Joint Parliamentary Under-Secretary of State for Commonwealth Relations, explained with regard to the NEACC in July 1961:

> While different considerations applied to each State in the area, it was in general necessary to exercise restraint in arms sales, though a complete embargo would invite further penetration by the Soviet bloc. It should remain our policy to remove the dangers of war and the spread of Communism in the Middle East and to produce a situation favourable to the West in general and to Her Majesty's Government in particular. Though our influence could not always be decisive, we should exercise political pressure on suitable occasions to persuade other supplying countries not to work against our policy.[8]

In effect, the system allowed its members to act as a cartel, at least until 1955. For example, Britain supplied Egypt, Iraq, Jordan, Oman and Kuwait. The US supplied Israel, Egypt and Saudi Arabia, while France supplied Syria and Lebanon, and later Israel. Member states would consult the committee before making major arms shipments to the region in order to ensure a rough balance was maintained between Israel and the Arab states. Their proposals would then be considered at a meeting, and unless agreement could be reached, the export would not, in theory, go ahead. However, the NEACC proved relatively ineffectual. Within a short period the committee was being informed only retrospectively of routine shipments, and co-operation was further reduced by the Suez crisis. By 1957, when the US and UK began to collaborate once again, the French were no longer fully reporting their arms supplies – particularly those to Israel – to the committee. Only the Italians were regarded as having kept to the rules. Moreover, the UK, with active US encouragement, failed to notify the committee of deliveries of Centurion tanks to Israel. In light of changing market circumstances, the NEACC was moribund by the early 1960s.

Towards the end, this phase witnessed the emergence of one of the most controversial arms export issues of the last 40 years – the question of arms sales to apartheid-era South Africa, and the UK response to efforts in the United Nations (UN) to restrict or embargo them. It is worth considering here events in the run-up to and immediately following the 1964 general election.

After the 1960 Sharpeville massacre British policy regarding the sale of defence equipment to South Africa changed. At Sharpeville, British-manufactured Saracens had been used for riot control, so any future sales were likely to meet with both parliamentary and public criticism. In future, weapons and equipment deemed suitable for internal repression were to be denied to the South African defence forces. However, such ethical considerations did not exist in a vacuum, and had to compete against more traditional great-power considerations, summarised in a June 1961 memorandum:

> It is an important United Kingdom interest that bilateral co-operation with South Africa be continued in the defence field. Apart from our strategic sea and air routes, there is the problem of access to the High Commission Territories for internal security purposes. For these reasons it is also important that South Africa should be able to defend her frontiers. Not only is South Africa a good customer in the defence field who could easily turn elsewhere: she is also our fifth largest export market.[9]

Hence British policy regarding export restrictions came to rest on maintaining a fine balance: sustaining close military and political relations with South Africa on strategic and commercial grounds, while at the same time not antagonising UK and Commonwealth public opinion. To this end, a distinction was employed between 'straightforward' items with a clear military use and items 'which might be readily connected in the public mind' with repression and crowd control (armoured vehicles, small arms, etc.).[10] The former could be exported, but not the latter.

This balance was threatened by the position adopted by the Labour Party. On 15 March 1963, Harold Wilson delivered a speech in Trafalgar Square, pledging that a future Labour government would ban the sale of all arms to South Africa and, furthermore, try to ensure that it could not acquire arms elsewhere. This generated fears in the Foreign Office (FO) that South Africa would respond by purchasing its arms elsewhere, particularly from France.[11] Hints were also dropped that the UK's broader trade with South Africa could suffer if arms, required as part of the Simonstown Agreement, were not supplied. The focal point of this concern was a 1962 order for 16 Buccaneer aircraft for the South African Navy, valued at £24

million. South Africa had already made one down-payment, with a second
(of £6 million) due in October 1963, but if a Labour government applied
a ban, the South Africans would have had no way of recovering these
payments.[12]

Macmillan's government had reassured the South Africans that only in
exceptional circumstances were existing contracts ever cancelled. Foreign
Secretary Alec Douglas-Home told them that he 'knew of no case where
in time of peace a British Government had cancelled a contract for political reasons', and that he 'doubted whether in practice a future
government would cancel the Buccaneer contract'.[13] Home's despatch to
Sir Hugh Stephenson, the newly accredited ambassador to South Africa,
summarised UK concerns:

> It must be expected that pressure from the United Nations for a complete
> arms ban will continue to grow, and would become intense if South Africa
> flouted an adverse decision of the International Court over South-West
> Africa. It would be very difficult for Her Majesty's Government to continue
> to supply arms to a country which was failing to comply with a decision of
> the International Court.
>
> For their part, the South African Government have been reviewing their
> position in the light of Mr Harold Wilson's and Mr Denis Healey's threats
> to cut off arms supplies altogether if a Labour Government came to power.
> The South African Ambassador has told me that although his Government
> do not intend any drastic steps it will be difficult now for them to place
> orders for delivery after a British General Election.[14]

From July 1963, the main issue regarding policy towards South Africa
was a resolution in the UN which sought to apply sanctions, including an
arms embargo. UK policy, which was co-ordinated with the US,[15] was to
resist economic sanctions and a blanket arms embargo, preferably
without having to resort to a veto.[16] At worst, any resolution had to be
non-mandatory, given that for 'aircraft alone current orders amounted to
£26 million, while orders worth £1½ million were currently under negotiation and further orders, worth £47 million, were in prospect'.[17]
Nevertheless, Macmillan was well aware that many African countries,
including Commonwealth members, would seek stronger terms,[18] and
that an economic embargo could have harmed the UK economy as much
as the South African, given the impact on the balance of payments, gold
prices, and sterling.

At the UN, two *ad hoc* coalitions formed. The US, UK, France and
Norway sought moderation, while a grouping of African and Asian states,
headed by Ghana and Tunisia, advocated a more strident course. The
Western coalition was not united in defining its goals, however, and the
US delegation shifted to supporting a full arms embargo, albeit one that
would allow the fulfilment of existing contracts. Hence the US offered to
cease arms shipments to South Africa by the end of 1963.[19] With the US

effectively undermining the UK negotiating position, the British line itself shifted to formally accepting an arms embargo and condemning apartheid, while stressing that the resolution was not mandatory, and that the government reserved the right to sell equipment required for South Africa's external defence, such as warships and aircraft, and would meet all existing contractual obligations.[20] In parallel, the African countries' position hardened to include a mandatory arms embargo and economic sanctions. This draft was tabled on 6 August, with Britain aiming to detach 'operative paragraph 3'[21] and ensure the resolution was presented as being non-mandatory.

The vote on the resolution took place on 7 August. Paragraph 3 was voted out of the resolution, and the UK and France alone abstained when the revised resolution came to a vote. Sir Patrick Dean's speech made it clear that the UK would be supporting the resolution in principle, but the exemptions it was prepared to make (on a combination of economic and strategic grounds, but couched in terms of the right of states to acquire the means of their self-defence inherent in Article 51) meant that it would not be supporting it in practice.[22] Dean's position would be effectively the same when the issue was voted on again in December. Home later defended the UK position to Dean Rusk in essentially strategic terms, telling him that that the UK 'could not stop arms shipments to South Africa, because of the need to maintain the Simonstown Agreement: the Agreement would become more important if we had to support Malaysia against Indonesia. The Suez Canal was a precarious link and there was little possibility of overflying.'[23]

The consequences of the UN resolution were discussed in Cabinet on 23 September. A recommendation from the Committee on the Export of Arms to South Africa 'that no arms should be exported to South Africa which would enable the policy of apartheid to be enforced' was accepted. However, arms useful for external defence (mainly naval equipment) would still be exported. While no new orders would be accepted for equipment clearly useful for riot control (the principle of the inviolability of existing contracts applied), enquiries concerning an intermediate category of equipment, including tanks and fighter aircraft, would still be considered on a case-by-case basis.[24] Typical of this third category was the proposed export of Vigilant anti-tank missiles and Bloodhound surface-to-air missiles, which had received prime ministerial backing in April 1963.

Through the last ten months of the Conservative government, Home attempted to maintain a policy which neither inflamed public opinion nor flagrantly overstepped the assurances given at the UN, while at the same time exporting as much as possible to South Africa, an ally with whom many Ministers had considerable sympathy. Home's claim in answer to a parliamentary question in December 1963 that Saracen spares were being supplied under the terms of existing contracts was untrue, although an official helpfully suggested that 'any supplier who sells a vehicle is generally understood to be willing to supply on request a reasonable supply of spares so as to enable the vehicle he has sold to operate during its normal expectation of life' – i.e. there existed a *de facto* contract if not a *de jure* one.[25] Home agreed, despite the reservations of his Overseas Private Secretary, who warned that the 'policy may well be right; the politics may be difficult'.[26] This fiction was maintained for the next six months. However, the issue was raised again by Barbara Castle in July 1964, by which time the UN Security Council had, on 18 June 1964, reaffirmed its December 1963 call on states to 'cease forthwith the sale and shipment to South Africa of arms, ammunition of all types, military vehicles, and equipment and materials for the manufacture and maintenance of arms and ammunition in South Africa'. Rab Butler told Home he thought Castle had 'detected an inconsistency in our policy'.[27] Given that Saracens had been used at Sharpeville, the continued export of spares clearly ran counter to the UK policy outlined at the UN the previous year. Butler recommended closing the loophole and refusing future requests for spares for armoured vehicles. Home grudgingly agreed to end shipments of spares for the Saracens and other armoured vehicles, albeit in the face of resistance from the Chief Secretary to the Treasury, who warned of the harm the decision would inflict on the UK's reputation for reliability of supply.[28]

Consistent with his pre-election pledge, just two days after Labour's October 1964 general election victory, Harold Wilson asked that the Board of Trade be instructed that the shipment of arms to South Africa should 'cease forthwith'.[29] However, as Wilson's officials were quick to point out, considerable sums were at stake, aside from the strategic stake in good relations with South Africa. Arms exports to South Africa in 1962 had been worth £7.85 million, in 1963 £7 million. Although Wilson was warned by his Private Secretary that the Bloodhound contract alone was worth £300 million,[30] this was untrue. As it stood, it was worth £10.9 million. Nevertheless, existing export licences for military equipment were worth over £39 million.[31]

Faced with this presentation of the financial implications and the impact of the loss of these orders on the balance of payments, the Cabinet's Overseas and Defence Policy Committee (OPD), decided on 9 November to allow existing contracts to proceed (with the exception of sporting weapons). However, there would be an embargo on fresh arms exports, including the Bloodhound. A decision on the Buccaneer (towards which the South Africans had already paid £11 million), about which Wilson and Healey had been so resolute in opposition, would be reviewed.[32]

Consideration of the Buccaneer sale was complicated by two factors. First and most important, Voerword publicly announced that failure to supply the aircraft would be a repudiation of the Simonstown Agreement.[33] At the same time, the Board of Trade was emphasising that Britain's strategic interests and ability to perform the global role it still aspired to would be affected:

> We have considerable interests in South Africa which would be at risk if our action over arms exports is so sharp as to provoke an emotional reaction by the South African Government. We stand to lose the facilities at the Simonstown Naval Base, including strategic communications, as well as the overflying and staging rights which we enjoy by agreement with the South African Government. These rights are important strategically and could be essential if we are to fulfil our commitments to the former High Commission Territories.[34]

Secondly, there was no UK requirement for the Buccaneers and apparently no prospect of finding an alternative customer. Hence there was also around £11.5 million of Export Credit Guarantee Department (ECGD) liability to consider, as well as the spectre of job losses at the manufacturers. In addition to these strategic and economic factors, Oliver Wright, Wilson's Private Secretary, came up with an ingenious third objection. The US and UK did not agree with economic sanctions, but many other states did. A decision to allow delivery would impact on any future UN sanctions on South Africa, as a force of Buccaneers on the Cape would make imposing a blockade prohibitively dangerous. In supplying them, Wright argued, Wilson would also be 'more or less [taking] a decision not to go along with economic sanctions since it would be madness to supply the weapons which will be making the effective application of sanctions almost impossible' but then also attempt to support them.[35] Wright admitted that he was biased in favour of sale, but the whole administrative apparatus, which had been preparing for the sale under the previous administration and was generally anxious to maintain good relations with South Africa, was weighed against Wilson's initial decision. After a weekend discussing the matter at Chequers, on 25 November Wilson announced that the Buccaneer contract would be honoured in full.

The government's commitment to a blanket ban on fresh orders was then tested when Defence Secretary Denis Healey raised the issue of the continued supply of spares to the South African Navy, of which Healey approved (drawing his customary distinction between 'sharp' and other equipment).[36] Suggestive of his later approach to arms sales issues, Healey made certain that, when this issue was discussed in the OPD, he gave his colleagues a thorough summary of the £21 million worth of orders that would be lost if the UK was to maintain the embargo.[37] The sense of erosion was heightened when the issues of spares for the South African Air Force and the export of Marconi radar were added, and when, on

10 February 1965 at an OPD meeting, Wilson concluded that the Wasp helicopter was an 'integral part of an anti-submarine weapons system' and as such should also be supplied.[38] These deliberations, and the divisions they revealed, set a pattern for the contests which lay ahead. In the meantime, government performance had failed to meet the expectations generated by pre-election pledges.

Phase two: 1966–80

The second phase in the post-war development of the international arms market was characterised by a shift of focus of Cold War tensions from Europe to the developing world. With the economic recovery of Western Europe virtually complete, in addition to France, West Germany, Italy, the Netherlands, and latterly Spain, began exporting arms in an expanding market. This growth was the result of a combination of factors: the consequences of the decolonisation process; reasons of prestige (by the mid to late 1960s jet fighters had become a defining symbol of statehood for newly independent states); the impact of the shift in the Cold War; and, later, the consequences of the 1973 oil crisis. These developments limited the potential for influencing behaviour through arms sales and at the same time placed a premium on the commercialisation of a supplier's arms promotion apparatus. For the Wilson government, greater emphasis on arms sales – for the most part selling-on ex-RAF aircraft like the Hunter, ex-army equipment like the Centurion and Saracen, and ex-RN vessels – helped finance their replacements and made a welcome contribution to a precarious balance of payments position, all for comparatively little extra outlay. Of course, as the market became more competitive, so the export promotion machinery and bureaucracy grew and the terms on which arms were offered became more generous, all of which impacted negatively on the profitability of arms exports. In short, what was seen as a quick fix to rectify an endemic balance of payments problem and help finance the continuation of a global role was to evolve into an unbreakable addiction where the mounting costs outweighed the diminishing benefits held to accrue from involvement, and where the addict would deny this vehemently whenever it was pointed out.

South Africa, 1967: profit or principle?

For the remainder of the 1960s and first half of the 1970s, the question of arms sales to South Africa figured prominently. A festering sore running throughout 1965 and 1966,[39] it erupted spectacularly in 1967, effectively leading to the resignation of George Brown as Foreign Secretary, and dividing Cabinet and party, according to Harold Wilson, in a way 'more serious than any other in our six years of Government'.[40]

Economic pressure, the implications for South African procurement of the UK's decision to withdraw its naval forces from the area, combined with forceful industrial and South African lobbying, suggesting that orders for naval and 'defensive' equipment worth over £120 million were imminent, forced the South African arms embargo back on to the political agenda in 1967. The scale of the potential orders was sufficient to convince Roy Mason. He argued that 'with such large sums at stake, we are bound at least to take a fresh look at the basis of our policy for sales to South Africa, so that the other Ministers concerned are aware of the sort of opportunities of which we are depriving British firms as things stand'.[41] A review of government policy was undertaken, leading to a meeting between George Thomson and Roy Mason on 13 July. At this meeting, Thomson confirmed that:

> After long debate in the Foreign Office, it had been decided to recommend that we should change our policy on the supply of arms to South Africa, to bring it in effect more or less into line with what it had been before October/November 1964. The Foreign Secretary had talked to the Prime Minister, who had agreed to this proposal, subject to careful timing and consideration by the Cabinet. The Ambassador in Pretoria had been authorised to let the South African Government know the direction in which we were moving, and he had reported that we could indeed benefit from such a change of policy ...[42]

Mason was in favour of the change in policy, in effect advocating a resumption of the policy followed by the Home government, wherein 'a reasonable distinction could be drawn between arms which could be used for internal suppression' and the rest. As Mason happily observed, 'the most valuable prospective orders ... fell clearly on the right side of the dividing line'.[43] The difficulty lay in getting the proposed change through the OPD and Cabinet. Mason instructed one of his officials to prepare a policy paper in the strictest secrecy, involving a minimal number of officials.

The following month, a first draft was distributed for discussion,[44] focusing on the potential strategic and economic losses if South African requests were not met promptly, and how the policy change might be presented publicly. Predictably, the Chiefs of Staff received the paper with delight,[45] even though, as the paper itself noted, the changes it proposed would undoubtedly lead to fierce criticism both at home and in the UN.

The paper was discussed at the OPD on 14 September 1967. Criticism of the paper was considerable: 'The decision involved a fundamental issue of principle, and one that could be regarded as critical to the future of our whole policy in respect of South Africa.' The government was 'giving precedence to an outdated concept of a British world military role over our support for the United Nations and all that it stood for'. In summing up, Wilson noted that the UK 'ban on supplying arms to South Africa had always been qualified, but the existing qualifications were of a different order from the relaxation now proposed'.[46] To accept the South African orders as proposed would effectively mean abandoning the embargo. Wilson concluded by saying that the issue had to be bound up in the wider context of relations with Rhodesia and southern Africa more generally, and would be discussed again on that basis.

Nevertheless, the perilous state of the economy continued to push the option along, and a revised paper was submitted to the OPD in early December.[47] While reference was made to the broader strategic dimension, the argument focused on the economic benefits of sales (worth at least £100 million in the short term) and the cost to civil trade of refusal. However, it recognised that a decision to sell 'would provoke a loud outcry in certain circles in this country and in the UN', and would not be without political cost.

The discussion at the OPD came down to the question of the price of principle. Foreign Secretary George Brown argued that the total trade loss to the UK would be as high as £300 million if sales of naval equipment in which South Africa had expressed an interest, and 'irrelevant to the maintenance and enforcement of the South African policy of apartheid', did not go ahead. The strategic importance of Simonstown, highlighted during the closure of the Suez Canal from June of that year, was a further consideration. Opponents of the sale argued that the moral costs were too great, that if the sales went ahead 'we could not avoid the charge that we put economic interests above principle',[48] and that sales would lead to economic retaliation by African and Asian countries opposed to apartheid. Wilson argued that arms sales to South Africa could be made politically palatable only if presented as part of a package of measures forced on the government by the economic crisis it was facing, and needed to be considered again in this context.

The Cabinet met to discuss the issue again on 14 December amid considerable media speculation, after Jim Callaghan had planted the idea with a group of Labour MPs that the ban on arms sales would be lifted. However, George Brown had been held up by bad weather in Brussels, where he had been attending a NATO meeting, and so a full discussion could not take place.[49] When the Cabinet reconvened the next day, it opened with what Richard Crossman called 'an hour and a half of mutual abuse'.[50] Denis Healey called it 'the most unpleasant meeting I have ever attended'.[51] The issues – virtually unchanged in twelve months except that devaluation had brought the economic considerations into even sharper focus – were restated, with George Brown pushing heavily for sale.[52] In summing up, and under pressure from half the Cabinet (Brown, Healey, Callaghan, Tony Crosland, Ernie Ross, Patrick Gordon-Walker, George Thomson and Ray Gunter) to abandon the embargo, Wilson said that the subject tested the moral credibility of the government:

To agree to supply the proposed military equipment to South Africa would be contrary to the principles for which the Government stood; and if they were to do so in order to carry economic credibility with British industry, they would risk being pushed into other policies advocated by the Opposition and thus lose all political credibility. They would not only destroy their standing with liberal opinion in the country, but also undermine the support of the Parliamentary Labour Party without which the Government could not survive.[53]

Securing their co-operation would be made much harder when the Cabinet was faced with the difficult decisions that would inevitably follow the previous month's devaluation. Therefore, Wilson concluded, the South Africa decision would have to wait until after the recess, from where it could be presented as part of the broad package of post-devaluation measures then being prepared. Hence although it was personally distasteful, and although his summing up at Cabinet had emphasised the problems rather than the benefits of sale, Wilson was prepared to accept the logic of the pro-sale advocates (although he mobilised backbench opposition to them), so long as sale could be presented as part of a series of measures aimed at alleviating the economic crisis facing the country.

However, on Monday 18 December, Wilson summoned the Cabinet again,[54] telling them that press speculation over the weekend, based on deliberately inaccurate leaks from Cabinet members (George Brown) to the effect that the majority of the Cabinet favoured a resumption of arms sales to South Africa, but that Wilson had used Brown's absence from the 14 December meeting to 'secure from the Cabinet a decision not to supply arms to South Africa', had made postponing the decision until after the recess impossible.[55] In light of this, Wilson no longer felt able to merely make the holding statement he had intended while the presentation of the decision was finessed over the recess. Instead, he felt he had to make a clear policy statement on the issue, as prompt action was required to prevent further erosion of confidence both in the government and in sterling. He also invited the Cabinet to recognise as inaccurate the leaks of the weekend and to support a statement repudiating them. For Wilson, in the context of the recent devaluation, simply to abandon the embargo on arms sales could well have fatally undermined his position, as some of his Cabinet colleagues knew only too well. Having outmanoeuvred his opponents in Cabinet, that afternoon Wilson told the House that:

> the Government have completed their examination of the question of the supply of defence equipment to South Africa and have decided that their policy on this matter, namely to conform to the Security Council Resolution of 18 June, 1964, remains unchanged. I should add that I have the authority of the whole Cabinet categorically to repudiate as inaccurate reported statements about the position taken by the Cabinet as a whole, by a Cabinet

Committee which met a week earlier, and also about the position taken by
the Prime Minister and other individual Ministers.[56]

In the final analysis, the arms-to-South Africa issue had merely been the
occasion for the working out of a power struggle within the Labour
government. Refusing to lift the embargo split the party and heightened
existing animosities in Cabinet, but a decision to go ahead with the sales
and thereby abandon the embargo would have had even more profound
consequences.

The F-1 1 1, arms sales, and partnership in global order

> One basic objective of the Government's defence policy is to ensure that the
> British balance of payments does not suffer unfair damage simply because
> of Britain's contribution to the security of the free world. (Denis Healey,
> May 1966)[57]

This phase also witnessed a significant decision which directly affected
perceptions of Britain's global influence and place in the world – the
decision to cancel the order for the US F-111 bomber. It was significant
for a number of reasons. In February 1966, during negotiations in
Washington on the possible UK purchase of the F-111 to replace the
cancelled TSR-2 programme, Denis Healey had urged the US to make
reciprocal purchases of UK goods to help offset the cost. When the
British government compared the cost of various arms purchases from
the US over the coming 12-year period with US expenditure on maintaining its troops in the UK they came up with a foreign exchange
balance of US$725 million in favour of the US. Coincidentally, this was
also roughly the cost of the F-111 programme. The Americans proposed
that the figure could be largely covered by setting a target for reciprocal purchases of US$325 million while also setting a target of a further
US$300 million worth of UK sales to the developing world, where the
US would step aside in favour of the UK. As we shall see later, this is
precisely what Robert McNamara had already offered to do with regard
to the sale of Lightning aircraft to Saudi Arabia in 1965, and the value
of this deal was to be included in the figure of US$300 million.[58]
Although the F-111 decision was some months away then, the minutes
of the OPD meeting of 9 February 1966 included the observation that
'there was no doubt that the United States Government had only agreed
to co-operate with us [over Saudi Arabia] in anticipation of this
purchase'. The UK finally agreed to purchase the F-111 on this basis
once the US had increased the ceiling on assisted sales to the developing
world ('co-operative sales to third countries' in the MoD's interpretation[59]) to US$400 million over 12 years (1966–77), thereby covering the
entire cost of the F-111 programme through reciprocal arrangements.

Hence British arms sales to Saudi Arabia served to maintain not only British influence, but also a global presence, by partly financing the F-111 programme. These sales brought economic benefits, but were intimately bound up with Britain's vision of its world role and foreign policy interests (and, indeed, with US perceptions of these).

However, in the face of the economic crisis, the F-111 programme became a key target of Chancellor Roy Jenkins, alongside accelerated withdrawal from military bases outside Europe, in particular in the Far East and the Persian Gulf. From Washington, Sir Patrick Dean warned that the Johnson administration was unlikely to accept cancellation or withdrawal lightly, and that 'they are unable for all sorts of reasons to acquiesce in this without making adjustments in their attitude to the UK. To them, these defence cuts can only mean a further general ebbing of Britain's ability to share the burden of Western defence and international peacekeeping which they have so often appealed to us to maintain.'[60] Any cancellation, Dean warned, would affect the offset arrangements and virtually close the American market to UK arms. In Cabinet, George Brown, Denis Healey, Jim Callaghan and Michael Stewart ('the four pygmies', according to Richard Crossman[61]) resisted the idea of cancellation and all that it implied for Britain's global role. Brown argued that 'Even if we ceased to be a world power, we should continue to retain world interests and to need friends and allies to defend them.'[62] With regard to the Gulf, for example, 40 per cent of British oil supplies came from the region – 50 per cent of Western Europe's – and 40 per cent of Gulf oil was in British ownership. Healey's argument did not just focus on the need for the F-111. (In truth, this was much reduced, as it had been intended primarily for defence east of Suez, from where the UK would now be making an accelerated withdrawal. Although Healey did try to defend it on the grounds of it being needed to defend Europe, Crossman 'got the impression that he could defend it just as brilliantly as essential to southern Irish defence'.[63]) Instead, Healey also focused on the consequences of cancellation on the offset agreement, both with regard to the US market and in the developing world. But, as Jenkins pointed out, the benefits of the offset agreement were limited to the value of the F-111 programme: 'Export earnings under the agreement did not bring any net benefit to the balance of payments; they simply prevented the deterioration which would otherwise result from purchase of the aircraft.' Similarly, the argument that the offset agreement opened up the US market to British military products did not overly impress Jenkins, who noted that 'it was certain that, once the target for offset sales had been reached, the barriers to sales in the United States would immediately reappear'.[64] Healey, who, less than a year earlier, had assured the Australian National Press Club that Britain intended 'to remain in the military sense a world power' and would remain 'fully capable of carrying out all the commitments we have at the present time',[65] was given one last chance to present alternative savings while leaving the F-111 programme intact, but these were rejected at a Cabinet meeting on 12 January 1968, after which Healey 'was on the point of resignation'.[66]

The decision impacted on Britain's standing as an arms supplier. For the smaller Gulf states, the news about British withdrawal had resulted in 'downright panic', according to George Brown. It was even suggested that some of the wealthier states in the region could contribute to the UK's defence costs if Britain remained. Once Britain went, however, its grip on the arms market would be weaker. From a US perspective, the withdrawal from the Gulf was much more serious than the cancellation of the F-111. When Brown travelled to Washington to brief Dean Rusk he was mauled, and told: 'For God's sake act like Britain.' As Brown told the Cabinet, Rusk 'had said that it was the end of an era; and by that he had in particular implied that it was the end of the age of co-operation between the United States and ourselves'.[67] This was a message also delivered directly by Lyndon Johnson to Harold Wilson. It was, Johnson said, 'fatal to the chances of cooperation between our countries in the field of defense procurement' and would lead to the 'complete cancellation of recent awards of military contracts to British firms'.[68] The era of what might be termed co-operative competition and of general co-ordination of arms sales policies was gone, ended by this decision as much as by the practicalities of the evolving arms market.

In his last-ditch argument to save the F-111, Brown also outlined the rationale for an active arms sales policy. This policy would pay for the F-111 and hence bring influence. This was the end to which the economic benefits of the arms trade were to be directed: sustaining global influence within a framework of gradual decline:

> it was essential that we should have the kind of military capability that would enable us to take political initiatives and play a part in shaping affairs, particularly in Europe, in the 1970s. The F-111 was an essential component of such a capability, which other countries would have to take into account and which would therefore give us the degree of influence that we ought to have; without it we should be opting out of any role in Europe and in the world generally.[69]

British arms and Vietnam

The F-111 offset arrangement brought to the fore another contentious arms sale issue: UK policy towards selling arms to the US that might be used in Vietnam. In practice, the government sought to perform another balancing act. On the one hand, it was keen to realise the full value of the offset agreement, and would have found it difficult to deny the US any specific arms request. On the other hand, Harold Wilson had made it clear that the government did not propose to 'supply arms directly or indirectly for the fighting in Vietnam'.[70] Wilson had told the OPD in June 1966 that the UK must 'reserve the right to refuse any orders for politically sensitive items if they were clearly destined for use in the present conflict in Vietnam'. Nevertheless, this did 'not involve a general refusal to sell lethal items as such to the US and in order to meet the target set in the offset agreement we should endeavour to promote the most extensive sale of arms and equipment to the United States which was consistent with the public declaration of the Government's policy of not supplying arms to Vietnam.'[71]

The government needed to find a way of limiting the range of arms the US could seek to buy under the offset agreement without giving offence. The solution, Healey suggested in a June 1966 memorandum to the OPD, lay in how 'arms' were defined. If the word was interpreted 'to include all military hardware our offset arrangements with the United States ... will be in jeopardy.' However, if a more 'realistic interpretation' of 'arms' was employed, the prospects looked better. Healey suggested a definition: 'All equipments whose specific purpose is to inflict death or injury, together with live ammunition for such equipments; except where the equipments are only capable of being used for purposes of air defence'.[72] This would allow the supply of a wide range of equipment (including radar, transport equipment, aero engines, etc.) while prohibiting the supply of 'sharp' equipment such as guided missiles, artillery equipment, and fighting vehicles.

A related problem was to what extent arms sales to Australia and New Zealand – providing around 4,500 troops and an artillery battery respectively to the US war effort – should be restricted. As Healey conceded, there were 'clearly strong grounds in logic' for applying the same restrictions to these countries as to the US. However, the situation was complicated by the fact that both Australia and New Zealand were then discussing the purchase of categories of weapons which it had been determined would not be sold to the US (including explosives, small arms ammunition, mortar bombs, and rocket ammunition), much of it clearly destined for the Asian war effort. Healey's solution was to argue that the consequences of not supplying the equipment would be serious; neither Australia nor New Zealand had domestic sources of supply, and much of this equipment was comprised of spares for equipment already sold by the UK. If the UK refused to supply, New Zealand and Australia might in future turn to the US for military equipment. And anyway, the government were 'under some moral obligation to keep up the supply of spares for goods already sold' – one of the few instances where Healey discussed morality and the arms trade in conjunction. At the end of June Healey's proposals were accepted by the OPD.[73] In line with this, in October 1967, the Ministerial Committee on Strategic

Exports agreed to supply 45,000 500 lb and 15,000 1,000 lb bombs for the Royal Australian Air Force's Canberras, a squadron of which were then serving in South Vietnam.

One ingenious possible line of defence of this sale, devised by Roy Mason, was that Harold Wilson's statement on arms sales to Australia had assured Parliament that if a situation arose in which 'the Australians were asking for bombs for bombing North Vietnam'[74] the decision would need to be carefully considered, and implicitly would result in refusal to supply. However, it was noted that 'the Australian Canberra aircraft have ... not been used to bomb North Vietnam despite their integration with the American Air Forces in South Vietnam', and so were not covered by the commitment.[75] Hence even though it was generally accepted that the bombs were required for Vietnam, or at best to replace bombs used over Vietnam, the OPD approved the sale, partly on the grounds that they 'had not been requested specifically for use in Vietnam and could therefore be regarded as coming within the terms of the Prime Minister's statement' to Parliament. There was 'no moral case for not supplying them' and the 'risk of opposition from some Government supporters' would have to be accepted.[76]

Isolated issues still arose. For example, at the beginning of 1967, it was agreed that herbicides, suspected of being required by the US for defoliation in Vietnam, should not be supplied, even though they were not subject to export licensing, and despite the fact that not only was the UK 'able to supply the particular chemical requested by the Americans but we believe that we could supply a better agent which would have a less harmful effect on the ecology of the region'.[77]

By 1967, the UK was willing to sell the US a range of lethal items in a bid to realise the full value of the offset arrangement, so long as they would not be ready for supply until 1968 at the earliest, working on the assumption that the Vietnam War could well be over by then. The government also approved the involvement of UK firms as subcontractors manufacturing forgings and casings for bombs and ammunition on this basis.[78] These were not subject to export licensing and, in any case, even though they would probably be used in Vietnam, they would be virtually impossible to identify as having been manufactured in the UK. However, as the end of 1967 approached with no end to the conflict in sight, consideration of lethal items reverted to a case-by-case basis.

Edward Heath's pro-European outlook drowned out Conservative calls for a reassertion of Britain's imperial role. However, Heath did enter office with a commitment to resume arms sales to South Africa on the same basis as the Home government had[79] (and George Brown had proposed in 1967), but the glittering prizes promised in 1967 failed to emerge. The only major items the South Africans bought were six Wasp helicopters, leaving Heath exposed to Harold Wilson's charge that he had been willing to 'stain our image in the world' for very little in return, by giving South Africa the international 'certificate of respectability' that supplying the helicopters amounted to.[80]

In general, the 1970s were lean years for British arms exporters. Britain's declining international status as a result of the withdrawal from the Gulf and the subsequent collapse of the 'special relationship' with the US made it a less attractive supplier. Nevertheless, the decade did witness the export of a significant number of Chieftain tanks to Iran, beginning in 1973. By 1979 that country had 875 of them. Kuwait followed up its purchase of the Centurion with a large order for Chieftains in 1977. At the same time, the old Centurion continued to find markets, with Israel ordering a further 400 in 1974. Latin America continued to be a valuable market for naval vessels. With few military aircraft orders unfulfilled by the beginning of the 1970s, it was a particularly lean decade for aircraft orders. The Hunters and Lightnings sold in the 1960s remained in service and would not be replaced until the 1980s.

Phase three: 1980–91

The third phase in the post-war evolution of the international arms market was characterised by a growing number of suppliers, including a number from the developing world, leading to increased competition in a contracting market, leaving a greater number of suppliers chasing fewer markets and resulting in the structural overproduction of arms. This phase was further defined by several other features, prominent amongst which was the rise in illegal and semi-legal arms sales, and governmental sanction of the export of military and related goods to sensitive areas, at times in apparent contravention of declared export policy. There were essentially two reasons for this. Firstly, the Iran–Iraq War created a massive demand for certain types of weaponry but also led to the imposition of various national restraints on their export. However, overcapacity gave governments, as well as manufacturers, an economic incentive to covertly approve exports. This was in addition to their geopolitical and security interests in covertly backing one side or the other – for example, Iran in the case of Israel, Iraq in the case of the US, France, Britain and West Germany, etc. Secondly, the proliferation of non-proliferation agreements designed to control the flow of advanced technology to the developing world of itself created a semi-clandestine market through which certain states sought to develop the technology for themselves. The relative ease of manufacture meant that this grew to be particularly true of chemical weapon production, with states such as Libya a particular focus of Western concern.

By the early 1980s, although arms sales continued to be an expression of Britain's desire to play some role in the world – to 'punch above its weight' – and guarantee some flexibility and independence of action n doing so, their importance was increasingly being defined by the government in terms of the economic benefits they brought. This was particularly true of the Thatcher years.

Batting for Britain: the Thatcher arms export revival
In 1972, the Managing Director of Marconi Radar Systems, J. W. Sutherland, outlined the assistance industry required from the government to sell defence electronics abroad thus: 'Provide the maximum flow of information; Give unstinting support and influence; Forget the "Queensbury Rules"; Buy British.'[81] In retrospect this advice could almost be taken as a blueprint for the behaviour of the Thatcher governments in this field in the following decade.

In part, this was a consequence of Mrs Thatcher's world view and vision of the role Britain should aspire to play in the world – a view markedly different from that of her predecessor. She failed to grasp that, as historian David Cannadine put it, the 'Empire, which was about serious power' had been replaced by 'the Commonwealth, which is about insubstantial sentiment'.[82] As she explained in *The Downing Street Years*, Britain had developed:

> what might be called the 'Suez Syndrome': having previously exaggerated our power, we now exaggerated our impotence. Military and diplomatic successes such as the war in Borneo – which preserved the independence of former British colonies against Indonesian subversion, helped to topple the anti-western dictator Sukarno, and thus altered the long-term balance of power in Asia in our interest – were either dismissed as trivial or ignored altogether. Defeats, which in reality were the results of avoidable misjudgement, such as the retreat from the Gulf in 1970, were held to be inevitable consequences of British decline ... The truth – that Britain was a middle-ranking power, given unusual influence by virtue of its historical distinction, skilled diplomacy and versatile military forces, but greatly weakened by economic decline – seemed too complex for sophisticated people to grasp.[83]

Having been shaped by the experience of Hitler and World War II,[84] having eagerly absorbed stories of Britain's imperial past at the feet of her father, Mrs Thatcher did not accept what Percy Craddock called the 'constraining facts of Britain's objective situation', that it was 'a small island off the north-west coast of Europe, with limited resources, a glorious but imprisoning past, an uncertain future and a host of economic problems'. The natural corollary of this perspective was that, as Craddock saw it, she viewed foreign policy;

not as a continuum, the stream largely beyond governments' control, on which ... the powers are borne, but rather as a series of disparate problems with attainable solutions, or even as zero-sum games, which Britain had to win. She regularly complained that her advisers brought her problems but no answers. The thought that for a middling power in a disorderly world there would be few answers in the crossword-puzzle sense, and many compromises, seemed not to occur.[85]

In recapturing the Falkland Islands, Mrs Thatcher suggested that reports of Britain's decline had, as she herself had long maintained, been greatly exaggerated. Britain had been seen to be willing and able to deploy force effectively in a far-flung corner of the globe. The implications for British arms sales were profound. Having re-established its credentials as a reliable supplier, Britain had also shown that it was a dependable ally. As Alan Clark noted at the time, the war had 'enormously increased our world standing. You asked about world opinion – I mean, bugger world opinion – but our standing in the world has been totally altered by this. It has made every other member of NATO say "My God, the British are tough."'[86]

This, of course, is why the Falklands example was so important to potential arms customers. Where the weapons they had bought proved insufficient to provide for their defence, they looked to a supplier with the political will and ability to intervene on their behalf. Also, they looked to a supplier with sufficient credibility that potential aggressors would themselves recognise the logic of this equation and be deterred from committing any aggressive acts. Britain now fell, once more, into this category for the states to which this applied. These were not merely micro-states, but states which, despite possessing the wealth which allowed them to spend lavishly on arms in the first place, did not have the strategic depth to defend themselves from a concerted assault. Many may even have lacked the strategic depth to operate to their full potential the systems they had paid dearly to acquire.

Explaining the Thatcher arms export revival: pursuing influence in the face of decline
By 1987, the Thatcher arms export drive had secured sufficient orders for the MoD to announce that (based on the value of orders) Britain had surpassed both France and the USSR to become the world's second-largest exporter, with 20 per cent of the global market. Measured by value of deliveries, the Stockholm International Peace Research Institute (SIPRI) at this time ranked Britain fourth – by the end of the decade it was ranked fifth, having been eclipsed by China.[87] However, as these orders turned into deliveries during the 1990s, Britain was unusual in seeing the value of its exports increase annually as that of others (including the US) fell.

In 1993, Defence Procurement Minister Jonathan Aitken told the House of Commons that: 'Britain's defence exports for 1992 were £4.5

billion, representing 20 per cent of the world market. Those were record figures. In the month of January 1993, British companies won orders in the middle and far east with a value approaching that of our world-wide defence exports for the whole of 1992.'[88] The post-Gulf War effect, deliveries under Britain's richest-ever arms deal – the Al Yamamah deal covering the supply of aircraft, infrastructure and training to Saudi Arabia – and high-profile and controversial deals with Indonesia and Malaysia ensured that this generally upward trend continued for the rest of the Major years. According to Defence Procurement Minister James Arbuthnot, in 1996 the UK secured 25 per cent of the world market, cementing its place as the world's largest arms exporter after the US. The £5.1 billion worth of equipment exported was an 'all-time record for the UK'.[89] Although the US Arms Control and Disarmament Agency (ACDA) offered a somewhat lower estimate of the UK performance for 1996, it nevertheless ranked the UK as the world's second-largest arms exporter (Table 1).

Table I

ACDA top ten arms exporters of 1996

Rank	Country	Value of exports (US$ million)	% of total
I	US	23,500	55
2	UK	6,100	14
3	Russia	3,300	8
4	France	3,200	8
5	Sweden	1,200	3
6	Germany	830	2
7	Israel	680	2
8	China	600	I
9	Canada	460	I
10	Netherlands	340	<I
			Total 95

Source ACDA, *World Military Expenditures and Arms Transfers* 1997, at http://www.acda.gov/wmeat97/wmeat97.htm

However, to an extent, the Thatcher 'revival' rested on an uncertain basis. Between 1985 and 1989, Saudi Arabia accounted for 20 per cent of all British arms exports (by 1997 the figure was up to 47 per cent), while during the same period BAe alone was responsible for 60 per cent of all British major weapons exports.[90] In 1996 BAe remained responsible for almost 20 per cent (£1 billion worth) of all arms exports.[91] If estimates that the Al Yamamah programme sustains 30,000 jobs in the UK are accurate, then this represents almost 20 per cent of all employment (both direct and indirect) sustained by arms exports.[92] Hence the British share of the market, and the health of Britain's flagship weapons manufacturer, remained heavily dependent on the continuation of the Saudi orders and very vulnerable to reductions or cancellations in them. Indeed, in the period after the collapse of his libel trial, Jonathan Aitken's co-defendant in the resultant perjury case, Said Ayas, argued that Aitken had been instrumental in securing the £5 billion second phase of the order, personally persuading King Fahd not to cancel it as Prince Sultan had urged, suggesting just how vulnerable the contract may have been.[93]

Table 2

Exports of British defence equipment by region, selected years, 1975–97 (£ million)

Region	1975	1980	1985	1990	1993	1994	1995	1996	1997
NATO and other Europe	52	111	247	396	704	592	617	1,055	1,460
Middle East and N. Africa	91	158	284	1,207	850	589	912	1,585	2,592
Other Africa	5	121	155	36	86	59	36	35	22
Asia and Far East	20	134	73	295	249	520	441	625	379
Latin America and Caribbean	30	13	54	46	24	38	69	102	145
Estimates of additional aerospace equipment	279	1,000	940	2,487	1,055	1,148	2,647	..	..
Total	477	1,537	1,753	4,467	2,969	2,946	4,723	..	..

Note Based on UK Customs and Excise data, and based on deliveries passing through UK Customs. Estimates of additional aerospace equipment are SBAC figures relating to items 'where official commodity classifications do not distinguish between military and civil aerospace equipment'. The table covers the following equipment: armoured fighting vehicles and parts; military aircraft and parts; warships; guns, small arms and parts; guided weapons, missiles and parts; ammunition; radio and radar apparatus; and optical equipment and training. Totals are rounded.
Source UK Defence Statistics 1998 (London, HMSO, 1998), p. 18.

Nevertheless, under Mrs Thatcher arms exports represented a reassertion of Britain's desire to play something of a world role. This in turn gave purchasing states confidence in British arms while Mrs Thatcher was in power. Closely related to this was Mrs Thatcher's dominance (after 1982) of British politics. For a purchasing state, political stability in the supplier state, and hence the prospect of uninterrupted delivery, are vital considerations. Mrs Thatcher's apparent domination of her party, clarity of vision (for better or worse) and large parliamentary majorities provided this.

Furthermore, under Mrs Thatcher, manufacturers began to tailor production to the export market. The Falklands conflict, in which certain British arms were seen to perform effectively, lent British arms the invaluable 'battle-tested' tag, fully exploited at the 1982 BAEE, which began only days after the Argentinian surrender at Port Stanley. Conversely, the experience of the Tornado during the 1991 Gulf War – where the insistence on flying low-level missions led to losses, as a proportion of aircraft flown, greater than those suffered by any other Coalition country sounded the death knell of any lingering hope of exporting it beyond Saudi Arabia.

The experience of the Saudis at the hands of the US Congress was also important. Their repeated attempts to secure the delivery of US aircraft tended to lead to their requests being examined and debated very publicly over a protracted period before finally being refused, and as such determined their decision to turn to Europe. Here, the nature of the British political system was attractive to the traditionally secretive Saudis. As discussed later, Parliament has been unable to oversee this aspect of foreign policy, guaranteeing secrecy for the purchaser, but also creating an environment in which corruption can thrive.

Mrs Thatcher's personal commitment to arms exports was a further factor. While previous governments had all had an interest in selling arms abroad, Mrs Thatcher displayed particular enthusiasm. She personally played a central role in securing arms deals and became personally identified with the British arms sales effort, 'batting for Britain' across the Middle East and Asia in particular. Linked with this was the desire to check what Mrs Thatcher saw as the advance of French arms exports at the expense of British. Following a visit to Riyadh in April 1981, she even went so far as to tell British businessmen that 'gradually one has come to see that there are times when the battle is not necessarily between company and company but also between country and country'.[94] Or, as the head of the Defence Export Services Organisation (DESO), Alan Thomas, put it, 'in defence exports our allies are also our competitors'.[95] Notwithstanding this world view, and the very real competition over Saudi Arabia, for example, it is also prudent to view the invocation of the 'French threat' as something of a mobilising device, designed to unite the nation behind an aggressive arms export strategy. After all, French manufacturers spoke of the British threat and called for increased governmental support in a strikingly similar manner.

Also important was the way in which the British intelligence machine was utilised to support the arms export effort. At the weeky meetings of the Joint Intelligence Committee (JIC), where the latest incoming intelligence is considered, technology transfers are of particular interest. Former

JIC official Robin Robison has recalled how the arms trade 'was a major piece of interest when I was there. GCHQ was constantly churning out stuff on the arms trade, not just the western arms trade [but] every aspect of the arms trade.' However, rather than monitor the actual end destinations and uses of British arms, the JIC's emphasis was on market opportunities and the activities of competitors, particularly the French. Intelligence on market requirements was routinely sent to DESO to help identify markets for British exporters, creating a potential conflict of interest for the JIC. Robison recalled how:

> It worried me intensely that the DESO were in receipt of GCHQ SIGINT on the arms trade ... because in theory – and I remember asking a senior officer about this – the JIC interest in the arms trade was to stop the illegal arms trade and to be part of an arms controlling network. The DESO has the opposite interest, and I don't believe they should have been in receipt of it because it must have given them an advantage.[96]

In addition to this, the reduction in the importance of human rights considerations in arms sales decisions became a defining characteristic of the Thatcher approach. While it would be easy to exaggerate the extent of Labour government linkage of arms sales with human rights during the 1970s (supplying, amongst others, Iran, Argentina and Brazil), it did take a stand over El Salvador, South Africa and Chile. Mrs Thatcher's early lifting of the arms embargo on Chile in 1981 served as an indication to authoritarian governments that the Thatcher government would do business with them and was unlikely to hold up orders over claims of human rights abuses. This proved of particular importance to Indonesia, faced with severe presentational problems over its continued illegal occupation of East Timor. Human rights considerations would not be allowed to get in the way of arms sales. The outlook of the government in this respect was summed up by Lord Strathcona's 1980 comment: 'Under some definitions there are practically no countries in the world which do not resort to what some people would regard as torture.'[97] A year later Douglas Hurd was arguing that: 'Most countries in the world have their problems and to use these problems as a reason for not supplying them with what they want would not be a sensible line to take.'[98] Colin Chandler, when head of DESO, thought that: 'The word repressive of course is a pretty subjective one. One man's repression is another man's defence of democracy. Is it really up to us to make these judgements?'[99]

Willingness to embrace flexible methods of payment, including offsets and counter-trade, also proved vital. 'Counter-trade' is the umbrella term applied to a range of compensatory trade arrangements, from barter, buy-backs and counter-purchases to offsets and licensed and co-production, intended either to reduce the amount of foreign exchange required to pay for arms or to link purchases with some form of inward investment. While

the Al Yamamah deals represent the most ambitious counter-trade deal
involving Britain to date, by the 1980s structural changes in the international arms market made some form of barter or offset almost *de rigueur*
as, in a buyers' market, states sought to limit their initial outlay and secure
something in return.[100] This is not to say that counter-trade has been
popular with arms manufacturers. Payments in forms other than hard
cash often do not realise the full value of orders. For example, the Al
Yamamah deals of 1986 and 1988 initially involved Saudi Arabia shipping 400,000 barrels of oil per day (b/d), later raised to 500,000 and now
standing at 600,000, to Shell and British Petroleum (BP) in part payment.
After they had taken a fee, this oil would be sold on the open market and
the proceeds eventually paid via the government to BAe or the relevant
arms manufacturer. However, fluctuations in the price of oil since 1986
have meant that in practice revenue has not been as high as anticipated
and that, for a time, there was a growing disparity between the value of
the equipment being supplied and the value of the 400,000 b/d of oil
received from Saudi Arabia. These fluctuations also led to periodic scares
that the future of the deal was in jeopardy. In practice, the situation has
resulted in periodic cash adjustments or adjustments to the volume of oil
delivered. Most strikingly, at the end of 1989 BAe was reported to have
received a cash payment of around £1.3 billion, while the Saudis upped
their payments in oil to 500,000 b/d.[101] Currently, 600,000 b/d represents
around 7.5 per cent of the kingdom's total 8 million b/d output.
Nevertheless, falling oil prices mean that this is of diminishing value. For
example, the value of the 600,000 b/d in September 1998 was up to £3
million a day less than a year previously.[102]

Under Mrs Thatcher, British companies became involved in a number
of counter-trade arrangements some of which bordered on the bizarre.
These took various forms and often represented a financial loss on the
contract of which they formed a part. For example, also under the Al
Yamamah agreements, Britain had to reluctantly agree to buy back from
the Saudis 24 1960s-vintage Lightning fighter aircraft, even though it had
no use for them or any prospect of selling them on. With Ecuador, Britain
took a quantity of bananas in part payment for Hawk aircraft. In selling
the Hawk to Finland, payment was partly in Finlandia vodka and metal
spiral staircases. To help offload them, a London department store,
Bentall's, was persuaded to hold a 'Friendly Finland Fortnight' featuring
Finnish goods at bargain prices.[103] (If these examples do not suggest that
the application of the counter-trade principle has come to have rather
opéra bouffe consequences, then the US company McDonnell Douglas's
agreement to accept part payment from Thailand for eight F-18 fighter
aircraft in frozen chickens surely does.[104]) One of the more bizarre mani-
festations of the close Anglo-Saudi military relationship involved the
England football team travelling to Riyadh in November 1988 to play a

friendly international with the Saudi national team as a condition of the Al Yamamah 2 deal.

Hence the structural imperatives of the arms market in the 1980s compelled arms exporters to enter into arrangements which were far from ideal, and which were not necessarily in their long-term interest. Nowhere is this more true than with regard to licensed and co-production agreements of the kind BAe has been obliged to enter into. As J. Fred Bucy has noted, the economic risks involved here increase over time because 'the release of know-how is an irreversible decision. Once released, it can neither be taken back nor controlled. The receivor of know-how gains a competence which serves as a base for many subsequent gains.'[105] Hence satisfying short-term interests can have a potentially harmful effect on longer-term interests. Contracts secured today help recipients compete with British exports in the future, and even consume British jobs in the short term as, for example, assembly work is taken out of the UK and licensed to a purchaser state.

Further factors which help explain the revival include the Thatcher governments' willingness to engage in constructive dispersal of the overseas aid budget and toleration of the payment of large commissions. While the payment of commission is standard practice in many industries when competing for foreign contracts, it is a deeply entrenched principle with regard to arms contracts. While the need to pay an official is viewed as corrupt practice when exposed at home it has been sanctioned as a necessary part of the process with regard to arms exports.

Finally, it is important to note the absence of political opposition or alternative vision with regard to Britain's global role in the context of the 'second' Cold War, and the role of arms sales within it. Defence was a Conservative issue, especially after the events of 1982 and the Labour manifesto of 1983. By extension almost anything relating to the military or to military equipment was a Conservative issue. There were few dissenting voices in Parliament, and anyway from 1983 to 1992 the government was insulated by large majorities. Furthermore, a number of arms sales relationships of dubious wisdom had actually been entered into by the preceding Labour government – most notably that involving the sale of Hawk aircraft to Indonesia.

Phase four: 1991–

Most recently, the post-Cold War, post-Gulf War era has constituted a further phase in the evolution of the international arms market, characterised by various features: the flow of former Soviet and Warsaw Pact weaponry on to the open market, generally at very competitive prices; the emergence of Eastern Europe as a potential market, especially in light of NATO expansion; a fresh bonanza for Western suppliers in the Gulf region; a continued high volume of semi-legal and illegal arms trafficking as the post-Gulf War 'new world order' was quickly supplanted by ethnic, tribal and regional conflict; the refocusing of export control concerns from the former Warsaw Pact states towards a small number of 'rogue' states such as Libya, North Korea, Iraq and Iran; and a shift in the focus of proliferation concerns from conventional to nuclear and, more immediately, chemical and biological weapons proliferation. Britain's performance in this market will be discussed more fully in Chapters 6 and 7.

Table 3
British major conventional arms exports to the developing world: leading recipients, 1964–97 ($ million)

1	India	6,364
2	Saudi Arabia	5,326
3	Iran	3,220
4	Brazil	2,805
5	Oman	2,354
6	Malaysia	1,984
7	Kuwait	1,619
8	Indonesia	1,462
9	Chile	1,429
10	UAE	1,294

Source Derived from the SIPRI arms transfers database. Figures are SIPRI trend indicator values in US$ million at constant (1990) prices.

Table 4
British major conventional arms exports to the developing world: leading recipients, 1964–97, by decade ($ million)

	1964–69		1970–79		1980–89		1990–97	
	Country	Value	Country	Value	Country	Value	Country	Value
1	India	949	Iran	2,913	India	2,857	S. Arabia	2,494
2	S. Arabia	606	India	1,848	S. Arabia	2,171	Malaysia	1,624
3	Libya	412	Brazil	1,613	Indonesia	931	Brazil	823
4	Kuwait	266	Oman	795	Turkey	821	UAE	760
5	Jordan	250	Chile	531	Oman	777	Oman	749
6	Israel	228	Israel	515	Nigeria	738	India	710
7	Iraq	226	Kuwait	444	Jordan	723	Kuwait	706
8	Malaysia	150	Argentina	416	Chile	664	Pakistan	532
9	Iran	136	Egypt	353	Egypt	480	Indonesia	522
10	S. Africa	115	Ecuador	277	Pakistan	371	S. Korea	418
Total of 10		3,338		9,705		10,533		9,338
Total UK in world market		5,596		17,212		18,959		13,624

Source Derived from SIPRI arms transfers database.

Understanding British arms sales

The economic argument

> My responsibility is to my own people and my own constituents, and I don't
> really fill my mind much with what one set of foreigners is doing to another.
> One has to say, what is it that is so dreadfully special about the people of
> East Timor to the people here? (Alan Clark[106])

One of the paradoxes of Britain's high-profile involvement in the international arms trade is that it is so difficult to find a rational explanation for
it. As defence economist Ron Smith has observed, this means that
'Whereas economists tend to think that weapons exports look unprof-
itable, and are driven by security factors such as military and political
interests, others tend to be more sceptical about the security benefits, and
think that they are driven by the economic advantages.'[107] In short, when
economists analyse Britain's involvement in the arms trade, they find
economic costs, when political scientists analyse it, they find political and
security costs.

Nevertheless, the preferred way of justifying some of Britain's more
problematic arms sales relationships has been through the invocation of
the number of jobs dependent on arms export success. This is the most
convenient line of defence, because the natural corollary is that any criticism of arms sales is held to be irresponsible and unpatriotic as it
jeopardises these jobs, rendering serious parliamentary debate virtually
impossible. Take, for example, this intervention in a parliamentary debate
from Lady Olga Maitland: 'We have a very clear policy on arms sales
abroad: they are for defence and for friendly nations. We will not sell to
a country that will use arms for an improper purpose. It is suggested that
it is somehow improper to sell police vehicles to Indonesia. Such a policy
would kill jobs – and that would be on the Labour party's conscience.'[108]
Or try this subtle variation from Ian Taylor, in answering Ann Clwyd's
question as to whether ministerial resignations would follow in the event
that 'the Minister is found to be at fault in his judgement that the
Indonesian Government will not use equipment exported from Britain
with licences granted by his Department': 'I am slightly puzzled by the
hon. Lady's question, given that the Labour party is in favour of selling
arms. If the Opposition are not in favour of selling arms, that would make
for an interesting statement by a Front-Bench spokesman as it would
threaten hundreds of thousands of jobs in this country.'[109]

The employment card was often a useful last refuge for Ministers being
pursued over the arms sales excesses of the Thatcher and Major years. For
example, under pressure over the Pergau Dam affair to say 'whether aid,
now or in the past, has ever been entangled with defence and arms sales –
yes or no?', the Foreign and Commonwealth Office (FCO) Minister of

State Alistair Goodlad turned the attack on opposition MPs, arguing that: 'They will not tell us whether they are in favour of defence sales, whether they are in favour of the aid and trade provision or whether they are in favour of destroying jobs – so we must assume that they are in favour of the latter.'[110]

For his part, Sir Geoffrey Howe told the Scott inquiry that in selling military equipment to Iran and Iraq the question was not 'shall the Iraqis or the Iranians get this or that?' but rather 'Shall we or shall we not stop British factories and workers from having the opportunity to supply?' Put another way, the question was not 'To what extent will Iraqis benefit?' but 'To what extent must Britons make sacrifices?'[111]

Employment has also been a focus of media reporting on the arms export industry. Take, for example, the BBC's *Westminster* television programme. On the day in 1997 when Robin Cook announced his new arms export criteria, Ann Clwyd, MP, appeared on the programme to provide comment. Presenter Nick Ross asked: 'Anne, let me ask you something. Suppose we've got people watching who, for example, are waiting to go on shift at British Aerospace who are making the Hawk: will you look workers in the eye and say "I am prepared to sacrifice your job in the short run in order for some principle overseas"?'[112]

There is no doubting the employment stake in exporting arms, although this is not to say that their export is a profitable exercise for the country as a whole. As a consequence of cuts in UK defence expenditure, and the policy of meeting equipment requirements through a vigorous process of international competitive procurement which does not automatically favour UK suppliers, the UK defence industry has lost an estimated 320,000 jobs since 1980/81. At the same time, though, those jobs estimated to be sustained through the export of arms has actually risen by 10,000. In the 1990s the number of defence jobs sustained by MoD expenditure declined steadily, from 405,000 in 1990/91 (itself a drop of 195,000 from a decade earlier) to an estimated 265,000 in 1996/97.[113] If defence companies were to survive in their current state – or, in some cases, at all – then export success was increasingly vital. Aided by vigorous government support during the Major years, and fuelled by Gulf rearmament and a number of valuable contracts in South East Asia (notably with Indonesia and Malaysia), the UK defence export sector had grown, in terms of employment, from a low of 80,000 in 1993/94, back to Cold War-era levels of 155,000 by 1996/97 (see Figure 1). Hence while the number of jobs dependent on MoD expenditure continued to fall, the total number of jobs in the UK defence industry in total actually grew by an estimated 60,000 between 1994/95 and 1996/97. In 1996/97, of the 420,000 jobs in the defence field, the government estimated that 155,000 were sustained by exports (75,000 directly, plus 80,000 indirectly)[114] – at 35.7 per cent of all arms-dependent jobs, the highest export-dependence

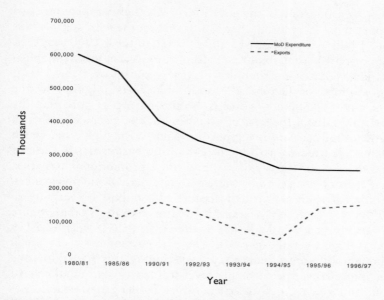

Figure 1 UK employment dependent on defence expenditure and exports.
Source Derived from figures in Ministry of Defence, *UK Defence Statistics, 1998*, table 1.11

rate in recent years, and up from 22.9 per cent in 1992/93. At the 1995 RN/BAEE, HDES Charles Masefield said that in future the defence industry would have to export 50 per cent of its output if it was to avoid further redundancies.[115]

However, creating or maintaining defence jobs has not necessarily rested on impeccable economic logic. Take this scene from Kenneth Baker's memoirs:

> On 18 June 1982 I was present at a meeting to discuss whether we should sell two frigates to Pakistan. Margaret [Thatcher] liked Pakistan, which was a good friend of Britain, but the Treasury ... and the Department of Trade ... were not in favour of finding the money to subsidise the cost of building the ships. Margaret was supported by John Nott, the Defence Secretary, and myself from Industry. She summed up by saying, 'You must find a way. You are accountants and accounting is all about taking a sum of money from one person and giving it to someone else. Sort it out.'[116]

In the light of such incidents it should come as little surprise that the 'economic defence' of UK arms exports has increasingly been called into question by analysts in recent years. In a 1996 study, Paul Dunne, Ron Smith and Neil Cooper set out to calculate the size of the annual government subsidy to the arms industry. Based on the cost of MoD support and promotional activity (£81 million), costs arising from ECGD cover (£303 million), and the proportion of the government R&D effort spent on arms that are exported (£650 million), they estimated that the total subsidy was in excess of £1 billion a year, or £12,500 for each of the 80,000 jobs then directly supported by arms exports.[117] In a more recent study, Stephen Martin has analysed the profitability of arms exports over the 1990s, considering a range of factors: the additional costs involved in the Government buying equipment so as to bolster its export potential; the cost of operating DESO; the cost of attachés' time in promoting British arms; the cost of military aid in support of exports; the high costs which the ECGD has incurred as a result of defaulting customers; the use of overseas aid to promote arms exports; and other promotional activities. Taking these factors into account, Martin argued that UK involvement in the arms trade carries a net cost of about £228 million – a subsidy of roughly £2,000 for each job 'sustained' by arms exports.[118] This figure overstates the current level of subsidy by taking an ECGD 'cost' of £239 million (an average over the period), when its current costs are much lower, although still substantial. Even susbstituting this figure for one reflecting its more recent performance level still leaves an annual cost of £23 million, and given the anticipated future higher costs as a consequence of the Asian financial crisis and depressed oil prices, this figure may well represent something approaching a best-case scenario.

The foreign policy argument

> It is the Government's policy to support the sale of British defence equipment overseas where this is compatible with our political, strategic and security interests. (Lord Clinton-Davis, March 1998)[119]

> Britain's political aspirations are linked to its defence sales efforts. (Frederic Pearson, 1983)[120]

Aside from the issue of employment, the other 'economic' arguments in favour of maintaining a healthy arms export sector (that they contribute to lower unit costs by yielding longer production runs, absorb some of the cost of weapon development for the UK, contribute to the maintenance of a broad defence industrial base) all have a single political underpinning. They arise only as a consequence of Britain's desire to afford and maintain an independent defence capacity sufficient for the country to continue to play a global role which allows for the pursuit of British interests, the assumption of a leading role in various defence groupings, and the need to justify Britain's continued occupancy of one of the five permanent (P5) seats on the UN Security Council. As former Defence Minister Alan Clark observed during a December 1997 defence debate, 'the objective of the Foreign and Commonwealth Office is that our military capability should carry sufficient weight to merit our place on the Security Council ... and, deriving from that, our place on the various other bodies that determine world policy, such as the Group of Seven'.[121] By extending influence and securing the ability to produce the means to achieve these ends, arms sales are clearly a political act, consistent with securing that objective. They are both an expression of Britain's continued desire to play a world role and a way of facilitating it. As Clark himself observed: 'as a general rule, countries that take in British equipment tend to be more closely linked to us in defence liaison matters ... it's part of an adjunct to your foreign policy, because if people are buying your equipment, they are to some extent dependent on you for the logistic train, and for repairing and servicing and training even – part of an integrated foreign policy.'[122]

As a former HDES, Charles Masefield, put it:

> The importance of the UK defence industry is for our own national security. We need a defence industry in order to have a secure nation, to provide defence equipment for our three services. Without defence exports it would be impossible to maintain our defence industry in its current form, in its current size, and we would be forced to go overseas to procure for our home defence and we would have to buy equipment which was not designed for our use or our needs and we would have to buy equipment which is more expensive.[123]

This vision was most recently reinforced in George Robertson's Strategic Defence Review, where the priorities outlined require continued arms sales success. Maintaining an independent military capability and demonstrating the willingness to deploy it in pursuit of UN or NATO goals allows the UK to retain influence over the definition of those goals. In this respect, the Labour government's intention to order two new 'super' aircraft carriers, twice the size of the current *Invincible* class carriers, serves as a key symbol. In the post-Cold War world, a healthy arms export industry is still a leading currency of international influence, a passport to a leadership role within NATO, influence over European Union (EU) defence and foreign policies, and the route by which the UK seeks to retain global influence.

Official policy statements

The rationales which the government itself offers fall into two categories: supplier-oriented and recipient-oriented. The former seek to justify sales in terms of British defence and national interests, as, for example, in the 1985 *Statement on the Defence Estimates*:

> with the rising cost of defence equipment, both our ability to provide the Services with the weapon systems they require and the continued strength of our defence industries depend more than ever on a vigorous but responsible overseas sales policy. The Government therefore supports British firms in

their efforts to sell defence equipment overseas, whenever this is compatible with wider political, strategic and security interests, since the unit costs of equipment we purchase ourselves are driven down both by competition and by the longer production runs required for overseas sales.[124]

The recipient-oriented rationale seeks to justify arms exports in terms of meeting others' legitimate defence needs, which, because they are legitimate, will be met by others if Britain chooses not to sell. As a result Britain will unnecessarily lose out on the related political and commercial benefits, in influence, as well as in employment. A good example is found in the 1991 *Statement on the Defence Estimates*:

> The United Kingdom's policy on arms transfers is to meet the legitimate defence needs of friendly countries provided we are satisfied in each case, on the basis of such criteria as the risks to our own security, regional stability and conformity to international obligations, that there are no good reasons for denial. Defence exports on this basis are of political and commercial value.[125]

This rationale is legitimised by reference to Article 51 of the UN Charter, as in the 1995 *Statement on the Defence Estimates*:

> The Government believes that the responsible transfer of defence equipment is consistent with Article 51 of the United Nations Charter, which recognises the inherent right of all states to self-defence if an armed attack occurs. That right cannot be exercised unless states also have the right to acquire the means by which to defend themselves. The transfer of conventional weapons, when conducted in a responsible manner, can enhance the ability of states to meet their legitimate defence and security requirements; contribute to the deterrence of aggression and encourage negotiation for the peaceful resolution of conflict; and enable states to join effectively in collective measures decided on by the United Nations for the purposes of maintaining or restoring internal peace and security.[126]

The difficulty, of course, is that, once delivered, arms are no longer under the control of the supplier, and self-defence is not the only use to which they can be put. In practice, arms exported from Britain in this period have seen more service in coercion, repression and aggression than in self-defence. An empirical study of arms imports by developing countries has added further weight to the argument that arms acquisitions contribute to repression, by 'making violent political acts more feasible' in environments where arms are used primarily to maintain order rather than guard against external threats.[127] In short, Britain's commitment to safeguarding the rights of states under Article 51 has been at the expense of violating the rights of individuals as enshrined in the Universal Declaration of Human Rights (especially Articles 3 and 5), adopted without dissent by the UN General Assembly in December 1948. Naturally, government justifications for selling arms do not address the two-sided character of the arms acquisition coin. Neither do they address the fact, suggested by statistical analyses, that arms races increase the likelihood that disputes between states may result in war.[128] Neither do they address the fact that the UK arms industry, along with its mainly Western counterparts, does not just passively respond to demand. It creates demand through weapon development, marketing weapons around a global network of exhibitions, and by selling to regional rivals.

For its part, in 1981, the FCO listed the advantages of exporting arms in the following foreign policy (rather than economic) terms:

(a) arms sales enable us to assist friendly countries to improve their ability to stand on their own feet militarily. This makes them more able to resist aggression or encroachment from countries whose policies are hostile to British and Western interests. Together with our programme of military training assistance, arms sales are a cost-effective way of providing continued support for pro-Western regimes. This applies particularly in areas where Britain has important political and economic interests but where we and our allies cannot provide direct military support;
(b) arms sales, because they enable friendly countries to defend themselves, can be an important element in promoting security and regional stability;
(c) our willingness to sell arms and to offer other indirect forms of military assistance can often be an important element in good political relations with customer countries. This sustains existing friendships and helps to create new ones;
(d) to deny countries which are important to us the right to buy our arms would be to risk opening up opportunities for countries hostile to British and Western interests to gain footholds in the third world. All countries have a right under the United Nations Charter to self defence and all exercise this right by purchasing the means to defend themselves. If they are prevented from buying arms from Britain or other allied countries they will look elsewhere.[129]

From an industrialists' perspective, the Defence Manufacturers' Association (DMA), the trade association which represents 370 defence and related companies in the UK, lists the benefits of exporting arms in a different way, emphasising the supposed contribution to the UK economy. Hence for the DMA, exporting arms: reduces the unit cost of equipment procured for UK armed forces by increasing production runs and exacts a commercial exploitation levy on exports of equipment developed at the taxpayer's expense; contribute to the balance of payments; account for almost 40 per cent of defence industry business and are therefore crucial to its survival; provide approximately 150,000 jobs; and finally are 'an important instrument of foreign policy for the Government in supporting allies, influencing other nations, helping to maintain regional stability etc.', and help in improving the prospects of civil exports to recipient countries.[130] As we have already seen, the core assumption underlying this argument (that exporting arms makes a positive contribution to the economy) has come under serious challenge in recent years.

The relative weight of political and economic considerations within any one decision on an arms sale is obviously affected by a number of factors: region, size of order, extent to which it ties the purchaser to the UK for its arms, absence of war, and so on. In reminiscing over British policy towards Iran under the Shah, Anthony Parsons' account illustrates the interaction of certain of these considerations, and shows how a combination of political and economic considerations underpinned British policy towards Iran:

> The Shah's human rights record was dismal. The public media were under strict control and free speech was a dangerous luxury. Arbitrary arrest, torture and executions were commonplace ... Moreover, the Shah's foreign policy verged on the hegemonistic toward his immediate neighbours, Afghanistan and Iraq, and to the smaller states on the Arab side of the Persian Gulf. For all these reasons, there was a strong strand in British public opinion which believed that it was wrong to supply arms to such a regime.
>
>   But Iran and Britain had been allies in a military treaty (the Baghdad Pact, later CENTO) since 1955 and Iran was a linchpin of Western strategy in the Middle East. The Shah was determined to build massive armed forces, principally in order to outstrip the armed might of the historic adversary, Iraq, and Britain badly needed arms export markets to sustain an indigenous defence industry, secure foreign exchange and promote industrial activity and employment.[131]

Recipient perspectives and leverage

Arms sales are also politically significant because they serve as an expression of approval of the recipient country. While a supplier may not regard the supply of arms as conferring approval, recipients clearly do, and the failure to acknowledge this was a factor in the collapse of Western relations with Iraq, for example. The arms sales relationship distorted both Iraqi perceptions of how the West would react to an invasion of Kuwait and Western perceptions of Saddam.

In 1971 Julius Nyerere offered what should have served as a warning to supplier states in this respect, when he offered the view that:

> the selling of arms is something which a country does only when it wants to support and strengthen the regime or the group to whom the sale is made. Whatever restictions or limits are placed on that sale, the sale of any arms is a declaration of support – an implied alliance of a kind. You can trade with people you dislike; you can have diplomatic relations with governments you disapprove of; you can sit in conference with those nations whose policies you abhor. But you do not sell arms without saying, in effect: 'In the

light of the receiving country's known policies, friends, and enemies, we anticipate that, in the last resort, we will be on their side in the case of any conflict. We shall want them to defeat their enemies'.[132]

Whether the British government considers this statement to be the reality is largely irrelevant. Its importance lies in the fact that Nyerere offers a recipient perspective.

A related consideration is the way in which arms sales relationships lead the supplier state to align itself more closely with the purchasing government thereafter in a number of ways. Firstly, as arms packages have increasingly, over the last decade, come to be tied to offset agreements, the conclusion of an arms deal tends to mark an increase in bilateral industrial and commercial ties. While these are notionally separate from the arms package, their fate is closely linked with it. Secondly, the negotiation of an arms package (often a lengthy process), discussions over training requirements, offsets, etc., require MoD, FCO and civil servants from other departments to visit the country in question. It is often also necessary for senior government Ministers, such as the Secretary of State for Defence, the Foreign Secretary and, increasingly, the Prime Minister to visit such countries, since the days of Mrs Thatcher taking along various captains of industry in a bid to fully exploit the opening. Such visits help cement closer bilateral ties, or create the perception of a close bilateral relationship, and can impact on the prestige of governments in the developing world. Those who doubt that this is so should reflect on the Iraqi media coverage given to Saddam Hussein's meetings with British Ministers of even the lowly rank of David Mellor (Minister of State at the FCO) in the late 1980s.

Furthermore, once such deals are concluded, they leave the supplier government vulnerable to cancellation or delays in the order until it is complete. Once a deal has been agreed, the relationship between supplier and recipient alters, as was evidenced, for example, in Britain's recent relations with Malaysia and Indonesia. This restricts the supplier government's room for manoeuvre in terms of criticising the activities of the recipient state. Any criticism has to be qualified and carefully weighed against the possible consequences. The necessity of avoiding such criticism has led to the British government playing down certain allegations or denying the validity of others. The supplier government is, whatever the private misgivings of those involved, obliged to support the recipient in its actions lest its military contracts, and any civil contracts that have developed alongside, should be jeopardised. Hence the threshhold for diplomatic expressions of displeasure and reaction is raised, generally dictating low-level responses to any excesses perpetrated by purchasers. Examples of this process are not hard to come by. In addition to the exceedingly mild reaction to the summary execution of Farzad Bazoft in

Table 5

Leading UK arms purchasers: democratic and human rights indicators, 1997

Country	Suffrage	Political parties	Ratified International Covenant on Civil and Political Rights (ICCPR)	Ratified Convention against Torture and other Cruel, Inhuman or Degrading Treatment or Punishment	Human rights issues, 1997
Bahrain	None	Prohibited	No	No	Several hundred arrests Following anti-government demonstrations. Torture and ill treatment of detainees continued.
Brunei	None	Inactive, banned or deregistered	No	No	No entry
India	18 yrs	Yes	Yes	Signed[a]	Thousands of political prisoners arbitrarily detained. Torture and ill treatment endemic, leading to at least 300 deaths in custody. 'Disappearances' continued; hundreds of extra-judicial executions reported.
Indonesia	17 yrs	Yes	No	Signed[a]	At least 300 prisoners of conscience detained. In East Timor 'disappearances' continued. Dozens killed by security forces in suspicious circumstances.
Kenya	18 yrs	Yes	Yes	Yes	Scores of people killed by police. During 1997 some may have been extra-judicially executed. Peaceful rallies calling for political reform violently broken up by police using tear gas, batons, live ammunition and rubber bullets.

Kuwait	Adult males naturalised for 30 years or more, or have resided in Kuwait since before 1920 and their male descendants at 21 years[b]	None	Yes	Yes	Status of scores of political prisoners arrested in 1991 remained unclear. The fate of more than 70 detainees who 'disappeared' in custody in 1991 remained unknown.
Malaysia	21 yrs	Yes	No	No	People continue to be detained without trial under the Internal Security Act
Nigeria	21 yrs	Suspended after 1993 coup Partially re-established in September 1996	Yes	Yes[a]	Hundreds of prisoners of Conscience detained during 1997 Most detained without charge or trial; others convicted in unfair political trials. Reports of torture and ill treatment of prisoners; at least two prisoners of conscience died as a result of prison conditions so harsh as to amount to cruel, inhuman or degrading treatment. People with links with political opposition or human rights groups attacked and threatened, allegedly by government agents.
Oman	None	None	No	No	At least 12 prisoners of conscience held; five of them were reportedly sentenced to prison terms following a secret trial.
Qatar	None	None	No	No	At least 117 charged in connection with February 1996 coup attempt. Forty were charged in absentia. 77 were held incommunicado. Torture of detainees alleged, in one case allegedly resulting in death in custody
S. Arabia	None	None	No	Yes	Scores of suspected political or religious opponents of government were detained. Hundreds arrested in previous years remained held without trial. Allegations of torture and ill treatment continued.
UAE	None	None	No	No	Torture and ill treatment reported and the use of cruel judicial punishments increased significantly

Sources CIA World Factbook 1997 (cols 1–2); Amnesty International Report 1998 (cols 3–5).
[a]Signed but not yet ratified (as of 31.12.97).
[b]Approx. 10 per cent of population.

Iraq, in the UK case this process has extended to the way in which it votes on relevant UN Security Council resolutions and the extent to which it has been willing to raise issues relating to purchasers there.

During the 1980s this was, for example, the case with regard to Chile and Indonesia. In the case of Chile, the British government found itself denying the validity of reports indicating that human rights abuses were on the increase after justifying a resumption of military sales partly on the basis that such abuses were in fact declining. With regard to Indonesia, the British government's freedom to criticise Indonesia's involvement in East Timor was circumscribed by its desire to continue selling the military equipment that aided the genocide of the indigenous East Timorese population. In the minds of many, the British government became so closely associated with the corrupt and repressive Suharto regime as to be regarded as one of its leading international supporters, a process aided by Mrs Thatcher's personalisation of the arms sales drive and high-profile visit to Indonesia in April 1985 (see Chapter 4).

Arms sales, then, are viewed by recipient governments as a mark of political approval. Such sales help underpin claims to legitimacy by supplying regimes with the means to retain power and satisfy the institutional demands of the military for state-of-the-art hardware. Where states have elected governments, are free of corruption, respect human rights, offer their populations the rights and freedoms those of supplier states demand for themselves, and do not order arms at the expense of necessary infrastructural development, this poses few problems. However, most major recipients of British arms have fallen far short of this model, as Table 5 shows.

Hence although government's role is not only to promote, but also to regulate, the flow of British arms abroad, there are compelling pressures which gravitate towards facilitation rather than regulation. As one commentator observed: 'Despite the fact that government involvement was originally intended to slow and regulate the arms trade, it has been responsible for massive expansions. Furthermore governments have their own "Midas touch"': they politicize everything they touch, and arms sales have been no exception.'[133] And as Frederic Pearson notes: 'Once in the sales business, government the nominal and ultimate controller, and the major defence customer for domestic arms industries, comes under intense pressure to become government the promoter.'[134] It is a role that has been taken up with enthusiasm by successive British governments, anxious not only to secure jobs, but to secure British influence abroad within a framework of gradual decline.

Notes

1 Hansard, 25 January 1966, col. 64.

2 *Financial Times*, 4 September 1980.

3 Andrew J. Pierre, *The Global Politics of Arms Sales* (Princeton, NJ, Princeton University Press, 1982), p. 3.

4 See John Callaghan, *Great Power Complex: British Imperialism, International Crises and National Decline 1914–51* (London, Pluto Press, 1997), esp. ch. 5. See also Correlli Barnett, *The Lost Victory: British Dreams, British Realities 1945–1950* (London, Macmillan, 1995), esp. chs 3–5.

5 John L. Sutton and Geoffrey Kemp, *Arms to Developing Countries 1945–1965* (London, IISS, Adelphi Paper No. 28, 1966), p. 9.

6 MoD: *Export of Surplus War Material*, end 9676, cited in Pierre, *The Global Politics of Arms Sales*, p. 101.

7 Public Record Office, London (hereafter PRO), FCO 371/177820, 'Arms Control in the Middle East', Paper circulated to FO Planning Committee, 30 December 1964.

8 PRO: CAB 134/2509, Minutes of Meeting of the Ministerial Committee on Strategic Exports, 4 July 1961.

9 PRO: PREM 11/4486, 'Supply of Arms and Military Equipment to South Africa', Memorandum by A. Clutterbuck, Chairman, SE(O)C, 10 June 1961.

10 PRO: PREM 11/4486, 'Supply of Arms and Military Equipment to South Africa', Memorandum, 22 June 1961.

11 PRO: PREM 11/4486, Telegram, FO to Washington, 9 May 1963; FO to Cape Town, 10 May 1963.

12 PRO: CAB 129/114, 'Export of Buccaneer Aircraft to South Africa', Memorandum by the Chief Secretary to the Treasury and Paymaster General', 23 July 1963. See also CAB 128/37/CC(63)49, 25 July 1963.

13 PRO: PREM 11/4486, 'Record of a Conversation between the Foreign Secretary and the South African Foreign Minister on July 9, 1963', 11 May 1963.

14 PRO: CAB 129/114, 'South Africa', Memorandum by the Secretary of State for Foreign Affairs, 28 June 1963.

15 PRO: CAB 129/114, 'South Africa and the United Nations', Memorandum by the Secretary of State for Foreign Affairs, 8 July 1963.

16 The Commonwealth Relations Office considered that an HMG veto at the UN could lead to retaliatory sanctions by the African Commonwealth nations against the UK. See PRO: CAB 129/114C(63)146, 30 July 1963.

17 PRO: CAB 128/37/CC(63)46, 11 July 1963.

18 See PRO: PREM 11/4486, 'Extract from Record of Conversation at Admiralty House', 23 July 1963

19 The relevant extract from Stevenson's speech is in PRO: PREM 11/4487, Telegram, New York to FO, 2 August 1963.

20 PRO: PREM 11/4487, Telegram, Home to Smithers, 3 August 1963.

21 'Calls upon all member states to boycott all South African goods and to refrain from exporting to South Africa goods, including strategic and other material, for the manufacture of arms and ammunition in that country.' PRO: PREM 11/4487, Telegram, New York to FO, 5 August 1963.

22 PRO: PREM 11/4487, Telegram, FO to Certain Foreign Embassies, 8 August 1963. Dean explained that: 'It is the view of my delegation that the right of South Africa to self-defence under Article 51 of the Charter and requirements which may arise from the maintenance of international peace and security must be borne in mind. In view of our arrangements of cooperation with South Africa for the protection of the sea routes, we must reserve our position in the light of requirements regarding the supply of equipment appropriate to these purposes.'

23 PRO: PREM 11/4487, 'Extract from a Record of Conversation' between Home and Rusk, New York, 26 September 1963.
24 PRO: CAB 128/37CC(63)56, 23 September 1963. In a memorandum to the Cabinet the chairman of the committee, Henry Brooke, recommended that 'because of our strategic, financial and commercial interests in South Africa, and the likelihood that African opinion will not be satisfied by anything short of a complete arms embargo, it seems desirable that at this stage any additional restrictions should be as few as possible'. PRO: CAB 129/114/c(63)158, 'Arms for South Africa', Memorandum by the Secretary of State for the Home Department, 17 September 1963.
25 PRO: PREM 11/5114, Memorandum, 'Supply of Spare Parts for Military Equipment to South Africa', 28 February 1964.
26 PRO: PREM 11/5114, Handwritten minute, J. O. Wright to Home, 28 February 1964.
27 PRO: PREM 11/5114, Memorandum, 'Export of Arms to South Africa', Butler to Home, 6 August 1964.
28 See his memorandum to Home, PRO: PREM 11/5114, 9 September 1964.
29 PRO: PREM 17/92, Minute, O. Wright to P. Carey, Board of Trade, 17 October 1964. The new Foreign Secretary sent Wilson a note two days later saying, 'I know what a rush you have been in these last few days ... but I think in normal circumstances it would have been right to consult me before issuing the instructions about an arms embargo on South Africa.' PRO: PREM 13/092, Walker to Wilson, 19 October 1964.
30 Handwritten comment on minute dated 19 October 1964. PRO: PREM 13/092.
31 PRO: PREM 13/092, 'Arms for South Africa', A. Hockaday to O. Wright, 23 October 1964.
32 PRO: CAB 148/17/OPD(64)/2, 9 November 1964.
33 PRO: PREM 13/092, Telegram, Pretoria to FO, 15 November 1964. A portion of the speech is appended to a letter from the South African embassy to Wilson dated 18 November 1964.
34 PRO: PREM 13/092, E. C. Redhead, Minister of State, Board of Trade, to Wilson, 30 October 64.
35 PRO: PREM 13/092, Minute, Wright to Wilson, 15 November 1964.
36 PRO: CAB 148/17/OPD(64)11, 25 November 1964.
37 PRO: CAB 148/17/OPD(64)4, 2 December 1964.
38 PRO: CAB 148/18, Minutes of OPD meeting, 10 February 1965.
39 The embargo had never been religiously observed. In addition to the exceptions discussed earlier, unarmed survey ships, naval spares, practice ammunition, aircraft spares, comunications and electronic equipment, and other items had all been sent during this period.
40 Harold Wilson, *The Labour Government 1964–1970: A Personal Record* (London, Weidenfeld & Nicolson and Michael Joseph, 1971), p. 470.
41 PRO: DEFE 24/256, 6 June 1967, John Peters, MoD Private Office, to Head, DS 13.
42 PRO: DEFE 24/256, 'Arms Sales to South Africa', Minute of meeting between George Thomson and Roy Mason, 13 July 1967.
43 *Ibid*.
44 PRO: DEFE 24/256, 25 August 1967, 'Arms for South Africa', O. J. Porter to AUS(M).
45 PRO: DEFE 24/256, 12 September 1967, Confidential Annex to COS Sixty-seventh Meeting/67, held on Tuesday 12 September 1967 at 2.45 p.m.
46 PRO: CAB 148/33, 'Arms for South Africa', Memorandum by the Secretary of State for Foreign Affairs and the Secretary of State for Defence, 11 September 1967. See also the briefing prepared for Denis Healey, dated 13 September 1967, in DEFE 24/256. The minutes of the meeting are at CAB 148/30/OPD(67)/30, Minutes of OPD Meeting, 14 September 1967.
47 PRO: CAB 148/34, 'South Africa: Maritime Defence Supplies', Memorandum by the

Secretary of State for Foreign Affairs and the Secretary of State for Defence, 5 December 1967.

48 PRO: CAB 148/30, 'South Africa: Maritime Defence Supplies', Confidential Annex to Minutes of OPD Meeting, 8 December 1967.

49 PRO: CAB 128/42/CC(67)/70, 14 December 1967.

50 Anthony Howard (ed.), *The Crossman Diaries* (London, Mandarin, 1991), entry for 15 December 1967, p. 422.

51 Denis Healey, *The Time of my Life* (London, Penguin, 1990), p. 335.

52 PRO: CAB 128/42/CC(67)71, 15 December 1967.

53 *Ibid.*

54 PRO: CAB 128/42/CC(67)/72, 18 December 1967.

55 Crossman commented that he had 'never heard anybody publicly scourged as George Brown was scourged by Harold this morning'. Howard, *The Crossman Diaries*, entry for 18 December 1967, p. 426. See also the accounts in: Wilson, *The Labour Government 1964–1970*, pp. 470–6; George Brown, *In my Way: The Political Memoirs of Lord George-Brown* (London, Victor Gollancz, 1971), ch. 9; Peter Paterson, *Tired and Emotional: The Life of Lord George-Brown* (London, Chatto & Windus, 1993), pp. 226–33; and Philip Ziegler, *Wilson: The Authorised Life* (London, HarperCollins, 1995), pp. 287–91. There was, of course, some merit in Brown's argument that he had been exploring a policy option agreed with Wilson but that Wilson had shifted his position and subsequently tried to portray Brown as the original and primary advocate of arming South Africa.

56 Hansard, 18 December 1967, cols 923–4.

57 Hansard, 11 May 1966, col. 471.

58 In May 1966, Fred Mulley, Minister of Aviation, faced a motion of censure for not informing the House that the Saudi Arabian deal would be included in the offset figure. See Hansard, 11 June 1966, cols 412–85.

59 PRO: PREM 13/2003, 'The Arrangements for Offsetting the Dollar Cost of the F-111 Aircraft', Memorandum by the Secretary of State for Defence, undated.

60 PRO: DEFE 13/511, Telegram, Washington to FO, 1 January 1968.

61 Howard, *The Crossman Diaries*, entry for 3 January 1968, p. 436.

62 PRO: CAB 128/43/CC1(68).

63 Howard, *The Crossman Diaries*, entry for 12 January 1968, p. 442.

64 PRO: CAB 128/43/CC1(68).

65 Healey, *The Time of my Life*, p. 292.

66 *Ibid.*, p. 273. See also the contemporaneous account from Tony Benn, *Office without Power: Diaries 1968–72* (London, Hutchinson, 1988), pp. 12–16.

67 PRO: CAB 128/43/CC6(68). See also the account of the meeting in PREM 13/1999, Telegram, Brown to FO, 11 January 1968.

68 PRO: PREM 13/1999, Telegram, Lyndon Johnson to Harold Wilson, 15 January 1968.

69 PRO: CAB 128/43/CC6(68).

70 Hansard, 17 May 1966, col. 1119. See also Healey's comment, Hansard, 23 June 1966, col. 919.

71 CAB 134/2798, 'Sales of Defence Equipment to the United States', Memorandum by G. C. B. Dodds, 12 December 1966.

72 PRO: CAB 148/28, 'Implications of the Vietnam War on Sales to the US and other Countries', Memorandum by the Secretary of State for Defence, 27 June 1966.

73 PRO: CAB 148/25, Minutes of OPD Meeting, 29 June 1966.

74 Hansard, 14 July 1966, col. 1716.

75 PRO: CAB 134/2795, 'Supply of Bombs to Australia', Memorandum by the Minister of Defence for Equipment, 12 October 1967. Another consideration was that 'The Australians would no doubt react against an expression of disapproval of their activi-

ties in Vietnam which are in support of policies to which the British Government in general adhere. It would be highly undesirable to strain our relations with the Australians on this ground so soon after we have, against strong Australian argument, revised our defence policy in the Far East in a manner unwelcome to them.' *Ibid*. See also the minutes of the Ministerial Committee meeting of 23 October 1967 in the same file.

76 PRO: CAB 148/30/OPD(67)/35, Minutes of OPD Meeting, 3 November 1967.
77 PRO: CAB 134/2795, 'Sale of Defence Equipment to the United States', Memorandum by G. C. B. Dodds, 30 January 1967. See also the Minutes of the Ministerial Committee on Strategic Exports, 2 February 1967, where the decision was formally taken.
78 PRO: CAB 134/2795, Minutes of Meeting of Ministerial Committee on Strategic Exports, 18 April 1967. See also, CAB 134/2799, 'Sale of Defence Equipment to the United States', Memorandum by G. C. B. Dodds, 13 March 1967, and his memorandum of the same title dated 11 April 1967 at CAB 134/2795.
79 Edward Heath, *The Course of my Life* (London, Hodder & Stoughton, 1998), pp. 477–8.
80 Hansard, 3 March 1971, cols 1722 and 1724.
81 J. W. Sutherland, 'Export Selling of Defence Electronics', Synopsis of paper read at Conference on Arms Sales and Political Influence, University of Southampton, 26–8 April 1972.
82 David Cannadine, 'This sceptic isle', *Observer Review*, 8 November 1998.
83 Margaret Thatcher, *The Downing Street Years* (London, HarperCollins, 1993), pp. 8–9.
84 For the impact of Hitler's rise on Thatcher's thinking, see Margaret Thatcher, *The Path to Power* (London, HarperCollins, 1995), pp. 24–34.
85 Percy Craddock, *In Pursuit of British Interests. Reflections on Foreign Policy under Margaret Thatcher and John Major* (London, John Murray, 1997), p. 22.
86 Quoted in Anthony Barnett, *Iron Britannia: Why Parliament Waged its Falklands War* (London, Allison & Busby, 1982), p. 135.
87 The value of China's arms deliveries began to fall after 1990, as the conditions that facilitated its rise changed. The Iran–Iraq War ended, the Iraqi market disappeared under the impact of sanctions, and China was displaced by Russia as Iran's preferred supplier.
88 Hansard, 9 February 1993, cols 810–11.
89 *Jane's Defence Weekly* (hereafter *J.D.W.*), 12 February 1997, p. 3.
90 *SIPRI Yearbook 1990: World Armaments and Disarmament* (Oxford, Oxford University Press, 1990), p. 226.
91 *J.D.W.*, 12 February 1997, p. 3.
92 Stephen Castle, 'Guns and football', *Independent on Sunday*, 24 May 1998.
93 See also the account in the revised edition of Luke Harding, David Leigh and David Pallister, *The Liar: The Fall of Jonathan Aitken* (London, Fourth Estate, 1999), pp. 189–90.
94 *The Times*, 22 April 1981.
95 Alan Thomas, 'Attacked from all sides: the UK 20 per cent in the arms market?', *RUSI Journal*, February 1994, p. 44.
96 Interview with Robin Robison, London, 27 March 1995.
97 Frederic Pearson, 'The question of control in British defence sales policy', *International Affairs*, 59:2 (1983), 228.
98 Foreign Affairs Committee, Minutes of Evidence, 4 March 1981, p. 45.
99 Cited in CAAT, *The Government and the Arms Trade* (London, CAAT, 1989)
100 For an overview of the different forms of countertrade see Ron Matthews, 'Countering or countenancing countertrade?', *Management Accounting*, October 1991, pp. 42–4.

For more detailed treatments see Ronald Matthews, 'Butter for guns: the growth of under-the-counter trade', *World Today*, 48:5 (1992), 87–92, and Stephanie Neuman, 'Co-production, barter, and countertrade: offsets in the international arms market', *Orbis*, spring 1985, 183–213.

101 *Sunday Times*, 10 December 1989.

102 See *Guardian*, 18 September 1998, *Sunday Times*, 13 September 1998, and *Guardian*, 19 February 1999.

103 James Adams, *Trading in Death: Weapons, Warfare and the Modern Arms Race* (London, Hutchinson, 1990), pp. 125–6.

104 *Guardian*, 21 August 1996.

105 Defence Science Board Task Force on Export of US Technology, *An Analysis of Export Controls of US Technology*, 1976. Quoted in Michael Klare, 'The unnoticed arms trade', *International Security*, 8:2 (1983), 68.

106 'Death of a Nation', *Network First*, ITV, 22 February 1994.

107 Ron Smith, 'The profitability of arms exports', unpublished paper, May 1991.

108 Hansard, 6 February 1997, col. 1222.

109 *Ibid.*, 14 June 1995, col. 779.

110 *Ibid.*, 28 February 1994, col. 652.

111 Scott Inquiry: Day 54, 12 January 1994, Evidence of Lord Howe, p. 13.

112 'Westminster', BBC2, 17 July 1997.

113 All employment figures are taken from, Ministry of Defence, *UK Defence Statistics 1998*, p. 17.

114 *Ibid.*

115 *J.D.W.*, 9 September 1995, p. 8.

116 Kenneth Baker, *The Turbulent Years: My Life in Politics* (London, Faber & Faber, 1993), p. 261.

117 CAAT, *Killing Jobs: Arms Trade, Economy and Unemployment* (London, CAAT, 1996). See also Neil Cooper, *How the UK Government Subsidises the Business of Death* (London, CAAT, 1997). Similar arguments are contained in World Development Movement, *Gunrunners' Gold: How the Public's Money Finances Arms Sales* (London, WDM, 1995).

118 Stephen Martin, 'The Subsidy Savings from Reducing UK Arms Exports', *Journal of Economic Studies*, 26:1 (1999), 15–37.

119 Hansard (Lords), 16 March 1998, col. 112w.

120 Frederic Pearson, 'The question of control', p. 225.

121 Hansard, 3 December 1997, col. 273.

122 Interview with Alan Clark, London, 3 February 1999.

123 BBC Radio 4, *File on 4*, 13 February 1996.

124 *Statement on the Defence Estimates*, 1985 (London, HMSO, 1985), p. 40. It is worth noting that the emphasis in these annual statements shifts from year to year in response to the prevailing climate. For instance, in the aftermath of the 1991 Gulf War, the emphasis on home defence was largely replaced by one on responsible, controlled exporting.

125 *Statement on the Defence Estimates, 1991: Britain's Defence for the '90s* (London, HMSO, 1991), p. 30.

126 *Statement on the Defence Estimates, 1995: Stable Forces in a Strong Britain* (London, HMSO, 1995), para. 446.

127 Shannon Lindsey Blanton, 'Instruments of security or tools of repression? Arms imports and human rights conditions in developing countries', *Journal of Peace Research*, 36:2 (1999), 233–44.

128 See, for example, Michael D. Wallace, 'Arms races and escalation: some new evidence', *Journal of Conflict Resolution*, 23:1 (1979), 3–16, and Susan G. Sample, 'Arms races

and dispute escalation: resolving the debate', *Journal of Peace Research*, 34:1 (1997), 7–22.

129 Memorandum submitted by the FCO to the House of Commons Foreign Affairs Committee, *Minutes of Evidence* 4 March 1981, p. 37.

130 Memorandum submitted by the Defence Manufacturers Association (July 1998), Foreign Affairs Committee, *Foreign Policy and Human Rights* III, Appendices to the Minutes of Evidence, First Report, Session 1998–99, HC100-III, p. 310

131 Anthony Parsons, 'An expense of money in a waste of weapons', *Index on Censorship*, 20:10 (1991), p. 25.

132 Quoted in Signe Langren-Backstrom, 'Arms trade and transfer of military technology to Third World countries', in A. Eide and M. Thee (eds), *Problems of Contemporary Militarism* (New York, St Martin's Press, 1980), p. 231.

133 Cindy Cannizzo (ed.), *The Gun Merchants: Politics and Policies of the Major Arms Suppliers* (New York, Pergamon, 1980), p. 15.

134 Pearson, 'The question of control', p. 213.

2

The administration and politics of British arms sales

Export control

National controls

The government's power to control the export of arms and related equipment is derived from the Import, Export and Customs Powers (Defence) Act of 1939. This was one of a number of Acts hurriedly passed at the outbreak of war to confer war powers on the Government, and is the source of the authority of the Department of Trade and Industry (DTI) today to make by order 'such provisions as it thinks expedient' to regulate the import and export of all goods. This authority is regulated through the application of the Export of Goods (Control) Order (EG(C)O) of 1994. As the DTI explained in 1990: 'The EG(C)O serves a variety of policy purposes and any of the goods listed are controlled for one or more policy reasons. Export controls are maintained for reasons of national and foreign policy and to give effect to international obligations and commitments.'[1]

The 1939 Act had two notable features. Firstly, it was clearly intended only as a temporary, wartime, measure.[2] Secondly, it made no provision for parliamentary scrutiny of or involvement in the export control process. In part, this was a reflection of the emergency nature of the powers. As Dingle Foot noted during the parliamentary debate on the Bill, 'we are all readily granting now to the Government powers which we should never have dreamed of granting in any ordinary time.'[3] Nevertheless, on the whole, Parliament acquiesced in the extension of these powers into peacetime without protest.[4] This has meant, for example, that Parliament has had no input into decisions on the imposition, duration or lifting of arms embargoes.

The most vocal challenge to the legitimacy of the continued use of the 1939 Act and the exclusion of a parliamentary role came not from Parliament itself but from Sir Richard Scott, in his 1996 'arms to Iraq' report. Scott was highly critical of continued reliance on the Act. It had been 'prompted by considerations of administrative convenience and political expediency', and its continued use was 'a reprehensible abuse of executive power by successive administrations'.[5] This represented some of the strongest language in the entire report, and the Major government accepted his recommendation of a comprehensive review. This process, which had led to the production of a Green Paper on Strategic Export Controls in July 1996, was inherited by the incoming Labour government in May 1997. However, while the new government prioritised the publication of new criteria for arms exports, and from there the negotiation of an EU Code of Conduct, the issue of reform of the export control system was put on a back burner. It was not until July 1998 that the DTI finally published a White Paper.[6] Even then, although the White Paper recognised the desirability of fresh legislation to supplant the 1939 Act,[7] the measure did not feature in the subsequent Queen's Speech, setting out the government's legislative programme for the 1998–99 session of Parliament. In December 1998, the Trade and Industry Select Committee (TISC) echoed Scott's call for the repeal of the 1939 Act.[8] Hence while Parliament has been alerted to its abdication of responsibility throughout the Cold War period, and seems prepared to assert its authority over the issue, the executive continues to drag its feet. Nevertheless, the supplanting of the 1939 Act with new legislation which will afford Parliament a greater role now seems inevitable.

The EG(C)O itself is divided into a number of separate lists which cover different types of goods. Part III of Schedule 1 (the 'Military List') covers arms and related equipment. Separate lists cover nuclear and dual-use equipment (the 'Industrial List'). This latter list also includes chemical precursors. Most of the equipment included on the Military List is derived from Cold War obligations defined by the Co-ordinating Committee for Multilateral Export Controls – COCOM – (identified by the prefix ML), with some additional, national, restrictions (prefixed PL). These lists provide the framework within which arms sales decisions are made. Any equipment featured on the EG(C)O must be granted an export licence by the DTI before it can be legally exported.[9] To take a couple of examples, ML6 covers vehicles designed or modified for military use, including tanks, self-propelled guns, armoured vehicles and components, while ML10 covers aircraft and aircraft equipment, including combat aircraft, engines, parachutes and crash helmets.

International control regimes

Throughout the Cold War era, the most important export control regime to which the UK belonged was COCOM, established in 1950 to restrict the flow of technology to the Warsaw Pact countries and their Cold War allies.[10] Its restrictions inform the core of the UK EG(C)O. The end of the

Cold War and collapse of the Soviet Union meant that COCOM was no longer a particularly appropriate vehicle for controlling the flow of strategic goods – nor were its former targets necessarily the destinations of greatest concern. Discussions on a successor regime eventually produced the Wassenaar Arrangement, which came into effect in November 1996. This mandates the maintenance of agreed lists of military and dual-use items with the aim of preventing destabilising accumulations of conventional arms and dual-use technologies, and provides a forum where member states (confidentially) exchange information on the denial and granting of export licences. In practice, for arms this is based on declarations made for the UN Conventional Arms Register. However, because (in theory at least) there are no specific target states, all decisions on licensing are the responsibility of national governments in line with their own export legislation. In practice, of course, there are targets, partly defined by non-membership. There are currently 34 member states in this loose grouping, the core of which are the former COCOM states, plus a number of additional states drawn from Eastern Europe, plus South Africa, South Korea, Argentina, and New Zealand.[11] Because there are no officially prohibited destinations, in theory any state can join, provided that it exports arms or dual-use equipment, and is deemed by a consensus of existing members to be able to implement effective export controls and to abide by internationally agreed norms regarding non-proliferation.

The UK is also a signatory to or member of a number of other international control regimes which help determine the content of the EG(C)O. These are: the nuclear Non-proliferation Treaty (NPT)[12] and, related to it, membership of the Nuclear Suppliers Group[13] and the Zangger Committee; the Missile Technology Control Regime (MTCR);[14] and the Australia Group.[15]

In the case of conventional arms there are few licensing problems. Armoured vehicles, ordnance and missiles cannot easily be mistaken for anything else. However, the bulk of the EG(C)O deals with products which of themselves are non-lethal. This is clear evidence of governmental awareness of the security implications of high-technology exports, and determination to exercise control over all aspects of the arms trade. Since the 1991 Gulf War the control of non-lethal and dual-use equipment has been further tightened.[16] Moreover, manufacturing companies are alert to government interest in this area. Even where they are not in the arms business themselves, they are well aware of the military implications of their products, as the Matrix Churchill and related cases made clear, and have some idea of the political respectability or otherwise of the importing country. In this latter regard, the quality of information made available through the DTI – both in printed form and through the internet – has improved greatly since 1991. Since exporters do not wish to run the risk of incurring production costs only to have a licence refused, they err on the side of caution and consult the authorities in advance of agreeing to any sale. Hence the British government has complete formal authority over arms exports and the active co-operation of the private sector. Its responsibility for the trade is therefore unconditional.

The role of the DTI

The DTI is charged with applying UK export control legislation and issuing export licences through its Export Control Organisation (ECO), established in 1988. Upon receipt of a formal order, a company will apply to the ECO for an export licence. When applying for a licence it is the duty of the exporter to provide the DTI with all relevant information regarding both the product and its intended end use. The ECO's Export Licensing Unit (ELU) would deal with this request. It is its job to ensure that the export licence application (ELA) is accompanied by the necessary supporting documentation, a copy of the contract (in the case of purchase by a government agency) or an end-user certificate, to confirm that the goods are for the purchaser's own use and will not be resold without permission. The ECO's Technologies Unit then checks the goods against a matrix matching goods with intended destination, and which identifies which goods for which destinations the other departments involved in the process have requested to see.

In general, if the product in question features on the Military List, information regarding the application will be sent to the MoD, FCO and, since September 1997, the Department for International Development (DFID), to assess whether export would be permissible and consistent with British security and foreign policies. Dual-use equipment (featured on the Industrial List) can also be dealt with in this way, although here the DTI has a degree of discretion about which combination of product and destination merits referral to these departments. Sir Richard Scott found that, in practice, the DTI relies completely on MoD assessments of the licensability of Military List goods (with some FCO input). If the MoD or FCO opposed a licence application, Scott found, the 'DTI could not override the MOD objections'. Hence 'the proposition that the Secretary of State at the DTI receives advice on ELAs from other government departments but then exercises his own judgement in deciding whether or not to grant the export licence has, so far as Military List ELAs are concerned, no connection with reality'.[17] Nevertheless, in theory at least, upon receiving advice to refuse an export licence, the ECO considers the case at a senior level to ensure that the refusal is 'soundly based', and the basis of the refusal can be challenged.[18] There would be nothing, in theory, to prevent a disagreement being discussed by Ministers, or being passed up to Cabinet committee or even Cabinet level, if the sponsoring department felt strongly enough about it, although in practice this is rare.[19]

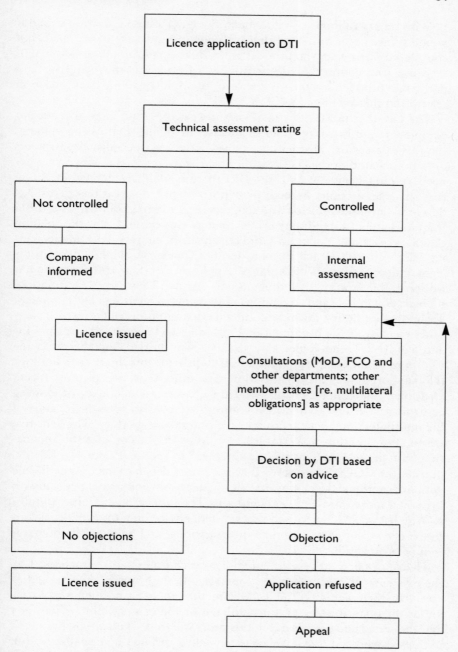

Figure 2 The export licence application process.
Source TISC, *Strategic Export Controls*, Second Report, Session 1998–99, Minutes of Evidence, diagram appended to 'Memorandum submitted by the Department of Trade and Industry'.

With regard to dual-use equipment, the ECO's stated position is that it would refuse applications on the following grounds: the consignee is not considered *bona fide*; the product is, in their opinion, intended for military use; the country of destination is of concern; the quantity of a particular product sought, or the level of sophistication, is excessive in relation to the stated end use.[20]

The fact that in all cases involving the export of military and nuclear equipment, and in a large number of cases involving dual-use equipment, the ECO passes on information for assessment to specialist departments does not mean that the DTI is without the capacity to make its own independent judgements. Within the DTI there is a clearly defined structure that analyses various aspects of export licence applications. This has developed in sophistication and scope in recent years. Following the 1990 Iraqi invasion of Kuwait, the DTI's capacity was expanded by the creation of a Sanctions and Embargo Enforcement Unit, charged with implementing UN Security Council Resolution 661. Currently, the ECO comprises eight units: Management Support; Applicant Services and Compliance; Military Licensing (including Small Arms); Sensitive Destination, Industrial Goods and Sanctions Licensing; Licensing Development; Technologies; Policy (including sanctions); and Enforcement.

As recently as the beginning of 1990, the ECO comprised just the ELU and Sensitive Technologies Unit (STU), since retitled, together with the Computer Unit, comprising three staff to provide information technology (IT) support across the organisation. The other units are all more recent creations. The Policy Unit is intended to ensure the adequacy of existing controls and ensure that British controls are consistent with the aims of the multilateral agreements to which Britain is a signatory. The Sensitive Destinations Section was established in May 1990 to process the applications for licences to sensitive destinations in the developing world (i.e. outside the COCOM-proscribed area). These destinations change in line with international developments, although certain countries are dealt with here on a more or less permanent basis. The Enforcement Unit maintains a 'Watch List' of suspect end users, offers advice on suspect destinations to exporters, supports Customs investigations, and helps in the preparation of prosecutions.

Hence the first stage of the administrative process is characterised by the existence of comprehensive controls. All applications are checked to establish their veracity and to ensure that there is nothing suspicious about the quantity of a product ordered or the compatibility of product and the stated end use. To aid in this process licence applications for destinations considered 'sensitive' are channelled through a specialist section which pays closer attention to such questions in their cases. Arms export requests, requests for sensitive destinations and known dual-use equipment requests are then passed on to the MoD, FCO or DFID, or all three, for advice, depending on the nature of the specific case. However, Sir Richard Scott's report did suggest that the process by which dual-use applications (Industrial List goods) were determined had the potential to be less than watertight. For example, by 1984, although the Iran–Iraq War had been under way for over three years, the MoD was still not sent all licence applications for goods covered by the Industrial List for those countries.[21] Moreover, despite the existence of this wide-ranging formal network, some doubts regarding the efficacy of the procedure surfaced in the early 1990s, as the nature of Britain's contribution to the arming of Iraq came to suggest that the process had been subjected to manipulation by politicians.[22]

The most extreme expression of this process occurred with regard to Iraq in January 1988 when Trade Minister Alan Clark met representatives of the Machine Tools Technologies Association and advised them on how to avoid having their export licence applications turned down, even though there was acceptance that their products were probably being purchased in order to manufacture munitions. Clark told the meeting that 'the intended use of the machine should be couched in such a manner as to emphasise the peaceful aspect to which they will be put. Applications should stress the record of "general engineering" usage of machine tools.'[23]

This points to the fact that export controls are only as effective as the government of the day intends them to be. While the lessons of Iraq are being absorbed into the regulatory structure, they also have to be absorbed at the political level. Clearly, the political will to apply the controls has to exist for the system to be effective. Comprehensive guidelines exist to aid those considering licence applications, but in borderline or sensitive cases their interpretation is a political act, and often reflects wider priorities. This also points to the fact that while the DTI is charged with export control, its *raison d'être* is export promotion, resulting in a conflict of loyalties, the resolution of which, recent history suggests, tends to favour exports over restraint. Hence there is a strong argument for suggesting that the ultimate export licensing body should not be the department charged with promoting British exports but the FCO, for whom exercising control over exports would throw up fewer conflicts of interest.[24]

The Ministry of Defence

In the case of a licence application being for military or dual-use equipment, the request is usually referred to the MoD and FCO for advice. The MoD evaluates the strategic and security implications of making equipment available to third parties, and offers technical advice as to whether specific goods are appropriate to their declared end use. Within the MoD, the Defence Export Services Secretariat (DESS) co-ordinates this process, which will also involve input from the Defence Intelligence Staff (DIS). To aid the process, the MoD maintains a standing classification for both arms and potential customers to which it refers when dealing with licence applications. Having separately classified arms and customers, during any negotiation it becomes necessary to merge the two sets of criteria – i.e. to enable a decision to be made regarding whether arms can be sold to country X, and, having decided this, to determine what level of sophistication of weaponry can be sold to country X bearing in mind its international position and the advancement and effectiveness of the technology behind the weaponry. This function is performed by the Release of Military Information Policy Committee. With regard to the Iran–Iraq War, in 1984 the MoD set up a further specialist committee, the Ministry of Defence Working Group, to consider licence applications just for those two states.

Another of the MoD's security functions is to ensure that, during the gradual process of sales negotiations, negotiators (whether DESO, attachés, or industrial) do not reveal too much information about a particular item at what the MoD considers to be too early a stage. Under the sales drive launched in the early years of the Thatcher governments, pressure to secure orders led to previously classified details being released earlier and earlier.

Ministerial roles

At a ministerial level, the Minister for Defence Procurement has responsibility for issues relating to arms exports. However, the contradictory tensions evident in the role of the DTI surface again here, as the Minister is responsible not only for export promotion, but also for advising against export where necessary. As with the DTI, there is a strong argument here that one person should not be required to pursue conflicting objectives. In such a situation, how is success measured? By the volume of arms sold, or the number of cases where restraint is shown? Again, recent history suggests incumbents measure their success in terms of the former rather than the latter. In addition to the roles performed by the Minister for Defence Procurement, the Minister for the Armed Forces can be called upon to consider cases where exports of arms could affect the security of British forces personnel. Particularly sensitive cases referred to either Minister could ultimately be passed on to the Secretary of State for Defence and, if contested by another department, to Cabinet committee or even the full Cabinet.

The Foreign and Commonwealth Office

The FCO retains an independent capacity to evaluate the politics of arms sales. It has the task of assessing the foreign policy consequences of agreeing to supply or refusing to supply countries outside NATO with British arms. The FCO's Non-proliferation Department (NPD) co-ordinates the activity of evaluating the impact of a proposed arms sale on the political situation within the purchasing country, and its likely effect on neighbouring countries and the prevailing balance of power. It checks to see that the licence application is consistent with multilateral treaty obligations such as the MTCR, etc. If it is not, it is rejected; if it is, it is passed on for further evaluation. This evaluation is provided by the relevant area desk. Area desks currently consider applications against the July 1997 criteria announced by Robin Cook and the EU Code of Conduct. Because the FCO is not staffed by technical experts (a constant complaint from industry, on the grounds that it slows down consideration of applications), DTI or MoD technical experts may be consulted.

Overseas posts may also be requested to supply information, for example where the stated end user is considered suspect. Any application with potential human rights implications will then be passed to the FCO's Human Rights Policy Department. Once it has received the area desk's advice, the NPD makes a final assessment. The Minister of State with geographical responsibility for the region in question would be responsible for this process, although particularly sensitive cases could be referred to the Foreign Secretary.

As Sir Richard Scott found, from 1984 the FCO maintained its own guidelines to assist officials in making licensing recommendations, but they were not published outside the FCO, and the DTI knew nothing about them. The guidelines were grouped under four headings. The first, 'Strategic/Political', included four considerations: 'would the sale introduce a destabilising factor in the area?' in terms of technological advance or volume of arms held; 'would the sale *severely* compromise HMG policy on arms control?' (present author's emphasis); 'would the sale create political problems with other more valued allies?' and whether special considerations applied, such as embargoes. The second grouping covered 'Britain's Allies and Collaborative Ventures', and considered whether a sale would infringe collaborative agreements or treaty obligations with allies. The third group covered 'British Interests'. Would an export weaken or compromise Britain's defences? What impact would the sale have on the economy or employment? Would a sale result in the release of weapons which might be used against British or allies' forces, or be passed on to a country which might use them in that way? Would a sale result in equipment sought by terrorists being acquired by a country 'which would be prepared to pass it on to anti-British elements'? The final grouping was headed 'Customer Country'. This advised that: 'Close attention should be paid to the recipient country if such a country has a bad record of human rights. If the equipment concerned is for internal security purposes ... officers should consider carefully whether it is likely to be used for internal repression.'[25] Hence the FCO operates according to clear guidelines in offering a recommendation to the DTI. Nevertheless, with regard to human rights considerations, one is bound to observe that either it has offered bad advice on more than one occasion, or its advice in this regard has been overridden by the DTI.

The Department for International Development

Currently, any licence applications to export goods identified as being of concern to 83 named countries are passed to the DFID for an assessment of the developmental impact of the sale, where human rights and internal repression issues are considered. The FCO may also pass on other cases for DFID scrutiny. However, questions about the weight which the DTI attaches to DFID opinion have been raised by the revelation that the DTI went ahead and issued export licences for Eritrea and Indonesia against the advice of the DFID.[26] The suggestion that its role is viewed by the DTI and MoD as subsidiary, and its existence as something of a necessary evil, is strengthened by the fact that while the Secretaries of State at the DTI, MoD and FCO all signed the annual report on arms exports, the Secretary of State for International Development was excluded,[27] although the department is notionally a part of the licensing process.

Interdepartmental bodies

In addition, the FCO is represented along with the MoD, DTI, Customs and Excise, MI6 and GCHQ on the Restricted Enforcement Unit (REU), an interdepartmental committee established in 1987 and chaired by the Director of the ECO. It meets fortnightly to discuss sensitive export cases of 'actual or suspected breaches of UK export controls or export control objectives'. This is an opportunity for departments to be made aware of intelligence findings, and to share their concerns on arms-related issues. One former chairman described it as 'essentially a clearing house for information and a forum for discussion which brought together a range of intelligence providers and potential users'.[28]

The FCO is also involved in the Security Export Controls Working Party (SXWP). Established in 1956, this is chaired by the MoD, and includes officials from a number of other departments, including the DTI, FCO, and Customs and Excise. It is the SXWP which effectively formulates government policy on export controls at a working level. In so doing it is aided by the operation of three sub-groups considering missile, nuclear, and chemical and biological weapons proliferation issues. Following the outbreak of the Iran–Iraq War, the government established the Interdepartmental Committee (IDC), which included DTI, MoD and FCO representatives, to scrutinise all export licence applications for either country. The IDC met monthly to interpret and oversee the application of the Howe guidelines. Its recommendations would then be circulated to the MoD and FCO for approval in the case of military goods, or to the DTI in the case of Industrial List products. As with the REU, disagreements would be referred to Ministers, although this proved necessary in only 5 per cent of the cases it considered.[29]

There is no evidence to suggest – as Mrs Thatcher seems at times to have believed – that officials in the FCO are fully paid-up members of the peace lobby. Their responsibilities include arms control, disarmament, the monitoring of embargoes, and regional peace issues, but they also take the view that arms can help cement relations with friendly governments. The record of the last twenty-five years suggests that the FCO has remained firmly under political control. Whatever private doubts officials may have had about the destabilising effect of arms sales initiatives, none (Mark Higson aside) was prepared to jeopardise his career by speaking out against the Downing Street line.

Customs and Excise

The final stage of the administrative procedure is played by Customs and Excise. It is responsible for enforcing compliance with the EG(C)O and the terms of end-use certification, by which a customer agrees not to pass on equipment to third parties without prior MoD approval.

Should a violator be formally identified, Customs and Excise are empowered to detain suspect shipments, seize unauthorised or illegal shipments, and press charges against individuals involved. Decisions regarding prosecutions are taken by Customs' Policy Division, but with the advice of the Solicitor's Office. Nevertheless, just because a prosecution is held to have a better than 50–50 chance of success that does not necessarily mean it will be brought. Wider political considerations can also apply. With regard to arms sales, this function has gained much publicity through the 'supergun', Matrix Churchill and Ordtec cases, the genesis of each of which indicates that Customs' role in the administrative process is confined to enforcement and does not intrude into policy formulation. Had Customs been more fully involved in the inner workings of the system, it is difficult to see how such prosecutions could have been pressed. This again points to the political nature of arms sales, and the difficulty identified by Sir Richard Scott that, while the purpose of prosecutions should be to enforce the law, 'the "law" where export controls are concerned has the appearance, and perhaps the reality, of being no more than government policy for the time being'.[30]

Sales promotion

The arms sales record and arms sales machinery, 1964

Prior to the production of the 1965 Stokes Report, what machinery existed to promote British arms sales abroad, and to what effect? The principles governing the export of arms at that time remained essentially those outlined in Parliament by John Profumo in January 1959:

> All applications for the supply of arms abroad are examined by the Government Departments concerned in the light of the political, strategic and economic implications of each individual case. Subject to these factors, the general principles followed are that sales are authorised to recognised and stable Governments which are in normal diplomatic relations with Her Majesty's Government. Sales are not authorised where the arms are, in the opinion of Her Majesty's Government, likely to be re-exported; or to be used for aggression against or subversion of other countries; or where such sales would have a generally prejudicial effect upon the stability of the area as a whole.[31]

Military equipment design was based solely on the requirements of the UK forces. No consideration was given to whether a design being adopted was also likely to fit the requirements of other states. Moreover, the demands of the UK forces in terms of quality were high, driving the price of equipment up to a level where few foreign buyers would consider it. Nevertheless, Donald Stokes was exaggerating somewhat in ascribing all UK arms export success at the time to luck: 'luck in producing a good weapon cheaply, luck in having the monopoly of some weapon, luck in finding another country prepared to bend its requirements to our own, luck in having captive customers as a result of political links such as those of the Commonwealth'.[32]

In terms of co-ordinating the sales effort, the key committee was the Ministerial Committee on Strategic Exports (SE(M)C), whose terms of reference covered arms export promotion as well as control. It was chaired by the President of the Board of Trade, and as such seems to have been designed to err on the side of exports where disagreement or division arose. This ministerial committee was supported by the work of the Strategic Exports (Official) Committee (SE(O)C), which was itself supported by the work of the Arms Working Party (AWP), chaired by the head of DS 13. There also existed a Committee on Export Policy, chaired by the Permanent Under-secretary to the Board of Trade, on which the MoD was not represented, and which discussed general export policy issues. Where appropriate, these bodies would liaise with or seek the advice of the Release of Military Information Policy Committee, although this was not primarily concerned with export issues.

Within the MoD, each of the three service departments had a responsibility for export promotion. In addition, the Ministry of Aviation (MoA) undertook export promotion, although it was the F6 branch of the Air Department which actually negotiated sales. The largest export promotion department within the service branches was the Army Department's Directorate of Sales, which numbered around 200 and which, in addition to an Executive Sales Director, who handled government-to-government sales, employed a brigadier as Military Adviser, Overseas Equipment, to advise foreign armies on the availability of British equipment. This directorate's primary task was to sell equipment produced by the Royal Ordnance Factories – essentially, armoured vehicles, guns and ammunition.

Overseas, the promotion of arms sales was primarily the job of the military attaché. However, in most countries, there was just one attaché representing two or all three of the services, who could devote only a limited amount of time to sales promotion. Contact between the service branches of the MoD and industry was, at best, limited and there were no formal arrangements for co-ordinated export promotion. In terms of credit facilities, in contrast to the flexibility which characterised credit arrangements during the Thatcher and Major years, the situation was somewhat rigid. The ECGD would normally provide credit for up to five years. While military aircraft were likely to qualify for the full five-year repayment period, items such as Scout armoured cars were more likely to qualify for just three. In addition, the ECGD was unable to offer insurance for government sales.

Furthermore, actual export performance was hampered by a number of institutional factors. British military equipment tended to be offered overseas later than that of competitors, delivery times were longer, and prices were generally higher. With regard to naval equipment, the requirements of the RN meant that naval producers were being asked to produce vessels which included many features which were not required by other countries which had no desire to pay for them. Hence the Navy Department had taken the first tentative steps in supporting producers in 'private ventures' – producing designs exclusively for the export market. Industry needed government assistance, though, as such items were considered unsaleable without some form of certification showing that the RN approved of the design and confirmed the capability. Hence while there was a willingness to support export industry and a growing realisation within the MoD that current efforts were inadequate, there was no structure capable of offering the support and co-ordination necessary to maximise the UK's share of the growing but increasingly competitive global arms market.

Towards the Defence Sales Organisation

In the last months of the Conservative government and the early months of the 1964 Labour Government, British manufacturing industry began to voice its frustration at what it saw as inadequate government support of the export effort. Already, in June 1959, the Select Committee on Estimates had produced a critical report which had concluded that while

> both the Ministry of Supply and the Service Departments appreciate the economic and strategic advantages of the sale to foreign countries of British military equipment and stores ... this appreciation has not always been fully translated into the determined effort necessary for effective sales promotion ... The market ... is increasing year by year and is becoming highly competitive. The situation demands a concerted effort on the part of the departments concerned if the United Kingdom is to increase, or even merely to maintain, its position in the export trade in arms ... [33]

In March 1964, Secretary of State for Defence Peter Thorneycroft told his private secretary:

> Both Lord Nelson of Stafford and Sir Charles Dunphie have told me recently that they think that there is room for much improvement in the liaison between the Government and Industry in the Field of arms exports. They say that time after time they are beaten by foreign competitors whose Governments have managed to exert influence either at the time when formal agreements covering defence matters are being signed, or in other ways.

Thorneycroft went on to say that there was a need to 'be clear on whether the object of the existing machinery of committees is primarily to promote the export of arms or to prevent it. Industry seems to be in some doubt about this.'[35]

As a result of these representations, the SE(O)C began looking into the US and French approaches to selling arms, and considering suggestions for 'stimulating sales of arms'. The question of whether the committee could be converted 'into an Arms Export Committee, with wider terms of reference, including the promotion of arms exports, and the task of giving special attention to what might be done to stimulate arms abroad'[35] was floated by Thorneycroft, but rejected by Prime Minister Alec Douglas-Home, who saw its primary and proper function as being one of control. Various suggestions for stimulating British arms exports emerged from the MoD. For example: making provision in defence votes to finance the visits of foreign buyers of arms; offering better credit facilities; producing a pamphlet for industry explaining how the government could assist arms exporters, and so on. (Most of these suggestions would be adopted in one form or another by Donald Stokes in his 1965 report.) In addition, meetings were scheduled between the MoD and the Society of British

Aerospace Companies (SBAC) 'to discuss the ways in which our representatives overseas, whether military or civilian, can help'. For its part, the SE(O)C concluded that there was a need 'for more people whose *primary* function was the promotion of arms sales'.[36]

Following the October 1964 general election, the incoming Labour Government inherited this ongoing review. Denis Healey, installed as Defence Secretary, told Douglas Jay, President of the Board of Trade, that the MoD were 'certainly very conscious of the need to export, realizing as we do that, if other countries can be induced to buy our weapons systems, the production runs will be longer and the cost to everybody reduced'.[37]

Export industry's concerns were summarised by Jay in a memo to Healey in December 1964. Jay told Healey that insufficient attention was paid to export potential in the specification and design of the products required by the domestic market.[38] But the clearest source of frustration was the apparent inertia of the British government when set against the dynamism of US administrations in this area, epitomised in US Defense Secretary Robert McNamara's setting up of International Logistics Negotiations (ILN) in 1961, which operated from within the Pentagon's International Security Affairs division. ILN was to become the model for the DSO.

Headed by Henry Kuss, and initially with a staff numbering less than 30, ILN divided the global market amongst four teams. In addition, each team was given a functional responsibility: the 'Gray' Team was given an industry liaison function, the Blue Team a finance function, the Red Team a long-range planning function, and the White Team an export support plans function. ILN also maintained direct lines of communication with the State Department where political clearance was required.

ILN's own figures suggest that its impact on US arms exports was immediate. Cash receipts from export sales rose from US$300 million in 1961 (the year in which ILN was established), to US$1.3 billion in 1963 and US$1.2 billion in 1964. As Kuss explained:

> Companies were spending thousands of dollars going overseas, coming back with the NATO telephone directory and thinking they'd done a marketing job. What we consider marketing, on the other hand, is a study that starts all the way back at tactical doctrine. Military sales are not and never have been very much like commercial sales overseas. Military sales are deeply imbedded in military-political thinking ... One of my most important jobs is to help bring the military men of the two countries together. That begins the process of resource utilization.[39]

As a result of these various pressures, in January 1965 an interdepartmental meeting was held, attended by representatives of the MoD, Board of Trade and MoA, to consider the issue of improved support for the export effort and air a number of key concerns. The Under-Secretary of

State for Defence (Army), Gerald Reynolds, noted that the promotion of arms sales was primarily the work of defence attachés, but that this network had been run down. There were also suggestions that British attachés were not as aggressive as their French and US counterparts, and that the MoD needed to take their sales role into account when making appointments ('sales promotion could not be effectively carried out, if it were regarded as a spare-time interest'). Moreover, Reynolds argued, the FO was sometimes 'over-sensitive' about arms exports, objecting, for example, to the sale of anti-tank weapons to Libya. He also pointed out that British industry was hampered where the Americans were not because in general British forces required only limited production runs. Hence it was not usually possible to sell equipment 'off the shelf'.

Some steps had already been taken by the MoD to promote the export of British arms. One of these was 'providing places on courses for young officers from overseas who would quickly reach high rank in their own countries'. However, this initiative had been limited by a shortage of instructors and criticism from the Estimates Committee that foreign governments were not being charged enough for the places.[40]

In June 1965, the government was on the verge of setting up a committee to consider the changes in policy and organisation needed to improve export performance.[41] In responding to this suggestion, Lord Shackleton, the Minister of Defence, RAF, compared the UK export effort with that of the US under Henry Kuss. Shackleton argued that the value of Kuss's role lay in that 'he is an operator within the American government machine providing essential co-ordination, clearing road blocks, seizing opportunities and thanks to his direct access to Ministers, especially Mr McNamara, he is able to bring to success what might otherwise get lost in what he calls the jungle of the Pentagon.' Having met Kuss, Shackleton was 'now firmly convinced that we need some form of central co-ordinating sales organisation'. As things stood, the UK lacked 'an effective focal point which must surely be essential to give direction and impetus in any sales campaign. There is a strongly amateurish "ad hoccery" about our efforts in contrast to the professionalism of the American Kuss organisation'.[42]

What was needed was a sales co-ordinating organisation. As to the question of who should head such an organisation, Shackleton suggested either 'a senior civil servant or perhaps, if he could be found, the right sort of ex-officer with some, but not necessarily too much, technical background and some experience of industry'. Again, this was modelled on the Kuss approach ('You will be aware that Henry Kuss and his team are career civil servants'). In addition, the organisation itself should be located within the MoD,[43] and its head should have direct access to a senior Minister in the MoD, and should be of 'sufficient status, personality and authority to conduct its operations'. Rather than set up a committee to discuss the options, on 7 July Shackleton met Donald Stokes, the head of Leyland

Motors. Stokes suggested that the head of any such organisation should be an experienced salesman rather than a civil servant or retired officer. One problem which Stokes anticipated was the need for the new organisation to build links with those who had influence over arms purchases in potential markets. Possibly with the contemporaneous Saudi example in mind, Stokes outlined how, when 'the right person had been found, effort would be concentrated upon him and in time a sale would be effected ... a great many arms sales were made not because anyone wanted the arms, but because of the commission involved en route.'[44]

The following day, 8 July, Shackleton suggested to Healey that they might offer the job to Stokes, who would only need two or three people to support him and, apart from that, would initially take over the running of the existing sales branches of the MoD and Ministry of Aviation. Healey said there were three options to be considered: Stokes could be invited either to conduct an investigation of the arms sales 'problem' and make recommendations – a process which would take three months; he could be asked to combine this with some operational work over a fixed term of six months; or he could be asked to reshape and head the arms promotion effort for the next two years.[45]

On 12 July, Shackleton took Stokes to meet Denis Healey.[46] Stokes presented Healey with six pages of 'quickly dictated first impressions of a possible method of dealing with the problem of export military sales' and Healey asked him if he would do a 'crash job' by advising the government on how best to organise its arms export promotion apparatus. On the one hand, Healey wanted advice on how to make the Whitehall apparatus more commercially oriented, on the other, how the 'jungle' of responsibilities and committees within Whitehall could be streamlined. He proposed that Stokes should take three months to conduct an investigation into and make recommendations on the arms sales apparatus both inside and outside Whitehall, and also on possible changes in arms sales policy.[47]

Stokes's 'quickly dictated first impressions' were, in fact, the template for the lengthier and more considered report he was to produce later in the year. In them he urged a more vigorous sales effort via the creation and operation of a 'Sales Organization'. They are replete with veiled references to the necessities of the market – the need to pay commissions, to cut through red tape and make instant decisions, and so on. Stokes warned that: 'A certain ruthlessness and disregard of convention in practice if not apparent is essential if any progress is going to be made against the formidable selling techniques now employed by the United States, French and other governments.' He suggested the establishment of a body, with complete executive authority, to promote British arms abroad, headed by a civilian chairman, 'not because there would be any shortage of gifted civil servants or military advisers' but because 'the position must be one held by a person who is more orientated to sales rather than respect for orthodoxy. Also, if the Organisation is going to be successful, it is going to get involved from time to time in situations where a position of independence will be indispensable.'

Assisted by a Private Secretary, A. W. Stephens, and an advisory group drawn from the MoD and MoA, Stokes began a programme of discussions with officials across government, outside government, and even outside the UK. These involved the Prime Minister, Foreign Secretary, Defence Secretary, Chancellor, and President of the Board of Trade, figures from industry, domestic and foreign – including the infamous British Aircraft Corporation (BAC) agent in Saudi Arabia, Geoffrey Edwards – and Ministers or officials in France, West Germany, Belgium and the Netherlands. He also had the opportunity to read in draft the contemporaneous Plowden Report on the aviation industry. In September 1965, Stokes also travelled to the Pentagon to get the advice of the man whose own organisation was the inspiration for his own proposals, Henry Kuss,[48] before finally delivering his report on 12 November 1965.

The Stokes Report

Stokes began by setting out his assumption that 'the Government is agreed firstly that the sale of conventional arms to friendly overseas countries is a desirable and necessary part of our trade and secondly that it is vital in present circumstances not merely to maintain our arms exports at their present level ... but to increase them substantially'.[49]

Stokes's report went on to recommend a fundamental change in approach to the question of exporting arms. The centrepiece of his recommendations was the creation of 'a small but very high-powered central arms sales organization in the MOD'.[50] The head of this organisation would be responsible, jointly, to the Defence Secretary and the Minister of Aviation.[51] This individual should be someone 'with a strong personality, drive, organizing ability, experience of exporting and an instinct for business' – that is, an industrialist. Supported by a senior civil servant and a military deputy, he would lead a team of 15–20, organised principally along geographical lines, as in Kuss's ILN. The organisation's key responsibilities would be: to collect sales intelligence; to survey the market; to monitor the sales potential of UK equipment requirements; to direct the overseas sales staff; to co-ordinate sales campaigns; to negotiate major deals; to cultivate foreign attachés in London; to arrange VIP visits to the UK; and to co-ordinate the activities of the sales divisions in the three services, which would be retained, although their lead role in export promotion would be assumed by the new organisation, which Stokes described as 'forming the spearhead in the thrust for important overseas orders'.[52]

Stokes was scathing about the existing sales culture in these divisions. For Stokes: 'One of the staff summed it up perfectly when he said to me, 'Hitherto we have not really existed to sell at all, but simply to supply on repayment.' The line of thought behind that phrase is all too clear; we only make our equipment available to other countries as a favour, it is up to them to come and ask us for it, we will only agree to make it available to them if we cannot find any use for it ourselves, and they will have to pay for the privilege of having it.'[53]

Having separate service divisions also had the disadvantage of reducing the potential for developing an overall market picture in a country or region, as the sales effort, such as it was, was compartmentalised along service lines. This was a disadvantage that Stokes's proposed organisation would overcome by being able to 'stand up for the sales interest ... comprehensively survey the market ... both collect and disseminate all information of sales value, [and] which can be regarded as the initial point of contact for other Departments and for industry on anything to do with arms sales, and which can direct the activities of all Government staff overseas who are concerned in selling defence equipment.'[54]

The overseas component of this effort would be spearheaded by 10 overseas sales representatives, each responsible for a number of countries within a given geographical area. Since their job would be to sell, Stokes warned that they 'should be readily removable if their performance proves them to be unsuitable'. These salesmen would have diplomatic status and be members of the staff of the relevant embassy or High Commission. Their role would be to 'establish contacts with the defence procurement authorities in those countries; to find out about their present and future requirements and to report them to London; to be fully informed about existing and projected British equipment and to promote interest in it; to look out for sales possibilities and report them; to cooperate with British firms and their agents; to call for specialist support from the UK and to organize visits and presentations; and generally to spearhead all British arms sales'.[55] Furthermore, they would 'suggest promotional gambits such as invitations to the UK', liaise with the service attachés, and work closely with agents of UK companies in the field. These agents would still have a vital role to play – as Stokes conceded, 'apart from providing an additional source of information, they are better placed than an official to dispense the less orthodox inducements'.[56]

The introduction of such salesmen necessitated some clarification of the role attachés were expected to play – up to this point the overseas promotion of UK arms having been solely their responsibility. Stokes recommended that attachés should support the work of the salesmen in two ways: by being alert to intelligence with a sales value and 'feeding it' to the salesmen ('they must be the eyes and ears of the sales organization'[57]), and by being more willing than Stokes believed they currently were to recommend British equipment to their hosts. It was only in recent years, Stokes concluded, that sales promotion had come to be regarded 'as even remotely their concern', and while some had adapted well to the new requirements, 'there are still some Attaches who have no interest whatever in sales, who regard the subject as unbecoming to them and who are reluctant to do anything at all to help'.[58] Some attachés, Stokes was appalled to discover, had even on occasion recommended foreign equipment in preference to UK equipment.

Attachés had pointed out that their time was limited and that their primary function was to gather military intelligence and pass it on to London, and to attend to representational duties. Furthermore, in a point 'which was repeated to me over and over again', attachés expressed concern that if they engaged too obviously in trying to shift British arms, regardless of the actual requirements of their hosts, they 'would compromise their position of professional impartiality in the Service circles in which they operated'. Stokes, who viewed their role less as involving 'professional impartiality' than as one of support salesmen in uniform, disagreed: 'I am perfectly sure that we do not gain any added respect by our reluctance to say that our equipment is best, but merely lose ourselves a lot of worthwhile business.'[59] He was also critical of the fact that in many posts 'the Attache jobs appear to be used as niches for people on the point of retirement or otherwise outside the main promotion stream and who therefore have little incentive to exert themselves'.[60] Nevertheless, attachés still had an important role to play, if for no other reason than that Stokes was proposing a body of only 10 overseas salesmen, and whenever they were out of a particular country it would fall to the attachés as the permanent UK military presence to, as he put it, 'keep the pot simmering' in their absence.[61]

Such an operation would obviously require a significant budget, which Stokes recommended should be generated by the imposition of a small levy on defence companies of around 0.25–0.5 per cent of the value of each sale concluded. This would replace the then current practice of *ad hoc* recovery of the cost of promotional assistance by the MoD or MoA. As Stokes argued, if the organisation was to be effective, it would need 'a good deal of freedom to spend money on activities conducive to sales promotion', including the ability to 'entertain generously' and 'extend official invitations to influential persons from defence circles in other countries to visit the UK, with their fares and hospitality provided and with their wives invited too'.[62]

Establishing the appropriate machinery with the appropriate authority was, however, only half the solution – the other half lay in having the right equipment to sell, at the right time, in the right quantity, and at the right price. 'No matter how efficient the sales organization,' warned Stokes, 'it will not be able to achieve substantial sales unless it has equipment to offer which other countries want.'[63] The role of the organisation was not just to sell the product, but 'also to ensure that the right product is available.'[64] Towards this end, the government had to be more flexible in acceding to a customer's requirements by, where possible, making its equipment requirements more compatible with the demands of the export market (in terms of specificiation, price, and credit facilities). Previously, the Army Department had explained its role in arms export promotion as being 'to explain the requirement which dictated the design of the equipment and ... to be able to convince the buyer that the equipment would meet his requirements'.[65] For Stokes, this was an approach whose time had passed. The government also had to be willing to divert equipment from the UK services to allow early delivery; to provide financial support to factories so that they could 'tool up' for extra production in anticipation of export orders; and to hold extra stocks in reserve.[66] The standard of after-sales service, maintenance and flow of spare parts were also key and had played a considerable role in the success enjoyed by the US in the field. Stokes warned that: 'To anyone who would say that the British forces must have exactly the weapon that they stipulate, or nothing, the answer must be that unless we can export our equipment it *will* be nothing.'[67]

Of course, UK manufacturers and the armed forces could not be expected to take into account the future requirements of the export market unless they knew what those requirements were likely to be. This was another role which the new organisation was to play; 'that is why it is absolutely essential for the organization to employ thorough market research and to have accurate information, cross-checked with the Defence Intelligence Staff, on which it can build authoritative forecasts ... '[68]

Being able to offer attractive credit terms was another important factor. The arms market was becoming a buyers' market, and hence credit terms were becoming increasingly significant in deciding sales. Decisions on arms purchases would no longer be made 'solely on the basis of the superior quality of our equipment. Countries with financial problems will purchase an inferior article if the financial terms are attractive. Political and financial needs sometimes override military assessments.'[69] Given that, on government-to-government business, there was at that point no history of bad debts being run up, offering credit terms over longer periods was not considered to represent too much of a risk.

Stokes's recommendations also sought to give the sales perspective an influential presence on the interdepartmental committees which considered arms exports, and to enable the head of defence sales to take his case on a particular export direct to Ministers where this presence proved insufficient. If the organisation was to be effective, it had to be made known that the relevant Ministers fully supported the sales effort. As he observed with regard to Henry Kuss, 'I am perfectly certain that he would only have achieved a limited amount were it not well known throughout American Service and industrial circles that he enjoys the full and active support of Mr McNamara.' Hence it was 'an absolute pre-requisite of any substantial improvement in our arms exports that Ministerial interest should not only be there but should be seen to be there'.[70]

Stokes also saw the political and commercial value of offering training to overseas military personnel, and recommended that the new sales organisation would need to investigate how this – at the time, limited – facility could be developed further. Today's junior officers were tomorrow's decision makers: 'In the long term, a foreign or Commonwealth officer who has undergone training in Britain, especially during his formative years, is more likely in later life to "think British" than if he has had no personal associations with this country.' So important was this consideration that Stokes recommended reducing or waiving fees for overseas officers 'where it would be of obvious sales advantage to do so'.[71] Even in the mid-1960s, training was recognised as an important adjunct to selling.

Stokes suggested there was also a need to consider how best to throw the full weight of the governmental apparatus behind 'private ventures' – those relatively few instances where manufacturers were designing weapons aimed solely at the export market. The key issue here was how to overcome the barrier of the weapons not having been proved in service by the UK armed forces for customers who were 'often very reluctant to act as guinea pigs'.[72] This was, and remains, a potent sales weapon, as does the related issue of the UK showing confidence in a product by – without equivocation – placing a significant order for it. Orders after equivocation send similar signals to a failure to order. The adoption of equipment by the UK armed forces, then as now, was crucial to export success. Stokes's solution was for the UK services to examine the design of specific private venture equipment and then certify that 'it appears to be a sound concept which should be capable of the performance which is claimed for it'.[73]

Ultimately, Stokes saw that no matter how able and enthusiastic his sales staff, and no matter how effective his new ideas on promotion were in theory, the volume of sales that could be achieved depended on the government's application of its strategic export policy. Stokes's strategy for success was predicated on a liberal approach to export controls, as the strict application of controls would militate against the aims of the new organisation. As Stokes himself put it, 'the more often an arms sale is ruled out for reasons of strategic export policy the more pointless it will become to employ valuable staff to sell arms'.[74] As he also pointed out, the UK was then 'excluded through political sensibilities from some of the most valuable defence markets of all', including South Africa and Franco's

Spain. The French 'do not find it necessary to suffer from similar sensibilities and are only too willing to cash in on ours'.[75] From Stokes's perspective, 'sensibilities' were needless impediments to the promotion of sales. Nevertheless, to a large extent, they could be countered by the new organisation having representation on the key committees. Stokes was, of course, advocating what George Bernard Shaw's Andrew Undershaft had termed 'the true faith of the armourer': 'To give arms to all men who offer an honest price for them, without respect of Persons or principles'.[76]

The government's reaction

The report was considered within the MoD and MoA and other departments, leading to Healey's January 1966 statement to Parliament. In essence, the MoD and MoA accepted Stokes's recommendations, notwithstanding some wounded institutional pride, reservations about the degree of autonomy proposed for the head of sales in pricing and his proposed direct access to Ministers, and with some wariness of the bureaucratic implications of increased government-to-government sales.[77] Their acceptance of his proposals represented something of an advance – as late as September 1964 the MoA had been arguing that there was no need for any new sales promotion machinery. At the same time, the Navy Department had voiced its objection to attachés spending so much time on sales issues that they lost their status, while the Air Force Department had observed that as a priority arms sales promotion ranked 'well below' the collection of intelligence. For its part, the Treasury believed that the role of the attaché was to collect intelligence. That was the basis on which they were funded – any promotional work was the province of the companies themselves.[78]

However, by the time the Stokes proposals were being discussed within the MoD and MoA, the Plowden Report had also been published, as had a report by the Estimates Committee on electrical and electronic equipment for the services, and their conclusions reinforced those of the Stokes Report regarding the inadequacies of the present system, the desirability of increasing arms exports, and for government to become more closely involved in their promotion.[79]

The government accepted the central recommendation of the Stokes Report on the need to create a central arms sales organisation under a Head of Defence Sales, drawn from industry at a suitably attractive salary (£15,000–£20,000 p.a.). The proposals dealing with the organisation of the overseas sales effort were accepted. Initially, the government proposed appointing four overseas salesmen, two each to be assigned to Washington and Bonn, from where their numbers would gradually expand. The government accepted, in principle, the need to take into account the requirements of the export market when formulating domestic equipment requirements. Flexibility in pricing was recognised as being necessary in principle, though debate continued on the best way to achieve it in practice. The importance of holding stocks or facilitating extra production capacity to enable rapid delivery was also accepted, as was Stokes's suggestion that the head of the new organisation should chair a Defence Exports Advisory Council, to facilitate liaison between government and industry.[80]

The proposals which were most readily accepted can be gauged from a draft directive setting out the new emphasis on pursuing the sale of arms abroad. The preambular section began with the obligatory and contradictory disclaimer to which successive administrations have shown an attachment, that the 'Government's policy in the long term is to bring about a climate in which the nations of the world no longer feel compelled to devote such a large proportion of their resources to expenditure on arms'. Nevertheless, 'while constantly working towards those objectives, we must recognize that there is still a vast demand for conventional defence equipment ... and that it is in the national interest that we should secure the largest possible share of this valuable market'.[81] It went on to outline the rationale for undertaking this arms export effort as lying in the opportunity to reduce the financial burden of Britain's overseas military commitments by enabling Britain to produce its own weapons more economically, recovering something of the initial R&D costs, and by recouping some of the foreign currency spent on the maintenance of British forces overseas. Hence the draft directive stated:

a   In formulating our own operational requirements, the present and future requirements of friendly powers must be taken fully into account.

b   Everything possible must be done to keep our prices at a competitive level.

c   The delivery requirements of overseas customer Governments must take priority over everything except the essential requirements of our own Armed Services.

d   There must be the fullest co-operation between the Government and industry, with particular emphasis on exchanging market information, on mounting presentations and demonstrations and on joint selling.

e   In negotiating collaboration projects with other countries, every care must be taken to ensure for Britain a fair share of sales to third nations.

f   Our posts overseas must assist to the full by passing back information and by supporting sales initiatives; they must in turn be kept fully informed about present and future British equipment.

g   Subject to overriding considerations of the national interest, every effort must be made to overcome, and to overcome quickly, difficulties of a political or military nature which stand in the way of releases of equipment or of information on which sales depend.

Finally, it reinforced the shift in thinking that Stokes had demanded by stating that 'it is of the utmost importance that everyone in the Government service who has the opportunity for military discussions with representatives of friendly Powers should make it his business to draw attention to British equipment and to stress the advantages of using it'.[82] This directive would eventually be released in Denis Healey's name in October 1966.

In January 1966, the OPD discussed the recommendations and the draft directive. There was general agreement on accepting the recommendations. However, conscious that the Labour Party was likely to be criticised for taking this step, it was recommended, without a hint of irony, that Healey's statement announcing it should be revised to 'give fuller and more positive emphasis to our disarmament policy'.[83] With this agreement, the way was clear for Denis Healey's oral statement of 25 January 1966. Healey told the House that: 'Increased sales of British equipment will help significantly to reduce the burden of our military commitments by enabling us to win back some of the foreign currency which we have to spend on keeping our forces overseas and equipping them for their tasks.' He then delivered the positive emphasis on disarmament, reassuring the House that: 'While the Government attach the highest importance to making progress in the field of arms control and disarmament' Britain had to 'secure its rightful share' of this market, then estimated to be worth £1 billion per year.[84]

Once the statement of intent was out of the way, the next issue to be resolved was, who should head the new organisation? The name of Raymond Brown was suggested by Fred Mulley, the new Minister of Aviation. Brown was the Chairman and Managing Director of Racal, which had exported £818,000 worth of defence-related equipment in 1965.[85] Brown was told that he would have to resign his directorship of Racal if he was to accept the new post, in order to avoid the appearance of a conflict of interests, and cut all business ties with the company (although not necessarily his shareholding). In May, Healey wrote formally to Harold Wilson recommending the appointment of Brown (representing Wilson's only involvement in the matter of the creation of the DSO).[86] Brown was offered a two-year contract, at a salary of £8,000 p.a. ('the maximum approved for industrialists recruited to the Department of Economic Affairs when it was set up' but well below the £15,000–£20,000 advocated by Stokes).[87] If a case arose in which Racal was in competition with another company over support for an overseas order, any decisions would be taken out of Brown's hands and made by the relevant Permanent Secretary, in consultation with Ministers if necessary.

Brown's job description confirmed that his role was 'to ensure that, within the limits of Government policy, as much British equipment as possible is sold overseas ... [,] to encourage overseas Governments to purchase commercially produced equipment from British manufacturers and to give every possible assistance through his organisation to facilitate sales by British firms'.[88] Beyond that, the Minister of Defence (RAF) would be responsible for the general oversight of arms exports. It was arranged that his appointment would be announced by Healey on 11 May 1966 in response to a question to be placed by the newly elected MP Kevin McNamara.[89]

The tension at the heart of the apppointment was wrestled with in a covering letter sent out to Heads of Mission together with the new arms sales directive, and which is worth quoting at length. They were told that:

> it is the Government's policy in the long term to bring about a climate in which nations will no longer feel compelled to devote so large a part of their resources to the purchase of arms. This is something we should all wish to work for, and we are constantly looking for ways of starting some advance towards this goal. It is therefore not unreasonable to ask whether the appointment of a Head of Defence Sales and the instructions in the enclosed directive are consistent with this policy ... we take great care about what equipment we sell and to whom we sell it, but ... what we do sell has importance for our defence industries, particularly as regards the level of employment, because of the smallness of our home market and, of course, for the general and essential purpose of earning foreign exchange. Mr Healey's directive makes it clear that we must exploit markets wherever this is possible. If we do not sell, others may be expected to do so. There are, of course, factors which inhibit the sale of arms ... in a number of cases considerations of policy, strategy or security prevent us taking full advantage of market opportunities ... but we should be clear in our own minds that where no positive reason exists for not selling arms the directive requires that we should do all that we can to sell them ... [90]

What kind of impact did Brown's appointment and the creation of the DSO have on arms exports? This is obviously difficult to quantify, but assuming at least some causal relationship between sales effort, improved infrastructure and staffing, and orders placed, it must have had some effect. Brown himself, in considering a target figure for 1967, thought £250 million 'not unreasonable',[91] but in reality the DSO fell well short of that. Denis Healey himself argued: 'I don't think you can show that the setting up of this organisation greatly increased ... our share of the world arms trade.'[92] As early as August 1967, the DUS (Pol) in the MoD was writing that 'it is almost impossible to set out in "concrete" terms what we have achieved as a result' of Brown's appointment.[93] Overall, sales had risen by around 25 per cent over those in 1965, although as a result of activity over which Brown could have had little influence. Nevertheless, there was general agreement that Brown should be offered a two-year extension of his contract.

However, this tends to ignore the fact that the DSO did not come into being, wholly formed, at the time of Brown's appointment in May 1966. Once Brown was appointed, most of the rest of the Stokes recommendations were only gradually implemented. For example, on 1 July 1966, the army and navy sales directorates were transferred to the Central Staffs to constitute what would become the Defence Sales Organisation, under the Head of Defence Sales. However, indicative of the gradual nature of the evolution of the DSO, although the Head of Defence Sales was being referred to in official minutes in that way (although Brown himself would have preferred the grander title of 'Head of Defence Exports and International Relations'[94]), as late as September 1967 the DSO was still being referred to as 'the new Central Sales Organisation within the MOD'.[95] The following month it was being termed the 'Office of Defence Sales'. Even by late 1967, sales activity was being pursued on a service basis (as before), rather than on the geographical basis recommended by Stokes. Moreover, Stokes's vision of a market research infrastructure was developing rather differently than recommended, although the compilation of data on a country basis to allow evaluation of market potential was under way.

The number of dedicated overseas salesmen recommended by Stokes – 10 – had also proved a problem. The MoD had recommended to the Treasury that initially four such posts should be created (in addition to one which already existed in Paris), but the Treasury had been willing to agree only to three. Appointments were therefore limited to Washington, Bonn and Ottawa, with temporary appointments for Libya and South America under consideration. More positively, the two deputies recommended – one a civilian responsible for sales promotion activities, the other a military deputy to act as a professional adviser on military issues and as a link between service and sales staff – had been appointed, and a number of the principles highlighted by Stokes – such as the importance of offering training, of logistic support, and of support for private ventures – had been accepted. Nevertheless, any impact on export figures was likely to be felt only in the medium term. Arguably, it is not until the early 1970s that such benefits become obvious, by which time issues surrounding commissions and the methods by which contracts were secured – for example, with regard to Iran – also begin to emerge.

In announcing the appointment of Raymond Brown as Head of Defence Sales, Healey had sought to reassure backbench critics 'that the sooner that we can arrange for a multilateral abolition of the international traffic in arms at all levels through the operation of some disarmament agreement, the happier we shall be'.[96] However, it soon became clear that Healey was not quite as eager as this suggested.

During 1966, under Foreign Secretary George Brown, the FO, in consultation with other departments, undertook an examination of the possibility of regulating the international arms trade. This resulted in a paper, sent to the Prime Minister in December 1966. Its conclusions were hardly encouraging. As well as Soviet and Chinese opposition:

> Recipient countries would resent the prospect of international regulation as a form of Great Power interference. Our friends and dependants would be particularly disturbed. Even an informal UK proposal put privately to the Russians could be exploited by them to our disadvantage in other countries; they are known to have passed to the Egyptians a version of the informal discussion which took place on this subject between the British and Soviet Governments in 1956. International regulation of arms exports might also stimulate local production.[97]

Despite the existence of such obstacles, the paper went on to outline the kinds of steps which might be considered. In doing so, its proposals anticipated the UN Register of Conventional Arms and the EU Code of Conduct. The 'least demanding of all forms of international action' would be a system whereby governments notified a body set up under UN auspices of all exports and imports of arms. Such a system would help dispel distrust and suspicion, and could form a firm basis for further action. However, given that such a proposal stood little chance of succeeding at the time, dangers lay in the UK being seen to propose such a move, including 'the resentment that would be caused in other arms producing countries, and fears that would be aroused of our readiness to sacrifice the interests of those we supply'. A further possibility was to pursue agreement on an effective licensing system for arms exports. While all governments exercised some powers over arms exports from their territories, some states were 'notoriously lax' in enforcing them.[98] Standardising around an agreed licensing system would obviously be an advance – although there was little that could be done to prevent the kind of divergence between public position and private practice which had been politically useful to a range of arms-exporting countries since 1945. The most promising, third, option, the FO advised, was to pursue agreement among the major powers on prohibiting the supply of sophisticated weapons to certain areas – implicitly, the Middle East. The FO advised that the US should be consulted as a first step.

This kind of multilateral action, the FO advised, was the only practical way of taking conventional arms control forward. Unilateral action by Britain 'would involve serious economic and political disadvantages for us. Foreign exchange earnings amounting to £119 million in 1965 would be put in jeopardy'. The cost of items for British forces would probably increase. Even restricting a unilateral ban to areas of tension carried unacceptable costs, as 'however carefully such qualifications might be drafted, serious uncertainty about UK policy would be likely to result'. Hence the FO concluded, 'the end result of unilateral action by us would be to hand foreign markets to our trading rivals and to cause discomfort to our friends abroad'.[99]

This paper was copied to Denis Healey, who wrote to Harold Wilson saying that he had no objection to the FO pursuing studies on the lines proposed, but 'in slow time', and without informing the Americans.[100]

The contemporary DESO

In 1985, the DSO's name was altered to the more opaque Defence Export Services Organisation. Its latest head is Tony Edwards, seconded from the TI Group at a salary of £165,000 a year, with a performance-related bonus of up to £15,000.[101] Although his job was advertised, Alan Thomas was earlier selected as HDES without the post being advertised, although two unnamed customers (one of them obviously Saudi Arabia) were 'kept informed'. This sensitivity to the reaction of foreign governments to UK appointments left the Defence Select Committee unmoved. It claimed that with 'some sensitive posts, it may be necessary to strike a balance between the requirement of fair competition and public accountability, and the need to maintain confidence overseas'.[102] During the 1990s, the numbers employed by DESO have gradually increased, from 541 in 1990–91 to 708 in 1994–95.[103] In April 1998 DESO employed almost 660 people.[104]

Table 6
Heads of DSO/DESO, 1966–94

Head	Years	Seconded from
Raymond Brown	1966–69	Racal
Lester Suffield	1969–76	British Leyland
Ronald Ellis	1976–81	British Leyland
James Blyth	1981–85	Lucas Aerospace
Colin Chandler	1985–89	British Aerospace
Alan Thomas	1989–94	Raytheon
Charles Masefield	1994–98	BAe
Tony Edwards	1998–	TI Group

Clearly, the defence industry is a special case – no other branch of industry receives anywhere near comparable support. Take, for example, the construction industry. It employs approximately 1.3 million people – around three times as many as the defence industry (in terms of both exports *and* domestic procurement) – and its exports are valued at around £4 billion per year. However, the support it receives from the Department of the Environment simply does not compare. The office charged with export promotion there runs on a budget of just £300,000 per year. For Sir Ian Dixon, chairman of the construction company Wilmott Dixon:

'The level of government support ... is in fact derisory ... compared with an industry like the defence industry.'[105]

Since 1995, in an increasingly competitive export environment, DESO has abandoned its role as provider of balanced support for all British companies pursuing a potential contract. It such cases, it now selects one British company to go forward, and supports it alone.[106] In 1998 the MoD Minister John Spellar described DESO's role as being 'to provide British defence exporters with the best possible Government support, within the framework of our defence, security and foreign policies'.[107] Building on its success in selling entire packages to Saudi Arabia and Malyasia, and in bundling arms packages elsewhere, DESO is focused on capitalising on the benefits of this approach. A more recent example of DESO's success is the £500 million 1996 deal to supply Qatar with Hawk aircraft, Vosper Thornycroft naval vessels, GKN armoured vehicles and Short missiles.[108] As Charles Masefield put it: 'Every order is fought to the death ... it is not products which the customer wants, it is solutions to requirements. In other words, the customer is looking for a package, which includes customer support.'[109]

Arms promotion is still undertaken by military attachés. In 1998 there were 127 military attachés and 239 support staff in 70 embassies and High Commissions, costing £30.8 million a year.[110] Their work falls into two categories, opportunity-led and demand-led. The former involves seeking out opportunities for exports and reporting them back to DESO, the latter responding to enquiries from British companies, either through DESO or directly (giving advice, involvement in promotional work, etc.). The amount of time an attaché devotes to selling arms depends on the scope for arms sales to the country concerned, and the overall workload and priority of arms sales within that. On average, an estimated one-third of an attaché's time is spent promoting arms sales.[111]

Key senior posts in DESO continue to be filled by secondees from industry,[112] while other staff are regularly posted from the MoD or the services for a tour of duty of generally three years. Some will serve in one of DESO's overseas offices.[113] The cost of operating DESO was £10.94 million during 1994–95 and £16.61 million during 1996–97. It is offset by receipts from a Commercial Exploitation Levy – a levy on the sale outside the MoD of equipment or designs whose development was funded by the MoD. Annual receipts from this vary wildly: in 1992–93 they were £15 million; in 1996–97, £90.5 million; in 1997–98, £54 million.[114] In addition, the government has estimated that the cost savings achieved in lowering the unit cost of equipment for British forces by selling arms abroad amount to £350 million a year, and that the 'total benefits generated by DESO for the MOD therefore more than cover the total cost of all its operations'.[116] Nevertheless, MoD claims as to the profitability or beneficial properties of arms exporting have, as discussed in Chapter 1, been vigorously contested.

Table 7
DESO: overseas offices, staffing and budget

Country	Established	No. of staff	Budget 1997–98 (£000)
Australia	1989	2	106
Brunei	1995	2	104
Germany	1991	16	340
India	1984	5	49.5
Indonesia	1991	3	190
Kuwait[a]	1988	9	149
Malaysia	1986	4.5	172
Philippines	1997	3	213
Saudi Arabia[b]	1985	99.5	104
South Korea	1988	2	108.8
Thailand	1992	2.5	110
Turkey	1988	1	74

Notes [a] Six staff are employed in the Kuwait Programme Office and are funded by the customer.
[b] Ninety-seven staff are employed on the Al Yamamah programme and are funded by the customer.
Source Hansard, 27 January 1998, col. 186w.

DESO today also arranges armed forces support for arms exports, including the use of British military personnel to demonstrate equipment to potential customers. An Army Sales Team was established in the late 1960s, comprised 60 staff in 1993,[116] and is designed to be available to assist British arms manufacturers in the sale and promotion of infantry equipment overseas. In addition, the division oversees the training of military personnel from countries that have purchased British arms.[117]

In conjunction with the defence companies, DESO has also developed a five year strategic plan, identifying the top 22 national markets within the UK's leading regional markets (the Gulf, South East Asia and North America), the major prospects there, and how contracts can be won. Its existence 'has helped DESO and companies to organise their resources more effectively and is improving our national performance in winning export orders which increased by 10 per cent in 1997 compared with 1996.'[118]

The Export Credit Guarantee Department

The ECGD was created under the Export Guarantees and Overseas Investment Act. Essentially, it has functioned as a governmental insurance and credit agency, providing exporters with credit, and covering companies against possible customer default, both of which services are guaranteed by the British taxpayer.

The ECGD's role is vital for British arms exporters in that the availability of loan finance is a key factor in making sales. Consequently, the relationship between DESO as the promoter of British arms and the ECGD as provider of cover is a close one, centred around their involvement in the Export Guarantees Committee, an interdepartmental committee chaired by the Treasury which determines individual country credit limits. The figure arrived at must cover both military and civilian sales. In reaching the figure, the committee may seek the advice of the Export Credit Guarantee Advisory Service, comprising prominent figures from the worlds of industry and finance.[119]

The country credit limit figures are calculated with reference to a series of four lists, A–D. List A contains those countries presenting least risk of default (in practice, most NATO and EC states); Lists B and C contain a cross-section of developing countries; and List D comprises past defaulters and a number of the poorer developing states which represent the greatest risk of default. The Export Guarantees Committee also considers the provision of ECGD cover in specific cases where it is not guaranteed.

However, the ECGD does not provide direct financing. The exporting company takes a loan with a bank, approved by the ECGD. The bank is then insured against risk by the ECGD. The bank is covered 100 per cent against risk, the exporter 90 per cent, although in the case of arms sales the figure tends to be closer to 75–80 per cent. If the goods are not delivered, the loan must be repaid. The ECGD's ability to meet the needs of British arms exporters involved in large contracts and still accommodate civil exports was becoming limited in certain cases (e.g. Saudi Arabia) by the late 1980s, because of the need to operate within the country credit limits. In response, in 1988 Trade Minister Alan Clark announced that a new £1 billion fund was to be established to cover these needs: 'Where in future ECGD's normal limits for individual countries cannot easily accommodate specific contracts, cover will, where appropriate, be made available under these new arrangements outside the country limit, but within the overall £1 billion ceiling.'[120]

Currently, the proportion of ECGD cover being allocated to defence and related exports is on the rise. While in 1980/81 the proportion of the ECGD budget dedicated to arms exports was under 10 per cent, in 1993/94 it stood at 48 per cent (£1,973 million). In 1997–98 defence accounted for 24 per cent of all ECGD cover.[121] Moreover, this has been a costly process for the British taxpayer. To take a few figures: between April 1990 and March 1993 the ECGD operated at a loss, paying out £2,314 million in respect of defaults. Between 1995–96 and 1997–98 it paid out £195.8 million in claims against defence equipment.[122] As of February 1999 the ECGD had paid out, but failed to recover, the value of arms purchases by a number of leading purchasers: in respect of Indonesia, £11 million; Kenya, £16 million; Egypt, £46 million; Algeria,

£98 million; Jordan, £253 million.[123] Many of Jordan's purchases, of course, were in reality destined for Iraq. In addition, there is the Iraqi default itself, the total cost of which to the British taxpayer has been estimated at £652 million.[124]

Arms sales and secrecy

If Parliament cannot get hold of the facts, it has no chance of engaging in or influencing the arms export policy debate. While, theoretically at least, there are a number of avenues through which it can be attempted, in practice there have been many barriers. Prominent amongst these are the use of procedures which favour the executive, the resort to opaque language and economy with the *actualité* and, under the Conservatives, the inherent weakness of the opposition in the defence field. While succesive governments have regarded these devices as legitimate, the Scott Report argued that their application to conceal details relating to Britain's role in the arms trade represented no less than a failure to fulfil the obligation of ministerial accountability.[125]

In the field of arms sales successive governments have invoked the 'national interest' or 'commercial confidentiality' to avoid scrutiny. This is not to suggest that, while contracts are being negotiated, there is no legitimate commercial confidentiality interest. The risks were summed up well by Malcolm Gale from the UK embassy in Lisbon in a 1966 despatch. Astonished to see a story in the *Daily Telegraph* trumpeting a sales victory for Short's over US competition, Gale complained that British companies;

> should, by now, have realised that it is a cardinal mistake during negotiations of this nature to divulge that discussions are taking place until the order has been signed and sealed. This is an elimentary [sic] rule when conducting such sales, especially when United States competition may be involved, as any leak permits the Americans, and even some of our other competitors, to mobilise their forces, trim their prices and also include such attractive and interesting side benefits that their offers are too compelling to be ignored.[126]

But the secrecy at work today goes beyond the requirements set out here. There is an implicit understanding between government and industry that secrecy is essential to arms sales success. After all, Britain has been able to secure its more lucrative contracts of the last 15 years only because extensive, public, discussion in the US Congress has led to suppliers turning away from the US.

Since the 1950s, the aim of departments involved in arms sales promotion has been to restrict as far as possible the flow of information to Parliament. In March 1964 the Board of Trade even complained that, in answering parliamentary questions, Ministers were indicating instances where no licences had been issued. While there was no reason why this information could not be made public (the dual rationales for secrecy – supplier preference and commercial confidentiality – clearly could not apply where no licence had been granted), the Board of Trade nevertheless argued that 'if negative information were given as a matter of course, a refusal to give information in other cases would indicate that licences *had* been granted. It is suggested therefore that ... even negative information should not be given without the strongest reason.'[127]

Hence despite the importance of this trade, information about it is hard to come by. This is understandable, given the legitimate national security concerns of purchasing governments, the desire for commercial confidentiality, the British tradition of secret government, and the widespread feeling that it is a dirty business linked with corruption, oppression and war. But if it is undebated, how can the public interest be established? As Fred Halliday has observed: 'What is in British interests is not a given, it's not in some drawer for some mandarin or minister to produce. It's a result of what people in this country think and the only way they can make clear what they think is by a public debate in the press, in Parliament, between the government and the population, about what they are and are not prepared to do ... '[128]

Predictably, official perspectives have been somewhat different. For his part, Sir Percy Cradock, one of the élite formerly charged with defining the national interest, has argued that:

> You cannot conduct a successful foreign policy on the basis of moral outrage or perpetual public scrutiny. You have to have realism and you have to have confidentiality. You have to deal with the world as you find it. Most of the countries we deal with would never pass an elementary examination in human rights or democracy; but we have to deal with them because that's the way to protect British interests, to protect British jobs and to look after security.[129]

In the 1970s, one defence official commented that: 'There's nothing to be gained by publicising sales, it's not like other businesses, where you need to advertise to get other people on the bandwagon. We don't want to give ammunition [*sic*] to our critics among the extreme politicians.'[130] As the House of Commons Defence Select Committee complained in 1990, the outcome of such perspectives was the existence of 'an element in the Ministry of Defence culture which appears to regard Parliament with suspicion ... principally demonstrated in an unwillingness to answer frankly, and in what seems to be a feeling that the less said to the Committee, the safer the Ministry will be'.[131] It is clear that the public do not support the sweeping invocation of secrecy to cloak the detail of arms sales. An opinion poll conducted in May 1998 found that 77 per cent believed there was too much secrecy surrounding arms exports, 79 per cent thought that tougher controls should be imposed on arms sales, even if it meant job losses, and 90 per cent disapproved of the government selling arms to countries, such as Indonesia, with poor human rights records.[132]

Despite this, the outlook exemplified by Sir Percy Cradock has extended right across Whitehall, as has been demonstrated by the TISC investigations into the 'supergun' affair and BMARC, and the Foreign Affairs Committee (FAC) investigations into the Pergau Dam controversy and the Sandline fiasco, and as was comprehensively exposed at the public hearings of the Scott inquiry during 1993 and 1994. At least until the Scott inquiry, this made finding out what weapons are sold to whom difficult. The standard government line up to that point is well illustrated by Tim Sainsbury, then a junior Defence Minister, in the House of Commons in 1989: 'It has never been the practice of this or previous governments to publish figures on individual companies' defence exports, for reasons of commercial and customer confidentiality.'[133]

As Sir Ronald Ellis, then head of the DSO, told an interviewer in 1979: 'Normally people do not like to have it revealed what they are buying. You do not announce in the newspaper how your burglar alarm works. Why should you? You are buying equipment to defend your country, why go and tell a potential enemy how many you've bought? That's the sort of thing your adversary spends half his life trying to find out.'[134] One commentator observed that this leads to a 'furtive approach, selling arms to other nation states as if selling contraceptives in Ireland'.[135]

However, partly as a consequence of the criticisms included in the Scott Report, the veil of secrecy was lifted up to a point under the 1997 Labour Government. Details of specific sales to specific countries are still withheld as being commercially confidential, but consolidated information of a limited nature was published in a first annual report on arms exports. Furthermore, enquiries in areas where it was the practice of previous governments to deny information can now yield more positive results. For example, the government was willing to list those countries attending the biennial RN/BAEE. Hence we know that 54 countries were invited to send delegations to the 1997 exhibition, including Indonesia, Turkey, China, Bahrain, Pakistan, Thailand, Singapore and South Africa. We also know that, for example, Russia, Sri Lanka and Algeria were not.[136] Details of training, and military and police assistance, are now given, where previously they were refused.[137] Other information is provided, but guaranteed a more limited circulation by being placed in the House of Commons library rather than published in Hansard. For example, in 1997 the government was willing to reveal that 63 UK companies attended the IDEX exhibition in Abu Dhabi, but the names of the companies were placed in the library rather than listed in the answer to the parliamentary

question.[138] Because the government has no interest in generating political inconvenience, there are categories of questions where answers are
only partially given, or where the answers are evaded. One category
regards evidence of British companies' involvement in supplying Iraq's
nuclear, chemical and biological weapon programmes, as uncovered by
UNSCOM, presumably on the grounds that unnecessarily airing such
matters would help galvanise support for a more restrictive approach to
arms exports. All holding replies on this question refer back to an answer
given to the indefatigable Llew Smith in February 1998. This answer
admitted that: 'British manufactured equipment has been found at a
number of sites inspected by UNSCOM and the IAEA', and that: 'Any
evidence of wrongdoing is investigated and, if appropriate, will be a
matter for the courts.' However, it declined to name any of the companies
identified by UNSCOM.[139]

This cat-and-mouse game of seeking the release of arms export information, analagous to the UNSCOM inspection process itself, is still being
played out in other areas. In May 1999 Ann Clwyd was told that a list of
UK arms exports to Yugoslavia or the former Yugolsavia between 1989
and 1991 and since May 1997 could be provided only at 'disproportionate cost'.[140] (Disproportionate to what? Ann Clwyd's importance?
Yugoslavia's importance? The importance of arms sales to the balance of
payments?) However, the previous administration had provided the information requested by the first half of Ann Clwyd's question in answer to a
parliamentary question from Llew Smith – a list which stretched across
nine columns of Hansard and included a vibrant trade in engine parts,
spares and ejector seats for the Yugoslav Air Force.[141] Given the prospect
of British troops going into combat in Yugoslavia, this evasion seems to
have had more to do with political convenience than the cost of compil-
ing the answer.

In general, evasion has been the norm when dealing with parliamentary
questions on arms-related matters. In *Yes, Minister* Jim Hacker remarks
to Sir Humphrey Appleby: 'Opposition's about asking awkward questions,' to which Appleby replies: 'Yes, and government is about not
answering them.' To take the case of Iraq, between 1985 and 1990
Parliament was apparently assured on numerous occasions that Britain
was not supplying weapons-related equipment to Iraq. This was done
through the carefully crafted reply which either avoided a direct answer
to the question posed, while containing a suitably affirmative statement
on some aspect tangentially related to the question meant to be taken as
an answer, or through answers which avoided admitting a change of
policy but were consistent with one. While this invariably involved
misleading the House, on occasion the process came perilously close to
lying.

The existence of such mechanisms was highlighted by William

Waldegrave in a moment of candour while giving evidence to the FAC in March 1994. He explained that 'In exceptional circumstances, it is necessary to say something that is untrue in the House of Commons,' and that 'Much of government activity is much more like playing poker than playing chess. You don't put all your cards up at one time.' In addition, he told the FAC that a Minister 'may not display everything he knows about the subject'.[142] There are numerous examples of these processes in operation over questions about arms and related sales to Iraq.

For example, in April 1989 Mrs Thatcher assured the Labour MP Harry Cohen that: 'The Government have not changed their policy on defence sales to Iraq.'[143] However, as Sir Richard Scott concluded, the guidelines *were* changed in 1988 following the cease-fire in the Iran–Iraq War. Despite this, John Major told Gerald Kaufman in February 1992 that the 1985 Howe guidelines 'remained in force until the invasion of 1990 when they were replaced with a total embargo'. While, strictly speaking, this was true, it omitted to mention the 1988 amendment of those guidelines, which represented a significant relaxation.

On 31 January 1991, against the background of the Gulf War, David Steel urged John Major to establish an inquiry into arms sales to Iraq 'so that never again will our forces be faced with an enemy armed partly by ourselves'. Major sidestepped the call by replying: 'For some considerable time we have not supplied arms to Iraq for precisely that reason.' 'Some considerable time', unbeknown to most MPs, was in fact six months (notwithstanding the narrow definition of 'arms' consistently applied). Furthermore, had Iraq not invaded Kuwait on 2 August 1990, further supplies of Matrix Churchill equipment would have been exported that month, and a relaxation of the guidelines agreed at a meeting chaired by Douglas Hurd less than seven months before Major made this statement would have resulted in a heightened flow of military equipment to Iraq. When the government's change of policy was finally revealed, no thanks to the government itself, it argued that it had not in fact tried to conceal the change, but did not consider it worth revealing to Parliament since it only involved a 'reinterpretation' of existing policy.

The Defence Committee, FAC, TISC and IDC, along with the Public Accounts Committee (PAC), have all had cause to examine questions relating to arms sales policy, yet the subject does not fall comfortably within the remit of any one of them. Several factors have combined to limit the effectiveness of efforts in this area. In general, committees have limited resources and powers, and hence have to rely heavily on the co-operation of the relevant departments. Too aggressive an investigation may lead to co-operation being withdrawn – for instance, through refusal to send key civil servants to give evidence.[144] Furthermore, even back-benchers who have transcended ambitions of Cabinet office have proved reluctant to press cases where government weaknesses are exposed, lest it jeopardise their chances of a knighthood or cause their removal from the committee and end the rewards (foreign trips, etc.) that membership offers.

The Scott Report was justly critical of this lamentable parliamentary record, which was, latterly at least, not so much a consequence of parliamentary disinterest or indifference as a consequence of the executive's use of blocking tactics, both in response to parliamentary questions and the operation of the select committee system. As Scott argued, where:

> the account given by a Minister to Parliament, whether in answering Parliamentary Questions, or in a debate, or in evidence to a Select Committee, withholds information on the matter under review, it is not a full account and the obligation of Ministerial accountability has, *prima facie*, not been discharged. Without the provision of full information it is not possible for Parliament, or for that matter the public, to assess what consequences, in the form of attribution of responsibility or blame, ought to follow. A denial of information to the public denies the public the ability to make an informed judgement on the Government's record. A failure by Ministers to meet the obligations of Ministerial accountability by providing information about the activities of their departments undermines, in my opinion, the democratic process.[145]

The politics of the pay-off

Commissions and corruption

Writing in the mid-1970s, the economic historian Clive Trebilcock complained that: 'Rational analysis of the armaments industry before the First World War has been complicated and frustrated by the persistence of what might be termed the "Merchants of Death" syndrome', which rested on 'a variety of sweeping allegations', principal amongst which was 'that they bribed their way into bloated weaponry contracts'.[146] If it was the case then that focusing on the role of agents, middlemen and commissions in the arms sales process was impeding serious investigation of the subject, it is equally true that today, when government-to-government contracts are increasingly the norm in the international arms trade, serious investigation of the subject can no longer dismiss these activities, for the issues they raise are of central importance.

The question of commission payments and the role of middlemen has attracted renewed interest recently, and partly this is a reflection of structural changes in the arms market which have resulted in heightened competition. As one commentator has noted: 'The most important influence on an industry's ethical practices is competition, both the amount and the kind ... Beyond a certain point (call it the ethical optimum of competition), as competition increases, so do unethical practices.'[147] For their part, Kugel and Gruenberg considered that commissions 'are acceptable in a particular country if they are consistent with that country's customs and laws. Thus, the customs and laws of a country determine what is "acceptable" conduct. The problem arises when decisions must be made in the face of different customs and laws of different countries.'[148]

The reliance on the payment of commissions and other inducements that this situation has encouraged has been aggravated by a further factor. Increasingly, competing Western major weapons systems, for instance main battle tanks, are remarkably similar in performance and price, with major producer governments all willing to be equally flexible over questions of credit and mode of payment, while the minor differences that remain are of themselves not a sufficient reason for ordering any one type over another. In these situations the purchaser may look to the range of additional inducements offered by the supplier company and government. These can be divided into two types; personal inducements and national inducements. (In certain states these can be one and the same thing.) Personal inducements cover the commissions or bribes paid to government officials, while national inducements cover a range of agreements, running from straightforward offset agreements, through various forms of counter-trade, to payments to official bodies, and other forms of investment. As a consequence, successful British arms deals have come to be discussed in terms of the payments and accommodations required to secure them and the probity of such arrangements, and deals that have fallen through have been explained away in terms of the activities and demands of middlemen and influential foreign nationals.

As the activities of pioneering arms salesman Sir Basil Zaharoff testify, commission has been used to secure sales for as long as there has been an international arms trade.[149] As long ago as the 1870s, Richard Jordan Gatling, inventor of the Gatling gun, was advising that: 'Our best policy will be to keep up the prices of the guns and give liberal commissions,' and that: 'We ought to give ten per cent commission on the guns – such a commission will make agents and gun men, consuls etc., whom we enlist in our interest work energetically in getting orders.'[150] Immediately, this introduces one consequence of paying commission – the price of the equipment being sold is increased to an artificially high level to accommodate the level of payment required while still protecting profit margins.

Why did the arms trade in particular become synonymous with such practices? As Anthony Sampson has noted, in the early twentieth century the majority of orders were placed by governments, 'where the decision [to purchase] could well depend on one or two individuals, whose support was therefore essential', and where 'the sales were usually conducted in secrecy, for reasons of national security',[151] thereby creating the conditions wherein corruption could thrive.

These characteristics still apply to the sale of arms and military equipment today, although the payment of commission to secure contracts is not exclusive to either the international arms trade or the Middle East, the geographical area where the two have joined in the popular consciousness. For instance, similar conditions make large capital goods, civil engineering projects, power station construction, etc., subject to similar influences. That the Middle East has come to represent the conjuncture of these in the popular imagination is partly a consequence of the oil boom of the early 1970s, which created lucrative markets and produced orders of a previously unknown size in the oil-rich states of Saudi Arabia, Iraq, Iran, Kuwait, Qatar, the United Arab Emirates (UAE) and Oman, and even in states with relatively limited or no oil wealth, such as Yemen, Syria and Jordan.

Ignorance of Arab culture and style of government, and of the decision-making processes in those countries on the part of the businessmen drawn to the Middle East led them to look to local representatives, preferably in positions of influence, to guide them successfully through the maze.[152] Given the then largely untapped potential of these markets the rewards were very high, and so the commission was correspondingly high. As this first wave of businessmen turned into a constant flow, the use of intermediaries became regular practice and from there a prerequisite for business success, as competing companies would enlist the aid of competing intermediaries with different sources of influence and entrées to the decision-making process. The intermediary, then, is the person with specialist access hired by a company to help secure an otherwise uncertain sale, although in the semantic fog which envelopes the arms sales process the term has come to be used interchangeably with terms like middleman and agent.

Those whom the intermediary must pay in order for a contract to be secured, and are otherwise in a position to block or veto any prospective deal, are termed skimmers.[153] In general, the agent will employ an intermediary on behalf of his company. The intermediary's fee will be a percentage of the value of the prospective deal, out of which it is his responsibility to pay the skimmer. Once this and other expenses are deducted from the commission paid by the company, the rest is profit for the intermediary. Said Aburish, himself a sometime intermediary, characterised the intermediary's role as one that 'consists of providing the company with an advantage over its competitors by securing the co-operation of someone in power, or with power and influence, to promote its interests ... in return for a commission/bribe which is shared by the intermediary and his political mentor'.[154]

One pioneer in this field was Geoffrey Edwards, who was instrumental in helping BAC win the contract to supply Saudi Arabia with Lightning aircraft. In return for his services Edwards, a former RAF pilot who had been living in Saudi Arabia, charged a 1.5 per cent commission, which it has been estimated amounted to over £2 million.[155] Edwards subsequently recalled that: 'The payments were normal practice, legal and out in the open. They were for business services rendered. Whatever criticism there might be, without this sort of business BAC's military division wouldn't exist today.'[156]

Because the commission paid to the intermediary covers the price asked by the skimmer, dealing with a reliable intermediary and a prominent, secure, skimmer produces a stable, albeit artificially high, price. However, difficulties can emerge which act to drive up the cost of the commission and complicate the deal. Firstly, deals can involve more than just one skimmer who needs to be paid before the contract will be allowed to proceed. Similarly, one intermediary could enlist the services of another to secure access to an influential skimmer, raising the cost of commission. Intense competition from another supplier state could drive up the level of commission by allowing the skimmer (and to a lesser extent the intermediary) to play off one exporter against another. Furthermore, difficulties can arise in dealing with Ministers or bureaucrats who may lose their position only to be replaced by individuals who also demand payment. The more companies are involved the more complex the picture becomes, the more so as the same intermediaries can be employed by different companies and, as is more often the case, different companies will be using different intermediaries to influence the same skimmer.

All this raises the question as to whether there is any place for ethics or morality in the arms trade. A peculiar kind of ethical code does seem to be evident from time to time. Compare the Western attitude to claims that King Hussein of Jordan received payments in return for awarding arms contracts (indifference) with the reaction to the case of the 'Three Guys' in Belgium over payments made to secure the purchase of the Italian Agusta helicopter (scandal). While Western governments were apparently unconcerned at accounts of the activities of Adnan Khashoggi's Triad marketing company in securing contracts in the Middle East, where the payment of commission and the hiring of intermediaries were considered a way of life, when Lockheed sought to apply these practices to Japan and Western Europe in selling the Starfighter (an aircraft with a safety record that earned it the nickname 'The Flying Coffin') the issue of commission came to assume a more unethical dimension. This was particularly true in the Netherlands, where a Lockheed agent approached Prince Bernhard, who requested commission of US$4 million to US$6 million. Subsequently, the Dutch set up a commission to investigate the prince's role and as a result he was removed from all public duties. In West Germany, it was alleged that Franz Josef Strauss secured payments from Lockheed in return for ordering the Starfighter.[157]

Fears that the process of offering or agreeing to payments to secure

contracts could infect the British system have been raised by periodic revelations. For example, in April 1976, Lieutenant Colonel David Randel, a
serving officer in the Royal Corps of Signals, who had previously worked
in the DSO and on secondment to the Sultan of Oman's armed forces, was
arrested. Randel appeared in court in April 1976 on two charges of
conspiracy – to corruptly receive money and to corruptly solicit and
obtain money in respect of orders for telecommunications equipment.
However, the charges themselves came to assume secondary importance
as the court case, which began at the Old Bailey in November 1977,
became the scene of embarrassing revelations about the involvement of
the British Government in the payment and co-ordination of commissions
on arms export contracts.

Randel denied taking around £25,000 in bribes between May 1971 and
October 1972 from two Racal executives, Geoffrey Wellburn, Managing
Director of Racal subsidiary British Communications Corporation (BCC),
and Frank Nurdin, BCC's sales director, who were charged alongside
Randel with corruptly giving him this money – charges both denied.
Ironically, Nurdin had been awarded the OBE in 1969 for services to
export industry. Wellburn and Nurdin claimed the money was intended
to be passed on to Iranian middle-men to secure the sale of Racal equipment, to be fitted to the Chieftain tanks Iran had then contracted to buy,
and something they claimed Racal chairman Ernest Harrison knew about.
This sum represented about 0.5 per cent of the contract value. In 1972
Racal BCC had duly been awarded a lucrative £4.5 million order for the
installation of its radar equipment in the Chieftain tanks.

A long statement by Nurdin, which was read out in court, alleged that
the Shah of Iran had established a special account to siphon off money,
and that the payment of 'bribes' was commonplace in Britain, the US and
France when dealing with the region. This embarrassing revelation about
the personal conduct of a close regional ally led the prosecuting counsel
to make it clear that 'it is not the Crown which is saying the Shah set up
a special fund, but it is Mr Nurdin's account of what he says was going
on',[158] explaining that 'reports of this kind have repercussions beyond this
country'.[159] Nurdin's statement recalled the keen competition which
Racal was involved in to secure the contract:

> Lt. Col. Randel was on our side in all these situations, and it became clear
> to Mr Harrison that the group had an extremely valuable contact in him ...
>
> It was mainly due to [Randel] that the Defence Ministry finally got the
> order for equipment, which was worth £4.5m to Racal BCC. We had to
> compensate him for all his work and expenses, including monies he was
> committed to pay to Iranians under the agreement ...
>
> Payments to key people able to influence decisions by Government is an
> accepted part of the price to be paid by any contractor or Government
> securing an overseas order.

The British, American and French Governments, to take the three most sophisticated countries dealing in arms sales, accept and operate this method of doing business with all under-developed countries. The bribe factor, as it is known in the commercial world, operates in many ways – from simple entertainment of visitors ... to very large sums of money indeed being transferred to overseas accounts.

It was a great achievement to sell British arms to Iran against formidable American opposition, and was achieved through the Defence Ministry sales organisation headed by Sir Lester Suffield.[160]

Thus was the government's role introduced to the trial, and it was here that the most explosive revelations occurred. When Suffield was called to give evidence a few days later, he revealed that commission of £1 million was paid by the MoD to Shapoor Reporter, who acted as an intermediary on the £100 million Iranian Chieftain tank deal, two years before he was knighted in 1973 – an honour he reportedly demanded as a reward for his services in securing the tank contract.[161] This payment was arranged by the government-owned Millbank Technical Services (MTS).

Suffield revealed that Reporter was a trusted 'confidant' of the Shah and that 'his advice is of tremendous importance to any British company trying to sell to Iran'. He went on: 'In business you have got to know all these people who are useful to you and he was very useful in Iran ... I knew of [Reporter] long before I came into the Defence Ministry job. It was standard procedure that he got a commission of 1 per cent on any successful commercial venture.'[162]

When asked directly if the £1 million payment to Reporter had been arranged by officials, Suffield replied: 'Yes. I approved it.'[163] As a result of the admissions, the Labour Government was forced to concede this point in Parliament through Defence Minister John Gilbert: 'Sir Shapoor Reporter, who is a British subject, has been retained for some years by Millbank Technical Services Limited as its sole adviser regarding official defence sales to Iran which are conducted by Millbank Technical Services on behalf of the Ministry of Defence. In that capacity he has received payments in return for those services.'[164] This had been the basis of Wellburn and Nurdin's defence. As counsel for Wellburn argued: 'My client's defence is that he honestly believed that just as in the top echelon money had to be paid to Sir Shapoor Reporter, so in the lower echelons, money had to be paid to the lesser fry.'[165]

Giving evidence subsequently, Oliver Prenn, Racal's deputy chairman, denied any knowledge of the practice of making commission payments to secure contracts in the Middle East, only to subsequently reappear at his own request and admit that he had misled the jury on this issue. He was then able to recall what had previously escaped him, that he had person-ally arranged payment of £20,000–£30,000 in commission to Reporter in return for his role in securing the Iran contract. This, it transpired, was in addition to the £80,000 commission paid to Reporter by BCC, which in turn was in addition to the £1 million paid to him by the British government.[166] Documents subsequently produced at the trial showed that in total Racal had paid Reporter over £255,000 in commission.[167]

When Nurdin came to give evidence, he developed some of the themes outlined in his written statement, recalling that: 'The American promoters were bribing key people in an enormous way and spending millions on bribes with top level people, both in Iran and other Middle East countries.'[168] Despite these arguments, and the clear evidence that the British government also paid commisions – or bribes, the term applied to Nurdin and Wellburn by the government's counsel – on 18 January 1978 all three were found guilty on corruption charges.[169] After the trial, the FO confirmed that Iran had contacted the British government but would not comment on reports that it was demanding repayment of over £1 million paid in commission (or bribes, as they also, ironically, viewed them), as it quite rightly considered that these would have been built into the purchase price. This meant that the Iranian government had paid vastly inflated prices in order to enrich officials, the Shah included, and that this fact had been broadcast worldwide. That this was the custom and practice was confirmed by a senior executive of a British arms exporting company at the time of the trial:

> We always have a scale for commissions, unless you happen to come across one of the top-liners who cost more. Up to £1 million [contract value] we normally pay up to 5 per cent. It's a ceiling, if you like, that we give our marketing director to negotiate. Providing he doesn't go above that, he has only to come back and say what the actual sum was – say, 4½ – and nobody outside the marketing department would be interested. All that matters is that it's allowed for in the overall purchase price to the customer.[170]

In a more recent case, Gordon Foxley was convicted of having received payments (described as 'backhanders' in this case) totalling £1.5 million while Director of Ammunition Procurement at the MoD in return for securing the award of MoD contracts to three foreign ammunition suppliers – Fratelli Borletti of Italy, Gebrüder Junghans of Germany and A. A. Raufoss of Norway. This figure was based on Foxley's alleged requirement of 5 per cent of the value of the contracts he secured between December 1979 and August 1984.[171] In a situation not unique in the international arms trade, Foxley's fee was paid into the Swiss bank accounts of three front companies he had established – Interep, Scientific and Confrere.

During Foxley's trial the prosecution argued that he 'agreed to take a series of substantial backhanders, and in doing so took dishonest advantage of his position, breaching the trust bestowed upon him by his employers', and that he had entered into 'corrupt arrangements' to do so.[172] This, of course, goes to the heart of the double standard being employed. It is acceptable commercial practice for British companies to seek, through well placed intermediaries, to offer payments in reward for placing contracts with them, but when such payments are offered to UK officials to place contracts, this amounts to 'corrupt' practice. On 3 November 1993, Foxley was found guilty on twelve charges of corruption during the 1979–84 period. On 27 May 1994 he was sentenced to four years in prison.[173]

Investigation

The PAC has looked into the question of commissions, but only when the issue has arisen during the course of investigating other matters. While it has had success in getting details on the record, there have been drawbacks to its efforts in this most sensitive of areas. Some concern the nature of the committee itself and the fact that it will not call Ministers to give evidence. In addition, the Comptroller and Auditor General (C&AG) can restrict the disclosure of reports to Parliament (including the PAC) when national security is invoked, an authority set out in a memorandum produced by the then C&AG to the PAC in 1981 in relation to the PAC's report *Chevaline Improvement to the Polaris Missile System*.[174]

Deriving from this authority to withhold information, Robert Sheldon, then Chairman of the PAC, during a debate on the Zircon affair outlined scenarios in which he would comply with C&AG requests for the suppression of information.[175] However, as then PAC member Dale Campbell-Savours pointed out, in practice this meant that: 'accountability to Parliament on highly secret projects is not accountability to the Floor, it is not accountability to the Public Accounts Committee; it is accountability to my right hon. Friend himself who has the specific role of examining these matters and other members of the Committee are precluded from doing so.'[176]

When in 1980 it was revealed that International Military Services (IMS), an arms sales quango intended to operate as commercially as possible but at arm's length from the MoD, had deposited £491,476.09 into a numbered Swiss bank account (No. 183118 LIGHT) as payment for 'consultancy services' on an arms deal,[177] the PAC turned its attention to the question of commissions. In doing so it questioned Sir Frank Cooper, Permanent Under-Secretary at the MoD. Prior to Cooper's appearance before the committee, the MoD submitted a memorandum to the PAC. This stated that:

> No bribes were paid. The payment of £491,476.09 made by IMS to a Swiss Bank on 14 January 1980 was in respect of an amount properly due for consultancy services entered into by IMS on behalf of the MOD. Such

arrangements have been made from time to time by IMS and occasionally
by the MOD directly where the legitimate services of consultants are necessary and helpful to the objective being pursued.

    Bribery, which is taken to mean payments for corruptly influencing a
decision, is something which successive United Kingdom Governments and
their agencies have not indulged in nor would condone.[178]

Cooper was asked how he could be sure that no part of the sum paid into
the Swiss account would be passed on as a bribe. He told the committee
that: 'There is not any way that one could be totally certain about that in
another country.'[179] Perhaps this was partly because the MoD had 'undertaken not to require IMS to supply documentation relating to the
company's commercial relationships with third parties'.[180] Furthermore,
Cooper conceded that the sum paid into the Swiss bank by IMS, as it was
not a round figure, was in fact a percentage of the value of an arms
contract. Despite these contradictions, and the critical line that some of
the questioning took, the Report concluded that: 'If, because of local practice or law, intermediaries are used to assist sales it would be unrealistic
to believe that there is never any risk that an agent might use some of his
commission corruptly. We consider that, short of banning the use of
agents, it is a matter for the Government to take into account in deciding
on arrangements for sales to countries where the use of intermediaries is
necessary'.[181]

    The question of the role of commissions and of middlemen in the sale
of British arms arose again in April 1989 when Sir Peter Levene, Chief of
Defence Procurement, gave evidence to the PAC during its investigation of
MoD support for defence exports. Chairman Robert Sheldon put it to
Levene that: 'There has been some comment on substantial commissions
paid on arms sales. Are you satisfied that no improper commissions have
been paid to United Kingdom citizens?' Levene replied: 'The payment of
any commission is a commercial matter for the firms involved. It is not
something in which my staff become involved and it is not something on
which I can comment.'[182] He later elaborated, saying that: 'We are not
involved in commissions; we are not involved. These are matters that are
negotiated between the commercial organisations and any representatives
they may have overseas. I must say that as we all know ... this is a very
competitive business. You have to be competitive to survive.'[183]

    When PAC member Michael Latham raised the question of intermedi-
aries with Levene and the nature of the advice offered to companies by
attachés and whether such advice 'relates to people of high ethical standards' Levene explained that:

The way in which this works is that a British company may well go overseas
and say they are looking for an agent in this country and who could be
recommended. I would be very surprised if any attaché said, 'You'd better

use Mr X.' What they may say is 'Look, here's a list of all those that I know. Some are better than others. I would not use this particular man at all.'[184]

While there was no parliamentary investigation of the activities of Geoffrey Edwards in Saudi Arabia in the 1960s, the Al Yamamah deals attracted considerable parliamentary interest. In April 1989, following a newspaper *exposé*, the C&AG, John Bourn (deputy head of defence procurement at the MoD at the time of Al Yamamah 1) ordered an inquiry into the MoD's handling of the deal.[185] The brief was to investigate allegations that commissions amounting to 30 per cent of the contract value had been paid to secure the contract and that 'backhanders' had been paid to middlemen in Britain.[186] The investigation was to centre on the way in which the MoD accounted for the vast sums of money it passed on from the Saudi Arabian government to BAe and other British companies.

On its completion in early 1992 the report was 'suppressed' with the agreement of Robert Sheldon. Sheldon told the other members of the committee – which included three Privy Councillors – that confidentiality had to be preserved because 'many jobs are at stake'.[187] He and Sir Michael Shaw, the PAC deputy chairman, subsequently met Sir Michael Quinlan, Permanent Secretary at the MoD, to discuss the report behind closed doors. Other members of the committee were unhappy with this arrangement and the implications for government accountability.[188] Clearly Sheldon and Shaw were not representative of the entire committee. Afterwards Sheldon commented that: 'I did an investigation and I find no evidence that [the MoD] made improper payments. I have found no evidence of fraud or corruption. The deal complied with Treasury approval and the rules of government accounting.'[189]

But did this answer the principal allegations, and if there was no evidence of fraud or corruption why not publish the report? Martin O'Neill, the Labour Party's defence spokesman, suggested that a future Labour government would reopen the inquiry, commenting that: 'The Government's attitude to defence exports is cavalier. It is based on a completely free-market approach. We need to reassess how we do this to ensure there is proper political control of who gets what and how.'[190] Former PAC members also voiced disquiet at the way in which the matter had been handled. Labour MP Dale Campbell-Savours stated, 'I am convinced that payments were made,' while another Labour ex-member, Jeff Rooker, argued that 'The Committee is supposed to be independent of political considerations such as jobs.'[191]

Despite its deep concern about the issue in opposition, New Labour in government has been markedly reluctant to look into the issue of commissions. Notwithstanding Martin O'Neill's comments at the time, neither has it been characterised by over-eagerness to publish the NAO report on Al Yamamah, although, somewhat ironically, Robert Sheldon has since come out in favour of re-examining the issue.[192] Nevertheless, when Harry Cohen asked the New Labour government about this he was told that 'the then Chairman of the Public Accounts Committee decided that the 1992 National Audit Office report into the Ministry of Defence's involvement in the Al-Yamamah programme should not be published as it refers to arrangements which are confidential between the Governments of the United Kingdom and Saudi Arabia.'[193] As with previous administrations, the government does not want to know. In answering parliamentary questions on commissions, DTI Minister Barbara Roche even went so far as to support such payments. In answering a question from Gordon Prentice, she admitted that: 'It is often advisable and sometimes legally necessary for exporters to enlist the services of paid intermediaries when seeking to win business over-seas. The Department gives appropriate advice to any British business person who requests it.' When subsequently challenged she remarked that: 'Nothing in my remarks attacks commission payments ... we realise that there are some circumstances where third parties are needed ... That is perfectly legitimate and is part of the process.'[194]

A number of more recent cases further illustrate the corrupting effect of the commission culture, especially in relation to Al Yamamah. Firstly, in 1994, Sir Colin Southgate, Chairman of Thorn EMI, admitted paying 25 per cent of a contract's value in commissions to secure a £40 million order for 4,500 bomb fuse assemblies for bombs for Tornadoes as part of the Al Yamamah deal. For Thorn EMI, as for all such companies dealing with clients like the Saudis, commission payments are such a way of life that the company regulates them. The Thorn EMI company handbook for senior staff stated that any proposed commission in excess of 12 per cent had to be cleared by the board. The Saudi commission avoided this fate by being paid through an offshore bank in the Bahamas in three separate stages. As a former managing director of Thorn's defence systems division observed: 'Commissions make the world go round. There's nothing illegal about them. I don't know of a [Saudi] royal who'll get out of bed for less than 5 per cent.'[195]

Secondly, in December 1997 and again in February 1998, Rolls-Royce were served with a writ in the High Court by a shadowy Panama-regis-tered company, Aerospace Engineering Design Corporation (AEDC), following allegations that it had not been fully paid commission (at 15 per cent) owed on contracts for Rolls-Royce engines for Tornado and Hawk aircraft in the Al Yamamah agreement. AEDC is controlled by members of the Al Ibrahim family, son-in-laws of King Fahd. While they had reportedly expected Rolls-Royce's £600 million stake in Al Yamamah to net them £90 million in commission, they alleged that Rolls-Royce had paid just £23 million, covering an unspecified number of engines at 8 per cent commission.[196] This case not only threatened to expose the core secrets of the Al Yamamah deal, it also made a further mockery of Roger Freeman's assurance that no commissions had been paid on it (see Chapter 5). Thirdly, stories concerning Mark Thatcher's involvement in the arms trade, and the Al Yamamah deal in particular, have been circulating for years. It has been claimed that, through his friendship with Wafic Said, young Thatcher became involved in the Saudi deal, acting as an intermediary, for which he is alleged to have received a cut of as much as £12 million.[197] Adnan Khashoggi explained that: 'Wafic was using Thatcher for intelligence. His value was his name, of course, and that whenever Wafic needed a question answered, Thatcher could go directly to his mother for the answer.'[198]

Finally, Jonathan Aitken went to extraordinary lengths to conceal the true purpose of a weekend visit to the Ritz Hotel in Paris in September 1993 while he was Minister of Defence Procurement, and the related question of who paid his bill there.[199] At the time, Aitken was also under the spotlight because he had been a non-executive director of defence company BMARC when it was exporting naval cannon to Singapore for onward transmission to Iran in breach of the Howe guidelines. The TISC investigation (deeply divided along party political lines) accepted Aitken's assurances that he knew nothing of this, but concluded that, as BMARC chairman Gerald James had claimed all along, the BMARC guns were sent to Iran.[200] However, the BMARC affair had brought the issue of Aitken's links with the arms trade to the fore.

In the course of the inquiry, a BMARC board minute of 2 November 1988 emerged. At item 3.8 this noted that: 'The agent acting for Mr Aitken [who] pulled off the Vosper contract is ambitious and is working hard at establishing relationships.' This agent was none other than Sheikh Fahad Al Athel, who acted for Saudi Prince Mohammed bin Fahd.[201]

When an April 1995 World in Action documentary, 'Jonathan of Arabia', alleged that Aitken's links with the Saudis were even more extensive and amounted to a dependency, Aitken issued his infamous pledge to 'cut out the cancer of bent and twisted journalism' and issued a number of writs. He remained sensitive to any suggestion that he had links with the arms trade. When Private Eye ran a small piece contesting Aitken's claim on BBC-TV's Question Time that 'Until I arrived on the board of BMARC in 1988 I had not been involved in the arms business,' Aitken's lawyers issued a further writ.[202]

When his libel trial collapsed, the court had just heard evidence from David Trigger of BMARC's parent company, Astra. Trigger had been the author and recipient of memos which suggested greater familiarity with the arms trade than Aitken had been willing to concede. In one dated 7 March 1989, written by Astra Sales Manager John Sellens, there was discussion of an 'agency agreement' for Al Athel: 'the Sheik will be asking

for a five year exclusive agreement for all Astra Group products supplied
to Saudi Arabia directly or indirectly at a commission rate of 15%,'
Sellens noted. 'I am happy with the fifteen percent,' he went on, 'which I
understand would also look after Jonathan Aitken's interests, although as
a director of one of our companies I am a little concerned that he is
included.'

A second memo, from Trigger and dated 22 March 1989, passed on
Aitken's advice on the payment of commission:

> In J.A.'s view we should seek to establish a relationship of trust with Fahad
> rather than try to pin him down with a written agreement. He put the view . . .
> that Fahad is a realistic businessman who is used to negotiating special terms
> to suit unusual circumstances. There may be occasions for instance, where a
> higher rate that [sic] 15% would be required to cover extraordinary in
> country expenses. There will also be other times where the deal is price sensi-
> tive and a rate of less that [sic] 15% would be necessary to secure the order.

Ultimately, because of the lavish commissions involved, arms deals like
Al Yamamah actually threaten to destabilise the systems they are intended
to sustain. In this respect, no one seems to want to face up to the lessons
of Iran in the late 1970s, of how the corruption engendered by massive
arms deals can become a focus for domestic opposition. To take one
current example, the Committee Against Corruption in Saudi Arabia
(CACSA) operate a web site which carries detailed allegations about each
leading member of the Saudi royal family, giving each a personal 'corruption index' based on alleged excesses. Obviously, the companies seen as
being involved in facilitating such corruption do not escape consideration.
CACSA characterises BAe as being 'a Saudi puppet company'. From
CACSA's perspective, Saudi Arabia is 'being used as a dumping ground
for weapons the Saudis cannot use or do not need, only so the royal family
and weapons companies can line their pockets ... Meanwhile, vastly
needed infrastructure improvements to the Saudi landscape are on hold
because of lack of funds.'[203] It is clearly not beyond the bounds of possibility that, as in Iran, lavish spending on arms will in fact destabilise
purchaser states from within, as the corruption and commission culture
they generate provide a rallying point for critics of the regimes.

Notes

1 The Right Honourable Sir Richard Scott, the Vice-Chancellor, *Report of the Inquiry
   into the Export of Defence Equipment and Dual-use Goods to Iraq and Related
   Prosecutions* (hereafter the Scott Report) (London, HMSO, 1996), para. C1.30.
2 That is, until the passing of the Import and Export Control Act of 1990, which made
   these temporary wartime powers permanent.
3 Hansard, 1 September 1939, col. 175.

4 There were some exceptions. For example, in 1988 the Trade and Industry Select Committee (hereafter TISC) advocated an annual parliamentary debate on the EG(C)O. TISC, 'Trade with Eastern Europe', Second Report, Session 1988–89, HC 51.

5 Scott Report, para. C1.64. In a November 1990 letter, the DTI's Mike Coolican referred to the absence of a parliamentary role as 'that happy state of affairs'. Scott Report, para. C1.117.

6 DTI 'Strategic Export Controls', 1 July 1998.

7 A DTI press release accompanying the White Paper recognised that: 'It is important in a modern democracy for Government to be accountable to Parliament for the way it uses its strategic export control powers.' DTI Press Release, 1 July 1998. The White Paper proposed the retention of the ability to amend the EG(C)O at short notice, and without parliamentary debate, but that such amendments would then require parliamentary approval within an agreed time scale for them to remain in force. DTI, 'Strategic Export Controls', 1 July 1998, para. 2.2.2.

8 TISC Strategic Export Controls, Second Report, Session 1998–99, 2 December 1998.

9 In addition to these controls, further restrictions can apply to the export of military equipment if it contains components or technology of US origin, through the need to secure a US re-export licence.

10 The COCOM-proscribed countries were: Albania, Bulgaria, China, Czechoslovakia, Hungary, Mongolia, North Korea, Poland, Romania, the former USSR (subsequently all 15 former republics), and Vietnam. In addition, although Afghanistan was not a proscribed destination, COCOM guidelines were used on applications. COCOM membership comprised all NATO members except Iceland, plus Japan and Australia.

11 The full membership of the Wassenaar Arrangement is: Argentina, Australia, Austria, Belgium, Bulgaria, Canada, Czech Republic, Denmark, Finland, France, Germany, Greece, Hungary, Ireland, Italy, Japan, Luxembourg, Netherlands, New Zealand, Norway, Poland, Portugal, Romania, Russian Federation, Slovak Republic, South Africa, South Korea, Spain, Sweden, Switzerland, Turkey, Ukraine, UK, US.

12 As it is a signatory, various materials vital to the production of nuclear weapons cannot be freely exported from Britain. These include, for example, quartz crystals, solid state switches, and high speed cameras. Countries that are not signatories to the NPT are prohibited from receiving such equipment.

13 The NSG has 34 members: all the members of the Wassenaar Arrangement except Turkey, plus Brazil.

14 As a signatory, export of items such as wind tunnels, analogue to digital converters, etc., is restricted. Essentially, the MTCR covers key items which were already covered by COCOM but through it were extended to countries in the developing world. There are 29 signatories to the MTCR. Membership comprises all of the Wassenaar members except Bulgaria, Czech Republic, Poland, Romania, Slovak Republic, South Korea, and Ukraine, but with the addition of Brazil and Iceland.

15 The Australia Group seeks to control the proliferation of the components of chemical and biological weapons. Under its listings, the export of items such as glass-lined vessels, glove boxes, protective clothing, toxins, etc., are controlled. Further restrictions on chemicals and biological weapons are provided by the EC's 1989 adoption of a Community Regulation on Chemical Weapons Precursors (Council Regulation EEC No. 428/89). This prohibits their export to states engaged in conflict or suspected of attempting to develop a chemical weapons capability. There are currently 30 members of the Australia Group: all Wassenaar members except Bulgaria, the Russian Federation, South Africa, Turkey and Ukraine, but with the addition of Iceland.

16 For example, see the measures outlined in TISC, Exports to Iraq – Memoranda of Evidence, July 1991, pp. 61–2.

17 Scott Report, paras C2.37–8.

18 See TISC, *Strategic Export Controls*, 'Memorandum submitted by the Department of Trade and Industry', paras 3.2.93–6.

19 Giving evidence to the TISC in November 1998, DTI Minister Barbara Roche said that, of all applications, 'it is about three per cent which actually goes to Ministers, and of that three per cent, there is a very, very small number ... which needs further discussion between Ministers to make sure that the process is correct'. TISC, *Strategic Export Controls*, Minutes of Evidence, 10 November 1998, para. 112.

20 See DTI: *An Exporter's Guide to Non-proliferation Policy and Controls*, 1991.

21 Scott Report, para. C2.17 and para. C2.33.

22 See: Mark Phythian, *Arming Iraq* (Boston, Northeastern University Press, 1997); Davina Miller, *Export or Die: Britain's Defence Trade with Iran and Iraq* (London, Cassell, 1996); Alan Friedman, *Spider's Web: Bush, Saddam, Thatcher and the Decade of Deceit* (London, Faber & Faber, 1993).

23 *Sunday Times*, 2 December 1990.

24 In his report, Sir Richard Scott suggested that, for goods licensable under the Military List, the licensing department should be the MoD, which, Scott considered, to all intents and purposes decided on the licensability of military goods (notwithstanding some FCO input) anyhow. Scott Report, para. K3.3. Nevertheless, the DTI's July 1998 White Paper predictably rejected this proposal. See DTI, 'Strategic Export Controls', July 1998, paras 5.3.1–3.

25 Scott Report, para. C2.44. These guidelines were amended in 1989 to cover issues relating to chemical and biological warfare and nuclear and missile proliferation.

26 International Development Committee (hereafter IDC), 'Conflict Prevention and Post-conflict Reconstruction', Sixth Report, Session 1998–99, HC-55-I, para. 151.

27 *Ibid.*, para. 152.

28 The DTI's Eric Beston, cited in the Scott Report, para. C2.69.

29 TISC, Exports to Iraq: Memoranda of Evidence, 17 July 1991, p. 19.

30 Scott Report, para. C3.5.

31 Hansard, 21 January 1959, col. 30w.

32 PRO: CAB148/24 'Export of Defence Equipment – Report of an Enquiry by Sir Donald Stokes', 12 November 1965 (hereafter, the Stokes Report), p. 38.

33 Select Committee on Estimates, 'Sale of Military Equipment Abroad', Second Report, Session 1958–59, HC-229, 17 June 1959, paras 39–40.

34 PRO: DEFE 13/284. Memorandum by Secretary of State for Defence, 23 March 1964.

35 PRO: DEFE 13/284. Peter Thorneycroft to John Boyd-Carpenter, 1 July 1964.

36 PRO: DEFE 10/460. Minutes of SE(O)C, 23 September 1964. Emphasis in original.

37 PRO: WO32/21301. Denis Healey to Douglas Jay, 22 December 1964.

38 PRO: WO32/21301. Douglas Jay to Denis Healey, 11 December 1964.

39 C. W. Borklund 'What military exports can mean', *Armed Forces Management*, January 1965, pp. 27–33. Quote at p. 31. As a US colonel also commented: 'These military ties can join with the economic and cultural interests to form strong bonds that will hold firm underneath the froth frequently stirred up at the diplomatic level.' *Ibid.*, p. 28.

40 PRO: WO32/21301. Minutes of Interdepartmental Meeting on Exports V (Defence), 30 January 1965.

41 PRO: WO32/21301. Minute from Parliamentary Under-Secretary to Defence Secretary, 8 June 1965.

42 PRO: WO32/21301. Lord Shackleton to Denis Healey, 29 June 1965.

43 *Ibid.*

44 PRO: WO32/21301. Minute of meeting between Lord Shackleton and Sir Donald Stokes, 7 July 1965.

45 PRO: WO32/21301. Minute of meeting between Denis Healey, Lord Shackleton and PUS, 8 July 1965.

46 Shackleton's thinking on the issue is clear from the heading of a memorandum he prepared for Healey in advance of the meeting; 'Further Thoughts on Kuss–Stokes'. PRO: DEFE 13/546. Memorandum from Lord Shackleton to Denis Healey, 9 July 1964.

47 Minute of meeting between the Secretary of State for Defence and Sir Donald Stokes, 12 July 1965. Stokes's terms of reference were: 'to examine what changes in policy and organisation are needed within the Ministry of Defence and the Ministry of Aviation to increase exports of UK arms. The examination should take into account sales policy; the relationship of overseas sales to R. and D. and production; relationships of the Ministry of Defence and Ministry of Aviation sales organisations with industry, with the individual UK Services, and with potential customers. In particular, the possibility of further centralisation of sales activities in the Ministry of Defence should be investigated.' Contained in letter from Henry Hardman, PUS, MoD, to Sir Donald Stokes, 14 July 1965. Appendix A to Stokes Report.

48 See PRO: WO32/21301. 'Summary of Sir Donald Stokes' Conversation with Mr. Henry J. Kuss, Jr., Deputy Assistant Secretary of Defense for International Logistic Negotiations, in the Pentagon on 21st September, 1965.'

49 Stokes Report, p. 10.

50 *Ibid.*, p. 4.

51 As Stokes noted: 'I think the Americans have proved fairly conclusively that a close-knit sales organization can operate successfully within a defence department and the French that it can operate equally successfully if shared between ministries of defence and aviation.' Stokes Report, p. 19.

52 *Ibid.*

53 *Ibid.*, p. 16.

54 *Ibid.*, pp. 17–18.

55 *Ibid.*, p. 5. See also p. 28.

56 *Ibid.*, p. 35.

57 *Ibid.*, p. 30.

58 *Ibid.*, p. 26.

59 *Ibid.*, p. 31.

60 *Ibid.*, p. 27.

61 *Ibid.*, p. 31.

62 *Ibid.*, p. 33.

63 *Ibid.*, p. 38.

64 *Ibid.*, p. 13.

65 PRO: DEFE 10/460. Minutes of the SE(O)C, 23 September 1964.

66 Stokes Report, p. 7.

67 *Ibid.*, p. 40. Emphasis in original.

68 *Ibid.*

69 PRO: WO32/20749. R. W. Browne (MoD) to L. V. Sumer (Secretary to Donald Stokes's Advisory Group), 25 August 1965.

70 Stokes Report, p. 12.

71 *Ibid.*, p. 53.

72 *Ibid.*, p. 46.

73 *Ibid.*

74 *Ibid.*, p. 48.

75 *Ibid.*

76 George Bernard Shaw, *Major Barbara* (London, Penguin, 1988 ed., originally 1905), p. 138.

77 PRO: DEFE 23/1/39050: Ministry of Defence, Defence Administration Committee: 'Sir Donald Stokes' Report on the Export of Defence Equipment', Paper by DUS (Pol.), 30

November 1965. Somewhat more critical, however, was a memorandum of 'IEL Views on Summary of Recommendations', dated November 1965. PRO: AVIA 65/1690.

78 PRO: DEFE 10/460. Minutes of SE(O)C, 23 September 1964.

79 Report of the Committee of Inquiry into the Aircraft Industry appointed by the Minister of Aviation under the Chairmanship of Lord Plowden, 1964–65, December 1965, Cmnd 2853, paras 304–15.

80 See PRO: CAB148/24. 'Sir Donald Stokes' Report on Exports of Defence Equipment', Memorandum by the Secretary of State for Defence and Minister of Aviation for the Cabinet Defence and Oversea Policy Committee, 20 December 1965.

81 PRO: DEFE 23/1/39050: Ministry of Defence, Defence Administration Committee: 'Sir Donald Stokes' Report on the Export of Defence Equipment'. Annexe A: 'Draft Directive for Issue by the Prime Minister'.

82 The directive was issued in Denis Healey's name on 4 October 1966. It added that: 'Political, strategic, economic and security factors will, of course, continue to be taken into account; but I hope that all unnecessary obstacles to sales will be removed as quickly as possible.' The original seven points (a–g) were retained, with changes to the wording in some cases but not to the sense or emphasis. See PRO: DEFE 13/509. 'Arms Sales Directive', issued by Secretary of State for Defence, 4 October 1966.

83 PRO: CAB 148/25. Minutes of meeting of OPD, 12 January 1966. See also the minutes of the meeting of 7 January 1966 in the same file. At this meeting Niall McDermot, Financial Secretary at the Treasury, cautioned that 'the importance of arms sales should not be exaggerated, since they formed a relatively small part of our total exports'.

84 Hansard, 25 January 1966, col. 64.

85 PRO: DEFE 13/509. Minute by Lord Shackleton, 22 April 1966.

86 PRO: DEFE 13/509. Denis Healey to Harold Wilson, 2 May 1966.

87 Ibid.

88 PRO: DEFE 13/509, 'Draft Letter to Mr Raymond Brown offering the Appointment as Head of Defence Sales', Annex II.

89 Hansard, 11 May 1966, cols 403–4.

90 PRO: DEFE 13/509. P. H. Gore-Booth, Covering letter to Heads of Mission, 27 October 1966.

91 PRO: DEFE 13/509. 'Note of Head of Defence Sales' Informal Board Meeting', 29 July 1966, para. 12.

92 Interviewed by John Pilger on 'Flying the Flag, Arming the World', ITV Network First, 15 January 1994.

93 PRO: DEFE 13/509. Memorandum: 'The Future of Ray Brown's Appointment', 1 August 1967.

94 See the correspondence regarding Brown's title in PRO: DEFE 13/509.

95 PRO: DEFE 13/509. 'Memorandum on Progress in Implementation of the Stokes Report', 21 September 1967.

96 Hansard, 11 May 1966, col. 404.

97 PRO: DEFE 13/546. 'Summary of Foreign Office Paper on the International Arms Trade', covering letter (George Brown to Harold Wilson) dated 30 December 1966.

98 Ibid.

99 Ibid.

100 PRO: DEFE 13/546. 'The International Arms Trade', memorandum from Denis Healey to Harold Wilson, 13 January 1967. Discussion of conventional arms control initiatives continued in the background throughout 1967 and 1968. See the correspondence in PRO: FCO 10/144.

101 Hansard, 14 December 1998, cols 327–8w.

102 Defence Select Committee, *The Appointment of the New Head of Defence Export Services*, Second Report, Session 1998–99, para. 4.

103 Hansard, 25 January 1995, col. 286w.

104 Defence Select Committee, *The Appointment of the New Head of Defence Export Services*, Second Report, Session 1998–99, para. 13.

105 Quoted on Radio 4, *File on 4*, 13 February 1996.

106 *Financial Times*, 17 March 1995.

107 Hansard, 8 April 1998, cols 279–80w.

108 See James Bruce, 'UK arms sales in Qatar challenge French trade', *J.D.W.*, 27 November 1996, p. 17.

109 *J.D.W.*, 7 February 1996, p. 24.

110 Hansard, 29 April 1998, cols 132–3w.

111 See Peter Levene's testimony in PAC: *Ministry of Defence: Support for Defence Exports*, Fortieth Report, Session1988–89.

112 For a full listing of those seconded from industry, see Hansard, 1 March 1994, cols 667–70.

113 In Europe, arms sales are co-ordinated through the British embassies in Paris and Bonn.

114 *Hansard*, 22 June 1998, col. 376w. Figures exclude VAT. Receipts for the second half of the 1980s were more stable at around £50 million. See Defence Select Committee, *The Appointment of the Head of Defence Export Services*, First Report, Session 1989–90, HC–14, 'Memorandum Submitted by the Ministry of Defence'.

115 Hansard, 21 April 1998, col. 556w.

116 *Ibid.*, 25 October 1993, col. 490. In 1991–92 it had a budget of £1.3 million, rising to £1.4 million in 1992–93. *Ibid.*, 30 November 1993, col. 530.

117 See CAAT: *The Government and the Arms Trade* (London, CAAT, 1989), p. 2.

118 *Hansard*, 16 February 1998, col. 486w.

119 The members of this body, since 1985, are listed in Hansard, 20 January 1994, cols 749–52.

120 *Ibid.*, 28 June 1988, col. 171. Also, see the House of Lords debate on the issue, Hansard (Lords), 13 July 1988.

121 ECGD, *Annual Report and Trading Accounts 1997/98* (London, Stationery Office, 1998), p. 5.

122 Hansard, 4 November 1998, col. 584w.

123 *Ibid.*, 2 February 1999, cols 581–2w.

124 *Ibid.*, 11 January 1994, cols 183–4w.

125 This failure is even more significant if Sir Robin Butler's distinction between minister-ial 'accountability' and ministerial 'responsibility' is accepted. This distinction rests on the proposition that, given the wide range of responsibilities which a Minister has, and the consequent need to delegate, the Minister cannot be held responsible for every deci-sion taken by every official in their department. However, acceptance of this proposition puts an even higher premium on a Minister conscientiously carrying out the obligation of ministerial accountability – giving Parliament timely and full details where required to do so, and ensuring full co-operation with select committee investi-gations. The Sandline/Sierra Leone imbroglio suggests that history will not regard this as having been a defining quality of the Cook Foreign Office.

126 PRO: FO 371/190847. Letter from Malcolm Gale, British Embassy, Lisbon, to D. S. L. Dodson, FO, 2 August 1966. The original *Daily Telegraph* story was published on 28 July 1966.

127 PRO: DEFE 10/460. 'Disclosure of Information about the Export of Arms and Military Equipment', Board of Trade Memorandum, attached to covering note dated 20 March 1964. Emphasis in original. The SE(O)C endorsed this argument. See PRO: DEFE10/460. Minutes of SE(O)C Committee, 13 May 1964, para. 2.

128 Fred Halliday, 'Taking the high road', *Analysis*, Radio 4, 2 October 1997.
129 Cited in Peter Hennessy, *Muddling Through: Power, Politics and the Quality of Government in Postwar Britain* (London, Indigo, 1997), p. 93.
130 Quoted in Anthony Sampson: *The Arms Bazaar*, second edition (Sevenoaks, Coronet, 1988), p. 294.
131 Quoted in *Index on Censorship*, 20:10 (1991), p. 16.
132 *Observer*, 24 May 1998, 1,000 people were sampled. Poll conducted by Opinion Research Business.
133 Hansard, 7 March 1989, col. 515. A separate rationale sometimes deployed is well illustrated by Margaret Thatcher's 1987 reply: 'Successive governments have agreed that it would not be in the public interest to disclose details of the operation of arms export contol procedures.' *Ibid.*, 13 July 1987, col. 317.
134 Sir Ronald Ellis, 'The future of defence sales', *Defence Attaché*, November/December 1979, p. 23.
135 Lawrence Freedman, 'The arms trade – a review', *International Affairs*, 55:3 (1979), 435.
136 Hansard, 5 June 1997, cols 220–1w.
137 *Ibid.*, 27 February 1998, cols 374–5w.
138 *Ibid.*, 27 June 1997, cols 658–9w.
139 *Ibid.*, 9 February 1998, cols 36–7w. See also, 16 February 1998, col. 489w, and 24 March 1998, col. 97w.
140 *Ibid.*, 4 May 1999, col. 333w.
141 *Ibid.*, 16 February 1993, cols 127–36w.
142 *Guardian*, 9 March 1994.
143 Hansard, 21 April 1989, col. 311. However, this reply also included the caveat that the guidelines were being applied 'in the light of developments in the peace negotiations with Iran'.
144 On this, see Davina Miller and Mark Phythian, 'Secrecy, accountability and British arms exports: issues for the post-Scott agenda', *Contemporary Security Policy*, 18:3, (1997), 105–27.
145 Scott Report, para. K8.
146 Clive Trebilcock, 'The British armaments industry 1890–1914: false legend and true utility', in Geoffrey Best and Andrew Wheatcroft (eds), *War Economy and the Military Mind* (London, Croom Helm, 1976), p. 89.
147 Raymond Baumhart, *An Honest Profit*. Quoted in Yerachimiel Kugel and Gladys W. Gruenberg, *International Pay-offs* (Lexington, MA, D. C. Heath, 1977), p. 34.
148 Kugel and Gruenberg, *International Pay-offs*, p. 15
149 The best of several biographies is Anthony Allfrey, *Man of Arms: The Life and Legend of Sir Basil Zaharoff* (London, Weidenfeld & Nicolson, 1989)
150 Quoted in John Ellis, *The Social History of the Machine Gun* (London, Pimlico, 1993), p. 29.
151 Sampson, *The Arms Bazaar*, p. 54.
152 Said K. Aburish, in his *Pay-off: Wheeling and Dealing in the Arab World* (London, André Deutsch, 1985), said that intermediaries tend to be non-desert Arabs from Lebanon, Syria, Egypt, etc., who are considered by desert Arabs to be more westernised and hence better equipped to deal with Western companies. See p. 7.
153 This is the terminology used by Aburish.
154 Aburish, *Pay-off*, p. 1.
155 *World in Action*, Granada TV, 26 January 1976: 'How to Sell an Air Force', II.
156 Sampson, *The Arms Bazaar*, ch. 6
157 *World in Action*, 26 January 1976.
158 *Financial Times*, 5 November 1977.

159 *Ibid.*, 21 December 1977.

160 Quoted in *Financial Times*, 5 November 1977, and *Guardian*, 19 January 1978. The former is a more sanitised version of Nurdin's statement, the latter (post-trial) account is fuller. Here the two are combined.

161 *New Statesman*, 17 October 1980, p. 14.

162 Quoted in *Financial Times*, 9 November 1977, and *Guardian*, 9 November 1977. After the 1979 Iranian Revolution, Reporter apparently went to ground. In 1980 it was reported that he 'is actually owed another £1.6 million ... but he has not been seen since a visit to London in September last year and his present whereabouts are unknown. In the unlikely event of his turning up to claim more of his loot, our sources indicate that MTS will not now be paying.' *New Statesman*, 17 October 1980, p. 14.

163 *Guardian*, 9 November 1977.

164 Hansard, 17 November 1977, col. 368.

165 Quoted in *Financial Times*, 22 November 1977.

166 *Ibid.*, 25 November 1977.

167 *Ibid.*, 29 November 1977 and 1 December 1977.

168 *Ibid.*, 17 December 1977.

169 Randel was sentenced to three years' imprisonment, Wellburn received a 12-month sentence, suspended for two years, and Nurdin was sentenced to 18 months' imprisonment. Afterwards, Wellburn commented that: 'If one stops making these payments then it would be disastrous for Britain and for any other exporting country.' *Guardian*, 20 January 1978. Wellburn and Nurdin appealed against their convictions, but were turned down on 14 February 1979. Nurdin was released from prison on the direction of the appeal judges in view of his age and health.

170 Quoted in *Observer*, 22 January 1978.

171 Foxley had retired in 1983 and was retained as a self-employed consultant until 1984, although his activities did not come to light until 1989.

172 *Guardian*, 27 October 1993.

173 *The Times, Independent*, and *Guardian*, 27 May 1994.

174 PAC: *Ministry of Defence: Chevaline Improvement to the Polaris Missile System*, Ninth Report, Session 1981–82, Appendix 1.

175 Hansard, 27 January 1987, col. 246.

176 *Ibid.*, col. 248.

177 See *New Statesman*, 'The bribe machine', 17 October 1980, pp. 12–17. The payment was thought to be for Saudi officials.

178 PAC, *Matters Relating to the Ministry of Defence*, Third Report, Session 1980–81, HC-125, p. 101.

179 *Ibid.*, p. 28.

180 *Ibid.*, p. xxiii. However, in 1977 the MoD laid down guidelines that IMS should observe in the payment of commissions to those they engaged in 'defence sales business'. These were: 'that public money is not used for illegal or improper purposes; that the agents employed are reputable in the area in which they are operating; that in cases ... where the total payment would appear excessive in relation to the work performed, the agent must not be engaged without reference to the Accounting Officer (there has been no such reference); and that fees and commissions paid to agents should not be in breach of the laws of the country concerned.' *Ibid.*, p. 105.

181 *Ibid.*, p. xxiii.

182 PAC: *Ministry of Defence: Support for Defence Exports*, Minutes of Evidence 26 April 1989, p. 2.

183 *Ibid.*, pp. 7–8. Levene felt unable to allow the PAC access to the memoranda of understanding relating to the Malaysian and Saudi Arabian Tornado contracts, subsequently advising the committee that: 'MoUs have not in the past been provided to Select

Committees, in accordance with the normal conventions applying to the inter-governmental negotiations.' *Ibid.*, p. 13.

184 *Ibid.*, p. 9.
185 *Guardian*, 13 March 1992.
186 *Independent*, 13 March 1992.
187 *Guardian*, 13 March 1992. Sheldon subsequently expanded on this, saying that: 'There were certain sensitivities about individuals – not in Britain, outside – which might have prejudiced some of the sales and of course might have led to a loss of contracts or, more seriously, a loss of employment opportunities in the companies concerned.' *Guardian*, 11 October 1994.
188 Interview with member of the PAC, House of Commons, 8 December 1993.
189 *Independent*, 13 March 1992.
190 *Ibid.*
191 *Ibid.*
192 *Guardian*, 25 June 1997.
193 Hansard, 2 June 1997, col. 15w.
194 *Ibid.*, 5 March 1998, cols 1188–9.
195 *Guardian*, 14 November 1994.
196 *Ibid.*, 7 February 1998. See also *Financial Times*, 20 December 1997.
197 For the fullest account of these allegations, see Paul Halloran and Mark Hollingsworth, *Thatcher's Gold: The Life and Times of Mark Thatcher* (London, Simon & Schuster, 1995), ch. 6.
198 *Sunday Times*, 9 October 1994.
199 The original story of the mystery of the Aitken bill appeared in the *Guardian* on 10 May 1994. The newpaper's account of the real purpose of the visit was contained in *Guardian*, 5 March 1999. See also the story on 6 March 1999, and the account in the revised edition of Harding *et al.*, *The Liar*.
200 TISC, *Export Licensing and BMARC*, Third Report, Session 1995–96, HC 87-I.
201 The reference to the 'Vosper contract' is to the sale of six Sandown minehunters to Saudi Arabia as part of Al Yamamah-2.
202 *Private Eye*, No. 892, 23 February 1996, p. 27, and No. 893, 8 March 1996, p. 24.
203 The website address is *www.saudhouse.com*. Quotes are from *www.saudhouse.com/al-yamam.htm*.

3

British arms sales to Latin America

Chile, 1973–79

Arms to Chile: responses to the 1973 *coup*

The military coup of 11 September 1973, during which elected President Salvador Allende died, ended an experiment followed closely by many in the Labour Party. For many on the Labour left it had a profound effect. Harold Wilson later recalled how passions were raised over Chile, 'where the socialist President Allende was murdered by the Fascist right wing'.[1] While Labour had been in opposition, Eric Heffer had led a delegation to Chile, taking a personal message from Wilson to Allende. 'We had lunch and spent three to four hours with the President in his Palace in Santiago. He said that Socialism in Chile would be pluralist and democratic and not bureaucratic as it was in the Soviet Union "If they let me". That was a chilling phrase because even then he understood that there were forces against him prepared to overthrow him.'[2] On hearing of the *coup* and Allende's death, Heffer 'wept unashamedly at the news, for an attempt to achieve socialism through the Parliamentary process had been murdered too.'[3]

In the wake of the *coup*, on 22 September, the Conservative Foreign Secretary, Sir Alec Douglas Home, announced that Britain had formally recognised the new Chilean military government. He also announced that arms for which contracts had already been signed – naval vessels and equipment ordered by the Frei government, and seven Hawker Hunter aircraft and related spares ordered by the Allende government – would be delivered so as not to impair Britain's reputation as a supplier, or jeopardise future trade with the region. During the 1970s the issue was to become a *cause célèbre* for the Labour left – the most controversial arms sales issue of the decade – not least because Hunter aircraft had played such a prominent role in the *coup*, attacking the Moneda Palace in which Allende died.

In November 1973 it was revealed that some of the seven Hunters on order had already been delivered,[4] and that, despite recent events, a group of Chilean servicemen had arrived in Britain to undergo training at the RAF Staff College at Bracknell. However, the fact that delivery neither of the Hunters, nor of the several naval vessels ordered, had been completed opened up the possibility of preventing further deliveries. The Chilean military were also aware of this potential and indicated their willingness to turn to the US if the aircraft order was disrupted.

On 28 November 1973, the House of Commons debated Chile around Judith Hart's motion calling for the imposition of sanctions, including measures, 'to prevent any sale of arms from Great Britain to the junta'.[5] Hart outlined the opposition Labour Party position, that:

> We believe that there should be no arms supplied from Britain for Chile, either on a Government aid or a credit basis or through private sales. We do not believe that any of the ships being built should go there, although my understanding is that the trade union movement is taking effective steps here.[6]

In response, Foreign Office Minister Julian Amery defended the sale of the aircraft and naval vessels:

> There are important naval contracts for the sale of arms to Chile worth about £71 million ... On what principle are we asked to suspend the sale of arms to Chile? There is no civil war in Chile. There is no war between Chile and her neighbours; nor is there a threat of war between Chile and her neighbours. There is no hostility on the part of Chile to Britain or to Britain's allies. I can see no reason why we should suspend these arms sales and why we should suspend the contracts into which we have entered.[7]

Amery defended the absence of sanctions in terms of events in Chile being 'a Chilean dispute settled by Chileans' and 'a quarrel of limited concern to the people of this country'.[8] He also hinted at the more substantial considerations at play. 'Our duty is to ensure ... the promotion of British interests ... This involves developing normal friendly relations with the Chilean Government of the day, whatever its political colour. This we have done.'[9]

The fact that the previous Labour government had acted similarly weakened the arguments of the parliamentary left – most vocally represented over this issue by Hart, Heffer and the firebrand Neil Kinnock. As Conservative MPs were keen to point out, the Wilson government had, after all, sold arms to South American military governments during the 1960s. As one noted:

> When at an earlier stage the Argentine forsook the form of democracy that it then had and endured a military *coup*, the Labour Government of the day used almost the same language, saying that the policies of Argentina were for Argentina to work out for herself and that if that country were not

hostile to us there was no reason for not maintaining arms deliveries to it, and the Labour Government continued arms deliveries.[10]

Although the motion was defeated by 280 votes to 262, the debate indicated just how emotive a subject Chile had become. In the event, delivery of the Hunter order was completed before the February 1974 general election, bringing the total number of Hunters in the Chilean Air Force to 39 – testament to the close arms sales relationship that existed between the two countries prior to the 1973 *coup*, but which was to remain highly contentious for the remainder of the decade.

Following the Labour victory in the general election, the Labour government was faced with a dilemma similar to that faced in 1964 over South Africa, and in 1997 over Indonesia. The new Foreign Secretary, Jim Callaghan, announced that no new export licences would be granted for the export of arms to Chile,[11] adopting the position that 'important arms' should not be sold to oppressive governments. But, as in 1964, the government was still faced with the dilemma of whether or not to fulfil existing contracts, in this case the Heath government's contracts to supply two *Leander* class frigates and two *Oberon* class submarines. Of these, one frigate, *Condell*, was undergoing trials in British waters, manned by the Chilean Navy, while the second, *Lynch*, was nearing completion. As regards the submarines, the *O'Brien* was due to be delivered in July 1974, while the *Hyatt* was only due to be delivered the following year.

With the personnel largely unchanged, it should come as no surprise that 'leaking' to the press remained endemic, and on 24 March the *Sunday Telegraph* revealed that the Labour government had decided to supply all four. With South Africa no doubt in mind, Tony Benn, then Industry Secretary, noted in his diary how:

> This is the beginning of the old game which I remember so well, where our moral position on foreign policy is completely eroded as soon as we get into office. It is a long uphill struggle against colleagues for whom the Manifesto is simply a piece of paper to be torn up as and when convenient.[12]

However, opposition to the completion of existing contracts forced what had initially appeared a *fait accompli* on to the Cabinet agenda:

> Cabinet, beginning with the question of warships to Chile. Jim [Callaghan] gave the case for supplying them, i.e., that there was a major export interest involved and that one of them had already been handed over to a Chilean Navy crew. Roy Mason [Defence Secretary] confirmed that we had orders worth £200 million in Latin America as a whole and we would be regarded as very unreliable if we reneged.[13]

Even so, the opponents of the hand-over secured an undertaking that Callaghan would canvass opinion from the back benches and then report back to Cabinet before a final decision was reached. In the event, this proved insufficiently strong to alter Callaghan's proposed course of action. As Benn recorded:

> At Cabinet, the Chile warships came up again. Jim Callaghan reported that he had met a group of Labour MPs the previous evening, half of whom had been in favour of releasing the existing warships. He said it would require legislation to stop the release, and how would you get the Chilean sailors off the ship already doing trials off the English coast, and so on and so on.
>   Michael Foot came out very strongly against and I said, 'It is absolutely untrue that it would require legislation ... What would we say if we discovered that the Russians had put in an order for some fighters from [the] British Aircraft Corporation? Of course we can do it, it is a decision we are absolutely free to take.'[14]

The unresolved issue of the warships was not the only one. The Cabinet was also faced with the question of what to do with a consignment of Rolls-Royce Avon engines for the Chileans' Hunter aircraft, which had been sent to Rolls-Royce's East Kilbride plant for overhaul by the Allende government, but work on which had been halted by the unions at the time of the *coup*. Callaghan favoured completion of both orders, but following discussions by the OPD on 1 May 1974 the issue remained unresolved.[15] Further Cabinet discussion of the Chile question was then delayed for two weeks while the Attorney General, Sam Silkin, prepared an opinion as to whether the government had any legal grounds for breaking the contracts.

The issue dragged on through May 1974. On 16 May, Tony Benn presented a paper to Cabinet arguing that Rolls-Royce should be instructed to terminate their aero-engine contract, and that the engines languishing in East Kilbride should not be returned to Chile. Benn had received a letter from the Chilean Air Force, passed on to him by Rolls-Royce, which asked if the engines could be returned to Chile if they could not be overhauled. This seemed to offer a solution, except that Callaghan continued to advocate fulfilling all contracts. A compromise was thrashed out whereby the Chilean Air Force would be denied any further spares or servicing requests, and Rolls-Royce would terminate its contract with the Chilean government. At the same time, so as not to injure Britain's standing as a commercial supplier (although, of course, the episode already had), the ships and engines would be supplied. In effect, the government had again accepted the principle of the inviolability of existing contracts over manifesto and public commitments made in opposition.

Ultimately, this compromise was unsatisfactory from all points of view. For the left, the delivery of the naval vessels was a clear defeat, whilst the decision regarding the aircraft sent precisely those signals to the Chilean Air Force regarding Britain's reliability as an exporter that Callaghan, Roy Mason and Denis Healey had warned against in Cabinet. Indeed, the Chilean Foreign Minister, Admiral Ismael Huerta, responded to the news by saying that Britain was 'not to be trusted' as an exporting nation, and that 'We too will have to revise to whom we sell copper – there is such a demand for it that we can select amongst those interested and will logically prefer countries that are friendly to us.'[16]

The compromise decision was formally announced by Wilson in the House of Commons on 21 May, leading to a spirited exchange with Edward Heath, who pointed out that servicing and overhaul of the engines would simply be done elsewhere, an argument which, Wilson suggested, was the 'traditional apology of the prostitute through the ages: "If I don't do it, somebody else will."'[17] However, the logic of the prostitute was also the logic applied to arms exports by the FO and in Cabinet committees throughout the 1964–70 Labour governments.

In his memoirs, Wilson presented himself as being firmly opposed to the sale of military equipment to Chile after 1973, except where international law dictated that such sales had to go ahead. However, his argument that the ships, and by implication any military equipment on order, had to be delivered was somewhat disingenuous, and not accepted by all in Cabinet at the time.[18] Wilson recalled that:

> Both the Foreign Secretary and I made clear in the Commons that our attitude to Chile involved a reversal of that taken up by our predecessors ... Aid was suspended. A projected naval training exercise arranged by our predecessors was cancelled. A review of existing contracts was in progress, but we said, 'We shall not grant new export licences for arms.'
>
> Ships they had ordered had already been handed over, and were engaged in trials. International Law would have forbidden us to take them back, or to instruct the Royal Navy to force them into port or sink them ... The Chilean Air Force had a contract with Rolls Royce Engines for the overhaul of aero-engines and the supply of spares, with a provision for three months' notice of termination. At the Government's request, notice was given to end the contract, and obligations to supply spares would also come to an end.[19]

Although highly criticised at the time, today it seems a bold political statement when considered in the light of the 1997 Labour government's decisions surrounding Indonesia. It is also interesting to compare the Wilson government's approach to arms sales to Chile with its approach to the question of arms sales to South Africa. As with Chile, the Heath government had sold weapons to South Africa, in that case reversing the qualified ban on shipments imposed by the 1964 Wilson government. Upon resuming office in 1974, Wilson reinforced the 'ban', symbolically cancelling the Westland Wasp helicopter order.

The issue of arms for Chile refused to go away. In 1975 Chile sought to re-schedule over US$300 million of its US$700 million debt, and hinted that unless its creditors agreed to accomodate it, it would default. Whilst the US, France, West Germany, Japan, Spain and Switzerland agreed to discuss rescheduling, Britain was joined by the Netherlands, Belgium,

Italy, Sweden, Norway and Denmark in refusing to meet Chilean representatives to facilitate such a move.[20] Consequently, Chile failed to meet
its 1975 debt repayment of £14 million to Britain, its largest creditor after
the US.

The Labour left saw in this an opportunity to reopen the debate and
withhold delivery of the outstanding naval vessels and aero-engines. In
July, Judith Hart and Ian Mikardo approached Trade Secretary Peter
Shore, in an attempt to persuade him not to allow the two submarines to
be delivered. Shore advanced the standard argument that unless the
government went ahead with the delivery, the chances of securing further
contracts in the region would be reduced.[21]

The issue was revivied again when, later in 1975, it was revealed that
a British doctor, Sheila Cassidy, had been arrested and tortured by the
Chilean secret police, after treating Nelson Gutierrez of the MIR guerrilla
movement. The resulting public outcry combined with the existing pressure regarding Chile to compel the government to act. Initially, the
Government had no success in attempting to secure Cassidy's release from
detention, but succeeded after suggesting that delivery of the remaining
naval vessels – the two submarines – and the aero-engines could be linked
with it.[22]

The government then moved to break off relations at ambassadorial
level, although it did not break off all diplomatic relations – a diplomatic
staff of 13 remained, trade relations were not directly affected and the
Chilean ambassador to Britain was not expelled. However, an official
arms embargo was imposed on all new orders. Neil Kinnock argued that
the government should go further in that direction: 'There are other more
forceful ways of registering British opposition to the barbarities of the
Chilean regime such as confiscating the warships now being built for
which Chile cannot pay.'[23]

Cassidy's case was not the only one of British citizens being detained
and tortured in Chile at the time. The Anglo-Chilean businessman and
British passport holder William Beausire was detained towards the end of
1974, and last seen alive in a torture centre in mid-1975. Even so, in 1976
Ted Rowlands announced that the two submarines would be delivered so
as not to affect Britain's reputation as a dependable arms supplier, even
though the Chileans had not kept up their payments on the two
submarines.

The arms-for-Chile controversy rolled on into 1976 with the revelation
that, during 1974, 53 Chilean naval officers and 223 naval ratings had
undergone naval training courses in Britain, that in 1975 a further 21 officers and three ratings attended the courses, and that in 1976 a further 12
officers and 40 ratings were expected to undertake similar training.
Although this seemed to run counter to the intent behind the more recent
government statements, the difficulties arose from the fact that this train-

ing provision was a component of the contracts already signed, the inviolability of which, as South Africa had shown, was regarded as sacrosanct by
leading members of the government. As Roy Mason was forced to explain:

> Requests for serving members of the armed forces of foreign Powers to
> attend Service training courses in the United Kingdom are considered in the
> light of the vacancies available and of the political, defence, sales and other
> relevant factors ... Training for serving members of the Chilean armed
> forces is limited to that deriving from naval sales contracts negotiated some
> years before.[24]

Mason was applying the same logic here that Callaghan had applied to
the wider question of supply, with the same concern about retaining
Britain's credibility as an arms supplier. Given the harm that the Labour
government's compromise position on arms-for-Chile had already done
to that reputation, the government could in fact have moved further to
cancel this provision without doing any further harm to its relations
with a military government already looking to the US for its future military requirements, especially in view of the latter's supportive role in the
1975 Paris Club debt talks. However, an overriding consideration was
that the Chileans had to be trained so as to be able to get the ships to
Chile.

Finally, in June 1976, the *O'Brien* became the first of the submarines
to be officially handed over, albeit two years behind schedule because of
fitting-out and political problems. This was followed in August by the
handing-over ceremony for the *Hyatt*, attended by Chilean Ambassador
and Admiral of the Fleet Kaare Olsen.[25] At this point, the Chilean Navy
still had a requirement for further submarines to add to its fleet, and so
Olsen's expressed hope that something of a normalisation of relations
could ease the way to further contracts (not a view shared by the Chilean
Air Force) was perhaps more than mere rhetoric. He explained that: 'We
would like to build ships again here, and we have had good relations with
most of the British people – but there are certain sectors that don't
like us. We look at it this way – we need certain things like ships and you
need to build them. It is a business transaction and has nothing to do with
politics.'[26]

However, the Callaghan government had authorised the hand-over
only at the last minute after demanding that Chile should 'regularise' its
payments within twelve months and receiving £7.5 million to clear the
debt on the contract. Although this marked the end of the most visible
element of the arms-for-Chile controversy, submarine spares were still
held up at Rosyth, and the aero-engines were still standing at the Rolls-
Royce plant in East Kilbride, 'blacked' by the unions.

In November 1976, to the embarrassment of the Callaghan government, the Chilean government made enquiries about the possibility of

ordering further submarines from Britain, at an estimated cost of £20 million,[27] a reflection of the conflicting signals the Labour government had sent to Chile through its attempts to both appease the left and honour existing contracts. From a recipient perspective, although the Wilson government had imposed a ban on fresh arms contracts, since then two frigates and one submarine had been delivered, with a second officially handed over and delivery only weeks away.

However, following the submarine enquiry, junta member and commander of the Chilean Air Force General Gustavo Leigh made it clear that Britain would receive no new aircraft orders given the continuing dispute over the aero-engines at East Kilbride. By 1978 pressure to return the aero-engines and to move towards normalising relations with Chile was growing. Conservative peers backed the decision of the Hamilton sheriff's court that the engines should be returned to the Chilean government. Viscount Masserine and Ferrard observed that: 'It is not a very good advertisement for our export trade if we deny our customers their property, presumably because their politics are not sufficiently Marxist to please the unions involved.'[28] Amid fears that there could be a legal battle over ownership of the engines during the likely period of the coming general election, the government indicated that it would support their return. The union convenor at the East Kilbride plant indicated that the engines were all rusting away anyway, because they had been left packed in crates and left outside the warehouse ever since the overhaul work had been completed in 1975.[29]

Finally, on 20 July 1978, the government granted an export licence for the engines, despite a motion signed by over 140 Labour MPs demanding that the engines should not be returned to Chile. The granting of the export licence did not solve the problem of how the engines were to be removed from the plant, but it did complete the legal framework for their removal. On returning from their annual holiday in early August, shop stewards still refused to move the engines despite these latest manoeuvrings and appeals from the government. Rolls-Royce then let it be known that it would not prevent the retrieval of the engines.[30] At this point a meeting of workers at the plant voted not to impede their removal.[31]

The episode came to an end when at dawn on Saturday 26 August 1978 (the beginning of the three-day holiday weekend), the engines were removed by a combination of police, haulage contractors, sheriff's officers and Chilean representatives. They were transported to an undisclosed destination, but were not shipped out of the country immediately, allowing the TGWU's Alex Kitson to make a final call to all trade unionists to ensure that the engines 'never arrive in Chile'.[32] Given the anticipated difficulty in moving the engines through a civilian airport or docks, it is thought that the government colluded in their storage at RAF Brize

Norton prior to landing rights being granted to the Chilean Air Force, in order that they could finally be returned to Chile. On 6 October 1978, General Carlos Degroux, head of the Chilean Air Force Supply Command, announced that the engines had finally arrived in Chile.

Why did the Chilean government decide that it needed the engines, which were in an uncertain condition, so badly as to make a minor incident out of their recovery? The answer lies, firstly, in the deteriorating relationship with Argentina over the Beagle Channel dispute, which threatened to escalate into armed conflict in 1978, and, secondly, in Chile's increasing difficulty in obtaining military equipment in light of the actions of the Wilson government and of the Carter administration following the assassination of Orlando Letelier and his US companion, Ronni Moffitt, in the US.[33]

In retrospect, the arms-for-Chile episode both soured relations with Chile and split the Labour Party. The fundamental flaw in the government's position – a consequence of trying to move far enough to appease the left while attempting to minimise the negative impact on Britain's reputation as an arms supplier across the region – surfaced repeatedly. The issue refused to go away. The Chilean debt position offered renewed hope of blocking delivery for the left after the cause had seemed lost. Then, as this issue died down, the cases of Sheila Cassidy and William Beausire led to renewed calls for the blocking of delivery in protest at their treatment. Finally, the sympathies of the trade unions involved were more in line with the efforts of the left than of the party leadership. With TUC backing, the unions at East Kilbride 'blacked' the Avon engines, creating a situation increasingly embarrassing to the government. The fundamental ambiguity of the government's position was a spur to each of these separate efforts to prevent delivery. In attempting to satisfy party interests and government commitments, it failed to satisfy either.

Arms to Chile: Pinochet and Thatcher

The Conservative government of Margaret Thatcher exhibited a different set of priorities and a different attitude towards relations with Chile. The one South American government most vehemently condemned by sections of the Labour Party became one of the South American governments to which the new Conservative government was closest. Indeed, its approach to the question of arms for Chile provided one of the earliest statements of its intent in the area of arms exports.

It moved quickly to improve relations by restoring full ECGD cover for exports in June 1979, even though at that time Chile remained one of the few casualties of the Carter administration's linkage of human rights and foreign policy. In fact, Chile's relations with the US deteriorated further in November 1979 with the announcement of a range of US sanctions, including the halting of all military deliveries and economic aid to Chile. New US military sales to Chile had already been blocked by the administration in 1976, so the new prohibition applied only to items ordered prior to that date. Hence Chile's relations with Britain began to improve just as those with the US deteriorated further.

It was in this context that on 16 January 1980 the Minister of State at the FCO, Nicholas Ridley, announced that relations would be restored at ambassadorial level,[34] the government having received assurances from the Chileans that they 'sincerely regretted' torturing Sheila Cassidy, and were continuing to investigate the case of the disappeared William Beausire. In his announcement, Ridley claimed that the human rights situation in Chile was improving, despite the discovery of over 600 unmarked graves in the main Santiago cemetery in November 1979. In defence of the move, he articulated the FCO line, that it would allow the British government to 'present our views on human rights and other matters at a higher level with greater impact'.

In September the Chilean Trade Minister, Hernan Cubillos, visited France to begin the process of shifting reliance from the US to Europe for Chile's military supplies. As a result, Chile announced that it was to purchase 16 Mirage 50s. The following month, the first group of Chilean pilots arrived in France for training. This was a process the Thatcher government was keen to be part of, but timing the announcement of the end of the embargo was always going to be problematic. In the event, the deal with France served to accelerate the announcement somewhat, and the announcement that the arms embargo was to be lifted was made by Ridley on 22 July 1980. In a clear effort to deflect attention away from the decision, the disclosure came in a written reply on the same day that the latest unemployment figures, the main issue of the day, were announced.[35]

However, resentment remained. Admiral José Merino was quick to state that, in light of the experience of the 1970s, 'Chile will not buy anything from England again in this area.'[36] This reflected the continuing doubts about Britain as a long-term supplier, fuelled by the unpopularity of the first Thatcher government, at least until 1982, the attendant prospect of disruption of supply if it were to lose the next general election, and the fact that opposition to relations with Chile, far from dying away when the Labour Party left office, had been rekindled by the indecent haste of the Thatcher government.

Indeed, the Labour Party's draft 1980 manifesto committed a future Labour government to a fresh withdrawal of the British ambassador and the reimposition of the arms sales ban. At the same time, Amnesty International and church groups were seeking to concentrate attention on the human rights situation in Chile. Prominent amongst this latter group was Cardinal Basil Hume, who had played a leading role the previous year in preventing the sale of armoured vehicles to the military government in El Salvador (see below), and who now lobbied Ridley on the Chile question, concluding that: 'Whatever may be the benefits of trade between our two countries, we should not close our eyes to the repression which so many Chileans are now suffering.'[37] However, an official at the MoD ingeniously noted that in this context the situation in Chile, 'is probably now no worse than that in other countries where we do not operate an arms embargo. The Government feels it is wrong to be selective.'[38]

As elsewhere – with regard to Indonesia, for example – voting performance at the UN was not always an accurate guide to foreign policy priorities. In December 1979, Britain had voted in favour of a General Assembly resolution expressing grave concern over the continued violations of human rights under the Pinochet government. Moreover, on 10 March 1980 the Minister of State at the MoD, Lord Strathcona, said that the government would not permit the export of military equipment to governments guilty of torture and repression.[39] In light of this, the government's ending of the embargo would appear to have been at odds with its principles. Ridley intervened in an attempt to paper over the cracks by suggesting that Sheila Cassidy had not been tortured, merely maltreated.[40]

To the government's subsequent embarrassment, it later emerged that Anglo-Chilean student Claire Wilson had been arrested and tortured by the Chilean security forces only six days prior to Ridley's announcement of the lifting of the embargo. Despite the fact that the British embassy helped to secure her release, Ridley claimed that he knew nothing of her plight at the time the announcement was made. The embassy, for its part, claimed to be unaware that the embargo was going to be lifted, and hence that London needed to be specially alerted to Claire Wilson's case.[41] It took the embassy a week (i.e. until the criticism over the resumption of arms sales had died down) to complain to the Chilean government about the incident, and a further eleven days before the ambassador was recalled to the FCO. Moreover, these responses were kept secret and when they were disclosed the indefatigable Ridley claimed that it was not the job of the FCO to publicise cases of British people being ill-treated abroad. The conclusion that the government had deliberately concealed the incident so as not to jeopardise the lifting of the arms ban borders on the irresistible. Ridley's handling of the issue contained several pointers as to the real rationale behind the lifting of the arms embargo, and the significance of human rights considerations within it. As he explained:

> The reason the arms embargo was lifted was that we do not place embargoes against any country except when there are special reasons for doing so connected with our security or matters like that. After careful thought and consideration, we decided to do the same as most other countries and trade with Chile, whatever we might think about their political system. We have, of course, strong reservations about much that goes on of a political nature

in Chile, but we don't mix up the two questions of trade and views of the political situation. Nobody does on Chile, and we don't see why we should be the odd man out.[42]

Notwithstanding these problems of domestic presentation, in August 1980 the improvement in relations was further cemented by the four-day visit to Chile of Trade Minister Cecil Parkinson, the first such visit since 1972. This positive approach to Chile was soon being matched by that of the incoming Reagan administration. In February 1981 the Carter-imposed Export–Import Bank ban was lifted, and Chile was invited to take part in inter-American naval exercises as a prelude to the lifting of the arms embargo. This formally occurred with the October Senate vote in favour, conditional on certification that the Pinochet government was making 'significant progress in complying with internationally recognised standards of human rights'.[43]

Also in October, the British government announced its first significant military sale to Chile since the lifting of the embargo the previous year, with the sale of the County class destroyer HMS *Norfolk* and the naval tanker *Tidepool*.[44] These had become surplus to requirements in the wake of John Nott's ultimately ill-fated defence review. Both were to be delivered in 1982 at a cost of over £10 million, which also included a commitment to supply the appropriate missiles, spares, and training for the Chilean Navy.[45] That month also saw the first official visit to Britain of a member of the Pinochet government, when Mining Minister José Pinera paid a four-day visit. He was followed by Labour Minister Miguel Kast on 17 November.

The Argentine invasion of the Falkland Islands in April 1982 accelerated the already heady pace of normalisation of relations. Geopolitical considerations dictated that it was in the Thatcher government's interests to pursue still closer relations with Chile in return for assistance in the conflict. The precise nature and extent of this assistance were, and remain, one of the most secret issues in the entire conflict.[46] Indeed, news editors were asked not to mention it.[47]

Co-operation and assistance took many forms. From the outset, a number of confidential points of collaboration were set out in classified telegrams from the British embassy to the FCO. These indicated that the Pinochet government would allow British forces the use of Chilean military bases and intelligence. In return, the British government would provide military equipment, cease any lingering criticism of human rights abuses, and help undermine UN investigations into these by opposing the reappointment of the UN's Special Rapporteur.[48]

The first fruits of this agreement were seen fairly quickly. In mid-April at least six Canberra aircraft were flown to Belize and repainted with Chilean Air Force markings, from where they were flown to an air base outside Punta Arenas. From there they were able to undertake regular reconnaissance missions over the principal Argentine airbases in the region. In organising this, Group Captain David Edwards liaised directly with General Fernando Matthei, Commander-in-Chief of the Chilean Air Force.[49] While both governments attempted to keep the arrangement as secret as possible, ITN reporter Jon Snow came across two Canberras complete with Chilean markings at Santiago airport in mid-May. Officially none was sold to Chile until after the conflict.

This co-operation also facilitated the establishment of a base near Punta Arenas from where SAS raids on Argentina could be staged. In addition, Chilean naval intelligence played an important role in the interception of Argentine military and navy radio signals. In return for this assistance the Pinochet government was anxious to acquire British military equipment. During April and May 1982, eight Hawker Hunter aircraft, the engines alone for which had been so controversial previously, were transferred to the Chileans, with an additional consignment of four departing in January 1983.[50] Prior to this, Britain had sold Chile 39 Hunters, around 23 of which were thought to still be in service.[51] In addition, RAF pilots were secretly sent to Chile to provide training for Chilean Air Force personnel.[52] Moreover, as many as six Canberra aircraft, by now complete with Chilean markings, were given to Chile in the aftermath of the conflict – three officially despatched from RAF Wyton on 15 October 1982, complete with Chilean markings, and up to a further three thought to have been left behind in Chile after British forces departed.[53]

Parliament was told nothing of this and Labour Party opposition was only mobilised some months later as a result of information coming to light through specialist aircraft publications. Nevertheless, the flow of military equipment to Chile was so great at this time that the Chilean Air Force decided to set up a depot at Luton Airport, with Chilean Boeing 707s using the airport to pick up spares.

Subsequently, Anglo-Chilean relations continued to be close. Despite the fact that none of this officially took place, Foreign Secretary Francis Pym told the House of Commons in November 1982 that: 'Chile was quite helpful to us in the [Falklands] conflict and we ought to bear that in mind when we consider our relations now.'[54] Further expressions of UK gratitude included the invitation of a Chilean delegation to the 1982 BAEE – the first since 1974 – and the invitation extended to General Matthei to head a team to attend the 1982 Farnborough Air Show. This provoked so much protest that the trip was cancelled (officially 'urgent legislation' at home was cited). However, Matthei did visit Britain in March 1983, when he met and was reportedly thanked by Air Marshal Sir Keith Williamson, RAF Chief of Staff.

In September 1982, Trade Minister Peter Rees followed in Cecil

Parkinson's footsteps by heading a British trade delegation to Chile, commenting that Chile represented 'a moderate and stabilising force' in the region with which Britain ought to be 'deepening and strengthening political relations'.[55] Towards the end of 1982, Britain further indicated its concern over human rights abuses in Chile – the ability to raise questions over which at an appropriately high level was a justification for the reinstatement of the British ambassador to Santiago in the first place – when the British delegation to the UN General Assembly attempted to downgrade the issue internationally by attempting to remove the Special Rapporteur – just as they had pledged to do in return for Falklands assistance.

Chile moved next to purchase a number of ex-RN vessels. It had already purchased HMS *Norfolk* in 1982, and in March 1983 expressed an interest in buying the aircraft carrier HMS *Hermes*, in order to counterbalance Argentina's possession of the *Veinticinco de Mayo*. The following month, Nicholas Ridley visited Santiago, and later in the year it was announced that Britain was selling another vessel from the Falklands campaign, HMS *Antrim*, for an estimated £5 million, with delivery scheduled for early 1984. Anglo-Chilean military relations continued to develop rapidly through 1983 (despite fears on the Chilean side of the consequences if the Labour Party were to win the general election), and were the subject of a parliamentary debate in November following rumours that a consignment of ex-RAF Jaguar aircraft, specially fitted to carry the Sea Eagle missile (giving Chile a capacity similar to that of Argentina with the Super Etendard–Exocet combination) were to be sold to Chile. Former arms sales enthusiast Denis Healey set the tone of the debate, arguing that: 'It really is quite extraordinary that at the very moment Argentina has elected its first democratic president, the British Government should be selling weapons to Argentina's deadliest enemy, a country run by the most hated dictator in Latin America and under heavy international pressure to resign.'[56]

Meanwhile, Britain's continued military trade with Chile, in the face of US protests, stood in stark contrast to the continued US embargo on sales of military equipment to Argentina in reluctant deference to the Anglo-American alliance. Laurence Birns, director of the Council for Hemispheric Affairs, commented:

> State Department officials told me they were alarmed that the Thatcher Government were heating up their relations with Chile at a time when the US was cooling its down. They said relations between London and Santiago were close and getting closer and the British were not telling the US a thing about it ... The British are working out a *de facto* military relationship with Chile, supplying arms and providing political credibility and respectability to a regime who are quite properly regarded as international pariahs.[57]

In March 1984 the government refused to grant Rolls-Royce an export licence for its V-8 Condor engines – intended to update Chile's fleet of M41 and Israeli-developed M-51 tanks. Then, in June, the AMAC Corporation was informed that no licence would be granted for the export to Chile of its AMAC-1 riot control vehicle. Despite the vehicle's repressive intent (it could carry a crew of 10, and boasted 16 grenade launchers, 18 gun ports, a high-pressure water cannon capable of knocking a vehicle over, searchlights and floodlights, and heavy body armour with a 7,000 V electrical charge running through it) not all Conservative MPs backed the government's decision to block the deal. For one, Nicholas Winterton argued that: 'We are playing the human rights game rather than thinking deeply about the issues. We should, perhaps, have called in the Chilean Ambassador and obtained assurances about the way these vehicles would have been used. In that way we could exert some influence over the actions of the Chilean Government.'[58]

In Chile, several days of national protest calling for the removal of President Pinochet and a return to democratically elected government took place in the autumn of 1984. As a response to the 30 October 1984 national strike a state of siege was declared on 6 November, involving a curfew, widespread press censorship, and a new wave of repression. In response to this changed situation the FCO produced a contingency planning document, which was leaked to Labour MP Jeremy Corbyn, outlining the range of responses Britain should consider. It grouped the 'Possibilities for Curtailment of Relations' under several headings, the first of which was arms sales. Here, the FCO ruled out the imposition of an arms embargo on the grounds that it would 'carry unacceptable penalties. The Chileans would regard an embargo as a major shift in British policy; and this could, in turn, hazard the defence and other co-operation we enjoy over the Falklands.'[59] This document again makes it clear that arms sales policy is determined not by objective or internationally recognised standards with regard to human rights or 'good government', but by its impact on British interests. The document ran through other possible defence-related sanctions: ending visits to Chilean ports by RN vessels; ending the loaning of personnel to Chile for training purposes; withdrawing the facility allowing Chileans to be trained in Britain. Instead of any of these measures, the FCO advocated a less expensive gesture:

In London. We might consider a Ministerial and senior official boycott of Chilean embassy social occasions. This could either be confined to FCO contacts or be extended to the wider range of business between Whitehall and the Chilean Embassy. We might also adopt a policy of only inviting opposition politicians to come to London and dropping our official visits programme as it relates to members of the Chilean government or administration.[60]

Hence there was no question of measures being applied which could impair the close military and political links between the two countries.[61] However, an attached summary of the exact situation regarding British arms exports to Chile revealed that a number of anticipated deals were considered unlikely to go ahead. For example, the Chileans' interest in the Jaguar had faltered when they decided that the price was too high. Chilean interest in the land-based Harrier was also likely to come to nothing because, while the British government were behind a sale, the aircraft contained US components, making its sale subject to US re-export certification, which, given the Reagan administration's now shifting position on the Pinochet government, was unlikely to be forthcoming. As regards naval sales, the FCO regarded the prospects as being low, and although the Chileans had an interest in purchasing 300 Centaur armoured vehicles, the human rights situation and stated British government policy made the situation 'politically difficult here. To be watched carefully.'[62]

Indeed, the proposed Centaur deal developed into something of a cause in its own right. Following press reports that one Centaur vehicle had been shipped to Chile for tests, George Foulkes, Labour spokesman on Latin America, protested, declaring that: 'The choice for Britain is now between human rights and arms sales. It seems likely that the government has chosen the latter.'[63] Following his visit, Conservative MP Keith Best reassured everyone that: 'The Chileans told me that they wanted it for use in the northern desert and the boggy areas in the south, and not for use against their own people,' adding for good measure that 'the Centaur is simply a truck; it is certainly nothing like that dreadful AMAC riot vehicle which the Government banned from being sold to Chile.'[64] However, critics pointed out that the Centaur would facilitate entry into shanty towns during demonstrations, something that existing vehicles found impossible in the face of makeshift barricades. The deterioration in the human rights situation in Chile following the granting of an export licence for a demonstration model in January 1984 guaranteed that issuing an export licence for up to 300 would prove highly controversial.[65]

Subsequently, the demonstration vehicle was returned to Britain. However, as Jeremy Corbyn told the House of Commons, the demonstration had not necessarily been without benefit to the Pinochet government, because although the Centaur had been returned, 'during the national strike this year, an identical vehicle was seen on the streets of Santiago ... It had apparently been manufactured by the Chilean junta one year after taking the design from the demonstration vehicle, and it was used to kill students who were taking part in the demonstration.'[66]

By this time, US–Chilean relations had deteriorated to the point that the Reagan administration had privately written-off the Pinochet government. Symbolically, in November 1985 the US ambassador, Harry Barnes, attended a human rights ceremony at Santiago Cathedral, and in December Elliot Abrams openly stated that the Reagan administration wanted the Pinochet government to be replaced by a democratically elected civilian government.[67] Throughout this, relations with Britain remained good. If the government's pronouncements were all taken at face value the situation would have been somewhat confusing. As Jeremy Corbyn complained: 'We cannot have it both ways. We cannot say that we oppose the human rights abuses in Chile if at the same time the Chilean Government know that there is a secret deal in the background to provide them with military and logistical support and know full well that the British Government will do nothing about human rights abuses in Chile.'[68] However, the Pinochet government had absorbed the lessons of the mid-1970s, and the consequence of their policy of diversification of supply and emphasis on establishing an indigenous capacity,[69] together with structural changes in the world market, meant that Britain would not be in a strong position if it sought to use arms sales as a political lever to influence domestic Chilean politics. Indeed, by the mid-1980s, Britain was arguably more anxious to secure sales to Chile than Chile was to buy from Britain. In September 1986 it sold the County class destroyer HMS *Glamorgan* for £8 million (renamed *Almirante Latorre*), and in 1987 HMS *Fife* became the fourth of the eight County class vessels to be sold to the Chileans, for around £10 million.[70]

In June 1987, General Matthei made another 'private' trip to Europe to discuss arms sales, visiting Spain, West Germany and Britain. While Matthei had some interest in the Sea Eagle missile, he was more concerned with acquiring modern avionics and Avon engine spares for the increasingly obsolete Hawker Hunters.[71] The timing of the visit was largely dictated by the imminent general election in Britain, which promised to be more closely contested than that four years previously, and going into which the Labour Party had again reaffirmed its commitment to blocking the further sale of arms to Chile. If contracts could be signed just prior to the election, the principle of the inviolability of contracts would ensure that at least existing orders would be honoured.

Although the Chileans need not have worried on that score, it was soon reminded that its close relationship with the Thatcher governments did not necessarily mean that it could obtain its weapons of choice all the time. Again, the problem was the need to secure a US re-export licence. Chile had shown an interest in buying 10 Westland Sea King helicopters, which were built under licence from the US manufacturer Sikorsky. When British government representatives made an informal approach to the Reagan administration on behalf of the Chileans, it ruled against it – even though the Chilean government was supportive of US efforts to covertly arm Iraq at this time, and had shown a willingness to become involved in the covert supply of arms to the Contras.

In October 1987, Trade Minister Alan Clark arrived in Santiago for a six-day visit intended to help boost British exports. Clark recorded in his *Diaries*: 'Earlier today a creepy official, who is "in charge" (heaven help us) of South America, came over to brief me ahead of my trip to Chile. All crap about Human Rights. Not one word about the UK interest ...'[72] There was a strong emphasis on the Sea Wolf missile for the navy, while the Chileans were also interested in the Javelin anti-aircraft missile (demonstrated in Chile in March 1988) as a replacement for their existing Blowpipes.[73]

Chile's relations with the US continued to deteriorate during 1988, following the announcement of a date to nominate a single presidential candidate to be put forward for ratification by plebiscite. Were that candidate defeated, an open election would be held. When the candidate turned out to be General Pinochet, the US National Endowment for Democracy made a decision to supply US$1 million to groups campaigning for a 'No' vote. This action was in direct contrast to that of Mrs Thatcher's government, which itself became the target of guarded criticism from Washington in the run-up to the vote by helping buttress General Pinochet's position through the continued supply of arms. Washington again urged Britain to end arms sales to Chile in the period leading up to the 5 October 1988 plebiscite. The State Department viewed the continued British sale of warships as affecting the balance of power between Chile and Argentina, as well as bolstering the 'Yes' campaign. Indeed, Britain had supplied the bulk of Chile's navy. Four of its eight destroyers were ex-County class, while two more were built in the 1960s in Barrow by Vickers-Armstrong. Of its four submarines, two were British (the others being West German), while Chile was also, at this point, negotiating to add to its fleet of two *Leander* class frigates by buying four more. In the event, the 'No' campaign prevailed by 54.7 per cent to 43 per cent, and, following the victory of Patricio Aylwin in the subsequent election, Britain felt able to justify the lifting of the informal restriction on weapons that could be employed for internal repression, even though General Pinochet remained Commander-in-Chief of the Armed Forces.

A closer relationship in the naval sphere was evident from the late 1980s. In September 1990, Chile completed the purchase of a third ex-RN *Leander* class frigate, HMS *Achilles*, renamed *Ministro Zenteno*.[74] In June 1992, it purchased a fourth *Leander* class frigate, HMS *Ariadne*, to be renamed *General Baquedano*.[75]

Another area of Anglo-Chilean military co-operation bore fruit in 1990, with the successful first firing of the Royal Ordnance/FAMAE (Fabricas y Maestranzas del Ejercito) Rayo multiple rocket launcher – designed as a cheaper version of the US Multiple Launch Rocket System – at RO's Aberporth range in Dyfed.[76] In May 1990, General Pinochet (who had not visited Europe since the funeral of General Franco in 1975[77]) toured the RO plant at Westcott near Aylesbury, landing at BAe's private runway in Hatfield. The Rayo programme was one in which Pinochet took a very personal interest. However, Pinochet's preference for British arms and interest in the Rayo seem to have contributed to his downfall, with a trip to inspect British arms leading to his detention.[78] Despite fears that the affair would impact on UK arms orders from Chile, beyond the Rayo there is little activity, and that appears to have been deemed too important to sacrifice as a gesture over Pinochet's detention.[79]

Ultimately Britain's renewed military relationship with Chile can be fully understood only in relation to the wider Falklands question. Not only did this relationship recognise an ideologically like-minded regime and reward it for its contribution during the Falklands conflict, it also kept the Argentine military occupied, and held out the prospect of this on-going co-operation being capitalised on in the event of any future conflict in the South Atlantic, however remote the possibility. Hence in the final analysis, while arms sales tended to be justified in terms of economic and employment arguments, with regard to Chile they clearly also served as an arm of UK foreign policy.

Argentina

Until the 1982 Falklands conflict, Argentina had been another good customer for British arms. From the nineteenth century it had regularly purchased British naval vessels and, more recently, the missiles to arm them. From 1982, however, the British government shifted its attention from leading the scramble for Argentine contracts to attempting to dissuade the US and West European suppliers from ending the embargoes most had imposed (in many cases, with some reluctance) during the Falklands conflict, and once more supplying Argentina with arms.

During the 1950s, 1960s, and early 1970s, Argentina purchased a range of military aircraft from Britain.[80] Even more significant was the naval arms trade, a trade which – in contrast to the Chilean experience – was not interrupted by the Labour government in response to the 1968 military *coup*. In addition to oilers and salvage vessels, Britain exported the ex-RN aircraft carrier *Colossus* in 1958, Short Sea Cat missiles in 1965, and six Ton Class coastal minesweepers from 1968. In 1970 Tigercat missiles were exported along with Sea Dart missiles, and a Type 42 destroyer, *Hercules*, built in Barrow by Vickers. At the same time, Argentina built another Type 42 destroyer, *Santissima Trinidad*, under licence in the Rio Santiago shipyards.

Preoccupied with Chile, the Labour Party showed relatively little inter-est in the equally brutal Argentinian regime, despite a possible conflict of interest over the Falklands.[81] During this period, Britain and Argentina were locked in negotiations over the purchase of six frigates (a contract ultimately awarded to West German company Blohm & Voss). This provided one incentive for portraying Chile as a case distinct from that of other Latin American military governments with which the Labour government could, therefore, legitimately pursue arms deals. As part of these negotiations, Admiral Massera made a 'private' visit to London in July 1978, meeting Admiral Sir Terence Lewin, the First Sea Lord, senior officials at the FCO, the Department of Trade, and the Bank of England. However, the visit was also marked by vocal demonstrations.[82]

In December 1978, Foreign Secretary David Owen invited General Orlando Agosti, Argentine Air Force chief, to London for a 'private' visit.[83] Argentina had embarked on a wide-ranging review of its military forces in response to heightened tension over the Beagle Channel. Given that Argentina reportedly had £450 million[84] to spend on arms, Britain was keen for further Lynx helicopter (two had been sold earlier that year) and naval purchases to be considered. While at this point Britain was content to arm Argentina whilst denying arms to Chile, in only five years the situation would be completely reversed, with Britain supplying Chile with a wide range of military hardware whilst refusing to supply Argentina with military equipment, and urging its Western allies to do likewise.

In 1979, a further eight Lynx helicopters were ordered. In addition, communications equipment continued to be a significant element of British military exports. In the late 1970s, Plessey Ferranti made modifications to Argentina's Type 42 destroyers to provide direct computer-to-computer radio data links and to improve control of the carrier-based aircraft, and in February 1979, Decca sold its Clearscan radar for fast patrol boats. In July of that year Redifon sold £750,000 worth of HF and VHF radios for coastal patrol boats.

Although Argentina experienced some difficulty elsewhere in its arms dealings, its relations with Britain continued to improve throughout 1979. In March that year, diplomatic relations were restored, and following the general election the thaw gathered pace. In November, Admiral Massera again visited Britain, expressing 'cautious pleasure' at the signs of improvement in bilateral relations. Indeed, 1979 and 1980 mark the high point of Anglo-Argentine military co-operation between the breach in diplomatic relations following the 1976 *coup* and the 1982 invasion of the Falkland Islands. By early 1981, this continued thaw was being matched by a thaw in US–Argentine relations, as the incoming Reagan administration moved to improve relations by lifting the Carter-imposed ban on arms sales and military assistance. By that time, it looked as if both Chile and Argentina, despite the existence of the dispute over the Falkland Islands, would enjoy a close military relationship with the Thatcher governments. Indeed, following the April 1982 Falklands invasion, controversy was stirred by the disclosure that the MoD had approved the delivery of naval spares to Argentina just 10 days before the invasion. Geoffrey Pattie, Under-Secretary for Defence, was called upon to defend this policy, explaining that: 'No major items of military equipment were supplied to Argentina in the six weeks prior to the invasion of the Falklands. Under the licensing arrangements in operation prior to the invasion, spares ordered direct from industry would not be monitored by MOD.'[85]

In the aftermath of the conflict, the government had two priorities with regard to arms sales. The first was to make full use of the 'battle-tested in the Falklands' tag. Defence Secretary John Nott set about this task immediately, beginning with the fourth BAEE, held at Aldershot in June 1982, the same month in which Port Stanley had been recaptured. Nott told those present that:

> Just one week ago British forces were in action in the South Atlantic and I believe that the history of the Falklands campaign will show it to be one of the most remarkable military achievements of this century. But our casualties were remarkably low, even though our men were faced with greatly superior numbers. This is a tribute not only to them but also to our equipment.[86]

The government's other concern in the area of arms sales was how to deny Argentina as wide a range of arms as possible for as long as possible – at least until the government had done all it was prepared to in order to guard militarily against any possible future invasion. While Mrs Thatcher recognised that the international embargo which resulted from the invasion would not hold together indefinitely, she at least expected it to see 1982 out. This was not to be. In August 1982, Italy announced that it was lifting its embargo on strategic exports to Argentina. In response, France also ended its embargo, opening up the way for the resumption in supply of the Exocet missile, for which France had an outstanding order for six, as well as for nine Super Etendard aircraft, ordered in 1979.[87]

On 18 November 1982, the Argentine freighter *Bahai San Blas* left Saint-Nazaire carrying five Super Etendards, 200 tons of light arms and ammunition, and 10 Exocets as France completed the first instalment of the order interrupted by the conflict.[88] The delivery infuriated Mrs Thatcher, who raged that 'we should feel very deeply hurt if the armaments of our allies were used against us', apparently ignoring the fact that British arms had just been deployed against British forces, and that the principle of the inviolability of contracts was being adhered to by Britain in a contemporaneous dispute over the Soviet gas pipeline. She added: 'We have asked our allies not to deliver arms until we have an undertaking from Argentina that hostilities have permanently ceased. We would prefer that people do not deliver arms because Argentina has not said there is a

permanent end to these hostilities.'[89] It took then Liberal leader David
Steel to observe that 'the French are merely pursuing the same aggressively
nationalistic policy as Mrs Thatcher and we should be furious at her for
having learned nothing about the need for international action to limit the
sale of arms'.[90]

However, the government's position on the inviolability of contracts
meant that it came to help in the manufacture of the West German
destroyers bound for Argentina at the same time that it was bemoaning
the French course of action. In September 1982, the Thatcher government
lifted its six-month-old embargo on the export of four Rolls-Royce
Olympus gas turbines intended to power two of the destroyers. In addition, Hawker Siddeley Dynamic Engineering (by now part of BAe) was to
supply electronic propulsion control systems for the ships, and David
Brown was to supply gear components. Furthermore, each destroyer was
to carry two Westland Lynx helicopters. If this were not enough, each ship
would also carry eight Exocet missiles, the plastic nose cones for which
were manufactured in Britain by British Aerodynamics, another
subsidiary of BAe.[91] John Silkin confronted John Nott with this information, to be told that:

> It would be wholly against our policy to supply equipment such as Rolls
> Royce engines direct to Argentina. However, those engines are part of a
> long-standing contract with a NATO ally and also with a most important
> trading partner. In making them available under the terms of an existing
> contract, we made it clear that we would be concerned about early delivery
> to Argentina.[92]

This led Labour MP Frank Allaun to ask: 'If it is wrong to sell Exocet
missiles to Argentina, why is it right to sell engines for destroyers made in
Germany which will go to Argentina? The Minister says that this is a long-
standing agreement, but did not the events of last spring alter all such
long-standing agreements?'[93] However, not all MPs saw the inconsistency
in the government's position over France, with MPs like Walter Johnson
and Bernard Braine urging people to boycott French wine, cheese and
apples, in order to 'hit the French where it hurts most – in their pockets'.[94]
The departure from Saint-Nazaire of the final consignment of four Super
Etendards in December 1982 did nothing to dampen this atmosphere.

While the French contribution to Argentine rearmament may well have
been the single most important, it was hardly the only one. It was estimated that Argentina lost over £500 million worth of military equipment
during the conflict. These losses included a cruiser (*General Belgrano*), a
submarine, a number of helicopters, and approximately 70 aircraft.[95] As
the air force suffered the heaviest losses, new aircraft and anti-aircraft
defences were a priority. In November 1982, Argentina purchased ten
Mirage aircraft from Peru and over twenty Daggers – the Israeli version

of the Mirage. In addition, it ordered a number of Brazilian Xavante trainer aircraft which were powered by the Rolls-Royce Viper 540 engine.

The first of the four West German frigates, *Almirante Brown*, was officially handed over on 2 February 1983, and set sail for Argentina exactly a week later. This prompted a renewed wave of attacks on the government. In the House of Lords, Lord Cledwyn of Penrhos complained that:

> It is becoming increasingly difficult to reconcile the Government's clearly declared policy toward the Argentine regime and these developments, the agreement to the sale of Rolls-Royce engines for destroyers supplied to Argentina and in the finance supplied to Argentina. It really is in danger of developing into something of a farce ... The fact that we have released these engines for the destroyers makes it increasingly difficult for us to make representations to our allies when they sell armaments to Argentina.[96]

Critics argued that the Thatcher government was responsible for more than just the confusion caused by these arms deals. They also argued that it was the government's policy of constructing a 'Fortress Falklands' that was spurring Argentine arms purchases on and encouraging Argentina to rearm so rapidly. With elections for a civilian government due to take place in October 1983, the Reagan administration indicated that this would mark the point at which it would lift its arms embargo on Argentina. However, the Thatcher government lobbied vigorously behind the scenes in opposition to this. With its objections in mind, a spokesman for the administration tried to calm fears by saying that arms would not necessarily be sold just because the embargo was being lifted – 'the Argentines won't be able to just walk in with a credit card and get what they want.'[97]

Although, as the focus of Britain's indignation, the issue was soon supplanted by the invasion of the Commonwealth island of Grenada without warning, the issue remained a delicate one. In early November 1983, Kenneth Dam, US Deputy Secretary of State, was despatched to London to smooth over relations. While the talks concentrated on Grenada and the imminent arrival of US cruise missiles in Britain, both these events strengthened Mrs Thatcher's hand in demanding that the US did not resume arms supplies to Argentina. Hence when the lifting of the US embargo was announced, to coincide with the inauguration of Raul Alfonsín as President, the US State Department was quick to stress that 'no arms transfers are contemplated which would increase the prospect of renewed conflict' over the Falklands.[98]

By 1998, and President Menem's October state visit, the New Labour government had decided the time had come to formally lift the 16 year old arms embargo on Argentina. In practice, over the previous months a steady flow of exceptions had been made to the ban, which had seen British military equipment provided to forces which were now serving

alongside UK forces as part of UN detachments.[99] Robin Cook told Sir
David Frost: 'We had an application to supply the Argentinian forces with
some vehicles. We found it ran up against the arms embargo. This is
plainly daft. We cannot be keeping the peace together and then withhold-
ing the equipment that is necessary.'[100] Hence as Tony Lloyd explained,
licences will be issued 'for exports that we are satisfied would not now, or
in the foreseeable future, put at risk the security of our overseas territories in the South Atlantic, or our forces operating there.'[101]

Peru

During the 1960s, a period of relatively close co-operation between the US
and UK on arms sales issues elsewhere, the Latin American market was
still regarded by the US as being its own preserve. However, as the case of
Peru shows, by the late 1960s, even with the grudging assistance of its
loyal ally Britain, changed market circumstances made it impossible for
the US to completely determine the shape of Latin American arms
procurement. As J. A. Thomson reported from the British embassy in
Washington in January 1966, 'the US could not be indifferent to arms
sales to Latin America; sometimes they considered it to be of the highest
importance that a particular country or a particular Armed Service should
have nothing but American equipment'.[102] However, the US Department
of Defense recognised the usefulness of British arms exports and suggested
a basis on which the two countries could proceed. The US would not seek
to prevent the UK from selling arms to Latin America, but 'whenever the
US badly wanted to supply a contract in Latin America for which we were
competing we would at their request withdraw provided they guaranteed
us at least an equal contract in some other part of the world'.[103]

This offer of compensating sales coincided with discussions on the UK
purchase of the US F-111 aircraft to replace the cancelled TSR-2. As
outlined earlier, in order that the UK could afford to buy these aircraft,
the US had agreed to buy more from the UK and stand aside in favour of
the UK in third markets, as it had at Defense Secretary Robert
McNamara's insistence in Saudi Arabia the previous year. As L. C. W.
Figg told Thomson: 'It is difficult to see what opportunities there may be
of this kind; but the equation begins to look as though in equity the US
would have to give us two opportunities elsewhere to one withdrawal by
us from South America.'[104]

Within this context, early in 1967 the issue arose of whether BAC
should be authorised to sell eight (supersonic) Lightning aircraft to Peru
(six Mark 53 fighters and two Mark 55 trainers) – a deal which was likely
to be worth £9 million in the first instance. There were a number of
factors weighing against authorisation. Such a sale would make Peru the

first Latin American country to acquire supersonic aircraft, and Chile, Argentina, Brazil, and even Ecuador and Bolivia could be expected to follow suit. The US position on the sale of supersonic aircraft to Latin America was well known – it did not want Latin American governments to acquire them until after 1969. Chile, traditionally another good customer for British arms, would also object. The UK ambassador to Chile advised the FO that 'the grudge which Chileans would bear us would be a lasting one', as their defence budget would not 'allow them to redress the balance with Peru'.[105] With Britain having only just sold Hunters to Chile in 1966, the sale of supersonic aircraft to Peru would make the Chileans 'look foolish'. Given the existence of one of the more serious border disputes in the region between Peru and Ecuador (which had flared up again at the end of 1966), the purchase of Lightnings by Peru would also probably lead to Ecuador seeking to acquire supersonic aircraft.

The arguments in favour of supply were familiar and, to officials, compelling. Firstly, the sale would represent a valuable export order which could open up other parts of Latin America to the Lightning and other British military products. Secondly, if the UK refused to sell the aircraft Peru would simply buy an equivalent elsewhere. Indeed, the former Peruvian air attaché in London, General Soldi, had warned the UK ambassador to Peru, Sir Robert Marett, that if the UK would not supply Lightnings the Peruvians would instead buy the French Mirage.[106] Furthermore, the FO argued that the sale could be interpreted as consolidating civilian rule in Peru, on the basis that the Belaúnde Government depended heavily on the goodwill of the armed forces for its survival (indeed, it was overthrown in a *coup* the following year), and the sale would allow it to satisfy institutional demands. However, the key consideration was the impact on the UK, not on Peru and its neighbours. As H. A. F. Hohler observed, 'given our present balance of payments difficulties, the political arguments against foregoing a valuable export order must be very strong indeed if they are to prevail'.[107]

At the same time, the Peruvian Air Force also expressed an interest in buying 12 Hawker Hunter Mark 9s, and had reportedly secured the funds to pay for them. At the Ministry of Aviation, John Stonehouse, ever keen to sell British aircraft, advised that:

> Peru has long been a good customer for the sale of British military aircraft, and with an eye on other expected sales to that country and the export potential in other South American countries, I am most anxious to maintain this relationship. Furthermore, having regard to the sale of Hunter aircraft to Chile some months ago, I consider the proposed sale to Peru to be most advisable if we are to avoid being accused of discrimination in that area.[108]

Supplying advanced equipment to regional rivals, therefore, was not necessarily to encourage an arms race, rather to engage in 'balancing'. In a later variation on the theme, the British ambassador to Ecuador advised the FO that the 'recent [Peruvian] invasion scare demonstrated that Ecuador is virtually defenceless against Peru so sale of supersonic aircraft would not materially alter the balance'.[109] Impartiality in the Iran–Iraq War would involve a similar logic. Hence Stonehouse proposed writing to the Peruvian Minister of Aviation, General Heighes, to the effect that 12 Hunters could be made available towards the end of 1967.[110]

The only difficulty was over availability, which was dependent on the numbers being relinquished by the RAF which could then be bought back by Hawker Siddeley, refurbished, and sold on. These aircraft then had to be apportioned among the several states queuing for them. In practice, for Hunters to be made available to Peru, India would be required to wait (it had a requirement for a further 24) or accept an earlier version than that which they were already operating. The principle of balancing sales to regional rivals also applied here. Pakistan had been enquiring about the possibility of buying 40 Lightnings. To sell Lightnings to Pakistan but only offer India dated subsonic aircraft would be to damage relations with India and prospects in the valuable Indian market.[111] A further obstacle lay in the need to secure US agreement to the respective sales, as the manufacture of a number of Hunters had been part-financed under the US Mutual Defense Assistance Program (MDAP), and so they were subject to US re-export restrictions.

Predictably, with the Punta del Este conference imminent, where the US was aiming to secure agreement from Latin American countries on arms restraint, the US response was not encouraging.[112] The US opposed the sale of partly US-financed aircraft, and urged the UK government not to sell any other Hunters. For the US the calculation was simple: mired in a conflict in rural, underdeveloped South East Asia, it had no wish to encourage Latin American governments – with the examples of Cuba and a series of imitation guerrilla movements still fresh – to divert spending from social, infrastructural and agricultural projects to military acquisitions. Of course, if it became clear that it had failed to prevent such diversion, its priorities could change to attempting to secure that market for itself, a possibility that the British government were only too aware of. Indeed, to combat the possibility, two Peruvian Air Force pilots were invited to the UK in March 1967 to evaluate the Lightning.

At the same time, the Air Force Department began a trawl to determine which of the Hunters deemed surplus had actually been funded by the MDAP programme, and whether sufficient numbers could be replaced by purely UK-funded Hunters if the government decided to go ahead with the sale in the face of US objections. Until this process was completed, the UK could muster only four surplus Hunters that were wholly UK-funded.[113] For its part, the manufacturer, British Aircraft Corporation (BAC), thought American actions were motivated by slightly different considerations. At the time, the US had no aircraft available to offer a Latin American country because of the demands of the Vietnam War, but had offered to sell the Northrop F-5 (supersonic) fighter to Venezuela, and possibly Peru and Brazil, in 1969.[114]

The need to sift out wholly UK-financed Hunters had meant that Stonehouse's draft reply to the Peruvian Aviation Minister's initial enquiry had not been sent, and the absence of a reply was interpreted as a snub by the Peruvians. In April, the UK ambassador advised the FO that the position was 'not only embarrassing but also unpleasant'. A reply from Stonehouse was quickly dispatched by diplomatic bag, explaining that 'regrettably the problem of determining the aircraft which could be made available for sale is unexpectedly taking longer to solve than I originally thought', and admitting that only four available Hunters had been identified.[115]

Meanwhile, BAC were pressing on with their efforts to sell the Lightning to Peru, and the sales and service manager, Hobday, visited Peru in April, where he informed the embassy – completely erroneously – that BAC had the government's approval to sell the Lightning (an impression quickly corrected by the FO). In pursuit of such approval, in April Stonehouse lobbied Fred Mulley, Minister of State at the FCO, telling him that:

> some Latin American countries, notably Peru, are seriously intent upon buying supersonic aircraft and, provided satisfactory financial terms can be agreed, I very much hope that we can get a share of this market through the supply of Lightnings. If HMG fail to give their approval, or give it too late to be effective, we will not prevent Peru (or any other Latin American country) from obtaining the aircraft they need. It will simply mean that we will lose the market to the French or the Swedes, or even to the Americans who may well re-cast their policy if they see that their present holding tactics are not having the desired effect.[116]

However, by the end of April, the Commander-in-Chief of the Peruvian Air Force and his chiefs of staff had made it clear that they were not interested in buying the Lightning, but instead were now interested in the Canberra bomber. Meanwhile, the British ambassador set out what he considered to be the reasons for the loss of a second potential order – for the Hunters. He saw the failure to respond promptly to General Heighes's initial letter of enquiry – the difficulties surrounding supply meant it took around 10 weeks and the ambassador's urging to secure a reply – as having been vital. Furthermore, 'my reception by the Minister of Aviation when I called on him on 19 April was very cool indeed and only just correct. General Heighes said then, plainly and brusquely, that the Hunter deal was off "because of the time that has elapsed" since his original letter, and that he was now looking for US aircraft. And, when I tried to draw him on the possibility of selling Peru other British civil or military aircraft, he permitted himself the luxury of pointing out the imperfections of each aircraft which my Air Attaché or I mentioned.'[117]

The Ministry of Technology complained that the delay had been caused by the US refusal to authorise the re-export of aircraft part-financed with MDAP funds, but acknowledged that this could not be disclosed to the Peruvians, as, 'apart from the bad odour it would cause, we have also no wish to appear to be puppets completely manipulated by American strings so far as defence exports are concerned!'[118]

Nevertheless, and notwithstanding Stonehouse's enthusiasm for exports, the US objections, the proximity of the Punta del Este conference and the impact that a sale would have on any agreement reached there, and the reaction of neighbouring countries – particularly Chile – made it far from certain that in this case Ministers would have authorised the sale. Instead, in June 1967 it was revealed that Peru was to buy 16 Mirage fighters (any doubts removed by the performance of the Mirage in the Arab–Israeli Six Day War of that month), and thereby become the first Latin American country to acquire supersonic aircraft. True to the suspicions of BAC, the US countered by offering the F-5 in 1970, the date when production would outstrip Vietnam demand.[119]

At the same time, attention in the UK now switched to the prospects for the sale of six Canberra bombers. Here too, the US seemed to have entered the competition. In July 1967 the UK ambassador in Lima met the US ambassador to discuss rumours that the US was offering Peru cut-price B-57 bombers from 1968 (once they had been withdrawn from service in Vietnam), at a time when the US was delaying a response to a UK request as to whether the Canberras (predictably, five of the six the UK wanted to sell had been part-financed through MDAP funding) could be sold to Peru. While the US ambassador 'gave no very convincing answer' on this, he did confirm that the US was now prepared to sell supersonic aircraft to Peru and other Latin American countries for delivery in 1970:

> That the United States should be publicly opposed to the sale here of super-sonic fighters by us or the French for delivery in 1968, on the grounds that Peru cannot afford them and that such a sale would only [lead] to a Latin American Arms race, yet be privately offering to supply the same sort of aircraft for delivery two years later seems to me to be more than a little unprincipled. I cannot help agreeing with British Aircraft firms view that United States authorities are not moved in this matter by regard for Latin American stability and well being but are only trying to stop the sales of a lot of aircraft by us until American manufacturers are less engaged in Viet Nam war and can once again turn to profitable market in which they have enjoyed a dominating position.[120]

The UK government's response to this news was to convey the importance it attached to the Canberra sale through the Washington embassy. The response was that the US was opposed to the sale of Canberras to Peru, notionally on the grounds of Peru's budgetary and balance of payments situation. At the time, Peru was approaching the US for a loan, which it would be unlikely to provide if Peru was to use it to finance the purchase of Canberras. Congress was particularly sensitive to the risk of fuelling local arms races in the context of the Arab–Israeli War of the previous month. In this context, Sir Patrick Dean was assured, there was no prospect of the US selling B-57 bombers to Peru. However, according to the British embassy in Lima, the Peruvian Air Force's purchases were paid for from the revenue from a tax levied on the sale of sweets and soft drinks, which could not be used for any other purpose.[121]

In the meantime, though, in the face of US delay over signalling whether it would approve the sale of Canberras (it took the US three months to respond in the negative) BAC had been continuing negotiations and was on the point of signing a contract. To pull out at that stage would have harmed commercial and military relations with Peru, caused wider damage in terms of Britain's reputation as a reliable supplier, and raised the kinds of questions in the developing world about UK independence from the US in matters of military supply that the FO was anxious to avoid having aired.

Hence in the light of the US refusal – apparently agreed upon at the level of President Johnson, Robert McNamara and Dean Rusk – Harold Wilson sent a personal message to Johnson asking him to approve the sale. He pointed out that the Peruvians already had Canberra aircraft, and that a refusal by the US to allow the sale of additional Canberras would not stop the Peruvians from buying them elsewhere ('indeed, in his present mood, De Gaulle might regard this as an excellent opportunity to make trouble for and between us'[122]). Johnson, however, was unmoved:

> I feel that I must do all that I can at this time to meet widely and deeply held congressional objections to unnecessary arms expenditures by countries such as Peru. This includes equipment of United States origin. Certain influential congressmen have for the moment expressed their concern about supersonic military aircraft ... but I am sure that if I did consent to the sale of the sub-sonic but medium-range Canberra, congressional reactions would be equally strong.[123]

The British embassy in Lima was instructed to tell the Peruvians that the deal could not go through because the Americans had blocked it.[124] General Heighes's reaction was to blame the US. ('Apart from making it obvious that we seemed not to be free agents but under United States control for sale of these aircraft, General Heighes put no blame on us'.[125]) He said that US denial was forcing Peru to seek aircraft from the USSR.

However, a trawl of the UK Canberra inventory subsequently revealed five Canberra aircraft which had not been part-financed through the MDAP and the story that the deal would go ahead was leaked to the press.[126] By October, the French press was also reporting news of a deal to sell 12 Mirage aircraft to Peru. In the same month, the contract for the sale of the Canberras (eventually for six) was also signed in Lima, from where the Peruvians immediately signalled their interest in acquiring a further 16.[127] The Peruvians asked that no publicity should be given to the purchase, and they finally announced that they were due to take delivery of the aircraft only in May 1968. In the wake of these purchases, the US immediately relaxed its position, telling the British government that it would no longer object to the sale of Hunters to the region, even if they were MDAP-funded. Nor would they object to non-MDAP-funded Canberras being sold in the region. However, they still opposed the sale of MDAP-funded Canberras to Peru, and asked that proposed sales of MDAP-funded Canberras to other countries in the region should be discussed with Washington on a case-by-case basis. As the FO told a representative of the US embassy in London, a key consideration in bringing about this *volte-face* had been that:

> while the US policy ... could have the effect of preventing sales of British aircraft, there was apparently no means by which the US could apply similar pressure to our competitors, particularly the French. It was also pointed out to him that [the] effect of US veto of MDAP-funded Canberra sales to Peru had been and would be to open that market to the French. He agreed that there was no sign at present of any desire on the part of Latin American governments to exercise restraint in arms purchases and that they were unlikely to be amenable to pressure from outside to do so.[128]

Brazil

While Britain profited less than other West European countries from the expansion of the arms market during the 1970s, British arms sales to South America nevertheless grew, largely thanks to the export of naval vessels to Argentina and Brazil. Indeed, Brazil was the third most valuable market for the UK, as measured by SIPRI, between 1970 and 1979, purchasing major conventional arms worth US$1,613 million.

This position reflected the close military ties that had developed from 1950 onwards. In 1953, Britain sold 62 Gloster Meteor F8 aircraft and ten Gloster Meteor T7s, followed up in 1958 by the sale of fourteen ex-RAF Lockheed P-2V-7 Neptunes and two Westland Widgeons. A further three helicopters, Westland Whirlwinds, were sold in 1960, and in 1961 Brazil purchased an aircraft carrier. Throughout the 1960s, Britain continued to sell aircraft. It sold six HS-748 Mark 2 transport aircraft in 1963, and further consignments of Westland helicopters – three Wasps in

1965, three more Whirlwinds in 1966 with another two in 1969 – two BAC–111s in 1968, and six HS-125s at the end of the decade.

During the 1970s, Brazil was by far Britain's most valuable customer for major arms in Latin America. According to SIPRI, Brazil's purchases amounted to over three times the value of those of either Chile or Argentina. Brazil had already bought Short Sea Cat missiles in 1966, but during the 1970s added *Oberon* class submarines, four *Niteroi* class frigates, four *Broadsword* class frigates, almost 400 Sea Cat missiles together with over 40 launchers, and more helicopters. When the return to office of a Labour government under Harold Wilson in February 1974 saw the imposition of sanctions against the military government in Chile, there were calls from within the party for the policy adopted with regard to one authoritarian government in the region to be extended to all. However, in practice, the Wilson government drew a clear distinction between Chile, on the one hand, and all other South American military governments – but particularly Argentina and Brazil – on the other. Not only was Brazil highly important as a trading partner, it was also an emerging regional power and international actor. President Geisel was even accorded a state visit in 1976, when he was received by the Queen, despite the opposition of the Labour left.

When James Callaghan replaced Wilson as Prime Minister, the Department of Trade produced a list of Latin American countries with which it was considered important to develop trade relations. Brazil headed the list, followed by Mexico and Venezuela. This assessment informed the Callaghan government's decision to distinguish between Brazil and the military government in Chile. As Ted Rowlands argued at the time:

> I do not ... believe that the situation in Brazil warrants the conclusion that it is comparable with that in Chile. For this reason I still believe that in the case of Brazil confrontation would serve neither our own interests nor those of the people of Brazil as a whole. In my view, our policy of encouraging contacts at all levels between the two countries has contributed towards a greater degree of understanding ...
>
> At the same time we have to recognise that Brazil is a country of increasing importance in world affairs which is making a sizeable contribution to multilateral discussion of world political and economic questions. I think it would be wrong not to work where we can with such countries in the search for solutions to the serious problems facing the industrialised and non-industrialised countries.
>
> Finally, I think we should bear in mind the important stake of British industry – and this means both sides of industry – in Brazil's economic development programme ... [129]

Here then, despite the obvious importance of economic considerations, Rowlands also articulated a set of complementary political considerations. On this basis, the lucrative military trade continued. As well as working to complete orders placed under the Heath government, and even the Wilson government in the late 1960s, new orders were received for BAC–111 aircraft and Lynx and Wasp helicopters.

This close military relationship continued after 1979. While Brazil was unsuccessful in its efforts to buy the Antarctic patrol vessel HMS *Endurance* after the announcement that it would be scrapped as part of the 1981 Nott defence review,[130] it did have more success later that year. In October, it was announced that the two countries had signed a memorandum of understanding for orders worth £370 million, to be financed by a Euro-currency loan provided by nine British banks, led by Lloyds Bank International.[131]

Although the arms trade relationship had survived the hostility of the Labour left in the 1970s, it did not emerge from the Falklands conflict unscathed, where Brazil had formally supported Argentina's sovereignty claim. In 1982, British Shipbuilders lost out on an anticipated contract to build two new submarines when the Brazilians announced they would turn instead to West Germany for an order worth around £88 million.[132] However, this did not mark a lasting cooling of relations. As Brazil's indigenous arms industry continued to develop, the traditional arms sales relationship came to be reversed, as Britain sought to purchase Brazilian equipment, most notably the Tucano trainer, to be produced under licence by Short's in Belfast.

Brazil's transformation into a significant arms exporter – by 1985 it was the world's fifth-largest exporter, competing in a number of areas with Britain – closed a number of export possibilities for Britain. However, there were still a limited number of orders and follow-on orders for British military equipment. In 1985, BAe sold 32 Sea Skua missiles, and in August 1987, Ferranti delivered the first of four KAFS action information organisation and fire control systems for the West German-built Type 209 submarines. The following year, Racal won a contract to supply Jaguar frequency-hopping radios to Microlab of Brazil in kit form, where they would be assembled and then sold on to the Brazilian army.[133] In the same year, Ferranti won its first contract for the AMX fighter, to provide video monitor display equipment for the rear cockpit.[134] However, it was not until late 1993 that Brazil placed a further substantial order with a British company, when it ordered nine Westland Super Lynx helicopters worth £150 million.[135]

The 1990s saw Brazil once again placing major naval orders with the UK, contributing to making Brazil the UK's third-largest market for major conventional arms between 1990 and 1997, with a value of US$823 million. In all, seven *River* class minesweepers were sold, together with four ex-RN *Broadsword* class Type 22 frigates (*Broadsword*, *Battleaxe*, *Brilliant* and *Brazen*), and nine Super Lynx helicopters for use with them.

El Salvador

By the late 1970s, Britain had not sold arms to El Salvador, where the limited market had been dominated by the US, much of it in the form of military aid. This reflected the types of government that dominated El Salvador in the 1970s and 1980s, the nature of US political and military support, El Salvador's weak financial position, and the international impact of the civil war and reaction to widespread human rights abuses. Even where this pressure was not felt directly by governments, popular opposition to the procession of military governments in El Salvador and attendant state-sponsored violence proved an effective barrier to trade. This was the case with Britain in the late 1970s, when the sale of £850,000 worth of military equipment was met by a well organised lobby both inside and outside Parliament.

In November 1977, the existence of a deal to supply El Salvador with 15 ex-MoD armoured vehicles – three Ferret and 12 Saladin vehicles formerly used in Northern Ireland – became publicly known. This was a period characterised by Ted Rowlands as one in which there existed a presumption that arms could be sold unless there was a specific ban.[136] Hence Rowlands, the relevant Minister of State at the FO, was not consulted over the decision to sell the vehicles to El Salvador, which was made on the basis that it was not one of the Labour government's declared priorities (these were Chile and South Africa), and there was no specific ban. Opposition to the deal centred on the Salvadorean government's appalling human rights record, but fears were also voiced over the Salvadorean government's support for Guatemala's territorial claims over Belize, which included a pledge to support a Guatemalan invasion.[137]

At this point the Callaghan government sought reassurance that the vehicles would not be used against British forces in the event of armed conflict over the British colony. Publicly the Salvadoreans agreed. Foreign Secretary David Owen announced that they 'would not in any circum-stances be used against Belize'.[138] Apparently, as one newspaper noted, the British government was 'satisfied with General Romero's promise that, if Salvadorean troops are sent to help invade Belize, they will leave their armoured cars behind'.[139]

The proposed deal arose at a time when the Salvadorean military was having to look elsewhere for military equipment after US military aid was suspended by the Carter administration in response to the human rights situation. Indeed, it was the fact that the armoured cars that Britain was proposing to sell could facilitate further human rights abuses, rather than fears of their being used in Belize, that generated most popular opposition to the sale in the UK, provoking a particularly strong response from religious groups. The Roman Catholic Bishops' Commission on International Justice and Peace was the first to object, in a letter to Ted Rowlands, pointing out the potential for heightened internal repression that the sale would create. This was followed up by Christians for a Just World, who, on 4 December, marked Prisoners' Day by holding a vigil outside the DSO's offices in London in protest at the deal. Given the dual concerns of internal repression and possible use against a British colony and British forces, opposition to the proposed deal was reflected in a fair degree of cross-party support in Parliament. In addition, a number of MPs from all the main parties signed a motion urging the cancellation of the deal.

The initial government reaction, a reflection of divisions within the Cabinet along lines predictable in sensitive arms sales cases, was to reiterate that assurances had been received from General Romero; that effectively the government had extracted a guarantee as to the conditions of their use – a line of defence identical to that mobilised in defence of Hawk aircraft sales to Indonesia in the 1990s. Further, deploying an argument later adopted by Mrs Thatcher with regard to Chile, the government argued that while the human rights situation in El Salvador was, admittedly, quite bad, it was nevertheless improving.[140] However, the entire government case was weakened when Salvadorean Foreign Minister Alvaro Ernesto Martinez stated that El Salvador 'was not interested in buying British arms if Britain makes the sale conditional on the formal promise not to use them against Belize'.[141] In a separate interview he reinforced the point: 'El Salvador will not submit itself to the criteria of any foreign power with respect to the purchase of military equipment or anything else . . . It is the buyer who should lay down conditions not the seller.'[142]

Opposition within the Labour Party continued to generate momentum. Kevin McNamara wrote to James Callaghan to point out the obvious – that Romero's assurances were hardly binding and could not be policed or enforced.[143] On 10 January 1978, the party's International Committee added its concern, unanimously passing a motion calling for the cancellation of the deal, 'even at this late stage'. (The vehicles had already been paid for and were stored at Sheerness Docks in Kent awaiting shipment.) Also in January, the Church resumed its pressure, with Cardinal Basil Hume appealing to the government to reconsider its position in a letter to Callaghan:

> I am distressed and perplexed that the government, having admitted that the situation of human rights in El Salvador is cause for grave concern, is nevertheless determined to go ahead with this deal. The expressions of concern by the Churches in Britain, by human rights groups and by politicians of all parties seem to have met with little response . . . It is still not too late for the government to reconsider this decision in the interests of the people of El Salvador. I would urge them to do so.[144]

The government's position was weakened by the fact that it could do little to enforce any conditions once El Salvador had taken delivery of the armoured cars. Another weakness in the government's position was that because the vehicles were second-hand, ex-MoD, vehicles it was deprived of some of the more traditional justifications for arms sales, as no jobs were at risk and the impact on the balance of payments would be negligible. David Owen's line of defence exposed some of these weaknesses. In a letter to Hume, he wrote that:

> The British armoured vehicles to which you referred are the subject of a contract approved in January of this year [1977]. Ministers reviewed this contract recently because of their concern about the situation. We found ourselves in much the same situation as has occurred in the past over the contractual position on arms sales [i.e. over Chile] and, with much reluctance, decided that in all the circumstances the contract should be fulfilled. Before doing so, we are stipulating that the vehicles will never be used in any circumstances against Belize and that their purpose is for re-equipping units of the Army with direct responsibility for frontier defence. Were there to be any change in these assurances it would be construed as a very serious breach of confidence. The Government of El Salvador would gravely damage their relations with this country if these vehicles were used for internal repression.[145]

However, by this time, the Salvadorean government was moving away from its cosmetic position and, by January 1978, Owen was siding with those in Cabinet advocating termination of the deal. However, in mid-January this group was outvoted on the issue by a group led by Defence Secretary Fred Mulley and Trade Secretary Edmund Dell, who invoked the traditional joint defences of harm to Britain's reputation for reliability of supply and the sanctity of existing contracts.[146]

Nevertheless, as a result of a shift in Cabinet support, on 19 January it was announced that the government had decided to cancel the vehicles' export licences. At Westminster, it was claimed that pressure from backbench Labour MPs had forced the rethink, while there were also suggestions that pressure might have been exerted by Washington. An FO statement gave no indication of either, simply stating that: 'The British Government has decided that the contract for the sale of armoured vehicles to El Salvador should be cancelled. This decision was taken because of the situation in Central America.'[147] It remains a unique case in recent times – the only one where, although it was invoked initially, the principle of the inviolability of existing contracts was overridden by political considerations. Contracts had been signed, the vehicles were at the docks awaiting shipment, the Salvadoreans had paid for them and would have to be reimbursed, but still the licences were revoked. This is precisely why the case is so important as a precedent. In an era where a Labour government has again used similar tried and tested methods to justify arms sales to Indonesia, the case of El Salvador represents a clear example of a combination of pressure and principle prevailing against the more entrenched interests in sale.

The whole arms-for-El Salvador episode lasted only a few months. Although the deal was concluded in April 1977, its existence became public knowledge only in November, and from then until the announcement of the reversal on 19 January 1978 the government was repeatedly and heavily criticised for insisting on going ahead with the deal. From the government's point of view, once the deal had been agreed (and the main question should be why the Foreign Office ever approved such a deal in the first place) the question of the government's reliability as an arms supplier became the overriding concern. Hence spokesmen were instructed to inform people that the deal would go ahead, but that General Romero had agreed not to use the vehicles in any invasion of Belize. This was a ludicrous position for a government to put itself in. How could such an agreement be enforced after delivery? How could the government respond if it was not? It was dealt a terminal blow when the Salvadorean Foreign Minister indicated that whatever might have been said previously, his government would not be constrained in how it chose to deploy its weaponry.

Ultimately, though, the government could afford to be seen to have accepted the wisdom of the human rights and Belize lobbies, as Central America and El Salvador were of such peripheral importance to Britain both as markets and international actors. The contract was of little value, there were no jobs at stake, and El Salvador could not afford the kind of major arms that made it worth defending. Similar lobbies had far less success when the object of protest was Argentina or Brazil.

Notes

1 Harold Wilson, *Final Term: The Labour Government 1974–1976* (London, Weidenfeld & Nicolson and Michael Joseph, 1979), p. 4.
2 Letter from Eric Heffer to the author, 15 February 1991.
3 See Eric Heffer: *Never a Yes Man: The Life and Politics of an Adopted Liverpudlian* (London, Verso, 1991).
4 *The Times*, 1 November 1973.
5 Hansard, 28 November 1973, col. 462.
6 *Ibid.*, col. 475.
7 *Ibid.*, cols 484–5.
8 *Ibid.*, col. 489.
9 *Ibid.*, cols 488–9.
10 Sir Frederic Bennett, MP for Torquay. *Ibid.*, col. 508. Furthermore, Conservative MPs were able to point to the swift recognition of the new government and absence of criticism that followed the 'left-wing' military *coup* in Peru in 1968.
11 On the same day, the Minister for Overseas Development, Judith Hart, announced that all bilateral aid, except for the financing of Chilean students in Britain, would be terminated.

12 Tony Benn, *Against the Tide: Diaries 1973–76* (London, Arrow, 1990), entry for Sunday 24 March 1974, p. 127.

13 *Ibid.*, entry for Thursday 28 March 1974, p. 130.

14 *Ibid.*, entry for Tuesday 9 April 1974, pp. 135–6.

15 *Ibid.*, entry for Wednesday 1 May 1974, p. 146.

16 *Keesings Contemporary Archives*, 1974, p. 26659.

17 Hansard, 21 May 1974, col. 188. See also cols 186–93.

18 Furthermore, his memory was failing him somewhat when he claimed in his memoirs that all of the ships ordered had been handed over to the Chileans and were undergoing trials. Benn's diary of the time records only one ship as having been handed over. See Benn, *Against the Tide*, p. 130.

19 Wilson: *Final Term*, p. 59.

20 For a Chilean perspective on this issue, see the letter from the Chilean ambassador, *Financial Times*, 8 April 1976.

21 When asked which countries in particular he had in mind, he cited Brazil and Bolivia, *Guardian*, 24 July 1975.

22 *Financial Times*, 31 December 1975; *Guardian*, 31 December 1975.

23 *Guardian*, 31 December 1975.

24 Hansard, 14 January 1976.

25 This process should not be confused with delivery, which was by that time due in January 1977 following sea trials. In the event, the *Hyatt* was finally delivered in February 1977.

26 Quoted in *Glasgow Herald*, 28 August 1976.

27 *Financial Times*, 17 November 1976.

28 Hansard (Lords), 27 June 1978.

29 The source of the continuing dispute was that no lorry driver could be found to transport the four engines away from the plant on the first leg of their journey to Chile. In addition, the unions had an agreement with Rolls-Royce that non-union labour could not be used at the plant. See *Sunday Telegraph*, 23 July 1978.

30 At the time, the Chilean Government was considering buying Lockheed TriStars for its commercial airline, which were powered by Rolls-Royce engines. Clearly, the company were concerned about the way this dispute could affect these prospects.

31 The original contract was modified towards the end of the dispute so as to scrap the usual clause guaranteeing 130 hours' flying time. The Chilean Government agreed to accept compensation in the, by all accounts likely, event that the engines did not perform properly, *Guardian*, 8 August 1978.

32 *Financial Times*, 29 August 1978; *Guardian*, 8 September 1978.

33 On this see, for example, Saul Landau and Sarah Anderson, 'Autumn of the autocrat', *Covert Action Quarterly*, 64 (1998), 33–7.

34 Hansard, 16 January 1980, col. 787w.

35 *Ibid.*, 22 July 1980, col. 123

36 *Daily Telegraph*, 28 July 1980.

37 *The Times*, 9 August 1980.

38 Letter from the MoD, 12 August 1980.

39 See Hansard (Lords), 23 April 1980.

40 *Tribune*, 1 August 1980.

41 *Daily Telegraph*, 9 September 1980. Wilson said that her torture claims were reported in the Chilean press on 21 July, the day before Ridley's announcement. *The Times*, 13 September 1980.

42 *Daily Telegraph*, 9 September 1980.

43 *International Herald Tribune*, 24 October 1981; *Guardian*, 24 October 1981. The previous month, the Carter-imposed ban on arms sales to Argentina had been lifted.

44 HMS *Norfolk* was equipped with Exocet missiles and Sea Cat and Sea Slug missiles. Subsequently, the Pinochet government allowed the handing over of the *Tidepool* to be delayed so that it could first serve in the Falklands conflict.

45 *Sunday Telegraph*, 11 October 1981.

46 In his autobiography, Norman Tebbit says somewhat cryptically: 'The full story of the Falklands War cannot be told for many years to come. There are no British skeletons in cupboards but it would be against our national interest to expose how, sometimes with the help of friends ... some things were achieved.' *Upwardly Mobile: An Autobiography* (London, Weidenfeld & Nicolson, 1988), p. 195. See also Nigel West, *The Secret War for the Falklands* (London, Little Brown, 1997), esp. ch. 6. Mrs Thatcher made an oblique reference to Chilean help in her photo-call visit to Pinochet following his 1998 detention. See, for example, the coverage in *The Times* and *Daily Telegraph*, 27 March 1999, and her letter to *The Times*, 22 October 1998.

47 *New Statesman*, 25 January 1985, p. 10.

48 *Ibid.*, p. 8.

49 *Ibid.*, p. 9.

50 *Scotsman*, 3 March 1983.

51 *Ibid.* Although dating back to the 1950s, they were revamped in the 1960s to act specifically as ground attack aircraft.

52 One of them, Flight Lieutenant Richard Thomas, was killed in a crash there in January 1983.

53 *New Statesman*, 25 January 1985, p. 9.

54 Hansard, 24 November 1982, col. 841.

55 Rees also visited Paraguay and Ecuador in an attempt to improve Britain's image in the region after the Falklands episode.

56 Quoted in *Scotsman*, 2 November 1983.

57 *Ibid.*

58 *Daily Mail*, 14 June 1984. The value of the deal was variously put at between £15 million and £40 million.

59 FCO: *Chile: Contingency Planning*, Annex A, internal FCO document, 19 November 1984.

60 *Ibid.*

61 Indeed, in December 1984 it was revealed that earlier in the year Britain had transferred one of its Antarctic bases, Adelaide Island, to Chile. See *Observer*, 9 December 1984.

62 FCO: *Chile: Contingency Planning*.

63 *Guardian*, 3 May 1985.

64 *Tribune*, 22 June 1984.

65 This concern was reflected in a motion introduced by Paddy Ashdown on 3 June 1985. This stated: 'That this House registers its deep shock at continued repression in Chile under the state of siege ... ; expresses its deep concern at reports of a possible sale of up to 300 Centaur military vehicles to the military government and at the fact that an export licence was granted for a demonstration model to be sent to Chile, thus implying that the contract in question would be allowed to go ahead; believes, on the basis of countless examples of recent repression in Chile, that such equipment will be used for internal repression, and would therefore break the Government's own criterion on arms sales to the military government ... ; and calls on the British Government to take urgent measures to undertake a serious review of present foreign policy towards Chile and to take urgent measures, including the reinstatement of an arms embargo, which would leave the military regime in no doubt as to its anxiety at the continued intensification of repression and the desire in Britain to see an early return to democracy and human rights in Chile.'

66 Hansard, 24 July 1986, cols 830–1.

67 In March 1986, when asked if the US was attempting to destabilise the Pinochet government, White House Chief of Staff Donald Regan replied, 'No, not at the moment.' See *Keesings*, May 1986, p. 34349.

68 Hansard, 24 July 1986, col. 826

69 For an assessment of the impact of these policies, see, for example, Cristian Marambio, 'In Defence of Chile', *Military Technology*, No. 2 1992, pp. 72–82. See also the interview with Carlos Cardoen in *Military Technology*, No. 3 1986, pp. 78–83.

70 HMS *Norfolk* had been sold in 1982, and HMS *Antrim* in 1984. Of the rest, HMS *London* was sold to Pakistan, HMS *Hampshire* was scrapped, HMS *Kent* was turned into an accommodation ship in Portsmouth, while HMS *Devonshire* was used for target practice for torpedoes and missiles.

71 *J.D.W.*, 6 June 1987.

72 Alan Clark, *Diaries* (London, Weidenfeld & Nicolson, 1993), p. 161.

73 *J.D.W.*, 9 April 1988.

74 *Ibid.*, 15 December 1990.

75 *Ibid.*, 13 June 1992, p. 1016.

76 On the development of Chile's domestic armaments industry, see, for example, *J.D.W.*, 7 March 1992, pp. 410–14.

77 Pinochet was the only head of state to attend. Paul Preston, *Franco* (London, HarperCollins, 1993), p. 780.

78 According to the *Sunday Times*, 25 October 1998, Pinochet was intending to inspect two frigates (HMS *Beaver* and HMS *Brave*) with a view to buying them.

79 See *J.D.W.*, 28 October 1998 and 6 January 1999.

80 In 1957 it purchased six ex-RAF Lockheed P-2E Neptunes, in 1966 one HS-748, in 1970 ten ex-RAF Canberra B.62s and two Canberra T-64s, and in 1971 one HS-125 and five Short Skyvans.

81 Interview with Ted Rowlands, MP, London, 20 January 1999.

82 Elsewhere, the flow of British arms to Argentina remained unaffected, at least as far as British willingness to sell was concerned. In 1976 Ferranti sold Isis sights for Skyhawk aircraft, and in 1977 sold its Seaspray radar for the Lynx helicopters.

83 The visit did not take place, first being postponed and then cancelled, possibly as a reaction to the reception of Admiral Massera during that summer.

84 *Guardian*, 19 December 1978.

85 Hansard, 21 April 1982, cols 111–12. In response to questioning from Labour MPs, he added: 'Routine releases of naval spares were made from Royal Navy store depots on February 19 and March 22, but a request on March 30 to expedite delivery of further naval spares already on order was declined at official level.' *Ibid.*, col. 112.

86 *The Times*, 22 June 1982.

87 *Financial Times*, 10 August 1982.

88 *Daily Mail*, 19 November 1982, *Sunday Times*, 21 November 1982. Of the original 1979 order for 14 aircraft, only five had been delivered by April 1982, when France imposed an arms embargo. All five survived the conflict.

89 *Guardian*, 20 November 1982.

90 *The Times*, 20 November 1982.

91 In the House of Commons, Labour MP Doug Hoyle claimed that 40 British companies supplied various components for the three different types of Exocet, a contention with which Geoffrey Pattie did not disagree. Hansard, 1 February 1983, col. 128.

92 *Ibid.*, 22 November 1982, cols 583–4.

93 *Ibid.*, col. 586.

94 *Observer*, 21 November 1982.

95 On this, see Martin Middlebrook, *The Fight for the 'Malvinas': The Argentine Forces*

in the Falklands War (London, Viking, 1989), and Bryan Perrett, *Weapons of the Falklands Conflict* (Poole, Blandford Press, 1982).

 96 Hansard (Lords), 15 February 1983.
 97 *Daily Telegraph*, 22 October 1983.
 98 *The Times*, 9 December 1983.
 99 For example, to allow the sale of 155 NBC suits and 50 pairs of boots for use by the Argentinian contingent of the UN task force in Kuwait. Hansard, 5 February 1998, col. 752w.
100 BBC-1, *Breakfast wth Frost*, 25 October 1998.
101 *J.D.W.*, 6 January 1999, p. 5.
102 PRO: FO371/190847, 'Anglo-American Arms Deal in Latin America', memorandum by J. A. Thomson, 25 January 1966.
103 *Ibid.*
104 PRO: FO 371/190847, 'Anglo-American Arms Deal in Latin-America', memorandum by L. C. W. Figg, 27 January 1966.
105 PRO: FCO 7/446, Telegram, Santiago to FO, 25 April 1967.
106 PRO: FCO 7/446, Lima to FO, 13 February 1967.
107 PRO: FCO 7/446, 'Sale of Lightning Aircraft to Peru', comment by H. A. F. Hohler, 24 April 1967.
108 PRO: FCO 7/448, John Stonehouse to Herbert Bowden, Secretary of State for Commonwealth Affairs, 23 February 1967.
109 PRO: FCO 7/446, Telegram, Quito to FO, 25 April 1967.
110 PRO: FCO 7/448, 'I am delighted to hear that you think so highly of Hunter aircraft, which continue to be a popular choice in a number of countries, and of course are still giving very satisfactory service in the RAF.' Draft letter, John Stonehouse to José Heighes, Peruvian Aviation Minister, attached to covering letter dated 23 February 1967.
111 These points were made in a reply to Stonehouse's proposal by George Thomas, Minister of State at the Comonwealth Office, 28 February 1967 PRO: FCO 7/448. See also PRO: FCO 7/448, Minutes of a Meeting to Discuss the Availability and Sale of Hunter Aircraft, 3 March 1967.
112 PRO: FCO 7/448, Jonathan D. Stoddart, Attaché, Politico-military Affairs, US Embassy, London, to D. V. Fielder, MoD, 10 March 1967.
113 PRO: FCO 7/448, Telegram, FO to Lima, 7 April 1967.
114 PRO: FCO 7/446, 'Aircraft for Peru', Memorandum by L. C. W. Figg, 31 March 1967.
115 PRO: FCO 7/448, Telegram, Lima to FO, 5 April 1967, and Letter from John Stonehouse to José Heighes, 10 April 1967.
116 PRO: FCO 7/446, John Stonehouse to Fred Mulley, 19 April 1967.
117 PRO: FCO 7/448, Telegram, Lima to FO, 9 May 1967.
118 PRO: FCO 7/448, R. Jardine, Ministry of Technology, to L. C. W. Figg, FO, 24 May 1967.
119 *Daily Telegraph*, 23 June 1967.
120 PRO: FCO 7/448, Telegram, Lima (D. Muirhead) to FO, 16 July 1967.
121 PRO: FO 7/448, Telegram, Lima to FO, 25 July 1967.
122 PRO: FCO 7/448, Telegram, Harold Wilson to Lyndon Johnson, 26 July 1967.
123 PRO: FCO 7/449, Telegram, Lyndon Johnson to Harold Wilson, 29 July 1967.
124 See the story by Chapman Pincher in the *Daily Express*, 'RAF jets deal is vetoed by US', 3 August 1967.
125 PRO: FCO 7/449, Telegram, Lima to FO, 1 August 1967.
126 See Chapman Pincher, 'Canberra jet deal with Peru to go ahead', *Daily Express*, 23 August 1967.
127 PRO: FCO 7/449, Telegram, Lima to FO, 12 October 1967.

128 PRO: FCO 7/450, Telegram, FO to Washington, 3 November 1967.
129 Ted Rowlands, letter to Jenny Little, 11 July 1977. Quoted in Richard Gott, 'Latin America: Labour Party policy and Labour Government practice', in Latin America Bureau, *Britain and Latin America: An Annual Review of British–Latin American Relations 1978* (London, LAB, 1978), p. 24.
130 *Daily Telegraph*, 12 October 1981.
131 *Financial Times,* 27 October 1981; *Guardian,* 27 October 1981; *Observer,* 1 November 1981.
132 *Daily Telegraph*, 13 August 1982.
133 *J.D.W.*, 30 April 1988.
134 *Ibid.*, 20 February 1988.
135 Hansard, 8 February 1994, col. 235.
136 Interview with Ted Rowlands, MP, London, 20 January 1999.
137 *Financial Times*, 20 January 1978.
138 *Financial Times*, 18 November 1977; *Guardian*, 11 January 1978.
139 *Observer*, 11 December 1977.
140 *Financial Times*, 15 December 1977.
141 *Guardian*, 11 January 1978.
142 *El Diario de Hoy*, 22 November 1977. Quoted in Latin America Bureau Press release, 12 January 1978.
143 *Guardian*, 11 January 1978.
144 Press release, 13 January 1978.
145 Letter to Cardinal Hume, 14 December 1977.
146 *Guardian*, 13 January 1978.
147 *Ibid.*, 20 January 1978.

4

British arms sales to South East Asia

Indonesia: jets, jobs and genocide

> We do not recognise Indonesian sovereignty over East Timor. We fully
> support the efforts of the UN Secretary General to find a just and compre-
> hensive settlement to the question of East Timor, and we continue to raise
> with the Indonesian Government our concerns about the situation in East
> Timor.
>   Along with several of our EU partners, we do not consider that
> Indonesia's annexation of East Timor precludes the sale of defence equip-
> ment to Indonesia. (Jeremy Hanley, MP, January 1997[1])

> The point of selling Hawk aircraft to Indonesia is to give jobs to people in
> this country. There is no doubt in my mind that a Hawk aircraft can do
> nothing to suppress the people of East Timor. The aircraft is not suitable for
> that purpose and we have guarantees from the Indonesians that the aircraft
> would not be used for internal suppression. (Archie Hamilton, MP, January
> 1993[2])

British interests in Indonesia have been both strategic and economic. In
terms of strategic interest, Indonesia – comprising thousands of small
islands – occupies a crucial position along and astride the major sea lanes
from the Indian Ocean to the Pacific. British assessments of the strategic
importance of the region and Indonesia within it have been similar to
those emanating from the US. In 1948 George Kennan had warned that
the US 'should recognize that our influence in the Far Eastern area in the
coming period is going to be primarily military and economic. We should
make a careful study to see what parts of the Pacific and Far Eastern
world are absolutely vital to our security, and we should concentrate our
policy on seeing to it that those areas remain in hands which we can
control or rely on.'[3] In the UK, in a memorandum discussed by the
Cabinet Defence Committee in December 1954, the region's importance
was summarised thus:

It is necessary to block the spread of Communism in South-East Asia. Politically the area is unstable and positive action is needed if the peoples and countries are to be retained in the Free World. Their loss to Communism would be a major defeat. Economically it is of great importance to retain the resources of South-East Asia and to deny them to the Communists. Strategically, control of the area with its sea and air communications prevents a direct threat to Australia and New Zealand. The focus of the communications through the area lies in Singapore. It is essential therefore that the surrounding territories remain in the Free World.[4]

The US and UK were both heavily involved in the events of 1965–66 which resulted in the overthrow of President Sukarno and his replacement by the little-known General Suharto. MI6 were closely involved in undermining Sukarno through covert operations and psychological warfare, while British sources liaised with army officers intent on overthrowing him.[5] Meanwhile, US officials compiled lists of thousands of Partai Komunis Indonesia (PKI) activists and passed them on to the Indonesian military, subsequently checking off the names of those captured and killed in the destruction of the PKI and massacre of around 500,000 people. As a former member of the US embassy's political section, Robert J. Martens, recalled: 'It really was a big help to the [Indonesian] army. They probably killed a lot of people, and I probably have a lot of blood on my hands, but that's not all bad.'[6]

On the very day of the December 1975 Indonesian invasion of East Timor, the *New York Times* further outlined the area's strategic significance: 'Indonesia, its islands extending from the Malay Peninsula to Australia, guards the western shore of the Strait of Malacca. The strait affords the most direct access for the United States' Pacific fleet to the Indian Ocean, where Soviet naval activity has been reported increasing.'[7] This importance also needs to be seen in the context of the experience of the US in Vietnam, Laos and Cambodia – all of which had been 'lost' by the time the US gave the go-ahead for the invasion of East Timor. Indeed, President Ford stopped off in Jakarta on 5 December 1975, *en route* from China, where he signed a joint communiqué which spoke of 'the intention of the United States to continue to provide substantial aid to Indonesia'. Ford's plane had barely cleared Indonesian air space when the invasion began. As C. Philip Liechty, a senior CIA officer based in Indonesia in 1975, told a 1994 television documentary, 'You can be 100 per cent certain that Suharto was explicitly given the green light to do what he did.'[8] As Daniel Patrick Moynihan infamously recalled in his memoirs, 'the United States wished things to turn out as they did, and worked to bring this about. The Department of State desired that the United Nations prove utterly ineffective in whatever measures it undertook. This task was given to me, and I carried it forward with no inconsiderable success.'[9]

Notwithstanding Moynihan's effort, the UN Security Council passed two unanimous resolutions (No. 384 on 22 December 1975 and No. 389 on 22 April 1976) which called on 'all States to respect the territorial integrity of East Timor as well as the inalienable right of its people to self-determination', and called upon 'the Government of Indonesia to withdraw without delay all its forces from the Territory'. Britain's arms sales relationship with Indonesia consistently undermined these aims.

In addition to Indonesia's strategic and Cold War importance, Mark Curtis, in his study of UK foreign policy, *The Ambiguities of Power*, has drawn attention to the economic significance the UK attached to Indonesia in the post-World War II period.[10] Having long been regarded as a valuable source of raw materials, the coming to power of the Suharto regime in 1965 created a highly favourable investment climate for Western companies. With strong US, UK, Japanese and Australian support, Indonesia began to emerge in the 1970s as a key regional player. Hence as elsewhere, Britain's relationship with Indonesia needs to be seen in terms of fulfilling Britain's perception of its world role – securing influence for Britain and at the same time helping to maintain a favourable, pro-Western, configuration of power in key areas of the developing world.

Sales of major British arms to Indonesia during the 1980s have been the most controversial of recent times, for several reasons. Firstly, British arms sales increased markedly during the 1980s as a consequence of the imperatives of Thatcherism. Between 1986 and 1990, Britain was Indonesia's largest single supplier of arms after the US, supplying US$522 million worth of major weapons.[11] Between those years, Indonesia became the third largest recipient of British arms, after Saudi Arabia and India. Indicative of the importance of Indonesia and the region in general, in 1991 DESO opened an office in Jakarta. During the 1990s, Britain went on to become Indonesia's biggest supplier of arms.

Secondly, Suharto's was an authoritarian and corrupt government, noted for its indifference to human rights, both internally and in respect of the illegal occupation and annexation of East Timor. As elsewhere, arms sales helped solidify Suharto's rule by satisfying institutional requirements within the Indonesian military. Finally, Indonesia exhibited expansionist tendencies which could be realised only if the Indonesian military were supplied with the means to occupy new areas and then 'pacify' any opposition. The West in general and, in recent years, Britain in particular supplied this capacity. Illegal occupation of East Timor was no barrier to Indonesia receiving arms from leading Western powers. Indonesia was hardly ostracised or punished for its invasion and the geno-cide which followed. Hence the actions of the UK hardly provided the impetus for Indonesia to reconsider its occupation.

Since the December 1975 invasion over 200,000 East Timorese – around one-third of the indigenous population – have been killed, 60,000 within the first five months.[12] In fact the figure of 200,000 was estimated as having been reached by 1981, and it has not been revised upwards since, despite a cycle of further atrocities, culminating in the post-independence referendum slaughter of September 1999. To put this figure in perspective, between 1981 and 1995 the war in Peru involving the Sendero Luminoso guerrilla movement, which has involved the use of scorched earth tactics, has resulted in an estimated 30,000 killed. Since 1969, 3,000 have been killed in Northern Ireland. In fact, next to the slaughter in Rwanda (810,000 killed since 1990), Somalia (350,000 since 1991) and Burundi (205,000 since 1993), more people have been killed on the tiny territory of East Timor than in any current armed conflict anywhere in the world.[13]

Obviously, every state has the right to define its own defensive requirements, and the threats it faces which make them necessary. There is no doubt that, comprising over 13,000 separate islands, with a coastline of over 54,000 km, Indonesia requires significant forces – particularly naval – to be able to police them. There is also a requirement for vessels to combat pirates and deal with the growing drug trafficking problem. Essentially, though, the Indonesian armed forces are configured to guarantee internal security, a fact recognised annually in the US State Department *Report on Human Rights Practices*. This means, effectively, that any military equipment sold runs the risk of being used for internal repression.

Britain used its position on the UN Security Council to refrain from condemnation of Indonesia over the occupation of East Timor, and never showed an interest in linking arms sales with Indonesian withdrawal. On the contrary, its arms sales relationship gave the impression of conferring a degree of legitimacy on a bloody and forceful occupation in the course of which British arms were deployed against the indigenous population. The combination of these characteristics in one state, coupled with the volume and type of arms sold, made Indonesia the cause around which opposition to Britain's arms trade under the Thatcher governments coalesced, the more so in the wake of the democratisation process in Chile.

However, the close military relationship of the Thatcher and Major years was not an entirely new one. Since the Second World War arms sales ties had been close, particularly during the 1950s but increasingly so under the Wilson and Callaghan governments of the 1960s and 1970s.[14] In 1978, the arms sales relationship took a quantum leap forward with the sale of eight BAe Hawk 'trainer' aircraft, in a deal estimated by SIPRI to have been worth US$4.5 million. The inevitable attacks on the Labour government were fended off by Foreign Secretary David Owen, who argued that 'the scale of the fighting [in East Timor] ... has been very greatly reduced'.[15] In addition, Owen argued that the Hawks were the trainer variant, despite BAe's contemporaneous marketing of the Hawk as a 'highly potent ground attack combat fighter'.[16]

As elsewhere in the region, it was with the election of Mrs Thatcher that British arms exports to Indonesia began to expand. In August 1981, Dunlop Holdings signed a joint venture agreement with Intirub (Indonesia Tyre & Rubber) worth £84 million to produce tyres for aircraft, cars, trucks and military vehicles. At the same time, Britain's trade with Indonesia was coming under the spotlight as human rights groups became increasingly well organised in their opposition to the continuing military trade. On 19 October 1981, for example, Labour MP Stan Newens 'asked the Lord Privy Seal if Her Majesty's Government will cease to supply military equipment to Indonesia in light of the armed invasion of East Timor and the refusal to allow any effective exercise of self-determination'. The government's reply came fom Humphrey Atkins: 'No, but all relevant factors, including political considerations, are taken into account in reaching decisions on defence sales issues.'[17]

During the same month, Trade Minister Peter Rees headed a 60-strong delegation of British businessmen who attended the second British–Indonesian Business Meeting on Trade and Investment in Jakarta. Afterwards, Rees told a press conference that the British government was expecting a 'large-scale expansion in Britain's trade with and investment in Indonesia'. This marked the healing of a rift which had occurred in 1980 over Britain's imposition of quotas on imports of textiles from Indonesia – a rift that the Thatcher government had responded to swiftly so as not to jeopardise the sale of the Hawk and other military equipment.[18] Further sales of the Hawk Mark 53 went ahead in 1981, 1982, and 1983. (See Table 8.)

Table 8
BAe Hawk sales to Indonesia

No.	Type	Year ordered	Delivered
8	Mk 53	1978	1980–81
4	Mk 53	1981	1981
5	Mk 53	1982	1983
3	Mk 53	1983	1984
8	100	1993	1996–97
16	200	1993	1996–98
16	200	1996	1997–[a]

Note [a] By the time of the 1999 suspension of sales, six of these aircraft were still held in the UK. See Chapter 7.

On 27 January 1982 the Foreign Secretary, Lord Carrington, began a three-day visit to Jakarta as part of a tour of the ASEAN states, accompanied by a number of leading industrialists, prominent amongst whom were Sir Frederick Page, Managing Director of BAe, Sir Arnold Hall and

Guy Checketts of Hawker Siddeley, and Edward Ashmore of Racal Electronics. While in Jakarta, Carrington signed what was then Britain's largest-ever export credit for Indonesia, worth £125 million and guaranteed by the ECGD. At the same time, the government found itself under increased pressure over arms sales to Indonesia. In December 1982, Lord Belstead wrote to the Labour MP Terry Davis to answer criticisms and set out the government's position:

> The Indonesian occupation of East Timor is of course one of the factors taken into account whenever we consider the sale of arms to Indonesia. In general, we sanction the sale of arms because this conforms with Article 51 of the United Nations Charter which provides that states have the right to act in self-defence and to acquire arms to protect their independence. But this is not to say that we are willing to sell arms indiscriminately. We consider proposed arms sales in the light of all relevant factors and we would not grant an export licence if we thought that the equipment was likely to be used for purposes of repression or to attack British forces or those of our allies.[19]

These aside, in the case of Indonesia, just what were the 'relevant factors'? In practice there were several. Firstly, in the event of Britain taking a human rights stand at odds with that of other principal suppliers and competitors – e.g. the US, France, West Germany – what would their reaction be? Secondly, the ideological orientation of the Indonesian government. Was supplying it with the means of maintaining itself in power consistent with the aims of NATO or, outside that, with the foreign-policy priorities of the West more generally? Related to this was Indonesia's growing regional importance. Thirdly, the balance between the size of the order, the dependence it would generate on British products in this area of defence, the likelihood of follow-up orders, training, spares requirements, etc., had to be weighed against the intensity and scale of the likely backlash from human rights campaigning groups and opposition political parties in Parliament. Fourthly, in relation to this, media (and particularly television) access to the areas where repression was allegedly occurring. Could any human rights groups' or MPs' allegations that British arms, contrary to the government's assurances, were aiding such repression be substantiated? Clearly, in the case of Indonesia in East Timor, the answer was no. The British government was hardly likely to actively seek out abuses. The onus was on the critics of government policy to provide proof that British arms were being used for internal repression and thus contrary to the government's stated policy. But what constituted 'proof'? Even photographic evidence, on the rare occasions it emerged, left the FCO unmoved. As an official of the South East Asian Department explained to one complainant in 1985:

The photographs enclosed with your letter, apparently taken some eight years ago, do not, in our view, show the [British armoured] vehicles engaged in combat in a meaningful sense of the term. Moreover, the temporary holding of an arrested person on an armoured car, or other vehicle, in itself scarcely constitutes conclusive proof of its use for 'internal repression'.[20]

Notwithstanding this, because the absence of evidence of British arms being used for repressive purposes was one of the main planks of the government's defence of its sale of the Hawk to Indonesia, there existed the possibility of a change in policy should such evidence emerge.[21] The government would then be faced with acting on or dismissing the evidence, on the basis of either its quality or who it came from. In practice, it was the latter alternative that the Major government preferred to follow.

By this time, Britain had enjoyed considerable success in selling armoured vehicles to Indonesia. By the end of 1983 Indonesia had 65 Saladin, 60 Saracen and 60 Ferret armoured vehicles. Furthermore, documents leaked from the Department of Overseas Development revealed that ECGD credits were being arranged to fund further armoured vehicle sales.[22] The possibility of their being used in East Timor prompted MPs Bob Parry and Bernard Braine, and Lord Avebury, to write to the FCO. The FCO reply to Parry stated that the vehicles 'can only operate on roads and in reasonably dry, open country. Their usefulness in the jungle and difficult terrain of East Timor would therefore appear to be limited.' This was a dubious assertion, as it was far from obvious that the vehicles could operate only on roads, and seemed to assume, in any case, that there were no roads in East Timor. The FCO went on to state that the bulk of armoured vehicle sales took place under the Labour governments of the 1970s, and so it could not comment on the terms under which they were sold, but noted that 'We do not normally seek assurances which can offer no reliable guarantee about the use to which the equipment might later be put,' presumably a conversion which had taken place since the El Salvador fiasco of the late 1970s and a view reversed in the 1990s when the Major government was under even more pressure to justify continued arms sales to Indonesia.

In August 1984, three British 'Tribal' Class 81 frigates (HMS *Zulu*, HMS *Tartar* and HMS *Gurkha* – all ex-RN and in service since the 1960s) were sold to Indonesia, and refitted by Vosper Thornycroft prior to handing over. In November, Sir Edwin Bramall, Chief of the Defence Staff, visited Jakarta to discuss this and other ongoing deals – primarily the BAe/MoD effort to sell Indonesia the Rapier missile system. These deals represented the British contribution to Indonesia's naval modernisation programme. In the previous five years, as part of that programme, Indonesia had purchased four submarines and two patrol boats from West Germany, three corvettes from the Netherlands, eight high-speed patrol boats from South Korea and twelve patrol boats from Belgium. In addition, it was planning to build a further six West German patrol boats in its own shipyards under licence.

The three British ships, due to be scrapped under the Nott defence review, had been reprieved, and had been on active service during the Falklands conflict. In the aftermath they had been refitted with up-to-date radar equipment and missiles, including the Sea Cat anti-aircraft missile. This made them ideal for the Indonesian navy. While ships have a 'hull life' of around 30 years, the rate of development of missile and radar technology means that the most attractive vessels are those that can be or recently have been adapted to take on up-to-date technology. The fact that such was the case with these ships also meant that the cost would be relatively low and delivery could be made quickly. Hence the ships were refitted and supplied within a matter of months at a total cost of around £26.6 million, and with around 10 years' hull life remaining.

In December 1984, BAe confirmed that Indonesia had been persuaded to sign a contract worth around £100 million for the Rapier missile system, making Indonesia the third ASEAN state to buy it.[23] One significant aspect of the deal, increasingly the norm in dealings with Indonesia, was that it allowed for the gradual transfer of technology, in effect, helping Indonesia to establish an indigenous defence electronics industry.[24]

For BAe in 1984, Indonesia represented a growing market, one of the most promising anywhere in the world. The British government termed the Rapier deal a 'significant breakthrough', with BAe anticipating further sales, as more Indonesian officers were to undergo training in Britain than were actually required for the number covered by this first sale.[25] In addition, BAe was trying to interest the Indonesians in the new Hawk 200 series – the dedictated ground attack version of the aircraft – against a background of US Congressional reluctance to supply Indonesia with F-16 aircraft (which, in any case, were three times as expensive as the Hawk 200).

In late 1984, John Lee, Parliamentary Under-Secretary for defence procurement, visited Indonesia, followed in January 1985 by Sir Keith Williamson, RAF Chief-of-Staff. The visits paved the way for the seminal event in the Anglo-Indonesian arms sales relationship – the April 1985 visit of Mrs Thatcher during her tour of South East Asia. This visit, delayed by the need to attend to the miners' strike at home, took place at the climax of a sales drive by British arms manufacturers, with the full backing of the Thatcher government, aimed at securing a major share of the arms market created by Indonesia's military reorganisation and modernisation. As one newspaper prophesied at the time, 'with commercial prizes like these, there will be little likelihood that Mrs Thatcher will be making strong representations over Indonesia's invasion of East Timor or the bitter resistance struggle that has been waged since then'.[26]

On 10 April 1985, Mrs Thatcher and President Suharto ('an immensley hard-working and effective ruler' in Mrs Thatcher's assessment[27]) had around two hours of talks. According to one report, 'Mrs Thatcher played stateswoman, discussing international issues, and saleswoman.'[28] During the talks Mrs Thatcher 'touched on, but apparently did not press' the situation in East Timor. Subsequently, Mochtar Kusumaatmadja, Indonesia's Foreign Minister, said that the issue was not 'even an irritant in the relations between our countries. We understand that the British can not do more than abstain [on the East Timor vote at the UN], and they understand what happened.'[29]

Before her departure from Indonesia, where she was 'mobbed and jostled by cheering students'[30] (seemingly bearing out Jim Callaghan's contention that the 'further you got from Britain, the more admired you found she was'[31]) Mrs Thatcher held a press conference. She suggested that Britain should become more involved in Indonesia's industrial and technological development, particularly rail, air, telecommunications, food technology, and aerospace, commenting that: 'I think Britain has not paid sufficient attention to Indonesia in the past and I hope and intend that my visit will be followed up by more ministerial visits so that we get to know each other better.' She ended by saying that the question of East Timor was 'not a matter for Britain'.[32] Out of office, in 1992, on being presented with an award by the Indonesians for 'helping technology' (i.e. approving licensed production of military and defence electronics products), Mrs Thatcher told her audience, 'I am proud to be one of you.'[33] In her 1985 meeting with President Suharto, Mrs Thatcher had told him that 'when it comes to defending independence and freedom, we are at one with you'[34] (an assertion with which many in Britain would have readily agreed), underlining again how the arms sales relationship served to give an aura of legitimacy to Indonesia's occupation of East Timor (not to mention what has come to be termed the 'crony capitalism' of the Suharto family and inner circle), and in practice served to align Britain closely with yet another authoritarian government.

In July 1985 future President B. J. Habibie, then Indonesia's Minister of Research and Technology ('a German-trained scientist of immense energy and imagination' according to Mrs Thatcher[35]), visited London, where an agreement on technical co-operation was signed. He was accompanied by General Surono, Minister Co-ordinator of Political, Defence and Security Affairs. The agreement was signed on Britain's behalf by Trade and Industry Secretary Norman Tebbit and Foreign Office Minister Richard Luce. It arose out of the discussions Mrs Thatcher had during her April visit, and was illustrative of the degree to which technology transfer was perceived as being vital to continuing export success.[36] While in Britain, Habibie, 'a key element in the battle for lucrative civil and military sales to Indonesia',[37] visited various companies, including Alvis (hoping to conclude a collaborative venture deal to manufacture 600 Scorpions in Indonesia – eventual sales would be substantially less) and Vosper Thornycroft. A close confidant of Suharto, Habibie had already visited several West European countries, and was being strenuously fêted by France and West Germany. However, once in Britain, he identified four categories of British equipment that Indonesia was interested in.

Firstly, fighter aircraft to fill the Indonesian Air Force's requirement for a new generation of fighters. Here, BAe's Hawk 200 was in competition with the US F-16 and F-20 Tigershark, which were the Indonesians' favoured option. The head of Indonesia's armed forces, General Benny Murdani, was a firm advocate of the F-16, the only perceived drawbacks of which (assuming Congressional approval) were cost and delivery schedule. Secondly, missile systems. The BAe Rapier was competing against the French Roland, while the Indonesians were also interested in the BAe Sea Eagle. Thirdly, tanks – hence Habibie's visit to the Alvis plant in Coventry to discuss the possibility of a collaborative venture potentially worth £250 million.[38] The fourth category was civilian aircraft.

By this time, a number of Indonesia's defence requirements were being met by its own fledgling arms industry – for example, 57m fast patrol boats, the assembly of Puma helicopters, and the manufacture of a range of small arms, artillery and ammunition. For Indonesia, this represented the beginning of the (long) road to self-sufficiency. As elsewhere, the impetus was the generally critical international reaction to aspects of its behaviour, which raised the spectre of the curtailment of supply in certain circumstances. Hence while there was a need to rely on outside supply, the reliability of the supplier was at a premium. This is not to say that financial support was not important in securing contracts, an area where Britain acknowledged that it lagged behind France and West Germany. It was 1985 before Britain pledged £10 million in soft loans as part of its contribution to the annual pledges of the Inter-governmental Aid Group on Indonesia, and Trade Minister Paul Channon visited Jakarta to negotiate a further soft loan package.[39]

On 16 December 1985 it was announced that Indonesia had, as expected after Habibie's visit, signed a further order for the Rapier missile. The deal included, 'further transfer of technology which will progressively enable the maintenance, and ultimate manufacture, of the system to be undertaken in country', and took the Rapier's export sales value for 1985 to over £450 million.[40]

During 1986 the pressure applied by human rights and campaigning groups increased. In January the first photographs to be smuggled out of East Timor since the invasion showing Indonesian military manoeuvres were printed in the British press.[41] At a time when Alvis was negotiating a potentially lucrative deal, these showed less agile Soviet PT-76 light tanks apparently coping adequately with the terrain, thereby disproving the FCO's earlier assertion that the nature of the terrain would severely limit the operation of any British armoured vehicles in East Timor. Further questions about the link between British arms sales and their possible use in East Timor were raised when, just as Indonesia was showing an interest in further Hawks, the Indonesian Air Force's chief of staff inaugurated a new squadron which included the Hawk – the sale of which had been defended on the grounds that they were only for training purposes – armed with air-to-ground missiles and machine guns, and announced that they were ready to undertake 'tactical operations'.

However, any immediate prospect of the sale of the Hawk 200 appeared to have been dented by the sale in early 1986 of 12 US F-16s, 35 per cent of the cost of which was to be covered by offset agreements. Notwithstanding this, the Indonesians were still looking to replace a squadron of 36 A4 Skyhawks and F-5s, and in so doing several factors suggested that the Hawk 200 would be the first choice. While Indonesia's drive to diversify its sources of supply and the cost of the F-16s were important reasons, even more significant was the personal enthusiasm of Mrs Thatcher, which compared highly favourably with the foot-dragging of Congress. Here, as elsewhere, the British system of government was itself an advantage to British exporters, as it allowed the government to maintain a level of secrecy which was to the liking of customers like Indonesia, but which could not be guaranteed by the US.

In April 1986, Indonesia took delivery of the ex-RN survey ship *Hydra*, following up its previous purchase of the three Tribal class frigates,[42] and in June Rolls-Royce signed an agreement authorising the Indonesian state aerospace company, IPTN, to repair and overhaul its aircraft engines. In December 1986, a year after it secured its second order, BAe won a third order for the Rapier missile, this time worth £40 million.[43] It brought the value of Rapiers supplied to Indonesia to £220 million. In line with the trend in dealing with Indonesia, offsets were again incorporated into the deal. Parts of the missile would be manufactured by the state aerospace industry, IPTN, and by Radio Frequency Communication. Indonesian staff would also be trained in Britain – thereby joining a long line of Indonesian visitors with an interest in British military hardware.

In February 1987 a team of senior executives from BAe and Rolls-Royce visited Indonesia as part of a British trade and industry mission headed by the Duke of Kent, vice-chair of the British Overseas Trade Board, to discuss greater co-operation with IPTN. The duke told the Indonesian-British Association that: 'Indonesia is one of the brightest long term prospects as a partner for Britain in the developing world ... because it is rich in natural resources and labour and has achieved sound financial management, political stability and military security.'[44] In March 1987, BAe announced that it had won a contract for five sets of its battery command post processor system. In November, Rolls-Royce signed a technical co-operation agreement with IPTN to consider possible areas for joint venture manufacturing and servicing of various engine parts. As the BAe Hawk had a Rolls-Royce engine, this was interpreted as a sign that Indonesia would purchase the Hawk 200 in the near future.[45]

In October 1987, Tim Sainsbury, Under-Secretary for Defence Procurement, visited Indonesia along with senior DESO officials, and was followed by Chris Patten, Minister for Overseas Development, underlining the extent to which Indonesia had become a major export market, one opened up by British arms and in which arms remained the centrepiece. At the time of Mrs Thatcher's 1985 visit, Britain's exports had been trailing behind those of Japan, the US, Australia, France and West Germany, but improved through the Thatcher government's use of the Aid and Trade Provision (ATP) and through the line of soft-loan credit extended to Indonesia.[46]

In mid-1988 BAe completed the construction of an Army College of Technology in East Java, at a cost of nearly £3 million, as part of the Rapier deals. As *British Aerospace News* noted:

> It will equip the students with the necessary basic skills for subsequent training in and maintenance of the BAe Rapier missile system being supplied under the contracts. But eventually its teaching will benefit other elements of the Indonesian Army and the level of technical education in the country generally ... The students will all be serving soldiers in the Indonesian Army ... Eleven instructors from BAe and four from Bell College in the UK have been appointed.[47]

Anglo-Indonesian relations remained close throughout the rest of the decade. In March 1989, Defence Secretary George Younger visited Jakarta to discuss joint ventures, with particular reference to the Hawk 200.[48] In July 1989, following another visit to Britain by Habibie, it was announced that BAe and IPTN were to set up an industrial co-operation programme. Under its terms a number of Indonesian students would study aeronautical and general engineering in British universities and be trained by BAe, again part of a process transferring technological know-how from the UK to Indonesia in support of arms sales.

The transition from Margaret Thatcher to John Major did nothing to dampen Indonesian enthusiasm for British arms. In June 1991, it was revealed that BAe and IPTN had signed a collaborative agreement on production of the Hawk.[49] The agreement was not accompanied by a formal order, but Habibie was quoted as saying that Indonesia required 69 aircraft. Hence the agreement was widely seen as opening the way to further sales of the Hawk 100, and the sale of the Hawk 200, at the time operated only by Oman and Malaysia.

At the same time, in the post-Gulf War environment, the posturing about arms control that many national leaders, John Major included, engaged in gave the question of arms sales to repressive and aggressive governments a new salience. Inevitably, Britain's relations with Indonesia came under renewed attention. In 1991 Lord Avebury wrote to John Major to protest over the continued arming of Indonesia. Major's reply was at best contradictory. He reassured Avebury that:

> Like you, I find the spread of weapons worrying. Britain has consistently operated a stringent policy of export controls and was not, for example, among those who supplied Iraq with arms in the past decade. But the experience of the recent conflict in the Gulf has underlined the importance of international action to restrain and regulate the trade in arms, while recognising the right, enshrined in Article 51 of the UN Charter, of every country to defend itself. This is why I took the initiative in proposing ... the creation of a register of arms sales at the United Nations to ensure greater transparency and thus making it possible to monitor and control the scale of arms build up in any one country.
>
> This does not, however, preclude the development of commercial links and economic co-operation between Britain and other countries. In the case of Indonesia, we recognise that the situation in East Timor, and the human rights dimension, is a factor ... We continue ... to do what we can to help efforts to find a solution to the East Timor problem ... We do not allow the export of arms and equipment likely to be used against civil populations. In the case of Indonesia, the criterion extends to possible use against the civil population of East Timor.[50]

Notwithstanding these concerns, on 19 September 1991 Defence Secretary Tom King met President Suharto to discuss co-production and other Hawk-related issues. However, shortly afterwards an event occurred which again raised the profile of Indonesia internationally, in a manner unlikely to aid the cause of British arms exporters.

On 12 November 1991 the Indonesian army massacred over 400 demonstrators in Dili, East Timor, beginning in the local cemetery and continuing later in the local hospital. Needing to act to deflect international criticism, the Indonesians set up a commission of inquiry, made up of local officials, which concluded – in an eight-page report, published on Christmas Day – that the soldiers involved had acted in self-defence. In Parliament, government and Conservative backbenchers joined together to commend the Indonesian government for this speedy investigation, and for the handful of light sentences imposed on a few of those involved, while the US praised its 'serious and responsible approach'.[51] Opposition MPs raised the matter through a series of parliamentary questions. For example, on 15 January 1992, George Foulkes asked whether the government would be reviewing 'policy in relation to the supply of all arms and provision of military training to Indonesia in light of the report of the massacre in East Timor'. In the most dismissive form of answer in the parliamentary armoury, he was merely informed that: 'The Government's policy on the supply of arms and the provision of military training is kept under constant review. All applications to export defence equipment are carefully scrutinised on a case-by-case basis.'[52]

In the wake of the massacre, the Labour Party demanded that the government should suspend aid to Indonesia (in 1991 worth £22.7 million) and impose an arms embargo. Given that the government was at this point publicly linking overseas aid with 'good governance', the timing of the massacre in Britain's key regional arms market could hardly have been more awkward. The demand coincided with the visit to Britain of Indonesian Foreign Minister Ali Alatas, who met the Foreign Secretary, Douglas Hurd, who stressed the importance of avoiding any repetition of the Dili massacre.[53] Sanctions, however, did not follow. The gravity with which the Indonesians should treat this message was further called into question with the announcement that the British government was to sell Indonesia the support ship *Green Rover*, in a deal worth around £11 million.

This announcement was to have been made in January 1992 but had to be delayed until the following month after a *First Tuesday* television documentary had shown footage of the November 1991 massacre at Dili cemetery, and presented first-hand accounts of the atrocities which followed.[54] Lord Avebury commented that: 'If the announcement had been made at the time of the *First Tuesday* programme there would have been a public outcry, but even with the lapse of a few weeks there will still be absolute outrage.'[55] This documentary also included a number of key witnesses who claimed to have seen Hawk jets being used over East Timor. Konis Santana of the Timorese resistance told of how 'British-made Hawk aeroplanes were used against the defenceless population. They launched bombs against defenceless people.' José Gusmao, a Timorese exile, recounted how 'The first time I saw two jet fighters, I was surprised. I realised that they were "Hawk" because we only saw [US] "Bronco". They flew over us, then minutes after we heard that strong blast, bomb and machine gun ...'[56]

But the government had no intention of imposing any restrictions on the sale of British arms – for one thing, lengthy negotiations on the sale of further Hawk aircraft were about to reach fruition. When part of the footage from Dili cemetery was incorporated into a new documentary by journalist John Pilger, broadcast in February 1994, it led to yet more letters of complaint, but these were barely entertained by the FCO. Take this example from June 1994:

> You refer to 'the evidence of John Pilger's visit to East Timor' which alleges, amongst other things, that British supplied military equipment and Hawk aircraft have been used for repressive and aggressive actions in East Timor. There is simply no evidence to support these allegations. The Hawk footage,

intercut with other material in Mr Pilger's film, was not shot in East Timor. There has never been any suggestion that air power was used at Dili in 1991 and the Hawk aircraft were not supplied until the early 1980s, well after the 1975 invasion ... It would be wrong to base, or amend, our policy on defence sales on the spurious allegations which have appeared recently in the media.[57]

In the aftermath of the documentary Lord Avebury had asked: 'What further restrictions, if any, [HMG] will impose on the export of arms and equipment capable of being used for military purposes to Indonesia, in the light of recent killings of civilians in East Timor, West Papua and Acheh by the Indonesian armed forces.' The Earl of Caithness replied for the government: 'None. We do not allow the export of arms and equipment likely to be used for repressive purposes against civil populations.'[58] For his part, Arizal Effendi of the Indonesian embassy in London explained: 'There is no war now in East Timor. Why should we use such an aircraft? It would be a waste of money and a waste of energy. To operate a Hawk is very expensive. I don't think that we need such kind of weaponry to fight a band of guerrillas in the mountains. To have this kind of military action against such small – is just like shooting flies with a cannon.'[59]

In a sense, however, it should come as no surprise if there was less of a need to use the Hawks over East Timor by then. Given the tactics adopted by the Indonesians in East Timor, it is also no surprise that the strength of the Fretelin forces was diminished. By 1996 the Indonesians estimated the group numbered no more than 70 armed insurgents, whereas five years previously its strength had been estimated at 200.[60]

By June 1992, with resentment within Indonesia at what was perceived to be outside interference in its domestic affairs subsiding, negotiations with BAe over the anticipated Hawk 200 order progressed once more. The eventual order, it was now suggested, would be for around 40 aircraft, which could be assembled in Indonesia. Hence in October 1992 the government informed Parliament that it 'did not believe that the imposition of trade sanctions against Indonesia would be an appropriate or effective way of promoting a solution to the East Timor question'.[61] Underlying this objection to any form of sanctions was the extent of UK trade with Indonesia, a high proportion of which was composed of military equipment. In fact, in 1992–93, British arms exports to Indonesia represented 98 per cent of all exports.[62] The same factors underlay the muted response to the Dili massacre. Even moderate diplomatic options such as the termination of UK training (conducted at the UK taxpayers' expense) of Indonesian military officers were discounted. In practice the British government restricted itself to agreeing to a June 1992 EC démarche on the subject – not even a slight breeze on the Beaufort scale of international diplomacy. Because its actions were circumscribed by the desire to continue arming Indonesia, any public criticism had to be expressed at a level and in a forum acceptable to the Indonesians. In such situations, multilateral rather than unilateral action was always the government's preferred response. As Mark Lennox-Boyd helpfully explained, 'the best way to influence human rights policy in Indonesia is by staying in there and maintaining our trade, and by discussing with them the matters on which we disagree, especially bearing in mind that in the first six months of [1992] we had £170 million of trade with Indonesia, which is double last year's amount'.[63] In reality, nothing could have been further from the truth. Not surprisingly, the East Timorese saw things differently, and labelled Britain 'the single worst obstructionist of any industrialised country' with regard to curbing Indonesian atrocities in East Timor.[64]

For the same reasons, neither was the government over-keen to use its occupancy of the presidency of the EC to pursue the issue of East Timor.[65] Moreover, when the European Parliament adopted a resolution in which the Indonesian occupation of East Timor was denounced as 'illegal', the government reminded MPs that it was under 'no obligation' to implement the Parliament's recommendations.[66] The government also made it clear that it would not support calls for either an EU or a UN embargo on arms sales to Indonesia.[67]

Nor was it prepared to act unilaterally. One reply to a question asking whether the Foreign Secretary 'will visit Indonesia to make representations about human rights violations in East Timor' was not only to decline the suggestion, but to argue that 'we believe that some of the figures' on deaths in East Timor 'have been exaggerated'.[68] The government itself repeatedly declined to put a figure on the numbers killed.[69] Not surprisingly, in view of the principle outlined above, the Conservative government repeatedly asserted that 'the question of East Timor's status and future is best addresed through the auspices of the United Nations' Secretary-General and through contacts between Portugal and Indonesia'.[70] However, when asked if it intended to bring the matter up at the UN, the government was far from enthusiastic.[71]

BAe used the platform afforded by the June 1993 Paris Air Show to announce its success in securing further sales of the Hawk: a £500 million contract to sell a further 24 aircraft (a combination of the 100 and 200, the latter being described as a 'dedicated, single-seat light fighter') to Indonesia as a replacement for the ageing fleet of US Skyhawks, and bringing the total number of Hawks sold to Indonesia to 44.[72] Only a few months earlier, Habibie had made it clear that the aircraft would 'be used not only to train pilots but also for ground attack'.[73]

Sensitivities over East Timor dictated that no announcement was made as to how many of the 24 would be the two-seater 100 and how many the single-seat 200, but in the event the order comprised a majority of 200s: 16 to eight 100s. The order took the number of Hawks in service or on order to 700. Once again, an offset component was included, with IPTN collaborating on the production of certain components.

The deal had been sealed by Defence Secretary Malcolm Rifkind during a necessarily low-profile visit to Indonesia. Responding to criticism of Indonesia's human rights record and its continued presence in East Timor, a BAe spokesman unveiled the dominant alibi of the 1990s: that the company had sought and received assurances that the Hawk would not be used by the Indonesian armed forces against East Timorese rebels – a reassurance as impractical as the one sought by the Callaghan government over the sale of armoured vehicles to El Salvador in the late 1970s.

John Major – who had opposed the sale of Hawks to Iraq in 1989 because of their potential for use as ground attack aircraft against the Kurds – told the House of Commons that the order demonstrated 'the excellence of the British defence industry'.[74] The announcement of the deal came shortly after Xanana Gusmao, leader of the East Timorese independence movement, had been jailed following what was widely perceived to have been a show trial. While Mario Soares, the Portuguese President, awarded Gusmao the Order of Liberty, one of Portugal's highest honours, the British reaction was to increase its aid to Indonesia almost fourfold, with a £65 million soft loan – a move difficult to reconcile with the leading role Britain had played in calling for aid to be linked with respect for human rights and 'good government'.[75] Moreover, it was subsequently revealed that the government had deliberately lied that it was pushing for Red Cross access to political prisoners in East Timor in order to 'stonewall' critics of its arms sales policy.[76]

In the climate of sustained criticism which greeted the Hawk announcement, the government now also began to cite assurances apparently sought from the Indonesian government regarding their use with increasing regularity. (The terminology itself is significant. These were 'assurances' rather than 'guarantees', hence their breach would not represent the breach of a guarantee, which might require a firmer response than that required in response to the breach of an 'assurance'.) What these assurances actually entailed remains somewhat unclear. In January 1993, prior to the announcement of this latest Hawk order, MoD Minister Archie Hamilton told Parliament that 'we have guarantees from the Indonesians that the aircraft would not be used for internal suppression',[77] although subsequent answers suggest that Hamilton was anticipating an arrangement rather than describing one already in place. In a written answer in June, just after the order was announced, Jonathan Aitken said that: 'Assurances as to the end use of the Hawk aircraft will also be sought prior to supply.'[78] By February 1994, Alistair Goodlad was assuring Parliament that the 'Indonesian Government have given us assurances that Hawk aircraft will not be used for internal security purposes.'[79]

However, previously Indonesian Air Marshal Sibun had said that the Hawks would 'be used not only to train pilots, but also for "emergency" air-to-ground attacks', further observing that 'the Hawks were made especially for air-to-ground assaults'.[80]

However, as Alan Clark – always far more frank about arms sales than many of his colleagues – pointed out: 'A guarantee is worthless from any government as far as I'm concerned. I mean, I wouldn't even bother with it, but it may look good in the formula, you know.' As he also noted, the Hawk might be classified as a trainer aircraft, but 'that's just a label you put on it ... The Hawk is a training aircraft, but it's actually an exceptionally effective aircraft and can be used in a whole variety of different roles.' The Hawk, he explained, 'is dual-use with a capital "D"'.[81]

Did the assurances extend beyond the Hawk? At times that seemed to be the government's message, at others the assurances were represented as applying only to the Hawk. In December 1994, Alistair Goodlad replied to one parliamentary question by saying that: 'The Indonesians have assured us that British supplied defence equipment will not be used against civilians in Indonesia or East Timor.'[82] So did the assurances fall short of covering the use of the Hawks over East Timor in any circumstances? Did this mean they could still be used against those the Indonesians labelled as belonging to the resistance movement, and who were therefore combatants rather than civilians?

Whatever, these assurances were invoked by the President of the Board of Trade Michael Heseltine in his rather defensive March 1995 announcement of his decision to licence the export of Alvis Scorpions. He told MPs, 'The Indonesian Government have given assurances that the vehicles will not be deployed in East Timor nor used in any form of repression of civilians anywhere in Indonesia,'[83] raising the question of just what Indonesia wanted them for?

Subsequently, in May 1995, Alistair Goodlad clarified the situation somewhat, telling Ann Clwyd that the government had 'received general assurances from the Indonesian Government that British defence equipment would not be used for internal repression in East Timor', that assurances regarding the Hawk were first sought on 24 June 1993 – i.e. to coincide with the announcement of that deal – and that subsequently, 'on several occasions, most recently on 2 February 1995, [the government] sought the assurance of the Indonesian Government that British-supplied defence equipment would not be used for internal repression in Indonesia and East Timor.'[84] In January 1995 Roger Freeman had gone so far as to tell MPs that Indonesia's assurances were 'an important factor in our consideration' of export licences for such equipment.[85] However, the government declined to reveal on how many occasions it had requested information in relation to these assurances, or whether similar conditionality had been applied to arms exports elsewhere.[86]

For its part, BAe was unequivocal. In 1994 the managing director of its Military Aircraft Division wrote that: 'There is no evidence to support allegations that Hawk aircraft, or other British defence equipment, is being used for repressive purposes against the people of East Timor ... So-called eye-witness accounts of two Hawk aircraft sitting on the tarmac in East Timor – even if credible – are hardly evidence of active service against the civilian population.'[87]

However, all these 'assurances' need to be viewed in the context of the role that air power played in Indonesia's efforts to eradicate the Fretilin movement and gain complete control of East Timor – something it was never actually able to achieve. In the 1970s, the Indonesians deployed US Bronco and Skyhawk aircraft in this effort. An offensive which began in September 1977 involved saturation bombing ahead of advances by ground forces, the use of defoliants to deny cover to Fretilin forces, and the use of chemicals to kill crops and livestock. Amongst many accounts of the impact of the bombing, one refugee testified to the situation in Natabora around 1978: 'Three aircraft – I think they were Skyhawks – bombed the region, killing thousands of people. In particular, women, children and old people were killed, people who couldn't run for cover. They were killed in large numbers. All we could do was pray for God's protection. The planes came in low and sprayed the ground with bullets, with their machine guns killing many people.'[88]

It was at this time that Indonesia sought to expand its aerial capacity, and in April 1978 the British government first sold the Hawk 'trainer'. As BAe's own press release of the time boasted:

> An overriding factor which will always determine whether an air offensive is a success or a failure is the quantity of ordnance that can be delivered accurately on to a target in a given time, and the cost of meeting this objective. Many of today's aircraft by very reason of their sophistication and complexity suffer not only from high initial cost but also from low cost effectiveness with long turn around times, protracted times to rectify defects and low percentage probabilities of successfully completing a mission.
>
> The 'Hawk' reverses this process. Its low initial cost and excellent design philosophy, which make minimum times on the ground possible, coupled with its impresive endurance/radius of action and weapon carriage capability make the Hawk an ideal ground attack aircraft.[89]

As the press release went on to note: 'Where Hawks have been acquired in the training version only ... they can be modified on site to the five pylon ground attack standard.' It would appear that Indonesia's Hawks underwent this conversion. Indeed, in the Indonesian Air Force 'Order of Battle', they are listed in the 'fighter-attack' rather than 'trainer' category, and are based at the Ishwahyudi military airbase near Madiun in East Java, from where East Timor is easily within range. Indeed, this is the very airbase from where the 1975 aerial invasion was launched.[90]

In November 1994 José Ramos-Horta issued a statement which included the following observation:

> I want to make it clear that Hawk ground attack/'trainer' aircraft fitted with missiles have been used in East Timor regularly since 1983. Hawk aircraft were first used in East Timor in the Summer of 1983, more precisely in August 1983, when the then Indonesian armed forces chief, Gen. Benny Murdani, announced a new military offensive after a three-month cease-fire negotiated by Xanana Gusmao, Leader of the East Timorese Resistance, and the East Timor Indonesian Army Commander, Col. Purwanto. The cease-fire was unilaterally broken by the Indonesians who thought that they could wipe out the resistance with the new aircraft they acquired.
>
> The 1983 offensive involved 20,000 Indonesian troops ... Two Hawk aircraft were used daily for almost six months. Hundreds of civilians and guerilla fighters were killed during that period. The Hawks, armed with missiles, were used in three main areas of East Timor: in the Same–Ainaro–Maubisse mountainous triangle in the centre of the country, in the Lauten–Lospalos–Tutuala corridor in the far east and in the Matebian mountain range between these two.[91]

In 1983, the Timorese resistance operated in units numbering approximately 100 and the Hawks had a key role in the Indonesian effort to break these units into smaller groups. According to Ramos-Horta, along with US Broncos and French Puma and Allouette helicopters, the Hawks were responsible for the deaths of hundreds of civilians between 1983 and 1986. Furthermore, it was claimed that during August and September 1994, two Hawks carried out at least six bombing raids in the eastern region of East Timor, and that in the latter quarter of 1994 Hawks made frequent raids, averaging six sorties a day. Both of these latter attacks took place well over a year after assurances had been sought that the aircraft would not be used over East Timor.

The intention of the Major government in apparently extracting promises from the Indonesians about the uses to which Hawks would or would not be put was not to guarantee an end to their use over East Timor, but to legitimise the continuation of their export in the face of widespread criticism. The assurances were sought as a convenient alibi with which the Major government sought to absolve itself of any responsibility for the manner of their use. However, even at the time, government assurances acknowledged that no comprehensive monitoring took place. For instance, in June 1994, Jonathan Aitken replied to a parliamentary question by admitting that:

> The United Kingdom could not monitor the use of these aircraft on a regular basis. But the Government have made clear their concerns and have received an assurance from the Indonesian Government that the Hawks will not be used against civilians. Staff from the British embassy in Indonesia regularly visit East Timor, as do representatives of various

human rights organisations. We have no reports from these visitors of Hawk sightings there, either in the air or on the ground.[92]

The truth of the matter was that comprehensive monitoring would be time-consuming and costly, and that it was not in the government's interest to spend money proving allegations that could lead to the cancellation of valuable arms contracts. In 1999, the Labour government came closer to admitting this truth : 'Post-export verification and monitoring is highly resource-intensive, and often requires a degree of technical expertise on the part of those carrying it out. Even if evidence of diversion is uncovered, the Government's only recourse is to take this fact into account when making future licensing decisions.'[93]

The value of Indonesia's assurances was further called into question by the observations of the highly respected journalist Hugh O'Shaughnessy. On 12 November 1995 he wrote an article from West Timor, telling of how, while he had been in East Timor on 10 November – the fourth anniversary of the 1991 massacre at Dili – two Hawk aircraft 'in close formation swooped low over Dili'.[94] Clearly, this represented a violation of the 'assurances' given by the Indonesians to the British government – and consistently invoked in Parliament – that they would not be used in this way. A few hours after this sighting, O'Shaughnessy was expelled from East Timor.

Table 9
Customers for the BAe Hawk, as of 1998

Abu Dhabi	38
Australia	33
Canada	18
Dubai	9
Finland	57
Indonesia	60
Kenya	12
Kuwait	12
Malaysia	28
Oman	16
RAF	176
Saudi Arabia	50
Switzerland	20
South Korea	20
United States	172
Zimbabwe	13
Total	734

Source François Prins, 'BAe Hawk', Air Forces Monthly, April 1998, p. 37.

In response to a question on the sighting from Lord Avebury, Baroness Chalker told the House of Lords, 'we have no evidence to support allegations that Hawk aircraft overflew Dili on Friday 10th November [1995]. Various enquiries were made of confidential sources which it would not be proper to disclose.'[95] The Indonesian government also formally denied that the flight occurred. This was good news for BAe, as it was again completing negotiations on a pre-election contract to sell yet more Hawks to Indonesia. The following year it announced the new deal: to supply a further 16 Hawk 200 ground attack fighters, in a deal estimated by SIPRI to be worth US$266 million, and bringing the total number of Hawks supplied to Indonesia to 60 – more than to any other single country except the US.

As the 1990s wore on, Britain's relations with Indonesia became an increasing embarrassment, leaving Britain, alongside Australia, Suharto's leading supporter internationally, and as such increasingly isolated. This isolation became even more apparent when the Clinton administration was obliged to distance itself somewhat from Suharto, particularly in restricting the supply of arms (for example, refusing Jordan's request to be allowed to sell-on F-5E fighters, leading instead to further Hawk purchases). These restrictions by the US obliged the Major government to explain that the continued supply of arms was a wiser course than discontinuation.[96] In subsequent questioning it stuck to the formula that 'we have not supplied any military equipment to Indonesia which is likely to be used for repressive purposes against the civilian population in East Timor'.[97] In the wake of the Indonesian repression in East Timor of the early 1990s, the Conservative government even claimed that 'the human rights situation in East Timor continues steadily to improve',[98] an assertion which could only possibly have been true if November 1991, the month of the Dili massacre, had been taken as the base month, and one not even remotely supported by the US State Department's annual human rights reports.

Another area of deep embarrassment lay in the fact that, in preparing to invade East Timor in 1975, the Indonesian armed forces had murdered two British citizens – Brian Peters and Malcolm Rennie – along with the rest of the Australian television crew to which they were attached, in particularly horrific fashion. Answers to parliamentary questions on this ranged from 'we pressed the Indonesians for information at the time'[99] to answers which deliberately avoided any indication that Rennie and Peters were UK citizens. For example, in reply to one 1995 question, Alistair Goodlad explained that: 'We have no plans to institute an inquiry. The Australians took the lead at the time in investigating the deaths of five members of an Australian television team working in East Timor ... In view of the circumstances then prevailing in East Timor, there was no means of ascertaining the precise circumstances in which they died.'[100]

This latter assertion was untrue; Goodlad could have read for himself the detailed reconstruction of events based on first-hand testimony put together by John Pilger.[101]

Nevertheless, arms contracts continued to be signed. In June 1994 Alvis announced a US$10 million deal to supply upgrade kits for its Saladin, Saracen and Ferret armoured vehicles (subsequent British government statements which implied that, because these vehicles were originally exported during the 1960s, they were practically antique and therefore not nearly as repressive as newer equipment, failed to mention this point), while its Helio Mirror Company subsidiary also won an armoured vehicle upgrade order, valued at $4.1 million.[102]

Having ordered the Alvis Scorpion in 1995,[103] the following year Indonesia awarded Alvis a second contract for a further 50 Scorpions, with Indonesia keen for approval to be pushed through before the imminent general election. Initially, Indonesian assurances as to their end use had provided a convenient alibi for the government, as in this letter from the DTI:

> A wide range of factors are taken into account in assessing an export licence application, including the capability of the equipment and any assurances we may have received about the intended end use. Critical to our considerations is an assessment of whether the equipment is likely to be used for internal repression. In the case of Indonesia, our assessment takes account of the likely use of our equipment for internal repression in East Timor ...
>
> We are ready, where necessary, to ask recipient countries on a confidential basis, about the location and use of defence equipment to be supplied ... the Indonesian Government has given assurances that the Scorpion armoured cars ... would not be deployed in East Timor nor used in any form of internal repression of the civilian population anywhere in Indonesia. We have no reason to doubt the Indonesian Government's assurance.[105]

But how did the government reconcile granting an export licence for this order (prudently secured well before the deal was publicised) with the fact that, despite such assurances, previously licensed Saracen armoured vehicles were used to break up student demonstrations in April 1996? According to Jeremy Hanley at the FCO: 'We have investigated the reports of the April 1996 incident in South Sulawesi and have discussed it with the Indonesian authorities. The Indonesians have themselves acknowledged that the way in which this equipment was used was inappropriate, and a number of soldiers have been tried and sentenced for excessive use of force.'[105] Yet he ended by falling back on the very assurances which the incident had suggested to be unreliable, saying that: 'We have received assurances from the Indonesian authorities that British supplied military equipment will not be used against civilians in Indonesia or East Timor.'

Indonesia's pre-election rush was completed with an order for 303 Tactica armoured vehicles, produced by Glover Webb in Southampton, a subsidiary of GKN Defence, and deployed by the British army in Northern Ireland. Foreign Secretary Malcolm Rifkind assured Sir David Steel that 'thorough assessments were made of the likelihood of this equipment being used for internal repression in Indonesia or East Timor. We concluded that it was not likely that they would be so used.'[106] Once more, this begged the questions of why Indonesia needed the vehicles and of the competence of those making the thorough assessments. In any case, Tactica vehicles were soon being deployed against civilians. In June 1996, they were used on pro-democracy demonstrators during a rally in Jakarta. During the demonstration at least three people were killed and 80 injured. Photographic evidence of their use was smuggled out of Indonesia and even appeared in the UK media.[107] For once, statements to the effect that the incident had been investigated but no evidence found were not an option. Instead, the FCO suggested that 'although the use of water cannon to stop violent demonstrations and riots must be preferable to the use of live ammunition, they can be dangerous and should not be used indiscriminately. We have ensured that [the Indonesian government] are well aware of our concern that such UK-supplied equipment should not be used to disperse peaceful demonstrations in violation of the universal rights of freedom of speech, organisation and assembly.'[108] However, the FCO did concede that 'Water cannon do not fall within the category of equipment for which we have obtained specific assurances from the Indonesian authorities.'[109] For GKN the matter was simpler. 'If you were in a crowd situation,' asked GKN's Head of Public Affairs, 'would you not prefer that the authorities used water as an early means of attempting to disperse or control the crowd, rather than more injurious or lethal means?'[110]

The continued training of Indonesian officers also proved controversial. To take just one example, perhaps the most notorious case of Indonesian officers attending courses at the UK taxpayer's expense has been that of Major General Mohammad Yunus Yosfiah. In 1989 he was a student at the Royal College of Defence Studies in London. But in 1975 he was the commander of the unit of the Indonesian Korps Marinier which, on 16 October 1975, murdered five journalists – including Brian Peters and Malcolm Rennie – in the East Timorese village of Balibó.[111] One well-worn argument has been that training allows beneficial exposure to Western notions of human rights, leading to fewer abuses. There is certainly a need for this, as the post-Dili massacre comments of General Try Sutrisno – subsequently made Vice-President – indicate. 'These ill-bred people,' he explained, 'have to be shot ... and we will shoot them.'[112]

In the aftermath of the Pergau Dam affair, the National Audit Office (NAO) investigated allegations of a link between aid and arms sales to Indonesia – a further embarrassment. Already, in September 1995, Labour MP Ann Clwyd had produced a detailed report on the aid–arms link regarding Indonesia, concluding that the government's 'continuing claim that there is no link between aid and arms sales is sophistry of the worst kind', and providing a framework for the NAO inquiry.[113] At the root of this lay the unavoidable fact that Indonesia was hardly one of the world's poorest countries – in 1994 it was ranked the fifty-fifth poorest.[114] Despite this, in 1993/94 Indonesia was the eighth largest recipient of UK aid, in 1994–95 the fifth largest. Between 1984 and 1993/94 it was the third largest recipient of the commercially motivated ATP funding, after China and Malaysia.[115] Furthermore, peaks in the provision of aid to Indonesia (especially ATP funding) coincided with negotiations on arms packages in 1982, 1984–85 and 1992–93. If there was no link, there was a remarkable chain of coincidence. Moreover, the projects which had been funded in Indonesia clearly had little to do with poverty relief and, in the best traditions of Pergau-style diplomacy, more to do with cultivating closer links between decision-makers in the Indonesian military and police and the UK.

The release of the NAO report was delayed at least three times as the government sought to time publication so as to minimise the impact of its findings. It was finally published in November 1996. Although it did not conclude that there was a direct link between aid and arms, it was clear that the types of projects funded had more to do with internal security than benefiting the local population – the intent behind all Overseas Development Administration (ODA) aid. For example, a police training programme was one of the projects funded. As the report noted: 'The Foreign Office, in providing support for the police training project, stressed how it hoped Indonesia would look to the UK for future defence equipment purchases.' It went on to say that: 'The close association between the Indonesian police force and the military establishment was felt by the Foreign Office to play a crucial role on future decisions by Indonesia on military procurement.' The ODA had decided to go ahead with this project despite human rights concerns, as these were 'outweighed by the potential developmental, political and commercial benefits' that would accrue from the project.[116] The report also noted how the British ambassador in Jakarta believed that not agreeing to release aid money for television and radio projects 'could have an effect on potential defence and commercial sales then being negotiated'.[117] As Robin Cook noted at the time, 'it is very difficult to ignore the pattern that is beginning to emerge. In a number of countries, big rises in aid to them have been followed by big arms orders by them.'[118] Also of concern, given the British government's formal position over East Timor, was the fact that the government had chosen to fund three projects in support of transmigration, the process of transferring Indonesians to East Timor – one of a number of means by which the Indonesians sought to impose their (Muslim) culture on that of (Catholic) East Timor, and in the medium

term reduce the indigenous Timorese to a minority, by which time a referendum on the question of East Timor's sovereignty might well have
produced the 'right' result.

A PAC report into 'Aid to Indonesia', finally published in January
1998, was heavily critical of the appraisal of projects funded under the
ATP prior to 1993. It concluded: 'We note the [Overseas Development]
Administration's assurance that the representations made to them by the
Foreign and Commonwealth Office, and by the British Ambassador in
Jakarta, about the potential benefits to defence and other UK business,
had no impact on their decisions about the provision of aid; and that these
decisions were not rushed through in order to secure defence contracts.'[119]
In practice, of course, acceptance of these assurances would not have been
compatible with the committee's criticisms of the inadequate appraisal of
key projects. Far from resulting in improvements in the observance of
human rights, the PAC report also noted how the police management
training programme was moved out of the UK's Bramshill Police Staff
College, at the insistence of the Home Office, and conducted in Indonesia
because of fears of the possible complicity of Indonesian police oficers in
extra-judicial killings.

Malaysia: alms for arms' sake

As with other major importer countries in the region, Malaysia, a country
to which Britain had exported arms moderately during the 1970s (exporting US$168 million worth of major conventional arms), took on increased
importance as a market under the Thatcher governments, although this
was not reflected in the value of deliveries until the Major years. Between
1990 and 1997, once these deliveries were under way, Malaysia became
the second largest customer for major British arms, after Saudi Arabia,
importing US$1,624 million worth. As with Indonesia, its importation of
weaponry came to be out of all proportion to any external threat.
Together with Indonesia, by the end of the Thatcher era Malaysia had
become a market of central importance to the British defence industry,
and particularly the continued health of BAe. Indeed, the government estimated that between 1989 and 1993 contracts worth in excess of £1 billion
were negotiated.[120] However, in the wake of the revelations about British
government connivance in clandestinely exporting arms to Iraq, the
government's role in promoting the sale of arms to Malaysia came under
renewed (and unwelcome) attention and official investigation in 1993 and
1994. At the risk of mixing metaphors, it became apparent that 'batting
for Britain' in Malaysia had not always involved playing by the
Queensbury Rules.

From the 1950s onwards, Britain conducted a steady military trade in naval vessels, armoured vehicles, missiles and aircraft with Malaysia. The growth of this trade in the 1980s was linked with the Malaysian armament programme of 1981–85, aimed at achieving a £2 billion expansion of Malaysia's military capability.[121] Britain was keen to capitalise on this, and in 1981 Defence Minister Lord Trenchard, the head of the DSO, Sir Ronald Ellis, and Defence Secretary John Nott were all despatched to Malaysia in an effort to sell aircraft and naval equipment. The visits came in the wake of a January 1981 package of interest-free loans and ECGD-backed credits worth £77 million over three years. At the same time, British companies were also bidding for the contract to build two new military bases – one for the Malaysian navy at Lumur, the other for the air force at Gong Kedak.

Progress on these fronts was, however, disrupted by Malaysian Prime Minister Dr Mahathir Mohamed's October 1981 'Buy British Last' proclamation – the decree that henceforth Malaysian government departments would have to submit all British tenders to his office, from where they would have to compete with a second, non-British tender. Mahathir termed it a policy of not buying British 'if we can help it'.[122]

While the long-term cause of this move seems to have been bitterness over the high tariffs and quotas imposed by the West on goods from developing countries like Malaysia,[123] the more immediate cause was Mrs Thatcher's 1979 decision to end subsidies on fees for foreign students in Britain, at a time when 20 per cent of Malaysia's university students studied in Britain. The stand-off jeopardised British companies' chances of winning defence contracts under Malaysia's £2 billion expansion programme.

However, a suggestion that the trade crisis might not spread quite that far came in December 1981, when a letter of intent was signed between Alvis and Malaysia for 51 Scorpion armoured vehicles, with an option on a further 30, in a deal worth £24 million. It was signed after the Malaysian government had already ordered £50 million worth of Belgian armoured vehicles, but suggested that, despite the boycott, Malaysia would not automatically look to change its sources of supply. Much existing defence equipment had been supplied by Britain, making a complete shift of supplier problematic.

The trade boycott was finally overcome when, in February 1983, Foreign Secretary Francis Pym removed its immediate cause, by announcing a £46 million scheme to create 6,000 scholarships for overseas students. A further signal that the freeze in relations (which had resulted in a 15 per cent drop in British exports to Malaysia in 1982) was over came with Mahathir's official visit to London in March 1983, where he met Mrs Thatcher and signed a contract for £14 million worth of British lorries for the Malaysian Defence Forces, and a £200 million contract with an Italian subsidiary of GEC. This was followed up in December

1983 by a visit to Kuala Lumpur by Under-Secretary of State for Defence Procurement Ian Stewart, who discussed the possible sale of Sea Harriers and Lynx helicopters ahead of the arrival of a floating exhibition aboard a RN aircraft carrier in October 1983.

Between 1984 and 1988, the value of British arms deals secured with Malaysia was put at £25.7 million, including a 1987 order for ex-RN Westland Wasp helicopters,[124] rumoured to have been sold at a knock-down price as a 'sweetener' for the sale of the Tornado, although the MoD denied this.[125]

By 1988 the trade rift of the early part of the decade had been healed by a succession of Ministerial and governmental visits to Kuala Lumpur, including one by Mrs Thatcher in 1985, and by Malaysian officials to London, including a further one by Mahathir in 1988. These also paved the way for the huge 1988 Malaysian defence order. In March 1988, Defence Secretary George Younger visited Kuala Lumpur for the Defence Services Asia Exhibition, and for further negotiations on the prospective order, which was set to include Tornado aircraft, submarines and artillery. At this point, the main elements of the proposed Anglo-Malaysian defence package comprised 12 Tornadoes (worth a reported £500 million); 12 Rapier air defence missile systems, two Marconi Martello 3-D radar systems (worth £145 million), 30 VSEL FH-70 155 mm howitzers, 20 Royal Ordnance 105 mm light guns, Plessey radio and sonar equipment, one refurbished *Oberon* class submarine and 48 Short Javelin ground-to-air missile launchers. It was also during this visit that Younger agreed to sign a protocol which complied with Malaysia's requirement that arms orders should be linked with future aid provision, and as such was at the root of the subsequent Pergau Dam controversy.

In June 1988, as negotiations were nearing completion, the Malaysian Defence Minister, Abdullah Ahmad Badauri, headed a high-level delegation to the BAEE at Aldershot. In August, Mrs Thatcher stopped off in Kuala Lumpur for two hours *en route* from Australia to Thailand to finalise the deal. When, in September, a government-backed global sales campaign, Golden Eagle, was launched, made up of an RAF Tornado team backed up by BAe and Rolls-Royce representatives, Malaysia was one of the stops it made.

As in the contemporaneous Al Yamamah deal, the contract would be accompanied by a British commitment to invest in Malaysia. Just as BAe emerged as the prime contractor on Al Yamamah, GEC was set to play the same role in Malaysia, with the British government again acting as lead contractor. However, the Malaysian government was also keen to secure further concessions from Britain before signing, the most important of which was to involve linkage with the question of landing rights for the Malaysian national airline, MAS (Malaysian Airlines System) at Heathrow Airport.

On 24 September 1988, Mahathir arrived in London for a four-day visit to hold talks with Mrs Thatcher and conclude the defence deal. The memorandum of understanding was signed at Downing Street by Mrs Thatcher, rather than at Defence Secretary level, as is customary, on 27 September and was estimated to be worth around £1.5 billion.[126] By 1993, the government estimated, the memorandum of understanding had resulted in the signing of contracts worth over £16 billion.[127] However, the following year this wildly optimistic figure had been revised to £1 billion.[128] The signing of the memorandum of understanding also coincided with an increase in the value of British exports to Malaysia, which, by 1992, were more than double their 1988 value (Table 10).

Table 10
Value of UK exports to Malaysia, 1982–92

Year	£m
1982	210.6
1983	248.3
1984	283.1
1985	281.7
1986	226.9
1987	258.0
1988	310.4
1989	441.5
1990	550.7
1991	582.3
1992	635.9

Source Hansard, 31 January 1994, col. 588w.

The scale and scope of the arms deal served to tie Malaysia firmly to Britain for its core defence needs, and in so doing the UK replaced France and the US as the country's major supplier. Again, as with Al Yamamah, in addition to the purchase of weaponry, British construction companies were invited to bid for several large construction projects to build military bases. The deal also paved the way for long-term co-operation and a degree of technology transfer. To oversee the contracts placed under the memorandum of understanding, a Malaysian Project Office was opened, comprising 22 staff – 10 based in London and 12 in Malaysia.[129]

Payment would be made partly in oil, natural gas and other products, like palm oil, tin and rubber goods, with instalments spread over at least 10 years. The Thatcher government's willingness to embrace counter-trade to this extent was an important factor in securing the deal, especially where the French had shown themselves to be similarly flexible. As the

Malaysian Deputy Defence Minister observed: 'It was particularly important for us to upgrade our air defence role but we were also interested in
a single package, government to government. The UK made us an attractive offer, both in the suitability of equipment and the aspect of
counter-trade.'[130] However, as with Al Yamamah, the nature of the agreement meant that the final package would be subject to expansion or
contraction (in the event, the reality) depending on the performance of the
Malaysian economy.

The fact that at the time of the deal the Malaysian Air Force was largely
equipped with dated US aircraft helps explain why Malaysia ordered the
Tornado. The deal was a prestige purchase, an act of national self-aggran-
disement, consistent with Mahathir's vision of Malaysia's standing as a
regional power. The Tornado had just been ordered by Saudi Arabia,
whose choices were influential across the developing world, given that the
Saudis could afford whatever they wanted, and also by Jordan and Oman,
but beyond these orders no country outside the Panavia consortium had
the aircraft at that time.

However, the issue of landing rights for MAS threatened to sabotage
the entire deal. Following the signing of the memorandum of understanding, British Airways (BA) and MAS failed to reach agreement. As a result,
Kuala Lumpur sent clear signals to the British government that it could
look elsewhere for its defence needs unless it were allowed to increase the
frequency of MAS Boeing 747 flights from Kuala Lumpur to London from
five to seven per week.[131] This was not viewed as an idle threat, as
Dassault had proposed the sale of the Mirage 2000 in a counter-trade deal
along the same lines as the British proposal. Hence while a Department of
Transport official was quoted as saying that 'there is no way that an arms
sale can be linked to landing rights', by 15 March 1989 MAS had been
granted the increase it had sought from five to seven flights, and Mrs
Thatcher even paid a 'courtesy visit' on Mahathir, who was on a private
visit to London, to confirm that there were now no further barriers to the
deal, as outlined in the memorandum, going ahead.[132]

However, following this settlement, Malaysia proceeded to reduce the
size of its arms order, a move which came at a bad time for the British
government. While the deal had been intended to blaze a path for the sale
of the Tornado throughout South East Asia, instead it was merely adding
to a growing problem, following decisions by Oman and Jordan to 'postpone' their planned Tornado purchases. Mahathir reduced the Tornado
order from 12 to eight and excluded the Rapier missile system from the
final package completely, while some artillery is also thought to have been
cancelled.[133] The government responded with an intense lobbying effort,
accompanied by strict instructions to the companies involved to maintain
complete secrecy about what they were or were not selling. In March
1989, Defence Secretary George Younger was despatched to Kuala

Lumpur, where he was able to secure agreement on 'the projects to be afforded first priority in the programme'.[134]

This episode nicely illustrates two characteristics of the contemporary arms trade. Firstly, large packages framed by memoranda of understanding can generate false expectations. This is itself an expression of the uncertainty that pervades the arms business, where changes in any one of a range of circumstances can lead to orders – which necessarily have long lead times – being cut or cancelled. The fulfilment of a deal as large as the proposed Malaysian one was clearly dependent on the continued economic and political well-being of the recipient. If, at any time during the at least 10 years that the deal was projected to run, the Malaysian economy began to under-perform for a sustained period, elements of the deal would be vulnerable to trimming in response, regardless of what stage production was at. This principle remains true even where counter-trade is involved. Uncertainty – also vividly illustrated over the serial scares over the future of Al Yamamah during the 1990s – is a defining feature of the international arms trade. Secondly, the episode also shows how striking a large package deal can be beneficial to the recipient, as it offers considerable scope for manipulation, as the continual threat of withdrawal or trimming is used as a bargaining chip. Clearly, this has major foreign policy implications.

The Malaysian case is also instructive, as it graphically illustrates how far the Thatcher governments were willing to go in using the overseas aid budget as a means of securing an arms deal, in this particular case, reportedly at the Prime Minister's personal insistence.[135] While Downing Street strongly denied any connection, and the government continued to deny there was any link between aid and arms,[136] there was at the very least a striking coincidental correlation. As the government was left clinging to a spurious distinction between 'entanglement' and 'linkage', Whitehall sources told the *Observer* newspaper that talks on a £100 million aid package had coincided with the signing of the memorandum of understanding in September 1988, adding that: 'If the Malaysians want to make the connection they can, but we do not.'[137] In 1994, Douglas Hurd presented the government's account of events thus:

> During discussions in 1988 about the proposed memorandum of understanding on defence sales, the Malaysians expressed their wish to make a reference to aid. A protocol was signed during the visit to Kuala Lumpur in March 1988 by the then Defence Secretary ... Lord Younger of Prestwick. This set out the Malaysian Government's intention to buy defence equipment from the United Kingdom ... The protocol included a reference to 'aid in support of non-military aspects under this programme'.
>
> After consultation with ministerial colleagues in London, the Secretary of State for Defence wrote to the Malaysian Minister of Finance in June 1988 to say that aid could not be linked to defence sales. As a result the issue was

not taken up in the memorandum of understanding on defence procurement which the British and Malaysian Prime Ministers signed in September 1988, and which did not cover aid. Our aid programme is not linked to arms sales.[138]

What Hurd did not say was that on the same day that Younger sent his letter (28 June) making it clear that aid could not formally be linked with arms sales, Sir Nicholas Spreckley, High Commissioner to Malaysia, also wrote to the Finance Minister assuring him that £200 million would be made available for aid projects. This ingenious 'separate but parallel' diplomacy meant that while a letter was sent in Younger's name explaining that 'the linkage of aid to projects was governed by international rules which would preclude the sort of arrangement which the Malaysian Minister of Finance had seemed to envisage', a letter in Spreckley's name was sent out confirming the provision of up to £200 million for developmental projects.

Strictly speaking, in so doing aid was, as Hurd contended, 'delinked', but the informal link was confirmed. Originally, Younger had agreed to a formula whereby up to 20 per cent of the price of the defence package agreed under the memorandum of understanding would be made available in overseas aid. The new arrangement was designed to secure this linkage while at the same time eliminating it from the memorandum, not remove it *per se*.[139]

Younger subsequently echoed the understanding of Malaysian politicians in conceding that: 'Each side had its own perception of whether there was linkage, and each was happy to keep its own perception', and that the 'British refused to make a connection but the Malaysians said there would be no military contract without the aid project'.[140] Spreckley recalled that: 'We were, I think, all of us, to varying degrees pretty convinced that if we showed hesitation then this deal would start to fall apart. I think it is well worth bearing in mind that we were talking as a result of what the Malaysians had said to us ... not only about £1 billion worth of arms sales and defence orders, we were also talking about the prospect of many hundreds of millions of pounds worth of civil orders which the Malaysians were prepared to put our way.'[141] Hence Douglas Hurd and John Major's 1991 insistence, at a time when lucrative arms contracts still had to be finalised, that £234 million in concessional loans should be provided for the Pergau Dam project, despite the objections of officials like Sir Tim Lankester, Permanent Secretary of the ODA.

In the wake of the arms-to-Iraq revelations, with arms sales issues more contentious and stoking greater than usual parliamentary interest, the FAC investigated the affair in 1994. (Mrs Thatcher declined to appear, on the spurious grounds that former Prime Ministers did not appear before select committees to give evidence on specific issues.[142]) Despite a wealth of evidence suggesting a link between aid provision and arms sales to

Indonesia, Jordan, Thailand and Oman, in its report (by coincidence, a Cabinet reshuffle took place on the day of its release, taking attention away from it) it concluded that the 1988 Younger Protocol with Malaysia was 'the only instance of which we were aware where the policy proscribing conditional linkage between defence exports and the aid and trade provision has been breached'.[143]

However, during the Thatcher years there does appear to have been a clear statistical correlation between states negotiating large arms deals and contemporaneous increases in bilateral aid to those states. As Table 11 indicates, bilateral aid to Oman, Indonesia, Malaysia, Jordan, Thailand, and Ecuador in particular increased over a 10-year period well in excess of the average increase in all UK bilateral aid during the same period, and at the same time that major arms packages based around memoranda of understandings were being negotiated.

Table 11
Growth in bilateral aid to major purchasers of British arms

Country	UK bilateral aid increase 1980–82 to 1990/91–92/93 (%)	UK arms sales 1988–92 US$ million	Rank
Average all	62		
Bilateral aid			
Saudi Arabia	0	3,116	1
India	14	1,044	2
Oman	75	367	3
Indonesia	111	201	4
Ecuador	267	193	5
Thailand	189	167	6
Pakistan	76	158	7
Chile	−47	141	8
South Korea	−90	106	9
Jordan	91	81	10
Malaysia	139	78	11
Venezuela	22,800	76	12
Nigeria	222	75	13

Note Arms sales values and rankings are SIPRI's and are based on the value of deliveries of major weapons systems. The high % rise in the case of Venezuela is due to the low level of aid donated (£2,000) in the base years.
Source Memorandum submitted by the World Development Movement to the FAC, *Public Expenditure: Pergau Hydro-electric Project, Malaysia, the Aid and Trade Provision and Related Matters*, HC-271-II, p. 116.

Such use of the aid budget, though, should not necessarily come as a shock in the light of the experience of Timothy Raison, who was sacked as Minister for Overseas Aid by Mrs Thatcher. In an open letter to his successor, Chris Patten, he observed that 'there are those who see the aid budget as simply a big pot to be used for buying businesses or impressing foreign rulers', adding that 'I can't say that over-enthusiasm for the aid budget' was one of Mrs Thatcher's qualities. However, by no means everyone considered the activities of the government improper, even though their views implicitly accepted that overseas aid had been linked with arms sales. For instance, *Times* journalist Peter Riddell's view was that:

> The whole episode is less a scandal than an example of Lady Thatcher's distinctive approach to securing contracts with foreign governments, relying on personal contacts with leaders and businessmen and understandings which bound her ministers and successors. Corners may have been cut, but orders were obtained for Britain, and jobs were safeguarded.[144]

However, the Malaysian deal remained controversial in other respects. One was the compensation demanded by BA in the aftermath of the landing rights issue. This payment was understood to be in excess of £1 million, and although BA claimed that MAS were to pay it, the Malaysians denied this. In February 1994 Transport Minister Steven Norris told Parliament that no 'public funding' was involved in the new arrangement.[145] As with the sale of the Tornado elsewhere, questions were also raised about the reasons behind its relatively high unit cost, and how much of this was accounted for by commission payments. It allegedly involved an up-front payment of around £60 million to Mahathir's UMNO Baru Party, as well as a further £40 million to agents and important individuals, obviously bumping up the overall cost. In 1989, the basic cost of a Tornado was between £17 million and £20 million, depending on the equipment included. The Tornadoes being sold to Malaysia were costing around £40 million each. Some of this (around £5 million per aircraft) could legitimately be accounted for by the cost of tropicalisation of the aircraft, but there remained a significant discrepancy. As one senior Malaysian defence official noted: 'Unusual people are involved in the deal, so we must expect unusual terms.'[146] One explanation for the large commission payments centred on the poor financial position of UMNO in the run-up to an election and the need to finance its campaign. Both issues led to a series of questions in Parliament and unwelcome publicity for the deal.[147]

The Thatcher government had some justification for fearing that parliamentary criticism could jeopardise the deal. The French had shown an interest in selling the Mirage and were also making a strong pitch for the submarine contract, and in July 1989 the French navy began a month-long deployment in Malaysian waters in an attempt to persuade the Malaysians to buy their products.

In September 1989, the first contract arising from the previous year's memorandum of understanding was signed, when GEC Marconi secured contracts worth around £170 million to supply two Martello radar systems. However, the rest of the £1 billion-plus order remained unsigned. Of most concern to the government was the failure to sign contracts for the Tornado, towards the sale of which substantial commission had allegedly already been paid. Sir Michael Quinlan, Permanent Under-Secretary at the MoD, was sent to Kuala Lumpur for three days of talks on the deal in December 1989. The pressure was kept up through the efforts of the MoD and Defence Secretary Tom King, and through the display given by RAF Tornadoes at the opening of the Defence Services Asia Exhibition in Kuala Lumpur in March 1990.

The delay in signing contracts was a setback to BAe, which considered the Far East to be a key sales area. According to its officials, it had a 46 per cent share of the total Middle and Far Eastern defence market at the time.[148] The sale of the Tornado to Malaysia had been intended to open up that market even further, by providing a platform from which to sell the Tornado to neighbouring countries. However, South Korea's defence needs were largely met by the US (despite some British penetration of the market – most notably through the BAe Hawk). Neither Thailand nor Indonesia had ordered the Tornado. Although both had shown some interest they had ultimately concluded that, if anything, the Hawk would be more appropriate to their requirements. This left Malaysia as the only firm regional order, although, as time passed without contracts being signed, this became less and less certain.

By 1990, Malaysia's economic deterioration since the signing of the 1988 memorandum of understanding suggested several possible outcomes. Firstly, its air force could opt for a standard export model Tornado, less expensive than the sophisticated model it had requested. Secondly, it could seek a bigger budget. Alternatively, it could make cuts in the other project areas in order to secure the Tornado deal. Finally, it could either reduce the Tornado order, or even cancel it completely so as to be able to afford the other five remaining elements in the package. In the event, this was the chosen option. On 21 May 1990, it was announced that the Malaysian government had cancelled its proposed order for 12 Tornadoes, making it the third country to cancel an order for the aircraft (after Oman and Jordan), and leaving the Saudi order for 120 the only one outside NATO.[149]

Why did Malaysia cancel its Tornado order? Firstly, the price had spiralled out of control once extravagent commission was added, making the export model twice as expensive as the RAF model – a fact confirmed by Malaysian Defence Minister Najib Razak when he visited London in June 1991.[150] Furthermore, in terms of its role and capabilities, it was not necessarily the most appropriate choice for states like Malaysia. This recognition was partly reflected in Malaysia's immediate switching of attention to the Hawk. The cancellation also reflected a changed world situation from that which prevailed at the time of the signing of the memorandum of understanding in 1988. Since then, developments in Eastern Europe had led to a radical reassessment of Western security needs, a reassessment which percolated down to the former arenas of Cold War alliance, paranoia and conflict in the developing world.[151]

Moreover, Mrs Thatcher's changed position could have been a consideration. In the early and mid-1980s, as she toured the developing world, 'batting for Britain' and taking a very personal interest in arms sales, she dominated party, Parliament and Cabinet. This fact, and her *rapport* with President Reagan, gave an air of authority to her dealings. By mid-1990, showing poorly in opinion polls, with a general election looming, she led a party and government divided over Europe, and over which her leadership was being increasingly called into question. Her reduced authority could have made any cancellation easier, as too could the precedents set by Oman and Jordan.

The suggestion of a sale of the Hawk provided an acceptable alternative to BAe, as it would not have to share revenue as it would within the Panavia consortium. The announcement that Malaysia would purchase a combination of 100 and 200 models was made in June 1990. Mahathir stated that any replacement for the Tornado would be British so as to abide by the spirit of the 1988 memorandum of understanding, although this still left the door open for either the F-16 or Mirage 2000 to replace its 14 F-5 Tigers.[152] By mid-1990, the number of Hawk aircraft under consideration was put at 28 – 10 Hawk 100s and 18 Hawk 200s – and was being valued at around £400 million.[153] At the same time, talks began on the purchase of the BAe Sea Eagle anti-ship missile to arm the Hawks. The contract for the aircraft included provision for a £76 million offset deal, the aim of which was to enable Malaysia to service its own Hawk aircraft. Given BAe's target markets at the time for the Hawk – Saudi Arabia, Indonesia, South Korea, Brunei, Thailand and Australia – the Malaysian purchase promised to be more significant in the long term than the sale of the Tornado could possibly have been.[154]

By 1991, the only equipment from the revised memorandum of understanding still outstanding was the requirement for two frigates. In addition to this outstanding equipment order, contracts for the construction of two military bases, with related training and equipment, also remained unsigned. In June 1991, Malaysian Defence Secretary Najib Razak visited London and met Defence Secretary Tom King and Defence Minister Alan Clark. He later explained that: 'The basic purpose of the visit is to underline the firm commitment of the Malaysian government that whatever has been agreed upon will be implemented and to have further discussions with . . . contractors and the ministry of defence at official and ministerial level. The . . . nuts and bolts of the agreement will be ironed out later.'[155]

The delayed award of the frigate contract to GEC-owned Yarrow Shipbuilders was announced by Tom King at the opening of the 1991 RNEE at Portsmouth. However, the announcement was made before the contracts had actually been signed, something which had been scheduled to happen during King's trip to Malaysia later that month, and the announcement reportedly irritated the Malaysians.[156] While King had spoken of Malaysia's 'excellent vote of confidence in Britain's shipbuilding and naval equipment industries', the announcement seemed to have been timed so as to push the Malaysians into a deal they had not finally decided upon. In the event, it threatened to do the reverse. The announcement was described as a 'historic political blunder' by one defence industry source, while a GEC executive condemned King, arguing that he had acted 'for his own political reasons ... you should never announce a contract until you've got it.'[157]

Hence when King did visit Kuala Lumpur in September 1991, he was unable to make the anticipated announcement, and instead merely referred to satisfaction at the 'progress of negotiations'. However, as these negotiations progressed, BAe scored an unexpected success by having the Sea Wolf reinstated in the package at the expense of the Matra system.[158] Finally, in April 1992, the contract, complete with the Sea Wolf missile system – its first export order – was signed. It covered two 106 m 2,200 ton frigates, rather than corvettes as originally planned back in 1988, to be delivered by 1996. In addition, a ten year offset programme covering technology transfer in shipbuilding, repair and defence electronics was included.[159]

In early 1993, Malaysia ordered the Short Starburst air defence missile system in a multi-million-pound order. However, following the publicity and allegations of corruption by Malaysian politicians surrounding the Pergau Dam affair, Malaysia revived its old 'Buy British Last' policy, announcing that, although existing contracts would be honoured, no new contracts would be awarded to British companies, opening up the prospect of France, Germany and the Netherlands benefiting from the unwelcome FAC investigation – once again highlighting the incompatibility between transparency, parliamentary oversight and success in the arms trade. At the 1994 Defence Services Asia Exhibition in Kuala Lumpur, attended by 81 British companies (the largest national contingent), Lord Cranborne, Junior Defence Minister, underlined this point, arguing that 'we must not let the press come between old friends', and that it was 'there for all to see how damaging this speculation has been to British interests'.[160] Exposing corruption and illegality should be no concern of the British press, at least where arms sales were at stake.

Notes

1 Hansard, 31 January 1997, col. 419w.
2 *Ibid.*, 12 January 1993, col. 749.
3 George Kennan, 'Review of Current Trends, US Foreign Policy', cited in Constâncio Pinto and Matthew Jardine, *East Timor's Unfinished Struggle: Inside the Timorese Resistance* (Boston, MA, South End Press, 1997), p. 19.
4 PRO: CAB 131/14, 'Defence in South-East Asia', Memorandum for Cabinet Defence Committee, 3 December 1954.
5 See Paul Lashmar and James Oliver, *Britain's Secret Propaganda War 1948–1977* (Stroud, Sutton Publishing, 1998), ch. 1.
6 Kathy Kadane, 'Ex-agent says CIA compiled death lists for Indonesians', *San Francisco Examiner*, 20 May 1990.
7 *New York Times*, 6 December 1975.
8 ITV, *Network First*, 'Death of a Nation', 22 February 1994. At the time, *The Economist* noted that 'a left-wing Timor, which could serve as a base for communist subversion and arms smuggling, was considered intolerable'. *Economist*, 13 December 1975, p. 20.
9 Daniel Patrick Moynihan with Suzanne Weaver, *A Dangerous Place* (London, Secker & Warburg, 1979), p. 247.
10 Mark Curtis, *The Ambiguities of Power: British Foreign Policy since 1945* (London, Zed Books, 1995). Also, Mark Curtis, 'Anglo-Indonesian Relations and British Foreign Policy', paper presented to a seminar on UK/Indonesian Relations, South Bank University, 13 July 1996.
11 SIPRI database. The US supplied only slightly more, $538 million worth, during the same period. Next largest suppliers were the Netherlands ($455 million) and West Germany ($11 million).
12 Addressing the UNSC on 15 December 1975, the Portuguese representative, Galvão Teles, estimated the population at 650,000. UN Security Council Official Records, 1864th Meeting, 15 December 1975, p. 6. The figure of 60,000 deaths was given by José Ramos Horta to the UNSC, UN Security Council Official Records, 1908th Meeting, 12 April 1976, p. 2. At the time, a former Australian consul to East Timor, James Dunn, called this 'an atrocity against a people, ranking with such crimes as the rape of Nanking and the wanton killings by Nazis in the occupied States of Europe during the Second World War'. *Ibid.*, p. 4. Dunn later wrote *Timor: A People Betrayed* (Queensland, Jacaranda Press, 1983).
13 Figures are from IISS, *The 1998 Chart of Armed Conflict*, 1 August 1998.
14 There were a number of major arms contracts signed in the 1950s. In 1953 Britain sold 10 Cessna 180 aircraft, in 1955 15 Alvis Saracen armoured vehicles, followed up in 1958 by 30 Alvis Ferrets and in 1960 by 15 Saladins. Throughout the 1960s, there existed a steady trade in naval equipment.
15 Letter to Lord Avebury, 19 June 1978, quoted in Helen Collinson, *Death on Delivery: The Impact of the Arms Trade on the Third World* (London, CAAT, 1989), p. 70.
16 BAe advertisement, *Flight International*, 4 March 1978.
17 Hansard, 19 October 1981, col. 75.
18 *Guardian*, 26 July 1980.
19 Letter from Lord Belstead to Terry Davis, MP, 29 December 1982.
20 Letter from South East Asian Department, FCO, 11 April 1986.
21 See, for example, Hansard, 24 June 1993, col. 276.
22 *Tapol Bulletin*, No. 55, 1983.
23 *J.D.W.*, 22 December 1984.
24 *Financial Times*, 3 January 1985.
25 *Ibid.*

26 *Guardian*, 10 April 1985.
27 Thatcher, *The Downing Street Years*, p. 503.
28 *Guardian*, 11 April 1985.
29 *Ibid.*
30 *Financial Times*, 12 April 1985.
31 Anthony Jay (ed.), *The Oxford Dictionary of Political Quotations* (Oxford, Oxford University Press, 1996), p. 73.
32 *Guardian*, 12 April 1985.
33 *Ibid.*, 12 February 1994.
34 *Ibid.*, 10 April 1985.
35 Thatcher, *The Downing Street Years*, p. 503.
36 *Jakarta Post*, 18 July 1985.
37 *Financial Times*, 8 July 1985.
38 *Ibid.*
39 *Ibid.*
40 BAe news release, 16 December 1985.
41 See *Guardian*, 16 January 1986.
42 *J.D.W.*, 24 April 1986.
43 *Financial Times*, 3 December 1986.
44 *Tapol Bulletin*, April 1987.
45 *Financial Times*, 11 November 1987.
46 This latter agreement, reached in July 1986, involved Britain providing up to £140m credit over three years at 3 per cent.
47 *British Aerospace News*, August 1988, p. 1.
48 By this time, France was pushing the Mirage to partner Indonesia's F-16s.
49 *J.D.W.*, 29 June 1991.
50 Letter from John Major to Lord Avebury, 23 July 1991.
51 For example, Hansard, 10 February 1993, col. 977, and 16 June 1993, col. 847. See also *Independent*, 28 December 1991.
52 Hansard, 15 January 1992, col. 584.
53 *Independent*, 6 February 1992.
54 *First Tuesday*, 'In Cold Blood: The Massacre of East Timor'.
55 Quoted in *Independent*, 17 February 1992.
56 'Death of a Nation', *Network First*, ITV, 22 February 1994. Also cited on *Channel 4 News*, 22 February 1994.
57 Letter from South East Asian Department, FCO, 22 June 1994.
58 Hansard (Lords), 19 February 1992.
59 *Channel 4 News*, 22 February 1994.
60 *J.D.W.*, 20 November 1996.
61 Hansard, 23 October 1992, col. 404w.
62 *Ibid.*, 8 February 1995, col. 319w.
63 *Ibid.*, 28 October 1992, col. 1012.
64 *Guardian*, 17 June 1992.
65 See John Major's reply, Hansard, 5 November 1992, col. 336w. See also col. 545w.
66 *Ibid.*, 18 January 1995, col. 497w.
67 *Ibid.*, 24 January 1995, col. 140.
68 *Ibid.*, 10 February 1993, col. 976.
69 For example, see Hansard 17 March 1994, col. 804w; 28 March 1994, col. 544w; 31 March 1994, col. 1019w. In this latter instance it declined to hazard a guess at the number of political prisoners held in East Timor on the grounds that: 'There is no agreed definition of a "political prisoner".'
70 *Ibid.*, 10 February 1993, col. 978.

71 For example, Hansard, 14 January 1994, col. 305w.
72 'Proven Hawk family looks to the future', *BAe Quarterly*, spring 1991, p. 3. These were delivered during 1996 and 1997.
73 Reuters, 7 April 1993.
74 *Hansard*, 10 June 1993, col. 430.
75 *Guardian*, 13 August 1993.
76 *Ibid.*
77 Hansard, 12 January 1993, col. 749.
78 *Ibid.*, 24 June 1993, col. 275w.
79 *Ibid.*, 9 February 1994, col. 285w.
80 Quoted in *Independent*, 23 February 1994.
81 ITV, *Network First*, 'Death of a Nation', 22 February 1994.
82 Hansard, 19 December 1994, col. 894w.
83 *Ibid.*, 2 March 1995, col. 716w.
84 See Hansard, 11 May 1995, cols 535–7w.
85 *Ibid.*, 27 January 1995, col. 449w.
86 *Ibid.*, 27 February 1995, cols 395–6w.
87 Letter, 23 May 1994.
88 Cited in John Taylor, *Indonesia's Forgotten War: The Hidden History of East Timor* (London, Zed Books, 1991), p. 87.
89 BAe press release, 5 April 1978.
90 See Hendro Subroto, 'Drop Zone Dili', *Air Forces Monthly*, January 1999, pp. 38–42.
91 José Ramos-Horta, Special Representative of the National Council of Maubere Resistance (CNRM), Lisbon, statement, 16 November 1994.
92 Hansard, 23 June 1994, col. 251w. See also 17 December 1993, col. 966w. In 1994, Alistair Goodlad told Sir Teddy Taylor: 'Obviously we cannot monitor the use of Hawk aircraft on a regular basis. But we have made clear our concerns and have an assurance from the Indonesian Government that they will not be used against civilians ... Our Embassy staff visit East Timor, as do human rights representatives ... and foreign journalists. We have no reports from these visitors of Hawk sightings – in the air or on the tarmac. It would be wrong to base, or amend, our policy on defence sales on the spurious allegations which have appeared recently in the media.' Letter, Goodlad to Taylor, 11 March 1994. In a variation on this letter, in November 1994 he added: 'Embassy staff who visit East Timor travel widely in the territory. They include our Defence Attaché who can, of course, readily identify the Hawk and other military equipment.' Letter from Alistair Goodlad, 16 November 1994. Another variation came from the FCO's South East Asian Deptartment in February 1995: 'Monitoring the human rights situation in Indonesia and East Timor is one of the priority tasks of our Embassy in Jakarta. Members of the Embassy staff visiting East Timor have seen no evidence of military aircraft in action there. Nor have they had any reports of sightings of planes in action from other Western colleagues who visit regularly, or from their extensive local contacts.' Letter from South East Asian Deptartment, FCO, 2 February 1995.
93 TISC, *Government Observations on the Second Report from the Committee (Session 1998–99) on Strategic Export Controls*, Fourth Special Report, Session 1998–99, Appendix, p. 6.
94 *Independent on Sunday*, 12 November 1995.
95 Hansard (Lords), 11 March 1996, col. 43w.
96 Hansard, 14 January 1994, col. 304.
97 *Ibid.*, 14 March 1994, col. 474w.
98 *Ibid.*, 29 March 1994, col. 617w. See also 30 March 1994, cols 806–7w.
99 *Ibid.*, 7 March 1994, col. 20w.
100 *Ibid.*, 27 February 1995, col. 394. See also, 14 March 1994, col. 473w, where the same

technique was applied. See also 23 February 1976, cols 109–10w. The situation was no different under 'New' Labour. *Ibid.*, 22 July 1999, col. 602w.

101 John Pilger, *Distant Voices* (London, Vintage, revised edition 1994), pp. 266–70. See also the account contained in Pilger's television documentary 'Death of a Nation' and the detailed account in *The Times*, 'Soldiers describe how two Britons were shot in back', 16 February 1976.
102 *Jane's Defence Contracts*, June 1994.
103 *J.D.W.*, 11 March 1995, p. 6.
104 Letter from Export Licensing Unit, DTI, 9 August 1995.
105 Hansard, 31 January 1997, cols 419–20w.
106 Letter from Malcolm Rifkind to Sir David Steel, 27 January 1997.
107 For example, *Observer*, 21 July 1996.
108 Letter from South East Asian Deptartment, FCO, 31 January 1997.
109 Letter from South East Asian Deptartment, FCO, 27 August 1996.
110 Letter from Head of Public Affairs, GKN Defence, 10 September 1996.
111 *Independent on Sunday*, 5 November 1995. See also, Shirley Shackleton, 'Planting a Tree in Balibó: a journey to East Timor', in Peter Carey and G. Carter Bentley (eds), *East Timor at the Crossroads: The Forging of a Nation* (London, Cassell, 1995), pp. 109–19.
112 Quoted in Allan Nairn, 'Free East Timor', *New York Times*, 26 October 1995.
113 Ann Clwyd, 'British aid to Indonesia: the continuing sandal', September 1995. Quote at p. 4. See also Paul Barber, *Partners in Repression: The Reality of British Aid to Indonesia* (Thornton Heath, Tapol, 1995).
114 Comptroller and Auditor General, 'Aid to Indonesia', Session 1996–97, HC-101, 29 November 1996, p. 1, para. 3.
115 Hansard, 2 February 1995, col. 773w.
116 C&AG 'Aid to Indonesia', p. 8, para. 25.
117 *Daily Telegraph*, 29 November 1996.
118 *Independent*, 14 November 1994.
119 PAC, *Aid to Indonesia*, Nineteenth Report, Session 1997–98, January 1998.
120 Hansard, 15 February 1994, col. 751.
121 *Financial Times*, 7 October 1981.
122 *Guardian*, 6 November 1981.
123 *Financial Times*, 7 October 1981.
124 *J.D.W.*, 8 July 1989.
125 An MoD spokesman said that it had secured 'the best price for a secondhand helicopter ... they certainly were not sold off cheaply'. *Flight International*, 9 April 1988.
126 *Sunday Times*, 25 September 1988.
127 Hansard, 5 May 1993, col. 145w.
128 *Ibid.*, 15 February 1994, col. 751w.
129 *Ibid.*, 21 February 1994, col. 69.
130 Quoted in *Financial Times*, 14 November 1988.
131 BA operated four Tristar flights per week between the two capitals at the time.
132 *J.D.W.*, 11, 25 March 1989, *Financial Times*, 16 March 1989.
133 *Financial Times*, 11 April 1989.
134 *Ibid.*
135 *Observer*, 7 May 1989.
136 For example, Hansard, 28 January 1994, cols 651–2.
137 *Ibid.*
138 *Ibid.*, 25 January 1994, cols 145–6.
139 See also 4 March 1994, col. 938.
140 *Economist*, 15 January 1994, p. 33.

141 FAC, *Public Expenditure: The Pergau Hydro-electric Project, Malaysia. The Aid and Trade Provision and Related Matters*, Third Report, Session 1993–94, HC 271-I, p. xiii.
142 FAC Report, Appendix 33, Letter from Baroness Thatcher.
143 FAC Report, p. liv.
144 *The Times*, 8 February 1994.
145 Hansard, 15 February 1994, col. 731w.
146 *Observer*, 7 May 1989.
147 For example, see Allan Rogers's questions in Hansard, 15 May 1989, col. 25w, and Joan Lestor's intervention at 11 July 1989, col. 796.
148 *J.D.W.*, 24 March 1990.
149 BAe's hopes of sustaining work on the Tornado were finally ended during the summer of 1990, when the British Government became the fourth within a year to cancel an order – for 33 remaining from a partially fulfilled order.
150 *Financial Times*, 14 June 1991.
151 A Malaysian official was quoted as saying that the cancellation 'forms part of a reassessment of Malaysia's defence needs in the light of the changed political climate in the South East Asia region.' *Ibid.*, 22 May 1990.
152 *Ibid.*, 8 June 1990. The Hawks were intended to replace the 31-strong fleet of Skyhawk aircraft.
153 The first of the 28 Hawks was officially accepted by Malaysia in January 1994. *J.D.W.*, 29 January 1994.
154 *Guardian*, 11 December 1990.
155 *Financial Times*, 14 June 1991.
156 *Independent*, 24 September 1991.
157 *Ibid.* On Malaysian doubts, see *J.D.W.*, 21 September 1991.
158 *J.D.W.*, 21 September 1991.
159 *Ibid.*, 11 April 1992, p. 607.
160 *Ibid.*, 30 April 1994, p. 8.

5

British arms sales to the Middle East

Israel

In 1982, the British government imposed an embargo on the sale of arms to Israel following its invasion of Lebanon. Even after the lifting of the embargo few British arms manufacturers were in a hurry to sell to Israel and risk damaging their prospects in the much more lucrative Arab markets. However, during the 1960s and 1970s, the UK was a not insignificant source of arms for Israel, and in the mid-1960s, and again in 1968, the government faced the dilemma of whether or not to sell Israel significant numbers of tanks.

In 1964, UK arms sales policy towards Israel and the Arab states was governed by the following considerations:

i   we should have regard to the balance of military capabilities between the two sides (which primarily means between Israel and the UAR);
ii   we should supply defensive weapons only;
iii we should avoid increasing the tempo of the arms race by raising the level of sophistication of the weapons held by the two sides;
iv   above all, we should avoid anything which might contribute to the acquisition of a nuclear capability, by either side; and
v   we should avoid becoming the exclusive or principal supplier of either side.[1]

With regard to Israel, the government was still following its 'driblet' policy, in place for two years, of allowing small numbers of Centurion tanks to be sent to Israel each month. A proposal to sell 45 more (later increased to 48)[2] was approved by Lord Carrington in January, a move it was hoped would prevent French sales of the AMX-30, and even pave the way for the future sale of the new Chieftain tank.[3] The Israelis had a requirement for more tanks than that – as many as 500 – and ideally wanted them from the US. However, there were divisions within the US over the wisdom of supplying what could clearly be construed as offensive weapons. By March 1964, the State Department had come to see the large-scale supply of British tanks, which Israel had purchased previously,[4] as a way out of the problem. Minister of Defence Peter Thorneycroft urged Rab Butler at the FO to be wary of US suggestions that there could be co-operation on this.[5] Butler warned that if the State Department had wanted to corner the Israeli arms market, no consultation would have taken place; what the Americans were looking for was for the UK to shoulder the political burden and 'take the heat' off them.[6]

Even though, by the end of the month, State Department officials were openly canvassing British opinion and looking at 'some kind of collaboration by which the political odium was spread',[7] it was not until May 1964 that the US government acted. A joint Defense and State Departments team of Frank Sloan and Robert Komer visited London on 4 May, before travelling to Bonn to assess the possibility of sourcing the tanks there, their credentials confirmed by telegrams from McGeorge Bundy and Robert McNamara. As Bundy explained, 'it is clear that if the US provides tanks to Israel, the consequence in the Arab world will be very severe, with resulting damage not only to US interests but to the whole Western position in the area ... Sloan and Komer are coming to explore with appropriate officers on your side what ways and means there may be of getting Israeli needs from British resources, and I repeat that the President simply asked me to report the great importance which he himself attaches to this Mission.'[8]

The Americans arrived in London, staying long enough to discover whether enough tanks even existed in the UK. Once the MoD had confirmed that over 200 would soon be available, they travelled to West Germany. In the interim, the FO produced a summary of the pros and cons of selling so many tanks to Israel. A sale of such magnitude had considerable advantages: the balance of power between Israel and the Arab states, disturbed by Soviet deliveries of tanks to the United Arab Republic (UAR), would be restored, reducing the likelihood of war and diminishing Israeli enthusiasm for missiles or nuclear weapons;[9] the order would have considerable foreign exchange value (£11 million to £12 million according to FO estimates); and a sale would represent a positive response to US concerns and could therefore yield benefits in other areas.[10]

However, there was no disguising the fact that the impact of such a sale on British relations with the Arab states was likely to be severe. Negotiations with the South Arabian Federation and ties with Jordan, Kuwait, Iraq and, in particular, Libya could all be jeopardised. Furthermore, it would be impossible to keep the sale secret. Even assuming the discretion of the Israeli government, the Johnson administration, in seeking to appease the Jewish lobby in an election year, was likely to let it be known that it had helped secure Israel's defence with foreign tanks. The only route out, it was suggested, would be to limit supplies to around 150 and present this, when it became public, as a continuation of the limited supply for self-defence agreed previously. Furthermore, it would leave Israel free to look elsewhere for the balance of their requirement, probably to France and West Germany, and therefore balance any 'ensuing Arab odium'. In commenting on the pros and cons, R. S. Crawford focused almost entirely on the publicity problem, stating that British tanks should be sold only if the government were able to 'secure an absolutely categoric understanding with the US government, that if we agree to supply some or all of the tanks needed they will say nothing in public indicating that this will happen and that it is made absolutely clear in private why this is so and why any publicity would be dangerous and unacceptable'.[11]

Komer and Sloan returned to London on 8 May,[12] by now leaning towards the supply of ex-US M-48 tanks from West Germany as a solution to the problem, even though there was some doubt as to whether these would be made available. For its part, the FO was still pushing for joint supplies from both countries (at the end of the day, the Israeli requirement was a convenient market for tanks that were due to be phased out and replaced by the Chieftain), while still emphasising the publicity problem.[13] With Bundy and the Johnson administration feeling the 'full force of Israeli and American Zionist pressure', British willingness to participate was gratefully accepted.[14] By mid-June, the Israeli defence attaché was conducting negotiations with the MoD for the 48 tanks authorised in January, and also expressing an interest in the purchase of up to 300 more, including a batch of Chieftains.[15] However, by this time, negotiations with the West Germans were under way in earnest, though, even from this early stage, there was considerable confusion about how, let alone whether, they should be involved. The West German government was divided over whether the transfer should proceed. Moreover, the tanks in question were not strictly surplus, but would have to be replaced from US stocks after they had been transferred to Israel. As the transfer would be part of the German aid/reparation payments to Israel, no one seemed certain whether a charge would be made for the tanks or the proposed upgrade.[16] Meanwhile, once the Israelis discovered that there was a possibility of acquiring free (or at least very cheap) tanks from West Germany they became demonstrably less enthusiastic about the UK option, at £18,000 per Centurion.[17]

This possibility of free or cheap German tanks complicated policy making in Whitehall, Washington and Tel Aviv. In the State Department, Phillips Talbot began to worry that, with so many surplus tanks apparently available in Europe, the Israelis might well be able to acquire enough to destabilise the equilibrium in the Middle East in their favour.[18] Ultimately, however, the German tanks would prove to be something of a red herring. In the meantime, August 1964 marked an important shift in both British and Israeli attitudes. Perhaps sensing that the West German deal was likely to collapse under its own weight, the Israelis renewed their interest in the British Centurions, doubtless encouraged by the MoD and Hubert, its energetic Director of Sales.[19] By that time, the supply of between 200 and 250 Centurions from the UK together with the West German tanks had developed into a firm package deal that the Israelis wanted to proceed with as quickly as possible. As an indication of their enthusiasm, Israeli Deputy Minister of Defence Shimon Peres visited London to discuss the package between 10 and 13 September, under conditions of strict secrecy.[20]

The FO was keen to explain to Peres that, while the government might agree to a deal, arms sales did not represent a British shift towards Israel on the wider issue of Arab–Israeli relations; Percy Cradock argued that only a meeting with Lord Carrington would be sufficient to ensure this point was adequately made.[21] Crawford feared, however, that any publicity for such a meeting would arouse Arab suspicion and could cause difficulties for British policy across a range of issues. In fact, the FO was so concerned about this that its officials went to some lengths to conceal it, including making a Jewish journalist give his 'word of honour' that he would not write anything about the meeting.[22]

The Peres visit achieved its aim. On 10 September, the sale of 250 Centurion tanks and associated equipment over the following three years was given ministerial approval.[23] The next day Peres met Carrington, who told him that 'he thought our position was well understood by the Israel government. We wished to be friends with every country in the area. We were particularly concerned with the preservation of peace and we were selling these arms to Israel because we considered that a balance of power in the area would help maintain peace.'[24] The more detailed negotiations were conducted at the MoD, leading to the signing of a memorandum of understanding on 15 September. The huge order, worth £7.5 million to £8 million, was to be processed in complete secrecy, and entailed a considerable commitment from the British government, though Peres himself succinctly described the essential *quid pro quo* as 'You will sell us the tanks and we will keep it a secret.'[25] Consequently, there was some debate over which foreign governments should be informed about the deal, and ultimately only the US and West German governments were told of it. Most notably, the French were not. Previous efforts to bring the French within the circle of the informal gentlemen's agreement by which the US and UK sought to direct the course of arms sales to the Middle East had not been entirely successful, and as a consequence the French were not considered particularly trustworthy in this respect.[26]

The election of a Labour government in October 1964 brought to power a party, which, in opposition, had argued that the major powers should seek to impose a *status quo* on the Middle East to reduce tension. However, once in office, Home's policy was continued seamlessly by Wilson. As elsewhere (for example, with regard to the contemporaneous issue of arms to South Africa) the weight of official advice was to discourage any notions of departing from the great stream of policy followed previously. (One official modestly characterised the new government's approach to sales to Israel as being 'generally accommodating.'[27]) Indeed, when Levi Eshkol met Denis Healey in March 1965 to enquire into the possibility of purchasing 200–300 Centurions in addition to the 250 already agreed on – a move which had clear implications for the policy of balancing Israeli and Arab armed forces that had underpinned US and UK arms sales policy to the region – Healey told him he could 'see no reason to think that we shall not be able to meet your needs'.[28]

As we have seen, the FO had always been concerned about the harm that would follow any publicity for the sale, and from December 1964 it received a salutary lesson in just how severe it could be when the West German element of the tank deal was exposed. Once the leaks began in December, the divisions between the German Foreign and Defence Ministries were soon exposed. The West German government was particularly vulnerable because (unlike the UK) it was committed to not supplying arms to 'areas of tension'. Foreign Minister Böker said the deal was a mistake, and denied that his department had been involved in the decision-making; if it had, he said, he would have opposed the deal.[29] The exposure provoked fierce criticism from Arab states, particularly Egypt, and West German resolve to proceed with the sale crumbled. By mid-February 1965, it was being reported that the deal would probably not proceed, and a month later Sir Frank Roberts in Bonn confirmed that such was the case. Even outstanding deliveries were to be cancelled,[30] illustrating how, for the Germans at least, political considerations could outweigh the attachment to the principle of the inviolability of contracts. Although several Arab states sought clarification of the British position on arms sales to Israel, their questions were politely evaded and because they did not vigorously pursue their investigations the British government escaped the inevitable criticism which would have followed exposure.[31]

Meanwhile, there were two consolations for Israel. The first was the offer of a secret loan of around DM 100 million from the West Germans. Secondly, in March, the US stepped in and offered to ensure the Israelis possessed 'an effective deterrent capacity', not only making up the shortfall of 110 tanks left by the West German cancellation, but offering 100 more to balance deliveries being made to Jordan.[32]

Even with the US absorbing almost all of the Arab criticism,[33] the UK government was keen to avoid too close an association with the Israelis. Fear of publicity and the dangers of too close a relationship pervaded all aspects of policy-making. For example, a proposal for annual talks between the Israeli Armoured Corps and the Royal Armoured Corps was rejected by the FO as representing just the sort of 'special relationship with Israel' that the government wished to avoid.[34] Even such matters as what sort of tanks the Israelis could parade at their Independence Day celebrations were felt by FO officials to be within the reach of their influence,[35] and when, in July 1966, Israeli Prime Minister Eshkol mentioned British tanks during a speech at the National Defence College, the FO sought to admonish the Israeli Ministry of Foreign Affairs for allowing a slip of this kind to occur![36] Furthermore, in keeping with the general policy considerations outlined at the beginning of this chapter, in late 1965 the Labour government took the decision not to sell the ('offensive') Buccaneer aircraft to Israel, a matter which involved discussion at ministerial level. Nevertheless, implementation of these guidelines left plenty of room for interpretation and hence manoeuvre. For example, the FO subsequently felt able to agree to the proposed sale of Saracens or FV-432 armoured personnel carriers,[37] while arguing against the transfer of surplus tanks.[38]

However, these guidelines were of little use once circumstances in the Middle East changed, as they did in November 1966, when Israeli troops attacked Jordan, destroying or disabling a number of British-origin aircraft in the process. Although ending arms supplies to Israel was considered as a possible British response, the US rejected such an option, and in the FO Morris produced a series of arguments against doing so which combined tradition with ingenuity: '(a) Israel, like other countries, has a right to acquire the arms she needs for her defence; (b) if we did not do so others would; (c) we need the business; (d) we believe a balance of defensive capacity is necessary in the Middle East if stability is to be maintained; (e) we believe that there is a particular danger that if Israel feels she is being abandoned by the West, she will either embark on some desperate military enterprise to destroy the Arab armies before she is overwhelmed, or go nuclear; (f) conversely, our position as suppliers gives us some moderating influence over Israel's policies generally.'[39] In short, a 'British embargo by itself would harm Anglo/Israeli relations and do us commercial harm whilst accomplishing nothing'. There would be no UK arms embargo.

As tension mounted in the region throughout May 1967, in particular through the Egyptian military build-up in the Sinai, the UK government was faced with a potential dilemma over continuing supplies of military equipment to Israel and the Arab states. At the time the UK was still supplying Israel with Centurion tanks from the 1964 order together with tank ammuntion. This ammunition was usually shipped, but from May the Israelis began to request that it should be airlifted. The government agreed to airlift 800 rounds, Harold Wilson approving the airlift, as 'there was no sign that the Israeli Government contemplated aggression'.[40]

Shortly after, the Israelis requested another 12 aircraft loads (a further 3,200 rounds).[41]

If total secrecy could have been guaranteed, it is unlikely the government would have had any difficulty in approving this suggestion. In practice, the fears about an Arab backlash if news leaked out made it very wary about any such agreement. In particular, George Brown 'had considerable misgivings' about both the initial airlift and approving any more.[42] The arrangements for the airlifting of the 800 rounds agreed to were evidence of this. They were to be flown out of the RAF base at Leeming, Yorkshire, by three Israeli Air Force Stratocruisers, the markings on which had been removed.[43]

The government decided that it would delay responding to this second request until it was satisfied that the first airlift had taken place in complete secrecy. Nevertheless, under pressure from the Israeli ambassador, a second airlift involving three aircraft carrying 880 rounds was approved by Wilson on 23 May.[44]

Although the Israeli ambassador had assured George Brown that this would be the last request for airlifting,[45] by 28 May he was requesting an airlift of a further 2,000 rounds, which was approved by Wilson the same day.[46] By 2 June, all this ammuntion had been picked up. By 1 June, the Israelis were requesting an airlift of 1,000 rounds of armour-piercing anti-tank ammuniton for their 105 mm guns, part of an order then being dispatched by sea.

When war broke out on 5 June, the British government had to decide how to respond, in view of the number of states involved that had arms on order from the UK. Denis Healey suggested that the government 'should not take a unilateral initiative by banning arms exports, but that we should act in concert with other nations through the [UN] Security Council'. However, he thought it 'might be desirable to impose some administrative delay on exports at least of certain types of equipment, such as the Hunter aircraft which were on order for Iraq and Jordan'.[47] Not to impose an embargo – as the US did at the outbreak of war – and delay arms requests for Arab states, having accelerated deliveries to Israel prior to the outbreak, clearly represented a tilt towards Israel, although one which the Cabinet did not acknowledge as such. The principles which had up to now guided UK arms sales policy to the region were discarded.

However, the Cabinet's decision to impose a 24 hour delay on shipments of arms to Middle East states did include a shipment of 10 Centurion tanks for Israel – part of the 1964 order, and then due to be transferred to Antwerp for shipping to Israel. Nevertheless, as Healey told his Cabinet colleagues the next day, 'it was important to ensure that we did not hold up supplies to Israel if the Soviet Union continued to supply the Arab states'.[48] Hence after 24 hours, in the absence of a Soviet commitment to end supplies, and in the face of strong Israeli pressure to airlift more ammunition,[49] the government lifted its delay (although without making a public statement to that effect). The Cabinet discussion of this illustrates the considerations at work:

> it was suggested that, while the fighting was still in progress in the Middle East, it would be wrong to resume supplies of arms to countries in the area. On the other hand it was argued that there were strong grounds for reverting to normal practice, particularly in view of the fact that Israel had shown herself willing to accept a cease-fire and that hostilities were not now likely to last long. Furthermore, some other countries, and especially the Soviet Union, were continuing to supply arms and the continued imposition of a delay on our part might lead to Israel suffering greater difficulties than the Arab states in maintaining her forces. In addition, if we were to default ... on orders which had been placed with us, we should cease to be regarded as a reliable source of supply and might put at risk large long-term orders already placed with us ... [50]

By 9 June, with war still being waged, the Israeli ambassador requested the airlift of 3,800 air-to-land rockets and 1,000 rounds of armour-piercing ammunition. Even though this was clearly required for offensive action, George Thomson felt it should be approved. [51]

In the aftermath of the war, amid widespread Arab perceptions that the UK had backed Israel, and the Arab ban on the export of oil to the US or the UK, the government's priority was to mend fences, using arms sales where appropriate – for example, with regard to Jordan, where it had been thought that King Hussein would probably fall, but whose position could be buttressed by agreeing to sell much-needed arms. At the same time, the Israelis needed to re-equip their forces to compensate for losses incurred in the fighting. In particular, they invoked Denis Healey's April 1965 letter, virtually assuring Israel of further sales of Centurions on demand, in urgently requesting a further 150 tanks.[52] On 28 July it was decided that an initial consignment of a further 18 tanks could go, but that it should be balanced by a sale of Hunter aircraft to Jordan to enable King Hussein 'to get his surviving pilots into the air'. Nevertheless, George Brown requested a Cabinet meeting to approve this course of action – 'to share the burden (and the risk!)', as he put it.[53]

The question of rearming the region exposed all the contradictions at the heart of British arms sales policy. As George Brown told the OPD:

> there was no immediate prospect that agreement would be reached among the major arms-producing countries on a controlled limitation on arms supplies to the Middle East; nor would Israel or the Arab States co-operate in any such arms limitation in the absence of a political settlement in the area. Although we must continue to work for arms limitation in the Middle East, we had to recognise that a unilateral refusal on our part to supply any arms to countries in that area would not be effective in military or political terms and would lose important export markets for our industry ...

Although he shared the widespread distaste in this country for the sale of arms in an area which had seen three Arab/Israeli conflicts in twenty years, he believed that in all the circumstances we should continue to supply arms to the Middle East.[54]

In addition, there was the omnipresent fear that moderate Arabs could be forced into the arms of the Soviets if they were denied legitimate arms supplies from the West. Given that there was no breaking out of the arms sales addiction, Brown highlighted principles that should guide the government's policy – an updating of the 1964 FO formulation. Firstly, as before, a guiding principle of arms deliveries should be to maintain a balance between Arab and Israeli forces. Secondly, the UK should not supply arms of 'a greater offensive power' than already deployed. Thirdly, the UK should avoid becoming, or being interpreted as becoming, Israel's principal supplier of 'any additional major types of arms supplies'. Fourthly, no arms or equipment that could contribute to the development of a nuclear capability should be exported. Finally, no arms should be sent to 'any Arab country which maintains a hostile attitude towards us'.[55]

Even these guidelines – hardly restrictive in terms of conventional arms – became a problem when the Israelis began to show a definite interest in the new Chieftain tank, which had been undergoing trials in Israel at the time of the 1967 war, and in the purchase of 1,000 lb and 500 lb bombs. These bombs were clearly offensive weapons, although the new Foreign Secretary, Michael Stewart, saw a way out of the problem, by taking account of:

the particular strategic circumstances of Israel in determining whether this definition should be regarded as sufficient reason for refusing supply. Israel is a small country hemmed in by her neighbours, for whom defence against an attack of any scale is likely to be impossible without very heavy civilian casualties. This enforces on her a strategy which concentrates on (a) the maintenance of sufficient forces to deter an Arab attack, and (b), if this fails, of attack on Arab armed forces and strategic targets at long range before they can themselves reach Israeli targets.

Hence Stewart ingeniously concluded, the 'distinction between offensive and defensive use if [sic] therefore an unreal one in relation to Israel', and as such the bombs could be sold.[56] This does, of course, beg the question of the utility of making this distinction the cornerstone of arms sales policy in the first place.

Even more difficult was a decision on the sale of the Chieftain tank, and whether this could be reconciled with the guidelines. Having agreed to the bomb sale, Michael Stewart argued forcefully against the sale of the Chieftain. The Israelis had enquired about the possibility of buying approximately 250 at around £100,000 per tank. There were obvious arguments in favour of supply: the Chieftain had undertaken trials in

Israel, and having approved trials a refusal to sell would offend the Israelis; the UK was the supplier of Israel's current main tank, the Centurion; the order was important to the UK tank industry, especially in the context of the then recent Dutch decision to purchase the West German Leopard rather than the Chieftain.

However, such a sale could not be reconciled with the 'greater offensive power' clause of the November 1967 guidelines, itself a considerable loosening of the relevant earlier guideline that 'we should supply defensive weapons only'. As Stewart acknowledged, supplying the Chieftain 'would undoubtedly mean giving an extra twist to the arms spiral in the area by introducing into it a tank of altogether higher quality than any which is now likely to be used there operationally', tilting the balance so far in Israel's favour as to contravene a further guideline – that committing the UK to aim at a balance of forces in the area.[57] It would also further set relations with Arab states back just as they were being rebuilt following the British military tilt to Israel in the 1967 war. Moreover, Jordan would take the sale particularly badly. Given that the government had just agreed to sell King Hussein 143 Centurions, as part of the bridge-building process and in an attempt to solidify the king's position, the sale of Chieftains to Israel would make him look stupid and either undermine him or drive him to seek arms from the USSR in order to secure his own position. A sale would also jeopardise the ongoing deal with Saudi Arabia, where King Feisal 'reacts more emotionally than almost any Arab leader to western gestures of support for Israel',[58] and whose co-operation in the recently announced disengagement from the Gulf was essential to safeguarding Western interests there. The value of arms contracts with Arab states which would be put at risk by agreeing to supply Israel with Chieftains was estimated to be around £400 million. Hence while the Israelis would be allowed further Centurions, Stewart concluded that they should not be allowed to buy the Chieftain.

This powerful argument seemed set to carry the day, but was contested vigorously by Denis Healey, one of the most forceful Cabinet advocates of arming Israel. He questioned both whether Arab orders would be lost, and also the FCO's judgement of the prevailing political balance in the region, suggesting that 'this balance had altered to the disadvantage of Israel since the war in 1967'.[59] Supplying the Chieftains would merely restore the balance.

Healey swung a majority of the OPD behind his argument. A decision was deferred and in the meantime Healey produced a detailed memorandum arguing in favour of the sale.[60] Hence even though it clearly contravened the government's own (revised) guidelines on arms sales to the region, at this point the government agreed that the Israelis should be allowed to buy the Chieftain tank, although Harold Wilson, recognising the 'obvious risks' of such a policy, urged that it would be 'essential to

maintain secrecy: failure to do so would have the most damaging consequences, and this must be impressed on all concerned, including not only
the Israelis themselves, but their sympathisers in this country'.[61]

Saudi Arabia: the dove of corruption

> Saudi Arabia is not just a trading partner, but a country whose foreign
> policy has shared similar objectives to our own ... Saudi Arabia has played
> a crucial role in the promotion of moderate and sensible policies. During the
> Cold War, Saudi Arabia, while at all times remaining staunchly indepen-
> dent, was a vehement opponent of communism and the spread of Soviet
> influence throughout the region ... [it] remains an important bulwark
> against any further Iraqi attempts to threaten or invade its neighbours. The
> Saudis share our suspicion of Iranian policies in the Middle East peace
> process. Saudi Arabia has been a bastion of stability and moderation in a
> region not always known for those qualities. (Jeremy Hanley, Minister of
> State, FCO, January 1996[62])

The charge of the Lightnings

The sale of Lightning aircraft and air-defence radar to Saudi Arabia in the
mid-1960s was a watershed in the British government's approach to arms
sales. The deal is particularly important in terms of the way in which it
highlights the political considerations involved in arms sales decision
making; the growing personal involvement of politicians; the importance
of selling package deals with effective after-sales service; of flexibility in
the credit terms available; and in the way it illustrates the role of agents
and commissions in the modern arms sales process. It was also part of a
period characterised by both competition and co-operation between the
US and UK in the Middle East, aimed at securing market share but, more
important, in securing the stability of Western interests in the region.

British relations with Saudi Arabia in the early 1960s were far different
from those of today and were in the process of being rebuilt following the
Suez crisis and the Buraimi affair. The Kingdom was in the first throes of
constructing its defences. The few arms transactions the UK concluded
with Saudi Arabia were governed by the overriding necessity of not
supplying equipment that could be passed on to rebel groups operating in
Oman and the Aden Protectorates. (Exports of Lee-Enfield rifles and
ammunition, for example, were blocked on that basis.) On the other
hand, Saudi Arabia was an emerging market, a state with which the UK
was moving towards normal diplomatic relations, one which had 'rallied
to the defence of Kuwait' during the 1961 crisis, and which, therefore, 'if
she is to carry out this task properly ... must have the necessary warlike
equipment', as one March 1962 FO minute put it.[63] At the time the bulk

of its 'warlike equipment' was obtained from the US, although the UK had sold it the Vampire jet trainer. The FO tended to defer to the US – the ultimate guarantors of Saudi Arabia's security – on arms issues, in practice a barrier to further UK penetration of the market.

This, then, was the situation at the time when the industrious Geoffrey Edwards, who had gone to Saudi Arabia in 1960, and quickly recognised the potential for making money from offering arms packages to the Saudis, began to negotiate a package that would see BAC sell the Lightning aircraft, AEI a radar system, and a company called Airwork the training. As John Stonehouse later recalled:

> Most people in Government frowned upon Geoffrey Edwards as an arms salesman grasping after his fat commissions. I did not. In an area such as Arabia much of the commission would any way have to be spent in bribes and, anyhow what was the point of adopting a 'holier-than-thou' attitude when Britain's factories sorely needed that business and our balance of payments needed the foreign currency.[64]

In July 1963 Edwards informed the British embassy in Jeddah that he was negotiating an arms contract with the Saudi Ministry of Defence worth £20 million to £25 million, involving the sale of 14 Canberra bombers, AEI radar equipment, military transport aircraft, small naval vessels and 100 Thunderbird Mark I surface-to-air missiles (for four to five batteries). At the time, the Saudis explained their need for the Canberra as lying in their intention of bombing the Aswan Dam if attacked by Egyptian forces.[65] A clearly sceptical embassy official noted that 'Edwards claims to have good relations with the [Saudi] Minister of Defence but it is difficult to know what to believe of all he says.' Given that the FO was anxious not to export types of equipment which the US was already supplying and training the Saudis to use, the embassy was 'concerned that Edwards' promotional efforts will do damage to our relations with the Saudis, that he will raise their hopes and that he will put the blame on us if no export licences are forthcoming'.[66]

In November 1963, Edwards confided to Sir Colin Crowe at the British embassy in Jeddah that what Saudi Defence Minister Prince Sultan really wanted was the Lightning Mark II: 'Sultan was fed up with the Americans, the Mystère people had not offered them all the necessary equipment with their aircraft and what he wanted to do was buy British.'[67] The same month, a team from BAC, AEI and Rolls-Royce organised by Geoffrey Edwards visited the Kingdom to give a sales presentation to the Saudi arms purchasing committee, which was favourably received.

At the time the Saudis were considering a range of aircraft (including the US Northrop F-5A, the Lockheed F-104G and the Mirage) to fill their requirement. However, Edwards told Crowe that the Saudis really wanted the Lightnings, in part because of 'how anti-American Prince Sultan and all the various Saudis were, how they wanted to get away from dependence on America and ... if they could not get what they wanted from us they might have nothing to do with either the Americans or ourselves.' Crowe was wary of such talk, reminding Edwards that 'the Saudis knew which side their bread was buttered. It was the Americans who were committed to defend the regime and they trained the Saudi armed forces. They would not take kindly to the Saudis being equipped with other than United States aircraft.'[68] This was the general perspective of most of those dealing with Saudi Arabia at the time. They believed that the Saudis merely wanted to play off the UK against the US in order to achieve the best possible terms from the US. This interpretation was certainly borne out by subsequent events, although it was not one in which BAC saw any merit at the time.[69]

In a November 1963 memorandum, Frank Brenchley set out the difficulties involved in considering selling the Lightning. The first Saudi interest in the Lightning had been reported in June 1962, but then it had been opposed by the Colonial Office, Air Ministry and Foreign Office on security grounds – primarily the threat it could pose to Aden and the fact that it was 'superior to fighter aircraft then available to defend the British protected States in the Persian Gulf.' By November 1963 these objections had been waived in the light of the advantages that could accrue: for example, the sale could help the RAF 'move from Lightning Mark IIs to IIIs rather than incur the expense and difficulty of converting the Mark II which they hold at present to model IIAs; this would spread the research and development costs, at present borne entirely by the British taxpayer, and might also encourage other foreign governments to buy the aircraft'.[70]

However, the British embassy in Jeddah was less enthusiastic about the idea, arguing that the fighter requirement fell within the scope of the US training programme. As Brenchley recognised, there were:

> clear political objections to HMG ousting the US Government from their training commitment or even appearing to contemplate doing so. Saudi Arabia is the Middle East country in which the Americans are most deeply involved and the only one of which they are virtually the sole Western supporter. Their commitment to Saudi Arabia is of the utmost help to us in the Persian Gulf and in Aden. We have therefore a positive reason for wanting to see the US Government remain deeply engaged in Saudi Arabia, as well as obvious negative reasons for not being prepared to take on the extra strain of defending Saudi Arabia ourselves.[71]

Hence Brenchley recommended telling the US that, while the UK recognised 'their readiness to defend Saudi Arabia and their provision of training facilities for the Saudi Regular Forces makes it natural that the Saudis should look primarily to the United States for weapons for those forces ... we cannot prevent British arms manufacturers from offering their products, more particularly as others, such as the French and the Swedes, are doing so'. Although the UK retained its distinction between offensive and defensive weapons, refusing to sell the former, the Lightning was considered to be essentially a defensive aircraft, and so would be unaffected by the application of this principle.

In early 1964 the head of the US air defence survey team recommended that the US should supply Saudi Arabia with either the F-5A or the F-104H for its fighter requirement. The State Department suggested that, of these, the F-5A would be more appropriate as it was the less difficult to operate. They claimed that it was essentially a defensive weapon, and therefore not to be compared with the Canberra. The State Department helpfully provided the UK government with comparative performance data showing that the F-5A had only approximately half the combat radius of the Canberra, and could carry only a fraction of the ordnance load. While, in theory, it could be converted for use as a bomber, the State Department considered that unlikely, convinced as it was that the Saudis would be unable to operate the aircraft in any capacity in the short run, and that 'in practice the United States' role in training Saudi pilots would give them sufficient control over the use to which the Saudis might put them'.[72]

On this basis, it was proposed to inform BAC that the Canberras, if requested, would not be licensed. However, the MoD contested the figures on which the State Department based its preference for the Saudis acquiring the F-5A. As Peter Thorneycroft complained to Lord Carrington: 'It is difficult to escape the conclusion that the State Department is trying to play down the capability of the F-5A. The performance figures they quote are greatly at variance with the published figures for this aircraft – the combat radius is half the published figure, the maximum speed is reduced by 30%, and the ordnance load by 20% ... The Air Staff in fact would still regard it as a more objectionable aircraft to have to face than the Canberra, because it is much too fast for the Hunter to deal with.'[73]

However, BAC's real interest now lay in selling the Lightning. For prestige reasons, the Saudis were determined to buy supersonic aircraft – either from the US or from the UK, or even France or Sweden. Even if the UK government broke with the informal understanding with the US that it would not normally licence offensive weapons for the region and agreed to licence the Canberra, the Saudis would in all probability find it politically expedient to buy the F-5A as well to appease the Americans. If they bought the F-5A anyhow, that would clear the way for BAC to make a pitch to sell the Lightning. Armaments, including 1,000 lb bombs, which would give them a ground attack capability, could also be approved, as the Americans could hardly object in the light of their sale of the F-5A.

What all this clearly illustrates is the complete dominance which the US enjoyed over the Saudi market, and the existence of a form of gentlemen's agreement between the US and UK to respect each other's market dominance in Saudi Arabia and Kuwait respectively. This principle was explicitly set out in a brief which the State Department passed to the British embassy in Washington at a meeting in February 1964 as a further part of the US campaign to dissuade the UK from allowing BAC to sell the Canberra, and instead secure the sale of the F-5A or F-104H:

> we would propose that neither party give special encouragement to salesmen who desire to deal in the other's area of primacy. However, if salesmen are specifically approached by the Saudis, or if they, on their own, obtain sales orders, the two countries before issuing export licences would mutually seek each other's views concerning compatibility of such equipment with that already in hand and with the training responsibility of the power concerned. Full, complete and continuing consultations in London, Washington and Jedda ... are required to carry out successfully this approach and to facilitate the rapid exchange between the two governments of any information concerning third country efforts to penetrate the Saudi Arabia and Kuwait arms sales area.
>
> The US accepts British primacy with respect to sales in Kuwait and would expect to be governed by the above guideline in its own sales activity in that country.[74]

In these pre-Stokes Report times, such an understanding was clearly not to the liking of BAC, and its chairman, Lord Caldecote, passed his view on to Lord Carrington. He told Carrington that:

> the Americans regarded Saudi Arabia as their sphere of influence. The American Embassy in Jedda were giving active and vigorous support to the efforts of United States arms manufacturers to sell arms to the Saudi Government. The Embassy had in fact brought strong pressure to bear on the Saudi Government to accept these offers, and were hinting that, if the Saudis met their arms requirements from other sources, the Americans might have to reconsider their present guarantee of Saudi independence.[75]

Caldecote went on to urge Carrington to encourage a similar commitment on the part of the British embassy. The Saudis wanted an assurance that BAC had the full support of the government before it would buy from them, but this had not been forthcoming. In fact, Caldecote told Carrington, some in the embassy even appeared 'actively hostile' to BAC agent Geoffrey Edwards. He was 'admittedly a 'buccaneer' rather than a gentleman; but he was the type of man needed if BAC were to do business effectively in Saudi Arabia.'[76]

On 12 March 1964 Lord Caldecote returned to the offensive, meeting Lord Carrington once more, again with little success. While, as mentioned above, Crowe was convinced that Saudi interest in Lightnings was bogus, and part of an effort to play the UK off against the US in order to get the best deal, Caldecote told Carrington that Saudi interest was genuine.[77] He then returned to the question of government support for the BAC sales effort, telling Carrington that 'his Company felt that her Majesty's Government had not done enough to give them support'. Carrington told him that the FO 'remained sceptical of the possibilities of sale, and thought that it would not be right for Her Majesty's Government to give their full backing to the project if its success were in any case very doubtful, and if the only end-product would be to cause irritation to the Americans.'[78]

However, in May 1964, Edwards told the embassy in Jeddah that the Saudi arms purchasing committee had now reported to Prince Faisal and Prince Sultan recommending the purchase of 40 Lightnings, Thunderbird missiles and AEI radar. Despite embassy and general government scepticism about BAC's prospects, by July 1964 the government's position was clear: it would license Lightning aircraft, Thunderbird missiles and AEI radar for Saudi Arabia, but would not itself become involved in any training programmes lest the Americans were further antagonised. This would have to be handled on a commercial basis. For their part, the Saudis had sought an assurance that the government would not intervene or restrict supply in the event of conflict breaking out, implicitly with Israel. The UK government could not give such an undertaking, especially as, in the event of such a conflict, it was deemed likely that the UN would call for a cessation of arms supplies. Nevertheless, as the FO's J. A. Snellgrove noted:

> The stability of Saudi Arabia is important to the stability of the Middle East as a whole which is essential to our economic and strategic interests; and the prospects for its maintenance are in turn largely dependent on the ability of the present Saudi régime to carry out the programme of reform and development which it has started. The acquisition of this defence system would increase its security and self-confidence.

And, with other recent cases no doubt in mind, he added: 'The Saudis look to the West for their supplies of arms. The United States of American [*sic*] have, for obvious reasons, hitherto been the main suppliers, but the Saudis have also approached the French, the West Germans and the Swedes. We do not wish to force them to look to the Union of Soviet Socialist Republics.'[79]

However, at this stage, the US continued to object to the British proposal. In October, the American embassy in London delivered an aide-memoire to the FO on the subject of the proposed Thunderbird sale, arguing that 'Saudi Arabia only has a low priority requirement for any such surface-to-air missiles. The purchase by Saudi Arabia of such overly sophisticated weapons would represent a short sighted drain on Saudi

Arabian financial resources, and a useless diversion of limited Saudi technical personnel and skills from the urgently needed Saudi development
program.' Showing a sensitivity it must have abandoned by the 1990s,
Eilts at the US embassy added a fresh argument: that 'the diversion of
large sums of money to these relatively useless weapons would be considered by the younger and better educated Saudis as evidence that the Royal
House was neglecting civil development for purely prestige expenditure'.
Brenchley dismissed these arguments as being 'pretty thin'.[80]

Hence this was the position at the time of the 1964 general election:
lukewarm support at embassy level for the sales effort but an emerging if
hardly proactive commitment to license the arms, despite continued US
pressure not to do so. When BAC made representations to the new Labour
government in December 1964, it immediately secured the expressions of
support it had sought in vain from the previous Conservative administration. A December 1964 meeting with Minister of Aviation, Roy Jenkins,
produced the expression of support BAC had long sought: a letter from
Defence Secretary Denis Healey to Prince Sultan:

> I would like to take this opportunity to reaffirm to Your Majesty the assur-
> ances which H.M. Ambassador has already given your Government orally,
> that we shall grant an export licence for Lightnings, Thunderbirds and ancil-
> lary radar equipment. We have found BAC and its associated companies to
> have a very reliable record in meeting their obligations under contracts both
> for the supply of aircraft and other weapons, and for training and mainte-
> nance.
>   We shall, moreover, stand ready to do everything we can to keep the firms
> up to the mark in carrying out to your satisfaction the work involved in
> discharging any contracts you may place on them.[81]

Then, at the end of December, John Cronin, MP, was sent to the
Kingdom, taking with him letters from Healey and Jenkins, and met King
Faisal. This was followed up in March 1965 by a first visit to the
Kingdom by John Stonehouse, Parliamentary Secretary to Roy Jenkins in
Aviation. He twice met Prince Sultan and King Faisal. At their first
meeting Sultan put a number of specific questions to Stonehouse. Firstly,
would the UK government allow RAF pilots to fly Lightnings until such
time as Saudi pilots were trained to do so? Secondly, he raised the question of whether the UK would 'continue to supply arms without
interruption even in unfavourable political circumstances, e.g. continued
Saudi support for the Arab League line against "imperialism"?' A further
question concerned payment terms. Finally, Sultan enquired as to the
prospect of immediate delivery of up to six Lightnings.

At the second meeting, Stonehouse offered his replies. As regards
credit, the Saudis would be required to pay a third of the full price as a
down payment, and repay the remainder over five to seven years. Sultan

countered that the American offer was for payments over seven years with no payment at all in the first year. Six Lightning Mark IIs could be released to BAC immediately for refurbishing, and delivered within three months. As regards guaranteed continuity of supply in the event of conflict, Stonehouse told Prince Sultan that 'he could agree to a formula suggested by Sultan to the effect that whatever the political circumstances there would be no interruption in our supply of arms to Saudi Arabia, it being understood that the arms offered to Saudi Arabia would be used solely in self-defence'.[82] The only exceptions would be in the event of a 'direct confrontation' between Saudi Arabia and the UK, or if Saudi Arabia committed an act of aggression, for example, by invading Kuwait.

On his return, Stonehouse produced a short report, summarising the Saudi requirement for arms. It was obvious, he said:

> that the Saudis are extremely concerned with the threat from Egypt through the Yemen. According to information the Ambassador gave me, land-mines had been planted by the Egyptians 15 miles over the border. The Saudis expect the Egyptians to launch a movement to out-flank the Royalists in the Yemeni mountains, and this would involve crossing Saudi territory. More troops and supplies are being deployed in the area to meet this threat ... The Saudis, although they do not wish to lose American support, are disenchanted with the degree of American assistance they can now count on in the event of an Egyptian invasion. ... In view of this hint of reduced support, I think that the Saudis are anxious to improve their own capability to meet an attack without being subject to the American political veto.[83]

Stonehouse ended by noting the vigorous sales campaign being waged by American officials on behalf of their companies, which had 'not stopped short of denigrating the British equipment on offer'. Despite this, the US and UK embassies in Jeddah came to an understanding whereby they would share information on Saudi approaches to them for arms, allowing them to monitor Saudi attempts to play one off against the other. For example, at the end of March the new British ambassador, Morgan-Man, sent a telegram to the FO outlining the substance of a conversation between Prince Sultan and the US ambassador following Sultan's meeting with Stonehouse. Sultan had told the US ambassador what Stonehouse had offered in terms of Lightning delivery dates, and that 'King Faisal had said this was not good enough and had instructed Prince Sultan to ask how soon the Americans could deliver between eight and twelve F-104 aircraft'. He had also asked – as he had of Stonehouse about the RAF – whether the USAF could provide pilots until Saudi pilots were trained, and told him that the British had refused. (Stonehouse had actually said he 'doubted' whether it could be done.) Sultan then raised the possibility of employing mercenaries to pilot the aircraft, saying that the British had told him that mercenaries could be employed through Airwork, to which the British government had no objections. (In reality, Stonehouse had stressed the need for the Saudis to train their own pilots as quickly as possible.) Sultan had also pressed the Americans on credit terms.[84]

This Anglo-US co-operative spirit reached an unlikely peak in September 1965. At a time when the UK seemed to have lost out on the Lightning order in favour of the Americans, US Defense Secretary Robert McNamara stepped in to gift the order to BAC and prevent US companies from taking it up.

On 23 September, Donald Stokes, then in Washington to meet Henry Kuss as part of the fact-finding mission for his report, met McNamara and Kuss, and the issue of fighter aircraft for Saudi Arabia was raised. McNamara said:

> that he, himself, had not been keen on the Saudi Arabian contract which he had hoped would go to the United Kingdom. The United States did not favour the acquisition of sophisticated aircraft like the F-104 by smaller countries, particularly in the Middle East and had discouraged the Saudis from buying it. He had assumed that the Saudis would settle for the second aircraft on their preference list (the Lightning) but for some reason they had gone after the F-5 which was their fifth choice.[85]

Henry Kuss interrupted to say that the negotiations had gone too far to be reversed, but McNamara 'instructed him to look into the matter more closely'. Later, of course, this would become a formal element of the F-111 offset arrangement. But there was another reason, besides the need to keep the UK involved, that underlay McNamara's generosity. The US was intent on applying a more restrictive arms sales policy towards Israel, and to be seen to be selling advanced aircraft to Saudi Arabia at the same time would have been politically difficult, and likely to arouse considerable opposition in Congress.[86]

King Faisal's decision to lean towards the F-104 had been governed by the fear that not buying American equipment would offend the US which, in the final resort, and whatever Prince Sultan thought, was publicly committed to the defence of Saudi Arabia – an obligation the British government had made clear it was unwilling to assume. Henry Kuss told Sir Patrick Dean, the British ambassador in Washington, that, 'both for internal political reasons and because of possible effects on Saudi/United States relations', the US could not simply instruct the Saudis to buy British, and suggested that the best solution would be to offer a new Anglo-US arms package involving the Lightnings, US Hawk missiles and US radar. Hence the UK would be invited to supply the component likely to be most offensive to US domestic opinion, and the US would supply the rest. Kuss told Dean that the US government 'was keen on supplying radar because of the opportunity it gave to penetrate remote parts of Saudi Arabia'.[87] He also told him that a joint US–UK package 'would be not only in our joint commercial interests but in our wider political interests' as it would 'keep out other countries' influence.'[88]

Although McNamara's offer was politically welcome, BAC was unhappy that its offer of an integrated package would now be replaced by offering different systems, adding to the difficulty of training, and harming its chances of following up a successful missile sale to Saudi Arabia with one to Kuwait. Given that the UK government had previously agreed that the Saudi arms market (except for the National Guard) was a US preserve, London regarded this outcome as a better one than did BAC, especially when Henry Kuss told Geoffrey Edwards that the package could include UK rather than US radar. Even Lord Caldecote came to agree that it was the best that could be achieved. He asked that Stonehouse should head a visit to Riyadh to present the new proposals to the Saudis (who had then just sent a letter to Robert McNamara formally accepting a US offer that unbeknown to them had been withdrawn of F-104s, Hawk missiles and radar equipment).

In November 1965, the UK and US Ambassadors to Saudi Arabia met Prince Sultan to discuss the details of the proposed deal, where Sultan gave what the British Ambassador described as 'an exhibition of righteous disappointment' over the credit terms on offer:

> Surely we could do much better than this. Saudi Arabia's critics abroad were watching the situation closely and if she accepted our terms the impression would be given that an Anglo/United States 'imperialist' deal was being forced upon Saudi Arabia. Here we were haggling like a lot of merchants in the souk when her British and American allies should be making every effort to be generous to Saudi Arabia. Was this the way to treat a friend?[89]

The companies involved in meeting the requirement for aircraft, radar and training now established the Saudi Arabian Air Defence Consortium, comprising Airwork, AEI and BAC. The value of the contract at the time was officially estimated at £75 million in exports, plus at least £50 million in spares and re-equipment over the following decade.[90] At the same time, Saudi haggling over credit terms brought complaints from the ECGD:

> This transaction would be the largest we have ever undertaken. It covers military aircraft, radar equipment and ancillary services, to a value of about £100 m. The potential losses could be significant to the viability of the Department's overall activities. The payment terms we are urged by the Ministry of Aviation to accept involve low pre-delivery payments and payments spread over as much as 15 years in all or 12–13 years from delivery. This relates to a country which is undoubtedly able to pay this large sum, but it is in an area where the risk of political disturbance is considerable.'[91]

Previously, arms had normally been sold on a cash or near-cash basis. The Saudi deal was to be a watershed – and even by this point the Saudis had barely begun a period of protracted haggling over credit terms. In the final event, the consortium accepted the Saudi proposal that payment should be spread over an unprecedented period of 14 years, with interest set at 5.5 per cent, and provision for payment of 2.5 per cent on the signing of the letter of intent, 5 per cent on the signature of the contract, 5 per cent one year thereafter, and the balance over the next 13 years, with no more than 10 per cent due to be paid in any one year. As Stonehouse told Prince Sultan, 'these terms go far beyond any which have ever been previously offered by the UK manufacturers for the sale of military equipment over-seas'.[92] In practice the annual payments over the 13 years broke down as 16 half-yearly payments at 5 per cent, one annual payment at 3.5 per cent and four annual payments of 1 per cent. The ECGD had refused to cover these last four payments, which were to be covered by the consortium companies themselves. As D. F. Hubback of the Board of Trade observed, 'the Saudis regard the longer terms as a sort of status symbol'.[93] As he also noted, up to then the outside limits on credit for military aircraft had been five years from delivery, and hence UK government actions here were 'bound to be quoted against us when other contracts come up and, to that extent, we have intensified the credit race. Clearly it is not in our balance of payments interests that we should have to wait so long for our money. But, as always in these cases, the question resolves itself into whether we could have got the contract on shorter terms and, if not, do we do ourselves more harm in the longer run by pushing out credit terms in this way?'[94]

Nevertheless, at the end of November, when the British ambassador and Geoffrey Edwards showed the Saudi Finance Minister these credit terms – the first time he had seen them – he complained that the payments were too heavy in the early years, and proposed a schedule that would have seen 19.5 per cent repaid over the final four years! Edwards immediately rejected this. For his part, the Governor of the Saudi Arabian Monetary Agency made a proposal along the same lines, which would have seen 13.5 per cent being repaid over the final four years.

In March 1966, against a background of growing regional tension and the risk of UAR attacks from the Yemen, Prince Sultan requested the immediate provision of a squadron of Lightning aircraft, a request he felt fell within the terms of the undertaking given by John Stonehouse the previous November. With contracts for Lightnings still to be signed, Sultan made it clear that in Saudi eyes there was a direct linkage between meeting this additional request and the contracts being signed. As Michael Stewart, the Foreign Secretary, noted:

> the American F-104 aircraft is now to be offered to Jordan; this develop-ment may give the Saudis second thoughts about the Lightning, to which they originally preferred the F-104 until the Americans showed some reluc-tance to supply. Indeed it may only have been the hope of involving us in

some kind of defence commitment that caused Faisal finally to choose Lightnings.[95]

To meet the Saudi request, the UK government would have to withdraw Lightnings then in service in Germany with the RAF. The question which remained was whether to supply just the aircraft (and armaments) or whether to also supply RAF crews and ground staff. Michael Stewart suggested that, in this instance, 'Our cover story would then be that this was a training mission, sent to demonstrate Lightnings to the Saudi Air Force'. Clearly, this option carried political risks, as Stewart realised. The UK could easily find itself 'engaged in war between Saudi Arabia and Egypt' which he rightly feared Cairo would portray as 'imperialist intervention in Arab affairs and this could affect our oil interests in Iraq and even perhaps in Kuwait'.

However, such considerations were outweighed by the importance of the Lightning contract. An offer to supply Lightnings complete with RAF crews (the 'training mission') could be used as a lever to force the Saudis to sign the Lightning contracts prior to their despatch:

> We must of course face the likelihood that the 'training mission' might have to conduct operations. I understand that the Lightnings would have to be based on Jedda and that their range is too small for them to become involved in operations in the frontier zone ... This has the political advantage that they could not be committed against Egyptian aircraft unless the latter had penetrated deep into Saudi airspace. There would be no question at all of our planes operating over the Yemen.[96]

Hence foreign policy was to be determined by arms sales interests.

For his part, Denis Healey was less enthusiastic about the open-ended commitment that sending an RAF squadron would represent, and suggested dispatching a squadron of eight RAF Lightnings complete with ground support (involving 250 personnel) for a maximum of two weeks, on a 'goodwill and training mission'.[97] The issue was discussed at the OPD on 9 March. It was agreed that the Lightning contract was of such importance that the Saudi request for assistance should be met.[98] The FO would inform Washington, which it did, stressing that:

> the potential foreign exchange earnings from the Lightning deal were an integral factor in our reckoning of our ability to afford the purchase of the F-111A. If the deal fell through, this would not affect the United States commitment to the agreed target for co-operative arms sales to third countries, but there would be no immediate prospect of replacing it with some other contract. This would be a grave situation.[99]

However, the dispatch of an RAF squadron was a last resort. The British embassy in Jeddah was told that BAC could make seven Lightning Mark Is available in five months, with four Hunter Mark VI aircraft available within four to five weeks, with Airwork able to supply pilots (although whether Airwork pilots would be prepared to operate them in a war environment was another question). Again, this was seen partly as a carrot to help secure the signing of the Lightning contracts, and such support was to be conditional on signature. In the event, Sultan was entirely satisfied with this offer, merely inquiring as to whether the delivery time for the Lightnings could be shortened, and for four Mark IIs to be supplied within two months (although he did subsequently request a later mark of Lightning).[100] However, the supply of the aircraft from stock was not without serious implications for the RAF. As the Air Force Department pointed out: 'Since the aircraft in store have already to some extent been cannibalized to keep the front line going, it is likely that our operational squadrons would have to be robbed of various items needed to bring the Saudi aircraft up to standard.'[101]

In April 1966 Sultan also requested the emergency despatch of batteries of Thunderbird missiles, even though under the terms of the 1965 carve-up the US was to supply the Saudis with missiles. The US government had been approached and asked to supply a Hawk battery immediately, but had offered only an October delivery date. The British government was therefore approached, and was willing to despatch two batteries of Thunderbirds within four to six months, but Sultan wanted faster delivery.[102] As he told the British ambassador, 'Jizan and Jedda were the vital places which required protection and Jizan even more than Jedda since it was in the South that Saudi Arabia would be required to meet [an] enemy assault on land and without protection against air attack Saudi forces could not be expected to hold an Egyptian advance into Saudi territory.'[103] Again, if neither the UK nor the US could improve on the delivery times already offered, Sultan implied that the Lightning contracts might not be signed, and even suggested that the Saudis could look to the USSR for weapons – a bluff that few in the FO were likely to take seriously. In addition, Sultan requested that British naval vessels should pay visits to Red Sea ports, at which the British government duly obliged. Once again, Saudi Arabia was looking to play the US and the UK against each other over the supply of weapons, and once again the response was the same: to share information on their separate meetings with Sultan and present a united front in terms of the weapons on offer and delivery dates. Given US unhappiness at the prospect of the Thunderbird deal – Raytheon saw this as a threat to its Hawk deal – the inclination was to tell Sultan that he should accept an American offer.

However, Rusk and McNamara themselves had no objection to the supply of Thunderbirds so long as it did not jeopardise the Hawk deal, and instructed the US embassy to tell Sultan that the US could not improve on its October delivery date.[104] From McNamara's point of view, this would eliminate any danger of the Saudis cancelling the Lightning contract which he had been so keen to facilitate the previous autumn. Denied the emergency despatch of Hawks, Sultan focused on the Thunderbird and immediately began haggling over the price (approximately £15 million). According to Sultan, King Faisal thought that this 'was tantamount to refusing to sell Thunderbird at all, so exorbitant was the price demanded'.[105]

Once the Lightning aircraft began to arrive in the Kingdom, questions about their suitability in a desert environment arose. From the Jeddah embassy Bill Cranston told Frank Brenchley of how:

> The manner of their arrival has not been very auspicious. Of the six ordered, Lightning No. 1 got through to Riyadh on 13 June at the first attempt backed by the large scale Royal Air Force flight re-fuelling and escorting operation. Lightning No. 2 landed at Amman with a technical fault and later reached Riyadh on the 16th. No. 3 ... reached Riyadh on the 18th, but its partner No. 4 remained unserviceable at Muharraq after both had been diverted there because of bad weather at Riyadh and reached Riyadh only about 28 July. Lightnings Nos. 5 and 6 arrived at Riyadh on 28 July. One of those originally at Riyadh is now unserviceable at Jedda.

This raised the question of the appropriateness of the Lightnings – an aircraft with a high proportion of electronics which demanded skilled servicing, and adequate facilities and spare parts – to the Saudi environment. As Cranston noted:

> There is no evidence here that I am aware of to show that the Royal Air Force, as the military experts in this subject, were ever formally consulted by those of our Government Departments concerned about the suitability of this type of aircraft and therefore the military wisdom of selecting it for Saudi Arabia. Had this been done, the Departments might perhaps have recommended another more suitable type of aircraft or air defence system, before the deal with the Saudis proceeded. The Royal Air Force, I am told, would not themselves have been likely to recommend the Lightning for use in the ground attack role.

Cranston concluded by warning Brenchley of 'the possibility of a situation being reached in which we will have sold to the Saudis a highly sophisticated weapon as part of a worthwhile commercial proposition yet one which, because of its sophistication, may not in the end be able to fulfil the purpose for which the Saudis bought it and, moreover, bought it in good faith that the weapon which we were supplying was one which could ensure their defence'.[106]

However, this was only the beginning of the problems that would emerge. In August 1966, the *Daily Telegraph's* air correspondent, air commodore Donaldson, wrote that the air defence scheme was ineffectual, and that it was not working properly because it was being run by civilians rather than the military. Prince Sultan was incensed and

Donaldson had to be persuaded not to follow up this scoop with further articles on the matter.[107] Then, in September, when a Lightning Mark II crashed on a demonstration flight over Riyadh, Sultan asked the consortium to replace it free of charge. However, most of the difficulties arose over Airwork's contribution, so much so that Prince Sultan cited problems between the Saudi Ministry of Defence and Airwork as one of the reasons why the Saudis placed an armoured car order with the French rather than buy UK Saracens.[108] At the same time, the Saudis were negotiating with the French over a tank contract that Vickers had hoped to secure, and over naval equipment. In addition, according to the Saudi ambassador to the UK, 'the French had been willing to deal with Saudi middlemen and to pay them the necessary 'commission', instead of relying on direct Government to Government contacts'. The ambassador thought that Vickers, for example, were not 'active and enterprising enough in their salesmanship' nor 'willing to consider similar deals through middlemen'.[109]

But Airwork's performance was not the only factor affecting sales prospects at the time: the announcement of the UK's intention to withdraw from the Gulf also had repurcussions. As the defence attaché in Jeddah reported:

> If withdrawal from Aden was unpopular it was at least accepted with the resignation tinged with disgust appropriate to an unpalatable event which has not occurred on the actual doorstep. The Gulf is different, as affairs here impinge directly upon Saudi Arabia and for all the outward calm with which our announcement was apparently accepted, the inside picture is very different. Resignation and disgust have given way to resentment and dislike. During very full discussions recently concerning various potential sales of military equipments the new position became clear and the Saudis need to make new friends who are prepared to show interest in the Arab world was evident.[110]

The attaché also reported on a military jingle that was doing the rounds in the Kingdom, which went thus:

> If you don't care for us,
> Do you think we'll care for you?
> We've got new friends in France
> And we'll see what they can do.

To help allay Saudi anxieties, John Stonehouse reaffirmed the UK government's commitment in answer to a parliamentary question, saying that the 'approval of the supply of defence equipment is not dependent on the disposition of our Forces abroad', and this reaffirmation was pointed out to Prince Sultan.[111] In March 1968 the government found out that the Saudis would not be renewing Airwork's contract, and instead had given the work to a team from Pakistan. The Pakistanis were cheaper and their government had guaranteed that they would take part in combat if required. The previous year, three Airwork pilots had refused to defend Saudi Arabia in the event of hostilities.

The Lightnings had all been delivered by 1969. However, the disarray caused by having to deal with a number of different companies – particularly Airwork – led the Saudis to insist in 1972 on BAC taking over the whole project under the co-ordination of the British government. Once this was done, a memorandum of understanding was signed[112] which outlined the 10 areas in which BAC would co-ordinate support under a £253 million deal. These were: Lightning and Strikemaster maintenance; pilot training courses at the King Faisal Air Academy; engineering courses at the Technical Studies Institute; on-the-job training for its Saudi graduates; provisioning and supplying personnel; motor transport maintenance; armament support; procurement; building construction; and aero-medical services.[113] Hence BAC's procurement responsibilities were considerable – it was to be responsible for the supply of everything except Rolls-Royce engines, involving it acting as prime contractor to around 700 British companies. Its building construction responsibilities alone involved £90 million worth of airfield work, technical buildings, domestic quarters and barracks. This relationship was to prove so fruitful that by 1976 there were 2,000 BAC employees working in Saudi Arabia. Another 250 were employed on the programme at Warton, Lancashire. It was no coincidence that it was Roy Mason, then Secretary of State for Defence, who was sent to represent the government at the funeral of King Faisal in March 1975.

Towards Al Yamamah

By the mid-1970s, in addition to the Strikemaster and Lightning contracts, British companies were working through orders for 250 Alvis Scorpion light tanks, eight SRN hovercraft, and a range of Rapier and Hawk missiles. The Callaghan government was anxious to build on this and persuade the Saudis of the wisdom of spending more of their US$6,700 million defence budget in Britain, a possibility discussed when Prince Sultan, Minister of Defence and Aviation, paid his first visit to London in November 1976. Now the government was interested in the sale of up to 100 Anglo-French Jaguar aircraft worth over £200 million, whereas in the past the FO had objected to any such sale on the grounds that in a fresh Arab–Israeli conflict the Saudis could hand the aircraft over to Egypt or Syria.[114]

The chances were that the Saudis would be looking to buy from the UK. In 1976, the US dwarfed all other Saudi arms suppliers, with outstanding orders for 80 F-5E aircraft, 250 tanks, six fast attack craft and Maverick ground-to-air missiles. However, this cosy relationship was jolted when, in 1976, Congress moved to block the sale of the Maverick. The election of Jimmy Carter as President in November 1976 further persuaded the Saudis that their reliance on the US could become as much a liability as an asset, and encouraged them to look to reduce their dependence on the US by diversifying their sources of supply.

Hence Prince Sultan's visit was regarded as of no little importance by the Callaghan government, as was evidenced by an itinerary which allocated a whole day to each of the three services, and also included meetings with Fred Mulley (Defence Secretary), Anthony Crosland (Foreign Secretary) and Eric Varley (Industry Secretary). This entire programme was informed by the trip to Saudi Arabia only the week before by the French Defence Minister, Ivon Bourges, also keen to capitalise on any tilt towards Europe.

In September 1977, Britain and Saudi Arabia finally signed a BAC follow-on contract. This four-year extension would carry British participation in the development of the Royal Saudi Air Force through to its scheduled transfer to Saudi hands and complete 'Saudisation' in 1982.[115] Even so, the Saudis' preference was still largely for US arms, specifically for around 60 McDonnell-Douglas F-15 fighter aircraft to replace the Lightnings by the early 1980s.[116] After all, relations with the US remained very close, politically and economically. Since the early 1960s the US had effectively guaranteed Saudi Arabia's independence. For its part, Saudi Arabia supplied the US with a quarter of all its imported oil, maintained around half of its estimated $60 billion assets in the US, and held around 85 per cent of its total reserves in dollars.[117] It lobbied for price restraint within the Organisation of Petroleum Exporting Countries (OPEC), helped prop up the Egyptian economy (and with it President Sadat), acted as a moderating force on the Palestine Liberation Organisation, and discreetly supported the Sadat peace initiative. Further afield, it financed the Moroccan troops who rescued President Mobutu in 1976, and had even supplied the Thieu regime in Saigon with cut-price oil. Hence the Saudis, with some justification, considered their relationship with the US to be close, albeit rather one-sided, and viewed the F-15 decision as a litmus test of US commitment.

However, during 1978 it became apparent that the US Congress was not going to grant automatic approval of the Saudi request. In January a draft letter was circulated in Congress, signed by a number of influential senators, calling on the Carter administration to delay the Saudi request on the familiar basis that the sale would pose a threat to Israel. In May, just 24 hours before the Senate vote, King Khalid sent a public letter, appealing to Congress not to block the sale. The letter played the card to which Congress had long been most receptive, but which in the Saudi case suggested desperation – defence against the 'Communist Threat'. In the event, the sale was approved, but only after Defense Secretary Harold

Brown had pledged that the aircraft would not be supplied with any equipment which would provide the capacity to strike at Israel.

While US–Saudi relations would continue to be affected by the highly effective pro-Israel lobby in the US, the Iranian revolution of 1979 left the Kingdom as the major pro-Western power in the Gulf, the principal defender of the pro-Western *status quo* and of Western oil interests. Given this, the Carter administration's priorities came to lie in supplying it with whatever military equipment it requested, even if that meant taking on Congressional opposition. From a Saudi perspective, the Iranian revolution reinforced the Saudis' desire to build up their armed forces, for which task US equipment was the first choice. This desire to secure advanced US weaponry, in turn, gave the Carter administration greater leverage over the Saudis.

One indication of this came on 15 July 1979, with the Saudi decision to increase oil production to 1 million barrels a day for the next three to six months. Within seven days of this announcement, the State Department recommended the sale of $1.2 billion of military equipment to facilitate modernisation of the Saudi National Guard.[118] A State Department official denied any link, explaining that: 'United States arms sales to Saudi Arabia have been conducted without any regard to any deals or links to the Saudi decisions on oil ... The sales are carried on within the context of our interest in helping the Saudis provide for their security and territorial integrity.'[119]

Beyond Britain and the US, the Saudis also maintained close relations with France. In May 1978 King Khalid travelled to Paris to meet President Giscard d'Estaing. In July 1979 French Defence Minister Bourges visited Riyadh, where he signed an agreement to supply around 500 AMX-30 and AMX-10 main battle tanks, ancilliary equipment, transport and training. By 1979 there were already 450 French military advisers in the Kingdom, and the number would increase as a result of the new contracts. In addition, a deal to sell a £400 million air defence missile complex, Shahine, developed partly with Saudi finance, was completed at around the same time. France viewed Saudi Arabia as a priority customer, and as such it was able to receive advanced military equipment even before the French military themselves. The Saudis also ordered the Mirage F1 and Puma helicopters, and asked France to draw up a whole coastal defence system for its maritime approaches to the Red Sea and the Gulf.[120]

During 1980, French military relations with the Kingdom improved further, just as British and US relations cooled dramatically. In Britain's case the damage was caused by a single event, the screening in April 1980 of the television programme *Death of a Princess*. The ensuing rift came at a particularly bad time for British companies. In 1979, Britain had sold £894 million worth of goods to Saudi Arabia (about 9 per cent of the market), and exports were up by 35 per cent in the first two months of

1980. In addition to the BAC work, Cable & Wireless was involved in a design, installation and maintenance contract worth £200 million for a communications system for the National Guard. Dunlop had been supplying the Kingdom, and GEC Marconi was involved in around £55 million a year's defence work. Moreover, the following month an announcement had been due on the Saudis' 'Third Development Plan', for which £131 billion had been earmarked.[121] In response to the screening, the British ambassador, James Craig, was recalled at the request of the Saudi government[122] and an impending visit to Saudi Arabia by Defence Secretary Francis Pym was cancelled. Even more significantly, a state visit to Britain by King Khalid was called off.[123]

In the US case, relations were strained following a further instalment of the ongoing F-15 saga. Following Congressional approval of the sale, the Saudis began to press the Carter administration for the inclusion of bomb racks, extra fuel tanks, and KC-135 tanker aircraft, to facilitate mid-air refuelling. However, the supply of this equipment would run counter to the assurances Harold Brown had given Congress to get the sale approved in the first place. While the administration was sympathetic to the requests, by October 1980 President Carter was trailing in the opinion polls in the run-up to the November presidential elections. So, although Brown and Zbigniew Brzezinski were amongst those in favour of supplying the equipment, the fact that candidate Reagan was campaigning to win Jewish support in New York by claiming that Carter was insensitive to Israeli security fears proved more important in the short run. The official Saudi press agency responded by saying that Washington should not take the Kingdom's friendship for granted, and added that if the US continued to refuse its requests for arms, it would 'knock on all doors' to acquire them, a point reinforced by the French confirmation of a massive £1.5 billion naval order just two weeks earlier. This new French order was designed to provide the Saudis with a small navy – four frigates, two supply vessels, and naval helicopters armed with missiles, plus training. The negotiations had taken over two years and involved 20 missions by French diplomats, as well as visits by heavyweights like Defence Minister Bourges and President Giscard, and the maintenance of an impeccably pro-Arab line in foreign policy, including support for an independent Palestine.

The victory of Ronald Reagan in the 1980 US presidential elections produced further twists in the US–Saudi arms sales relationship. On 20 January 1981, the new administration announced that it had authorised the sale of over US$2 billion worth of military equipment and services to the Kingdom, including US$900 million for support and maintenance of the 114 F-5 and 60 F-15 fighters for the Royal Saudi Air Force. In addition, the US announced a US$846 million programme for the building of 'facilities essential to support the Royal Saudi Navy', and the sale of US$299 million of related equipment.[124]

More controversy was stirred in April with the announcement that the Reagan administration proposed to sell five AWACS (airborne warning and control system) aircraft to the Kingdom. The administration brushed aside Israeli requests for the sale to be reconsidered, but the scale of Congressional opposition raised the prospect of the AWACS proposal being defeated in Congress. That the administration was all too aware of this was evidenced by the decision to delay the formal announcement of the proposed sale until after the June 1981 Israeli elections. Once the deal was announced, Congress would have 30 days to reject the sale.

In June 1981, King Khalid and Prince Sultan visited Britain, the climax of the Thatcher government's 18 month campaign to repair relations after the *Death of a Princess* controversy. High on the agenda was the renewal of the former BAC, now BAe, deal covering servicing and training for the Kingdom's Lightning and Strikemaster aircraft, which was due to expire in August 1982. BAe was confident of renewal up to 1985, worth an estimated £150 million to £200 million a year, because if the aircraft were phased out (the alternative) the Kingdom would be dependent for its front-line aerial defence on US F-5Es and F-15s, something the Saudis had sought to avoid. Furthermore, BAe had devised a way of lengthening the projected life of the Lightning up to 1985,[125] although the company recognised that its continued involvement in Saudi Arabia after that date was dependent on selling a new generation of aircraft. The Saudis were provided with another incentive by the destruction by Israeli aircraft of the Iraqi Osirik nuclear reactor on 7 June 1981, just two days before the visit. The aircraft had crossed Saudi air space to carry out the raid, but US AWACS apparently 'failed' to detect them.

British arms companies knew that securing orders in Saudi Arabia would require high-level governmental involvement and commitment. As one sales executive commented: 'We can beaver away at our level forever, but that will be useless without a political decision at the top.'[126] However, the Thatcher government had embraced the lessons of the past and had paid particular attention to King Khalid's visit to Paris in May 1978, where French assurances of uninterrupted delivery in times of conflict and sympathetic attitude to the question of Palestine had been pivotal in securing the £1.5 billion naval contract. In this respect, the British visit came just one month before Britain assumed the presidency of the EEC, from where it would be expected to give an indication of its seriousness by, for example, persuading its European partners of the need to involve the PLO in regional peace initiatives. Furthermore, the Saudis wanted the British to secure the Reagan administration's acceptance of the principle of self-determination for the Palestinians. With this in mind, on the eve of the visit, it was leaked that the Foreign Secretary, Lord Carrington, would be holding talks with Yasser Arafat at an early stage of his term at the helm of the EEC.

Saudi confidence in the US was being further eroded by the Reagan administration's attempt to impose conditions on the sale of the AWACS. In an attempt to secure Congressional approval of the sale, the administration proposed a form of dual control whereby US technicians would control the use of the aircraft in certain circumstances, a proposal which predictably did not meet with Saudi approval, especially in the wake of the Osirik incident. This stalemate led to suggestions that the Kingdom might instead purchase the Nimrod from Britain. However, Prince Bandar held talks on a possible compromise which involved guaranteeing that at least one US 'technician' would be involved in the operation of the surveillance equipment every time the aircraft flew.[127] This, together with the hint that the sale was in jeopardy, was considered by the administration sufficient to secure the deal's passage. Having abandoned the House of Representatives as a lost cause, the administration concentrated on the Senate, emphasising the cost of losing the order in economic, employment and intelligence terms. Although the administration lost the vote in the House (by 301 to 111), in the Senate the proposal passed by 52 to 48.[128] While this marked an undoubted success for the Reagan administration, the experience did not endear it to the Saudis, merely confirming their view that they needed to diversify their sources of supply by pursuing a European option, or risk leaving themselves vulnerable in the event of conflict in the region. France again benefited from this decision. In January 1984, Saudi Arabia signed a contract for between £3 billion to £4 billion worth of anti-aircraft defence systems – a deal even more valuable than the massive naval agreement of 1980, with Thomson-CSF the prime contractor, Matra and Giat supplying the missiles and the armoured vehicles to carry them.

Al Yamamah

Throughout 1984 and 1985, negotiations were also held over what would ultimately become the Al Yamamah deal. Once again, France was well placed and looked to have secured a deal based around the Mirage 2000, partly through offering a better price and earlier delivery dates than Britain. Defence Secretary Michael Heseltine was despatched to Riyadh in an effort to save the deal. However, Heseltine was reportedly given a rough reception, as King Fahd drew unfavourable comparisons between Britain's Middle East record and that of France.[129] Heseltine was despatched on further missions, but was unable to persuade King Fahd of the advantages of buying British. The deal was wrested from the French only at the last minute when Mrs Thatcher interrupted her holiday in Salzburg, Austria, to hold talks in Switzerland with the Saudis. Not only did this meeting secure Britain's most lucrative export order ever, it also became the source of much speculation as to what was offered to save it.

On 17 February 1986, Britain and Saudi Arabia formally signed the £5 billion Al Yamamah deal in Riyadh, under the terms of which Britain was to provide 132 military aircraft. The contract was signed by Saudi Defence Minister, Prince Sultan, and Colin Chandler, head of DESO. The deal was to be paid for almost entirely in oil, which would be processed by BP and Shell (who would take a fee), from where the money would reach BAe, and from there the various subcontractors (see Figure 3). However, it was widely rumoured that both BP and Shell had to be pressured by the government before agreeing to take, refine and sell the oil.

Initially, it was agreed that the Saudis would supply 400,000 b/d of oil to pay for the package. However, difficulties with this arrangement arose when, almost as soon as the agreement was signed, the price of oil on the world market collapsed, and the Saudis abandoned their oil-pricing policy, on which payment for the deal had been based.

The deal provided for the sale of 48 strike (IDS) Tornadoes, and 24 air-defence (ADV) variants, together valued at over £2 billion. In addition, it included 30 Hawk trainers, worth £150 million to £200 million, 30 Swiss Pilatus PC9 trainers, worth around £50 million, the Sea Eagle missile and 155 mm artillery shells. BAe was to be the prime contractor for the entire deal. Between 50 per cent and 60 per cent of the value of the deal went to the subcontractors – for example, Rolls-Royce, Plessey, Ferranti, GEC and Dowty. However, other countries also benefited – the Swiss in particular, as only 5–10 per cent of the value of the Pilatus PC9s would accrue to Britain, and also the West Germans and Italians, with whom Britain jointly produced the Tornado in the Panavia consortium.

The Al Yamamah agreement dwarfed even the French naval and tank and the US AWACS deals. More important, in terms of procurement trends, it marked a shift away from Saudi reliance on the US for major items of defence equipment. In reality, the deal was concluded only because of the Saudis' experience at the hands of the US Congress. Their first-choice package had been a combination of the US F-15C and F-15E aircraft, which would have had the advantage of complete compatibility with the AWACS system and the US Peace Shield command, control and communications system operated by the Kingdom. However, by 1984 it had become apparent that any such deal would be blocked by the pro-Israeli Congressional lobby, and that even if the deal succeeded it would only be because such restrictions had been attached to the sale in order to get it through as to deny the Saudis the level of security they sought by buying the aircraft in the first place.

The Tornado deal gave them the advanced aerial attack capability they sought with no restrictions on the area of operation. For instance, the aircraft would be free to operate in the north-west of the Kingdom (unlike

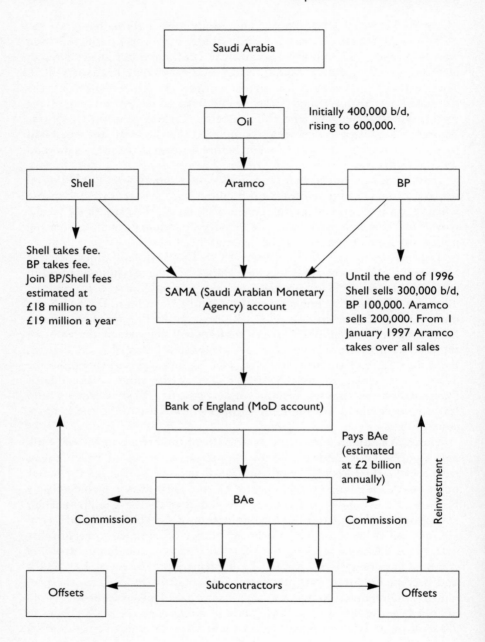

Figure 3 Al Yamamah: the system of payment for arms.

the AWACS), and from the Tabuk military base close to both the Jordanian border and hence Israel. The Saudis had long regarded this base as a likely target of an Israeli pre-emptive strike in the event of further Arab–Israeli conflict, but the US electoral system had always meant they were denied the aerial technology they sought to defend it.

A deal of such magnitude had far-reaching implications for the British defence industry. Until the deal was agreed, it had been expected that the Tornado production line would close in 1989. Together with British, German, and Italian replacement orders the deal held out the prospect of the line remaining open into the 1990s. British subcontractors also stood to gain significantly. Almost all the Tornado's weapons were produced by British companies (for instance, the JP 233 runway-cratering bomb made by Hunting), while BAe also produced weaponry for the Tornado and the Hawk. However, the deal also had an impact on the RAF, one which was informed by the French approach to arms sales. Four Tornadoes were to be delivered to the Saudis almost immediately. Already built for the RAF, they would be diverted to Saudi Arabia. In total, the RAF would be obliged to forgo 20 of the strike Tornadoes which would that year have formed the first of two reconaissance squadrons.[130]

In January 1987, following a visit to the Kingdom by Trade and Industry Secretary Paul Channon, an offset supervisory commission was created at the urging of the Saudis, who were keen to use the Al Yamamah deal to ensure that British industry participated in joint ventures in areas of Saudi interest.[131] However, there was no contractual obligation on the part of BAe in this respect. The government had agreed to encourage UK companies in general – not just those with a stake in Al Yamamah – to invest in Saudi Arabia, with the aim of achieving £1 billion worth of investment – around 25 per cent of the technical sales cost.[132] However, progress was slow, and when King Fahd paid a state visit to Britain in March 1987, the subject of offsets, none of which had materialised by that point, was again raised.

On 8 July 1988, a new phase of the Al Yamamah deal (Al Yamamah-2) was announced, with a value estimated at up to £10 billion, potentially twice the value of the earlier deal, and hence the richest export order in British history. Once again, BAe would be the prime contractor, with the government the main contractor. The deal further signified that the Kingdom was no longer prepared to be subjected to delays, refusals and what it regarded as public humiliation by the US Congress, especially when the more discreet British alternative, where legislative probing was not allowed to interfere with a good thing, was available. Between the signing of Al Yamamah and Al Yamamah–2, several further Saudi arms requests had been rejected by Congress. (Table 12.)

Table 12
Saudi arms requests refused by the US Congress, 1986–88

Weapon	Value ($ million)	Date
48 F-15 aircraft	n.a	February 1986
1,600 Maverick missiles	360	November 1987
800 Stinger missiles	89	May 1986
88 Lance missiles	n.a.	1986–87
Armour-piercing uranium ammunition	n.a.	May 1987
Ground equipment/maintenance of AWACS	325	April 1988

Source *Jane's Defence Weekly*, 23 July 1988.

As a result of this second deal, Britain overtook the US as the Kingdom's largest single arms supplier. Had the F-15 been available, with no strings attached, it would again have been the Saudis' first choice. As one Saudi official explained: 'We would prefer buying weapons from the USA. American technology is generally superior. But we are not going to pay billions of dollars to be insulted. We are not masochists.'[133] While Saudi sensitivity over the release of details of the new contract meant that MoD spokesmen could talk only in general terms of 'a significant enhancement to project Al Yamamah', the initial 'wish list' comprised: 48 Tornadoes (both strike and air-defence variants), complete with armaments and spares; 60 Hawks (a combination of 20 100s and 40 200s); 88 Westland helicopters (mainly the Sikorsky Black Hawk, built under licence); six *Sandown* class minesweepers (to be built by Vosper Thornycroft); a small number of BAe 125 and 146 aircraft for communications; the construction of an airbase (eventually dropped as a result of depressed oil prices); and facilities for the minesweepers (to be built by BAe's then recently acquired construction arm, Ballast Nedam); as well as training programmes for both the RSAF and the navy. The deal, signed by Defence Secretary George Younger and Prince Sultan on 3 July, followed discussions which again involved Mrs Thatcher.

To finance it, the current oil barter arrangements were to be extended. This meant that the proportion of Saudi oil production allocated to arms purchases would again increase. In addition, what the MoD referred to as 'a positive and constructive offset programme' was to be a feature of the deal, aimed at the reinvestment of a minimum of 25 per cent of the value of the deal's technical content. While a memorandum of investment was signed by Prince Sultan and George Younger on 23 November 1988, the negotiations over the precise nature of future offsets were to take a considerable amount of time. In the meantime, one of the more bizarre consequences of the close Anglo-Saudi military relationship manifested itself when, as part of the Al Yamamah 2 deal, the England football team travelled to Riyadh in November 1988 to play a friendly international with the Saudi national team.

The England team flew to the match in a Concorde chartered by BAe and 'topped up with the company's officials, customers and clients'. The Football Association's Chief Executive, Graham Kelly, was quoted as saying that: 'The FA are more than happy to assist the Government to fulfil its obligation to Saudi Arabia. We have considerable expertise to draw on, not only in the establishment of coaching and educational schemes but also in sports medicine.' This was good news, as BAe was also involved in securing deals with other Gulf states which would see the company sponsoring the expansion of the FA's coaching and educational scheme in the Middle and Far East, and result in a visit by the England under-16 team to Oman in February 1989.[134]

It was not long after the signing of the Al Yamamah 2 deal that the manner in which the British government had secured the Saudi deals came under scrutiny. Perhaps unsurprisingly, this richest-ever export order seemed to have been accompanied by unprecedented levels of bribery. From the British government's point of view such scrutiny was particularly unwelcome, as the secrecy it could afford the Saudis was one of the attractions of doing business with Britain in the first place. It was even more unwelcome in that it concentrated on the role of middlemen and commissions, allegations that named members of the Saudi royal family had required payments before agreeing to place the deal with Britain, and that at the UK end of the deal people had benefited personally from the arrangement.

As we have already seen, the question of the role, scale and propriety of commissions in securing arms contracts goes to the very core of the business. While there is no doubting that they are paid, governments seek to ensure that the arm's-length principle applies, and hence that commissions are deniable in terms of a contract being a commercial venture between two parties, confidential to them, about which the government has no particular inside knowledge. Only where this arm's-length principle is called into question through a proven link between a member of a government or someone close to it and the original contract can serious difficulties over commission arise, as the case of Prince Bernhard of the Netherlands illustrates only too well.[135]

The fact that the UK had secured the first Al Yamamah deal at the eleventh hour, when the French manufacturer Dassault was convinced that its bid had been accepted, only for Mrs Thatcher's personal intervention to swing it Britain's way, had left a Dassault spokesman talking of the outcome as being 'unexpected, incomprehensible, and catastophic'.[136] L'Express attributed the Saudi decision to British willingness to pay 'exceptional commercial expenses',[137] while those involved on the British side moved quickly to deny such allegations. For example, Michael Heseltine argued that: 'What you have to remember is that arms sales are commercial warfare at its most acute. Anything goes – rumours, smears, allegations – you can be absolutely sure that our rivals are trying to undermine what we have done. The Government had no knowledge and no dealings involving commission arrangements.'[138]

However, given the assurance of anonymity, some involved in the Al Yamamah deals were prepared to be more forthright. As one arms industry source explained: 'When you sell to Saudi Arabia, you are really selling to the Saudi royal family – a limited company with 200 shareholders. It is quite simple. In some countries you pay import duties of 30 per cent, in others you pay commissions.'[139] Clearly, if it is to succeed in a field where such payments are the norm, a government must be prepared to compromise standards it might otherwise seek to apply to the conduct of business. In the Middle East, though illegal in Saudi Arabia (and hence arranged and banked in Switzerland), commissions are claimed to be a source of income for the massed ranks of the Saudi royal family.

In May 1989, Prince Sultan again visited Britain, this time to review the progress of the deal, and in particular of the offset arrangements. Progress here was slow. By June 1989, the first proposals were being put forward to the British Offset Committee, not surprisingly with BAe in the vanguard. The Saudi Arabian Offset Committee accepted the offsets of BAe and Dowty, who proposed the establishment of a missile engineering facility to repair and maintain weapons supplied to the RSAF. It also accepted a deal for the inclusion of a Rolls-Royce engine maintenance and overhaul support site. Jointly, the deals had an estimated value of no more than £100 million.[140] By 1990, just eight proposals had been put forward, of which BAe was involved in five. Hence the progress of the offset programme has, to date, been rather disappointing from a Saudi perspective. In practice, many companies have been reluctant to invest in what they see as a potentially unstable area. Nevertheless, further initiatives involving Tate & Lyle, Glaxo and BP have now been implemented. However, by the mid-1990s, the number of jobs created as a result of these programmes still only numbered in the low hundreds.[141]

Meanwhile the very nature of the Al Yamamah programme, and the context in which it was secured, led to periodic scares over whether the Kingdom would really require all the equipment originally indicated, and whether the payment arrangements were satisfactory. Given the fall in the price of oil on the world market from almost the minute the first deal was struck, a situation developed in which there was a growing disparity between the value of the equipment that was being supplied and the value of the 400,000 b/d of oil received by the MoD. By the end of 1989, it was estimated that rectification of the situation would already require an additional 100,000 b/d.[142]

This situation posed difficult choices for the Saudis, one of which would involve cancellation of parts of the programme. While it had placed

great emphasis on defence spending, the Kingdom, which had traditionally been unwilling to engage in large-scale foreign borrowing, was
running a budget deficit. The end of the Iran–Iraq War also placed
elements in jeopardy, as, according to defence industry sources, several
components of Al Yamamah were intended for onward passage to Iraq in
the first place. Most prominently, at least part of the Westland helicopter
element was alleged to have been intended for Iraq. Notwithstanding
these considerations, the Saudis' commitment to defence, and the royal
family's reliance on commission payments to help fund lavish lifestyles,
proved the stronger. By the end of 1989 the Saudis moved to adjust their
payments. BAe received a cash payment of around £1.3 billion, and the
Saudis increased their oil flow to 500,000 b/d.[143] As mentioned in Chapter
1, at the time of writing it stands at 600,000 b/d, but even this is not real-
ising the value of the equipment covered.

Again though, immediately prior to the Iraqi invasion of Kuwait, and
with Al Yamamah 2 contracts still to be signed, the fortunes of British
arms companies involved in the programme seemed to be in decline, again
underlining the general sense of uncertainty that pervades the arms trade.
It was not a good time to be trying to sell the Tornado (or generate
contracts from promises to buy). While delivery of the 72 ordered under
Al Yamamah 1 was due to be completed in 1991, the requirement for a
further 48 remained vulnerable to cancellation – a vulnerability highlighted by the cancellation of Tornado orders by Oman, Jordan and
Malaysia – leaving Saudi Arabia the only purchaser outside the Panavia
countries. A further blow to the aircraft's export potential came with the
announcement that, as a result of the *Options for Change* defence review,
the government was cutting its purchases of the aircraft.

Moreover, the Iraqi invasion of Kuwait completely altered the strategic
balance in the region.[144] As the US undertook its huge airlift, ostensibly to
defend Saudi Arabia against further Iraqi aggression, domestic US perceptions of the Kingdom were changing. From the US point of view, the crisis
highlighted the importance of Saudi Arabia as the defender of Western
interests in the region, and also underlined its vulnerability to attack. This
perception, at least in the short to medium term, increased the likelihood
of future Saudi weapons requests being treated more sympathetically.
Further, the conduct of the war, the role of the US and the perceived high
performance of US military hardware meant that US weaponry would top
the region's post-war shopping lists. In turn, these facts, coupled with the
perceived poor performance of the Tornadoes (notwithstanding the
debate regarding the wisdom of such a large number of low-flying
missions) led to months of anxiety at BAe, lest the Kingdom abandon its
plans for further Tornadoes in favour of US equipment.[145] Of particular
concern was the reliability record of the RSAF Tornadoes deployed at
Dharhan. Reportedly, during the conflict, US aircraft had been obliged to

fly additional sorties because the Tornadoes were continually incapaci-
tated.[146]

The fact that almost immediately after the invasion, US Defense
Secretary Dick Cheney was promising Saudi Arabia a whole bevy of
sophisticated equipment, most of which had previously been opposed by
Congress, on the grounds that 'the situation in the Gulf region has
changed dramatically',[147] heightened British fears about the future of Al
Yamamah. This fear was informed by the fact that much in the Al
Yamamah agreements existed only in the form of memoranda of understanding dating from 1988 – no contracts had been signed. Rather, the
entire arrangement was viewed by the Saudis as constituting an ongoing
defence relationship that would extend into the next century. In
September 1990, with British forces stationed in Saudi Arabia, Prince
Bandar sought to defuse the Tornado scare by explaining that: 'We have
no intention of scaling down our British purchases. If anything, we might
be looking for more co-operation with our friends in Europe, including
Britain, and for more equipment to equip our armed forces.'[148] The
following year, Prince Bandar announced that the Kingdom would sign
contracts for the equipment still outstanding on the Al Yamamah 2 deal,
and paid tribute to the performance of the Tornado in the conflict: 'We
were very pleased with the performance of the Tornado in the Gulf war.
When we first ordered the fighter in 1985 we needed strike capability and
it proved itself during the conflict. We are also grateful for the support
shown to our country by Mrs Thatcher and for the continued support
from Mr Major.'[149] In reality, this latter consideration was the more
important.

There was never any question of 'good government' initiatives or the
application of human rights criteria getting in the way of the Anglo-Saudi
arms relationship, so central to the corporate health of BAe, and hence
also to the maintenance of a defence infrastructure which allows Britain
to realise its vision of its place in the world. As Jeremy Hanley explained
quite clearly in 1995: 'Her Majesty's Government have no plans to link
the UK's trade and defence policies with Saudi Arabia's performance in
the area of respect for human rights. Her Majesty's Government have no
plans to link the UK's trade and defence policies with Saudi Arabia's
performance in the area of respect for religious liberty.'[150] In the post-Gulf
War scramble for contracts too much was at stake. Britain had to secure
its rightful share of the market.

Jordan

Compared with its Arab neighbours, Jordan has suffered from two significant disadvantages which have limited its ability to acquire the arms

of its choice. Firstly, it is a poor country compared with its oil-rich neighbours, and has relied in part on gifts from them and Western suppliers alike, not to mention over-generous credit terms, to equip itself. Secondly, its proximity to Israel has imposed clear limits on what the US has been prepared to sell. While the US had no wish to undermine King Hussein, successive administrations preferred to express their support in currency other than arms. In practice, as this case study shows, neither of these was a barrier to Jordan receiving British arms. In particular, Jordan's economic circumstances were no barrier to the £270 million Anglo-Jordanian arms deal of 1985. In practice, however, as the figures cited in Chapter 2 illustrate, Jordan has been unable to pay for these arms.

In the years leading up to Jordanian independence and beyond, British officers formed the backbone of the Jordanian armed forces. Britain was instrumental in the creation of a Jordanian Air Force capable of a combat role through the sale of a squadron of Hawker Hunters and Whirlwind helicopters in 1958. In the mid-1960s Jordan sought further Hunters.

Late in 1966 the British government told the Jordanians it would supply one Hunter free of charge. In early 1967 the Jordanians intimated that they would like to purchase two Hunter aircraft. In addition, they wanted to buy a range of other equipment, including Saracen and Ferret armoured cars, together worth around £2 million to £3 million. As the British embassy in Amman noted: 'Quite apart from our political interest in helping to maintain the present régime in power by co-operating with the Americans in providing arms and equipment, thus strengthening the loyalty and confidence of the armed forces who remain the one guarantee of continued stability in Jordan, there is also the fact that this Jordanian request could represent a considerable British export order.'[151] However, the Jordanians themselves could not afford all the equipment, and so placed their hopes on Kuwaiti and Saudi Arabian contributions.

The requirement also has to be seen against a background of rising tension in the region. An Israeli attack on the Jordanian village of Samu in November 1966 had demoralised the Jordanian armed forces, a result of both the attack itself (which decimated the air force) and King Hussein's decision not to retaliate.

In this context the FO was keen to do something to show support for King Hussein. The UK already provided a £2.4 million annual subsidy to Jordan, while the US supplied a range of military equipment for free, and had loaned a number of F-104s to fill a gap until F-104s on order could be delivered.

In February 1967 it was decided that, in an effort to shore up King Hussein's position, the UK government would offer him three Hunters free of charge (superseding the earlier offer of one, and meeting the total number the Jordanians had suggested they were seeking), making up for the two shot down in the Israeli attack. All that the Jordanians would have to pay for was the MoD refurbishment, estimated at £200,000. The total cost to the UK of this gift was £100,000:

> The calculation was that an immediate gesture of this kind would have an effect on the morale of King Hussein and his Government and on his people out of all proportion to the actual cost to HMG. It would make the armed forces feel that they were in a better position to resist further raids; it would enable them to demonstrate that friendship with the West produced results in terms of actual equipment just as well as friendship with the East.[152]

The first of the Hunters was officially handed over in April 1967. Neither of the other two had been delivered by the time of the June 1967 Arab–Israeli War. However, the war itself was not to be allowed to impede the delivery of arms to Jordan. As the FO told the embassy in Amman:

> The policy on arms sales to the Middle East does not differ much from our policy prior to the recent war. However we shall scrutinise with great care all requests from Middle East countries and will ensure that supplies of any particular type of equipment are not delivered at a greater rate than before hostilities. Subject to this condition we would expect to be able to approve all reasonable requests from Jordan provided they could afford to pay.[153]

The continuation of King Hussein's rule was not something about which the UK government was dispassionate. As the British ambassador observed, support for King Hussein was at least in part premised on 'the desirability of the continuance of a relatively moderate Jordan as an encouragement to other like-minded Arab states in the face of revolutionary Arab nationalism, demonstrably antagonistic to the maintenance of British interests in the Middle East'.[154]

The best way, the ambassador suggested, for Britain to show its support for the king would be to offer up to 20 Hunters quickly, and preferably as a gift. This would also 'help explode the myth that the USSR is the only great-power "friend" of the Arabs', a myth gaining ground due to Soviet rearmament of Syria and the UAR.

The difficulty, as elsewhere, was securing sufficient Hunters from the RAF to meet the various demands for them. The ambassador was told that all Mark 6 and Mark 9 Hunters likely to be available by 1970 had already been allocated. However, the MoD did have 20 earlier Mark 4 Hunters mothballed, the cost of refurbishing each of which would be £100,000.[155] The problem lay in the delivery times. Delivery of the first batch could take place in 12 months, but it would be around two years before all 20 could be delivered. Jordan's requirement was more immediate. In the aftermath of the June 1967 war, it had just eight Hunters left, some of which were undergoing refurbishment and one of which was damaged. Only one was serviceable. In view of both this and their preference for either Mark 6 or

Mark 9 aircraft, Jordan turned the Mark 4 proposal down.

Jordan's requirement was all the more immediate in view of the attitude of the Johnson administration. Despite his desire to assist King Hussein and prevent the emergence of a radical Arab regime, Johnson's hands were tied by Congress, and it would be the beginning of 1968 before the US released any further arms for Jordan.

A further complicating factor was that King Hussein, convinced that the UK would not release any further Hunters, planned to visit Moscow in August 1967, where he was thought likely to accept Soviet offers of replacement aircraft. On this basis, Foreign Secretary George Brown felt it 'important both for the survival of King Hussein and the maintenance of a Western-orientated Jordan that we should accede to the King's request for Hunters' before he visited Moscow.[156] (Indeed, when General Khammash, the Jordanian Chief of Staff, subsequently visited Washington in January 1968, after the Johnson administration had agreed to resume supplies to Jordan, he described to Walt Rostow his reception in Moscow. There, Marshal Grechko had 'apparently put down a blank page in front of Khammash and said to him: "Write down whatever you need in the way of supplies and training and you shall have it"!'[157])

Hence the search for available Hunters began. It revealed that three Mark 9s could be made available to Jordan within three weeks by withdrawing them from a Middle East squadron. These would be three of 16 which would in any case have become available once withdrawal from Aden was complete. In anticipation of the withdrawal all the aircraft had been allocated to customers. In this respect, Jordan's gain would be India's loss. As Denis Healey warned George Thomson: 'In view of the political nature of the transaction we shall naturally need to have a firm assurance from you that payment will be forthcoming either from the Jordanians (who still owe us money on earlier orders for Hunters) or, failing that, from Foreign Office votes.'[158] Once refurbished, the Hunters would cost around £120,000 each.

As George Brown observed, 'together with the Israel order for eighteen Centurions, [this] makes an arrangement we might just get away with. However, there should be no underestimation of the political criticism this combined deal at this moment could provoke both here and elsewhere.'[159]

The ambassador in Amman was instructed to inform King Hussein of this decision before he left for Moscow, together with a warning on the need for circumspection in dealing with the Russians in view of their aim 'to support the revolutionary regimes and undermine the moderate Arab Governments which favour peaceful development and co-operation with the West.'[160] Jordan accepted the offer. However, as General Khammash pointed out to the British ambassador, notwithstanding the fact that the UK had sacrificed front-line aircraft to meet Jordan's requirements,

Jordan still had a fighter force comprising just eight aircraft, whereas it needed a minimum of 18. Khammash took his case to London in August 1967.

The problem for the British government was that the only way in which additional Hunters could be made available was through withdrawing aircraft from active service. To supply the additional 10 that Khammash sought would involve disbanding an entire squadron, and would risk affecting relations with India and Kuwait, which were already awaiting Hunters when they became available. (The aircraft had not been in production for some time by then.) In the event, Saudi Arabia decided to forgo six Hunters on order, releasing more for Jordan. This supply was doubly important, as all US arms sales to Jordan were still suspended, and even a visit by King Hussein to Washington had failed to get the suspension lifted. With Jordanian plans to buy the F-104 shelved, the Johnson administration informed the British embassy in Washington 'that they would warmly welcome it if we could find enough Hunters to satisfy Jordan's immediate requirements'.[161]

At the beginning of 1968, the Jordanians turned their attention to the question of acquiring supersonic fighter aircraft. BAC had already been trying to interest the Jordanians in the Lightning for some time, although King Hussein did not seem interested. Such a sale would be advantageous to the British government as it would maintain the Warton production line, which was otherwise coming to an end. Other arguments in favour included, of course, the UK's commitment to maintaining King Hussein's moderate Arab influence in the region. This depended on him being able to command the loyalty of the Jordanian armed forces. It could 'only be maintained if these forces can see the prospect of their being supplied with modern equipment comparable to that available from Soviet sources to the armed forces of other Arab states.'[162] The sale would also offset criticism of the continued UK supply of arms to Israel.

At the same time, the Johnson administration finally approved its long-awaited arms package for Jordan, compiled on the basis that the king would not buy arms from the USSR. However, wider regional and Congressional considerations meant that 'the State Department would still much prefer the Jordanians to buy Centurions and Lightnings and will press Khammash to do so. But they are not hopeful and for this reason felt obliged to include tanks and aircraft in the offer for which they sought approval.'[163] Indeed, such was the degree of Anglo-American co-operation over arms sales to the region that both willingly exchanged details of prices, credit terms and the availability of the goods which would comprise their respective aircraft and tank offers.[164]

However, the Jordanians' interest in buying American rather than British had less to do with price than with the political symbolism of buying from the US, and thereby securing what they regarded as the best possible demonstration of US support for King Hussein's position. Nevertheless, this did not deter the industrious John Stonehouse from pursuing the sale of the Lightning, with a personal letter to King Hussein:

> I understand that you are considering whether you would also need supersonic aircraft and are examining the types at present available. If this is so, I should like to commend the BAC Lightning to your attention. This aircraft has shown itself to possess a unique interception performance, coupled with a high degree of reliability in worldwide service ... I can further assure you that if you decide to acquire some Lightnings, you may rely upon our consent, for we look forward to continuing the close relations that have been built up over the years between the Royal Jordanian Air Force and Royal Air Force.[165]

Even so, King Hussein decided to buy the F-104. However, Jordan did continue to purchase additional Hunters into the early 1970s, and to press for their earliest possible release.

During the 1970s, these deliveries aside, British arms exports to Jordan fell dramatically, as Jordan came to rely more on the US, regarding the purchase of US arms as having a deterrent value to Israel. However, it began to move away from this reliance from 1980 onwards.[166] The move coincided with the election of the first Thatcher government, complete with its commitment to securing new markets for British arms, and the subsequent revival in the fortunes of British arms manufacturers in the region. The first signs of revival in Jordan were not long in coming.

In October 1979, following a visit to London by King Hussein, where he met Mrs Thatcher and DSO head Sir Ronald Ellis, it was announced that Britain would sell Jordan 200 Shir-1 tanks, in a deal worth up to £200 million. The Shir-1 was the tank Vickers had developed from the Chieftain for sale to the Shah of Iran, the order for which had recently been cancelled by the new revolutionary government.[167] The tank order stemmed from something of a change of mind on the part of the Jordanians, who had been considering the purchase of the US M–60 tank. Interviewed on US television, King Hussein explained that the change of mind had been brought about partly as a result of conditions the US had sought to apply as to the use of the tanks.[168] In September 1981, Defence Secretary John Nott visited Amman to follow up this sale and try to sell the Jordanian Air Force the BAe Hawk.

When, in 1983, the Reagan administration announced that it would not be going ahead with its projected sale of 1,600 Stinger ground-to-air missiles, because of Congressional opposition, the Thatcher government immediately moved to plug the gap. During the March 1984 visit to London by the Jordanian Foreign Minister, Taher al Masri, Richard Luce, Minister of State at the FCO, tried to sell him the Javelin missile, even though it was not yet in service with UK forces. Then, in October 1984,

Defence Secretary Michael Heseltine visited Amman and held talks with King Hussein on the possible purchase of British arms. In terms of the competition to secure the anti-aircraft missile contract, there was thought to be little to choose, in the absence of the Stinger, between the British Javelin, the French Matra Mistral and the Soviet SA-7 Grail. Hence the final decision, as Heseltine was well aware, was more likely to rest on the credit terms available than on operational criteria. In the event, Jordan opted for the Soviet SA-7, on highly favourable credit terms.

In 1985, in advance of a visit to Jordan by Mrs Thatcher, IMS concluded a £270 million loan package for Jordan, backed by the ECGD, which included a substantial subsidy element. Under the terms of the deal, the average rate of interest to be paid by Jordan would be just 8–9 per cent, considerably below the minimum export finance rates agreed by the OECD for Jordan.[169] The memoranda of understanding establishing the facility were to be signed by Mrs Thatcher during her visit. Clearly, the lessons of the anti-aircraft missile contract had been quickly absorbed, with Mrs Thatcher reported to have personally approved the credit cover.[170] In September 1985, Mrs Thatcher duly visited Jordan and signed the memoranda of understanding.[171] A second memorandum of understanding was signed on 9 June 1987, valued at £40 million.[172]

The lessons to be gained from Mrs Thatcher's success were not lost on the Reagan administration. On the eve of a meeting with King Hussein in Washington in September 1985, Reagan told Congress that his adminis-tration still wanted to sell Stinger and Hawk missiles to Jordan, as well as either F-16 or F-20 aircraft.[173] This was intended to wean the Jordanians away from their developing military relationship with the USSR. However, in February 1986 the Reagan administration admitted defeat and decided against presenting its arms-for-Jordan package to Congress. This opened up the way for Britain to sell the Tornado.

The Saudi purchase of the Tornado under the Al Yamamah deal was of great symbolic importance in trying to sell the aircraft to Jordan. Already, in late 1985, Jordanian air crews had flown both versions of the Tornado in Britain. In December 1987 a British MoD team travelled to Jordan to try to sell the Tornado, amidst fears that King Hussein's imminent trip to the USSR could otherwise result in Jordan purchasing the MiG-29. However, the sales effort proved successful and, following a meeting with Mrs Thatcher in London in March 1988, it was announced that Jordan would purchase eight Tornado strike aircraft in a deal worth over £400 million.[174] At the time, Jordan was reportedly interested in buying 40 Tornadoes, although the price seemed prohibitively high for such a small country. In addition to the eight aircraft, the contract – signed at the Farnborough Air Show by King Hussein in September 1988 – also covered the construction of support facilities and the provision of training, giving the whole package a value well in excess of the price of the aircraft alone.

However, there had been disagreement over which aircraft to buy. While the contract had been signed for the Tornado, the Royal Jordanian Air Force had opted for the Mirage 2000, which meant that, in practice, Jordan would pursue a 'split procurement policy' by also purchasing twelve French aircraft.[175]

Just six months after the Tornado contract was signed, claims surfaced in the *Observer* newspaper that led to the cancellation of the entire deal. In early March 1989, Norbert Gansel, a West German SPD MP, asked his government if it possessed any information on the payment of commissions in connection with the sale of the Tornado to various Middle Eastern states.[176] The question had its basis in two letters, the first of which had been written by Mrs Thatcher and leaked to *Der Spiegel*. In it Mrs Thatcher berated the Kohl government, a partner in the Panavia consortium, for not providing sufficient export credit for the sale of the Tornado to Jordan, thereby leaving the Thatcher government with no alternative but to bear most of the financial risk itself if the deal was to go ahead. The letter read:

Dear Helmut,
I was glad that your Government approved the sale of the Tornado IDS (strike) aircraft to Jordan. But I am disappointed that you felt unable to provide official credit support for this sale which we both agree – as do the Americans – is strategically important ...
[Therefore,] to preserve this valuable order, the United Kingdom is being obliged to shoulder a considerably larger than expected share of the credit burden. I must tell you that for the future I would find it difficult to accept such credit arrangements. Risks associated with export sales should be shared according to the work ratio.[177]

The second letter was somewhat more mysterious, and had been sent to the West German Foreign Minister from an address in London. Although it was signed by a 'Charles Langley', no such person lived at the address from which it was sent, leaving its authorship open to question. It read, in part:

Jordan is at present suffering the most severe financial crisis of its existence and the last thing it can afford is a contract for an aircraft that because of the small number involved makes no sense in any case apart from the gross over-charging. The basic price for a Tornado is around £22 million, the Jordanian price is in excess of £35 million basic. The difference is covered by hidden commissions to middlemen and politicians.[178]

The newspaper article went on to quote published German references to the Tornado deal which put its value at around £500 million (DM 1.6 billion). British sources quoted the deal as being worth £420 million. Allowing £100 million for support and spares, this left a figure of around £40 million to £50 million per aircraft. The figure compared unfavourably with the unit cost of the 394 Tornadoes in the then current

British Defence Estimates (£10,260 million), which worked out at £26 million per aircraft. The conclusions reached were reinforced by subsequent statements on the price of the Tornado. For example, in April 1993, Sir Christopher France, Permanent Under-Secretary at the MoD, told the PAC that the price of a Tornado was 'about £20 million'.[179] While there was some truth in the claim of Colin Chandler, head of DESO, that any discrepancies could be explained by different levels of spares and support, these alone could not account for such a large discrepancy. The letter to the German Foreign Minister offered an alternative explanation, which included the kinds of claims that were also to surface with regard to the Al Yamamah deals: 'The contract between the Panavia consortium lead for this deal, British Aerospace, includes commissions approaching 50 per cent of the contract value. These commissions are largely payable from the first payment and include approx 30 per cent (as in the Al Yamamah 1 Saudi contract) for ..., and approx 7 per cent payable to ... and various smaller sums for Jordanian officials'.[180]

This would explain the West German reluctance to bear more than 23 per cent of the deal's total cost. Norbert Gansel himself claimed that it was the West German government's refusal to condone the large commission paid on the deal which led it to refuse to fully finance it. Four days after the article appeared, Jordan indefinitely postponed its order for eight Tornadoes, claiming that it could no longer afford the deal.[181] Indeed, Jordan's ability to pay had been a worry within Whitehall and was clearly behind Mrs Thatcher's lobbying of the West Germans to share the credit burden more fully. As negotiated, the British taxpayer stood to pick up the bill had the deal gone ahead and Jordan then been unable to pay (which is, in effect, precisely what has happened).

Why did Jordan effectively cancel the Tornado? Officially, the cancellation was unconnected with the newspaper reports, although in reality the timing clearly suggested otherwise. The disclosures compounded existing misgivings brought on by Jordan's economic difficulties and demands for financial restraint from the IMF. Furthermore, the allegations were personally embarrassing for King Hussein. While the payment of commission is generally accepted to take place, specific allegations, and even worse the citing of specific figures, obviously dents the credibility of a leader, and unless that leader acts to distance himself from the allegations by in some way being seen to refute them (regardless of whether they are true), his position is undermined. Finally, there is also the question of the extent to which the purchase was necessary and to which it was a prestige project motivated by the Saudi purchase and, to a lesser extent, the proposed Omani purchase.

At the same time, this setback was not the only one facing the Tornado. Rumours were rife about the future of the Saudi deal, and Oman was looking to 'postpone' its purchase, thereby creating a precedent for

Jordan. Mrs Thatcher broke the news to the House of Commons thus:

> I have discussed the possible sale of the Tornado to Jordan with King
> Hussein on a number of occasions, most recently on 13 March. I understand
> that the Jordanian Government, after reviewing their financial commit-
> ments, and in the light of the current economic situation in Jordan, have
> informed us that they would like to postpone further negotiations on the
> sale until more favourable circumstances prevail. This has been agreed.[182]

Questions in the House predictably failed to shed any further light on the
real reasons for the decision, although the Commons did provide a platform for Labour MP Dale Campbell-Savours to attack the owner of the
Observer, Tiny Rowland, who had first brought the story to the attention
of his editor and journalists, and which several had apparently declined to
write. Campbell-Savours argued that, given his links with Dassault,
Rowland had sought to use the story to undermine BAe's sales prospects.
Rowland was, he said, an arms dealer with 'a direct interest in the
fortunes of the Dassault company'.[183]

All that this attack served to achieve, however, was to allow junior
Defence Minister Tim Sainsbury to launch into an attack on detractors of
the arms export industry and attempt to rubbish suggestions that excessive commission had been paid by arms manufacturers in the Middle East:
'I suspect we would agree that it is not surprising that the losers of a
contract seek to discredit the arrangements of the winners ... This sort of
speculation could damage an extremely important project that means a
great deal to British industry.'[184]

This did not mark the end of British arms exports to Jordan, though,
and neither did it seem particularly to strain bilateral relations. However,
following the Iraqi invasion of Kuwait, arms sales to Jordan inevitably
came under closer scrutiny. Jordan's close military relationship with Iraq
was not just a one-way affair, with Iraq supplying Jordan with captured
Iranian arms. Jordan was, within the arms business and in government
circles, a well known conduit for arms to Iraq, which Iraq would otherwise have been prohibited from receiving because of the various national
restrictions imposed on sales to it in response to its war with Iran.[185]

The Scott inquiry was told that Britain's historic relationship with
Jordan, the country's contemporary geopolitical significance and the
importance of not undermining King Hussein's position were all important factors in the turning of a blind eye to Jordan's conduit role and the
muting of any criticism of it. During the Iran–Iraq War, the Jordanian
port of Aqaba was a favoured route through which military equipment
was rerouted to Iraq. So extensive was this trade that Iraq had a whole
section of the port to itself, fenced off from the rest and known as the Iraq
Ports Authority. Nevertheless, the British embassy in Jordan was not
instructed to investigate the use of Jordan as a diversionary route. Ian

Blackley told the Scott inquiry that the FCO 'were aware that Jordan, Kuwait and Saudi Arabia were being used as transshipment ports for goods destined for Iraq'. The FCO's Simon Fuller, in his written statement to the inquiry, said that there was 'a general knowledge that Aqaba was a major route for the supply of military equipment', and that 'Jordan was a strong and consistent supporter of the Iraqi war effort against Iran'. This support extended to the upgrading of the road from Aqaba to the equivalent of a dual carriageway in order to cope with the volume of traffic coming from Iraq to pick up military and other supplies, and take them back along it into Iraq. The inquiry was also given MI6 reports which indicated clear knowledge of Jordan's role. A Jordanian perspective on its involvement was provided by the Jordanian ambassador to the UK, Fouad Ayoub, in a radio interview cited by Scott in his report. Ayoub explained that:

> Really, it's no secret that during the years of the Iran–Iraq war, many countries, including Western countries and Arab countries, were keen to see that the Iraqi military capabilities then remained undiminished. Jordan operated within this context and as such we helped to purchase and send some arms and equipment to Iraq. And, in point of fact, those arms and equipments were financed by other Arab countries as well as they were done with the full approval of Western powers and other Arab countries too.[186]

Former FCO official Mark Higson told the inquiry that 'it was long suspected amongst FCO officials that Jordan was being used as an arms conduit. Indeed, even during my time in the British Embassy in Kuwait [March 1983–July 1986] we knew Jordan through Aqaba was being used for imports of hardware from the UK, which was then going on to Iraq.' David Mellor told the inquiry how he 'knew that all the rest of the Arabs wanted Saddam to win [the war with Iran], and of course knew that he was being provisionally supplied through contiguous countries, Kuwait and Jordan'. In his statement Alan Clark conceded that it was 'certainly true that a lot of illicit traffic was going through Jordan at this time'. Despite this high level of informed suspicion, the battle within Whitehall between those eager to promote arms or not harm bilateral relations and those arguing that evidence existed which should be met by refusal to sell was a very uneven one.

In view of this kind of evidence, what did the Scott Report say about the use of Jordan as a conduit? Scott traced British government knowledge of the use of Jordan as a conduit back to 1983. As early as May 1983, an MI5 note he cites observed that 'in view of the restrictions imposed on the sale of war material to Iraq and Iran, Iraq has been using Jordan as an intermediary'.[187] Scott went on to record a series of instances, stretching across six pages of his report, indicating ever-growing governmental awareness of Jordan's conduit role. However, there is no evidence that this awareness translated into concern when the September 1985 Jordanian arms deal was being concluded. It is fair to assume that elements of this, as with the Al Yamamah order, were intended for onward transmission to Iraq. Scott confined himself to observing that 'the possibility that military exports to Jordan might be diverted to Iraq represented a continuing threat to the integrity of the Government's policy on restricting defence related exports to Iraq'[188] – an unduly restrained conclusion in view of the weight of evidence presented.

Kuwait

From its independence until the 1970s Kuwait relied on Britain as its primary supplier of major conventional arms, and in this its experience was similar to that of most other Gulf states. Similar too was the pattern of post-oil boom diversification of supply and subsequent displacement of Britain by the US and France. However, this displacement did not necessarily indicate a fall in the value of British arms exports to Kuwait, rather that Kuwait looked elsewhere to fuel its expansion. So, while Britain monopolised a market worth just US$27 million between 1956 and 1960, its 17 per cent share of a market worth US$1.66 billion between 1976 and 1980, and 7 per cent share of one worth US$1.3 billion between 1981 and 1985, were nevertheless of greater value.

Kuwait was another arena where the hegemonic designs of the Tripartite Declaration impacted on the arms market. When, in the mid-1960s, Kuwait was looking to buy a squadron of fighter aircraft, its preference was for the US Phantom. The US had told the Kuwaitis that they would not sell them military aircraft, claiming not to want to fuel a fresh spiral in the regional arms race with Israel. However, the British embassy in Kuwait was told that 'the United States Government's real reasons were their desire not to trespass on our territory and the agreement with the Defence Secretary [McNamara] to assist sales of British Equipment in appropriate cases' – that is, the agreement which would fund UK acquisition of the F-111 in order that the British could continue to perform their role as junior partners in maintaining global order. 'For all these reasons,' the ambassador continued, the 'United States Government would be willing to support Her Majesty's Government's efforts to sell British aircraft, to the exclusion of others, if her Majesty's Government were willing to meet Kuwait's needs.'[189] Buoyed by this news, and regardless of the government's notional commitment to arms restraint, the ambassador suggested that Britain might also be able to sell them the Buccaneer.[190]

Although talks with BAC about Lightnings continued, US–UK attempts to maintain a monopoly of influence in the region were proving more and more difficult. As the ambassador warned:

> We know that they regard the Lightnings as second best, and are only considering it because the United States Government told them that Phantoms would not be supplied. There seems to me therefore that there is a risk that despite the language problem ... the Kuwait Government might turn to the Mirage, which we believe to be about £1 m cheaper overall, for a larger number of aircraft. This would certainly have adverse effect on our defence relationship with the Kuwait Government ... [191]

While in this case the UK sales effort prevailed, and Kuwait bought 14 Lightnings, the Kuwaitis became adept at playing the UK off against the French to exact the most favourable sales terms, and the threat of French penetration of the Kuwaiti market became a preoccupation of the ambassador's dispatches to London. Moreover, with the advent of the 1967 war, the Kuwaitis came to wish they had bought the Mirage in the first place.[192] When the Kuwaitis sought tanks, armoured cars and small naval craft in 1968, they again turned first to the US, which again told them 'that they should in the first instance seek to meet their requirements from British sources'.[193]

However, changed market circumstances meant that the US could no longer guarantee that in forgoing the deal the Kuwaitis would turn to the UK, and hence the agreement by which they had sought to control the region began to break down (a process accelarated, of course, by the contemporaneous UK decisions to scrap the F-111 order and pull out of the Gulf).

Nevertheless, Kuwait remained an important market for UK arms in the 1970s, one important element of Britain's market share being the Callaghan government's 1976 £100 million agreement to sell around 150 Chieftain tanks, making Kuwait the first Arab country to buy them.[194] In part this purchase had been motivated by the 1973 border clashes with Iraq, as a result of which Kuwait also sought to develop its defensive capabilities in other areas. At the time of the Chieftain order, it also ordered US A-4 Skyhawk aircraft in preference to the Jaguar, the markets agreement being by now moribund and, more significantly, 36 Mirage F-1s to replace its Lightnings. It was also in the market for naval equipment, having taken the decision to develop its own navy. Uniquely for a Gulf state at the time, it also concluded an artillery deal with the USSR, seen as representing a warning to the US after Congress had stalled a proposed sale of the Sidewinder missile. As the Kuwaiti Minister of the Interior and Defence, Sheikh Saad al Abdullah, indicated at the time: 'Our policy is to purchase suitable arms from any available source, provided we can determine the types convenient to us and provided that the source does not impose any conditions or limitations upon concluding the arms purchases.'[195]

Mrs Thatcher visited Kuwait on her 1981 Gulf tour, observing that 'There's a tremendous lot for Britain here.' Her discussions were dominated by the twin themes of trade and defence, and by efforts to sell the Kuwaitis Tornado and Hawk aircraft, as well as further Chieftain tanks. Later, with customary modesty, she told a press conference that: 'We could be of particular help in things like a full military communications system. As you know, we are very good at radar and all defence electronics. After all it's we who discovered radar.'[196]

Kuwait looked to extend its arms purchases following the outbreak of war between Iran and Iraq in 1980, partly as a consequence of Iranian threats in response to its support for Iraq. On 31 October 1983 Britain and Kuwait concluded a contract for 12 Hawk aircraft, then already in service in the UAE, to replace the BAC Strikemaster. At a later stage in the Iran–Iraq War, the Kuwaiti Defence Minister, Sheikh Nawaf al-Ahmed al-Sabah, announced that Kuwait was negotiating to buy both additional Mirage aircraft and an arms package from the US that included the Maverick missile and F/A-18 aircraft, Congress allowing. In an attempt to improve their chances of securing the deal, the Kuwaitis again sought to play off the US against the USSR, signing an arms deal with the latter on the eve of Sheikh Saad al-Abdullah al-Sabah's four-day visit to Washington in July 1988. Nevertheless, in July 1988, the Senate voted to strike the Maverick from the package on the traditional grounds that it posed a threat to Israel. The Kuwaiti response was that it must be the entire package or nothing, and to remind the US that 'We will never beg to obtain arms.'[197]

This hint that Kuwait could turn away from the US and towards other suppliers, as Saudi Arabia had just done in concluding Al Yamamah, was given greater immediacy when Defence Secretary George Younger arrived in Kuwait on the same day that the Kuwaiti Prime Minister left for Washington. Younger met the Emir, Sheikh Jaber al-Ahmed al-Sabah, and various Ministers, and tried in vain to interest them in the Tornado, then recently ordered by Oman and Saudi Arabia. However, alongside King Hussein, the Kuwaitis were masters at playing one side off against the other to secure the arms they wanted (and at the right price), and the whole trip was effectively a charade. This interpretation was borne out when, in August 1988, the Reagan administration, Congress, and the Kuwaitis, finally agreed a $1.9 billion sale of 40 F/A-18 aircraft and 300 Maverick missiles.[198] Yet the agreement was not without strings. Firstly, delivery would be delayed by one year, from 1993 to 1994. Secondly, for every F/A-18 delivered, Kuwait would have to return one of its 30 US Skyhawks. Thirdly, Kuwait would not be permitted to buy in-flight refuelling equipment (also a hurdle in negotiations with Saudi Arabia), which would have given the aircraft the ability to strike at Israel. In return, the Maverick was returned to the package although the version included was the less sophisticated Maverick-G anti-ship missile rather than the advanced Maverick-D anti-armour version.[199]

By this time the Kuwaitis were already negotiating with Vickers over the possible purchase of the Challenger II tank. Vickers approached these negotiations with some confidence, as it had manufactured Kuwait's existing fleet of Chieftain tanks. Around the same time, the French had stepped up their efforts to secure a share of the Kuwaiti market, reportedly offering to undercut any prices quoted by British companies.[200] In early September 1988, the French Defence Minister, Jean-Pierre Chevenement, visited Kuwait to discuss replacing its existing 34 Mirage F-1s with the Mirage 2000. Following this, the Emir paid a state visit to France. In December, a delegation headed by the vice-chairman of Dassault-Bréguet, Huues de l'Estoile, also paid a visit.[201]

Following the August 1990 Iraqi invasion, elements of the Kuwaiti Air Force managed to escape to Saudi Arabia.[202] Between then and the outbreak of war in January 1991, France supplied the government-in-exile with a range of weaponry, as a prelude to securing a slice of the market – ideally including the sale of the Mirage 2000 – when the conflict was over.[203] Of course, this overt arms sales support was markedly different from the actual French military support for the coalition war effort, which was necessarily more qualified as a consequence of French arms sales policy towards Iraq.

Oman

British links with Oman date back to 1800, when Captain John Malcolm confirmed a treaty in Muscat with Sayid Sultan which secured friendship with Britain, 'until the end of time or the sun and moon cease in their revolving careers'.[204] Oman has remained the one state in the Middle East where Britain's traditional links have translated into sustained dominance of the arms market. Until the end of the 1950s Britain supplied all of Oman's limited arms imports, and still provided 83 per cent between 1965 and 1970. However, it was not until the 1970s that Oman began to import significant items of weaponry – the Jaguar aircraft, Rapier missiles and patrol craft, for example. During the 1980s the UK remained by far Oman's leading supplier of major conventional arms.[205] Although, as elsewhere in the region, both the US and France had penetrated the market, until the Gulf War they had not done so extensively, and their exports have still remained limited to clearly defined defence fields.[206]

Throughout the 1970s Oman maintained a steady flow of orders for British military equipment, and bilateral relations were given a further boost with the election of Mrs Thatcher, whose world view was peculiarly similar to that of the Sultan. Their relationship was confirmed by Mrs

Thatcher's visit on her 'Batting for Britain' tour of 1981, which subsequently created controversy at home when Mark Thatcher's presence resulted in Cementation International, a civil engineering company to which he was a 'consultant', winning a £300 million contract to build a new university under unusual circumstances.[207] At the time, one journalist noted how:

> After the push and shove atmosphere of the other Arab countries, where Britain is only one of many contenders for the ear of government, Oman is like a great stranded chunk of that 19th century imperial world of which Britain was a part. In Oman, British influence is pervasive, the British position in trade is still commanding, and a Tory Government's views on standing up to the Russians or even on the Arab-Israel question meet with wholehearted local approval.[208]

Indeed, of all the Gulf states, Oman most visibly displayed the trappings of its colonial past, and British armed forces personnel continued to play a dominant role in the Omani bureaucracy, especially in relation to military matters. The Omani army was still commanded by British officers, British advisers answered the telephone at Ministries, and the palace royal staff included a healthy British contingent, including someone to tend to the Sultan's fleet of bullet-proof Cadillacs. The royal bodyguard was commanded by a Brigadier Tom Harcourt, who had been Sultan Qaboos's sergeant instructor at Sandhurst. The head of the Omani CID, Commander Cook, was also British, as was the head of the intelligence service (the Oman Research Department). In the military itself, notwithstanding the ultimate aim of Omanisation, the heads of all three services were British. Hence British influence permeated the armed forces.[209] In addition, at the time of Mrs Thatcher's visit, 700 British servicemen were based in Oman, and while there Mrs Thatcher announced that the number was to be increased, again underlining the link between arms sales and the perception that the supplier's military commitment extends beyond the business relationship.

This environment goes a long way to explaining why Britain exercised a grip on the Omani arms market that it was unable to maintain elsewhere in the region. Nowhere else was the military decision-making apparatus so dominated by the British. The British community in Oman (numbering 6,000 in 1981) may have been far smaller than that in Saudi Arabia (numbering around 30,000 at the same time), but it was much more influential.[210]

When Mrs Thatcher arrived in Oman, her discussions with the British ambassador, Ivor Lucas, hardly represented a meeting of minds. He told Mrs Thatcher that in his opinion Sultan Qaboos was spending too much on defence and too little on economic development, risking a situation analogous to that in Iran prior to the 1979 revolution. Mrs Thatcher dismissed these concerns, telling him that building up Oman's military forces (with British equipment) and standing up to the Soviet threat to the region were more important. Also present on a number of these occasions was Mark Thatcher.[211] He had first shown up in Abu Dhabi, then appeared again in Oman, pursuing business interests in a part of the world where family ties are considered of the utmost importance. Cementation International (to whom he was acting as a consultant) was awarded its university contract after Mrs Thatcher reportedly raised the project with Sultan Qaboos during a private talk. She later denied there was any conflict of interest, explaining: 'I bat for Britain. I don't distinguish between British companies. When I'm trying to secure contracts it is to try to get business for British companies and not overseas companies.'[212] A former trade minister has noted the irony 'that she intervened at all in foreign contracts . . . in 1981 most of us were monetarists and we couldn't understand why she kept going on about "batting for Britain". Let the market decide was our view.'[213]

Britain's military relations with Oman were also informed by Britain's willingness to provide weaponry as well as British forces to fight a limited counter-insurgency operation to defend the rule of Sultan Qaboos's father in the 1950s, and again to defend Sultan Qaboos in the 1970s.[214] British officers trained and led the Omani forces which defeated the Popular Front for the Liberation of Oman insurgency. When British intelligence suggested that in early 1981 Dhofar rebel activity was again on the increase, an SAS contingent was sent to Oman to spearhead attempts to bring it to an end.

The supply of naval equipment had always been an important aspect of the military trade with Oman, and in the early 1980s the sultanate ordered several new vessels. In 1980, Vosper Thornycroft won an order for a Province Class fast patrol boat, and the following year won orders for a further two.[215] Each ship would carry two triple launchers for Exocet missiles supplied by France, as well as small guns. In early 1986, the sultanate ordered a fourth Province Class vessel, once again armed with Exocets and Racal–Decca radar.[216]

In the wake of Mrs Thatcher's 1981 visit, a contract was also concluded for the purchase of Chieftain tanks valued at £35 million. Furthermore, in relation to the defence assurances Mrs Thatcher had given the Sultan, it was announced that General Sir Timothy Creasey, former commander-in-chief of British land forces, had agreed to waive retirement plans to become Chief of Defence Staff to the sultanate.[217] The appointment came at a time when Omani defence expenditure was increasing as a consequence of the Iranian revolution and anxiety over relations with South Yemen, following the Soviet invasion of Afghanistan.

Creasey's appointment soon attracted unwelcome publicity, however, when Jeremy Cripps, a Briton who had formerly been director of budgets in the Omani MoD, claimed that he was removed from his post for challenging the way Creasey was spending millions of pounds on importing arms without proper financial controls.[218] He alleged that the Omani procurement system had been manipulated by the British in Oman to favour British products and that, given the price of certain equipment, commission was clearly being paid. He recalled: 'The procurement system was a complete shambles. We were not providing the Omanis with the best equipment at the best prices.'[219] He alleged that the competitive system of bidding under the Omani defence tender board had been bypassed, citing five specific cases.

The first involved the eventual purchase of Alvis Scorpion armoured vehicles. Cripps had been asked to compare the Alvis bid with that of a French Renault armoured vehicle. Cripps concluded that the French wheeled model would be less expensive initially, easier to maintain, and would also be more appropriate for desert conditions than the tracked Scorpion. His report was apparently well received by the tender board in February 1982, but two days after being delivered all papers relating to the deal were removed from his office on the instruction of Creasey's staff. The Scorpion was then purchased.

A second case involved the purchase of Chieftain tanks. The sultanate already possessed US M-60 main battle tanks, but a decision was made to purchase the Chieftain as well. Cripps argued, 'It didn't make sense to me. There was no strategic plan, no questioning about whether the country needed or could use them.'[220] The tanks were purchased at a cost of £1.5m each, and while the price was partly determined by the combination of weaponry included, Cripps discovered that the tanks had been sold elsewhere in the Gulf at £1 million each. Amongst other cases, Cripps recounted the order for a consignment of Blowpipe missiles. He was asked to personally negotiate with Short's, recalling that 'I didn't know anything about Blowpipes. The man from Short's said he had never negotiated in this way, he always had to face a team. There was no consideration of cost but they told me they were going to buy Blowpipes and I was told to go and do it.'[221]

The tight British grip on Omani defence contracts was something which came to bemuse the US. A US$50 million maintenance contract for work on three US-constructed bases in Oman was given to a British company and its US partner, Airwork, at the insistence of the Sultan, despite the fact that the contract was supposed to be open to competitive bidding. This led to protests from other US companies, although, given its desire to hang on to the bases, the Pentagon considered there to be little room for manoeuvre. The situation was further complicated by Omani demands (backed up by their British advisers) to be given complete access to the bases where classified material was stored.

A further sign of the close military relationship came in 1985, when

Oman became the first country outside the Panavia consortium to order the Tornado, following a four-day visit to the sultanate by Defence Secretary Michael Heseltine. The order was for eight ADVs, with an option on a further four, together with support and weapon systems worth over £250 million.[222] However, just six months after placing the Tornado order, the Omanis asked BAe to delay delivery by three years because of financial difficulties caused by a fall in the price of oil, the effect of which was exacerbated by the reluctance of other Gulf Co-operation Council (GCC) members to pay Oman an agreed annual grant to facilitate arms purchases.[223]

Notwithstanding this, in December 1985 Marconi won a contract to supply communications for the armed forces, to include a nationwide network of interconnected 'Radio Bearer' systems, telephone exchanges and priority switching systems, together with the associated buildings, antennae, power supplies and support activities.[224] Shortly afterwards Ferranti secured a £7 million contract to install its FIN 1064 Inertial Navigation System (INS) in the Omanis' fleet of Jaguar aircraft, then undergoing an overhaul.[225] At around this time, Plessey was completing work on the Watchman air traffic control radar for the Omani Air Force,[226] and in February 1986 it was announced that Plessey had also won an order worth over £500,000 to supply a number of advanced circuit switches to the Omani MoD.

By 1987, Oman was once again negotiating to delay its projected purchase of eight Tornadoes, by now until 1992 at the earliest. The Deputy Prime Minister for economic and financial affairs, Qais bin Abdul Munim al Zawawi, indicated that the sale would go ahead then so long as there was sufficient money available. In the meantime, the sultanate suggested that the aircraft put aside for Oman might be delivered to another buyer instead. Meanwhile, the Omanisation of Oman's defence took a significant step forward in late 1987 with the departure of the armed forces' commander, British General John Watts. Watts had effectively acted as Defence Minister. His association with the sultanate extended back to 1970, and he had played a prominent role in the 1976 counter-insurgency campaign. Watts had also acted as commander of the combined Anglo-Omani forces during the November–December 1986 Exercise Swift Sword. This had been Britain's largest out-of-area deployment since the 1982 Falklands conflict, and again underlined the close relationship between arms sales to a country and the perception that the supplier was able and willing to intervene further if required. When he left, Watts was replaced by a triumvirate under the Sultan. However, both the air force and the navy remained under the command of British officers,[227] although a schedule had been devised by which they would be replaced by their (Omani) deputies in the near future. By 1988 most army officers were Omani, while all major air bases had Omani commanders and most fighter pilots (trained in Britain) were Omani. The navy too had made progress to the point that most ships' commanders were Omani. However, technical support staff in all areas still tended to be British – and hence British influence could still be forcefully exerted over procurement decisions. Notwithstanding this, the logic of the process dictated that the day was coming when Britain would no longer have such a grip on the military bureaucracy, and when its share of the Omani defence market would more accurately reflect Oman's perception of British willingness and ability to continue to defend the Sultan's rule.

During 1989, Oman again postponed its purchase of the Tornado. This time, the sultanate announced that it intended to purchase an unspecified number of BAe Hawk aircraft and Shorts Javelin surface-to-air missiles, effectively confirming that the postponment was a cancellation. A statement from the Omani government read:

> The Omani Government is taking the opportunity to replace the ageing Hunter fleet with the Hawk fighter and equip the Oman Army with Javelin missiles, for which there is a pressing operational need. During recent talks with the British Government, the Sultanate of Oman has expressed its wish to postpone for the present the purchase of Tornado aircraft, and this matter is being reviewed by both Governments. Declining oil prices prompted the Omani Government to opt for prudent financial management in order that a reasonable economic balance be maintained.[228]

The British government issued its own statement, clarifying the position:

> We confirm that, after extensive consultations with us about their defence needs and financial position, the Government of Oman has decided to alter its air-defence procurement plan for the 1990s. This will involve the suspension of the Tornado purchase. Discussions will begin shortly for the early purchase of Hawk aircraft to replace Oman's Hunter fleet, together with Javelin missiles.[229]

However, concern surfaced that Sultan Qaboos was merely cancelling the Tornado in order to pursue the French Mirage when he visited Paris (the first European country other than Britain he had ever visited) less than a month after the announcement. While this fear was not realised, Oman and France did conclude a framework accord on defence co-operation that allowed for the training of Omani military personnel in France and the provision of unspecified equipment.[230]

In February 1990, the Omani navy shortlisted three European yards to bid for the construction of patrol vessels. Vosper Thornycroft was joined on the short list by the French Société Française des Constructions Navales (SFCN) and the Dutch Royal Schelde. Vosper, with the advantage of having already sold several vessels to Oman over a number of years, was offering a version of the *Vigilance* vessel which had already been sold to Brunei.[231] In September 1991 it was announced that Vosper had won the order, to construct two 1,400 ton, 83 metre corvettes, worth £150 million.[232] The official announcement was made by Defence Secretary Tom King, who also announced the imminent deal with Malaysia at the same time. Together, King trumpeted the agreement as 'the largest warship export orders for Britain for over 20 years ... It is an excellent vote of confidence in Britain's shipbuilding and naval equipment industries. It is a further extension of our highly successful Defence Equipment understandings with both countries and the close and friendly relations we have with them.'[233]

Finally, on 30 July 1990, the contract was signed for the supply of 16 Hawk aircraft to replace Oman's ageing Hunter fleet, comprising a mix of Hawk 100 'trainers' and the Hawk 200 dedicated attack aircraft, at an estimated cost of £150 million.[234] This sale was as much a milestone as the sale of the Tornado had been intended to be, in that it represented the first firm order for the new Hawk 200. Furthermore, BAe stood to make a larger profit out of the deal than it would have under the proposed Panavia Tornado deal.

Hence on the eve of the Gulf War, Britain's military relations with Oman had been informed by an unusually close relationship, even by Gulf standards. The Sultan's trust in and preference for all things British extended to the purchase of arms, and was so all-embracing as to create a climate where other countries found penetration of the market extremely difficult. However, the process of Omanisation of the armed forces had already had something of an effect on this relationship, and the impact of the Gulf War was to further loosen the UK grip on the Omani arms market.

United Arab Emirates

The UAE was formed in the wake of Britain's withdrawal from the Gulf and the granting of independence to the old Trucial states (Abu Dhabi, Ajman, Dubai, Fujaira, Ras al-Khaima, Sharja and Umm al-Qaiwain) in 1971. Discussions aimed at establishing a federation were held between these states and Bahrain immediately prior to and after independence, but came to nothing. Consequently, the seven emirates established an independent federation (the UAE) between December 1971 and February 1972.

The British withdrawal meant that these states now needed to provide for their own defence. As the Director of Army Sales noted after a visit to the area in August 1968, their 'knowledge and judgement in defence matters are vestiginal and even those who are poor seem little concerned with costs. They all want to run too far too fast.' In stark contrast to the post-1990 attitude to arming these states, he went on to note that: 'The

British aim is to restrain their ambitions as far as possible to reduce costs, to avoid buying a lot of equipment which cannot be operated or maintained, and to avoid the build up of a number of local forces which will then battle, however ineffectively, for local supremacy.'[235]

The UAE has relied mainly on Britain, France, the US, (West) Germany and Italy for its arms imports, but has also purchased from Brazil (96 EE-11 Urutu armoured personnel carriers), Canada, Egypt, Spain, Sweden and Switzerland. As elsewhere in the region, Britain was the dominant supplier until the 1970s, controlling 84 per cent of the market in major conventional arms from 1966 to 1970,[236] before French marketing techniques and what was viewed as the more progressive French position on the Arab question helped secure France's presence in the market.

During her 1981 Gulf tour, Mrs Thatcher made a point of discussing arms, trade and the Palestine issue, thereby seeking to combat the French advantage. Indeed, Mrs Thatcher even secured an order for the purchase of the Hawk after talks with defence chiefs in Abu Dhabi, despite a concerted French effort to sell the Alpha trainer – an effort which had included a visit by President Giscard d'Estaing.[237] This represented another personal success for Britain's premier arms salesperson. As one observer noted: 'Mrs Thatcher's tour of the Gulf states is turning into a highly personal arms sales drive which yesterday produced an on-the-spot commitment from the United Arab Emirates to buy British jet trainers. Mrs Thatcher describes herself as "delighted" at this result of face-to-face commercial diplomacy.'[238]

However, it later emerged that Sheikh Zayed and his family had been irritated by Mrs Thatcher's aggressive 'batting for Britain' and by what they considered a premature announcement of the deal. It was not to be the last example of either. The contracts for the deal were eventually signed in 1983.[239]

During the 1980s the UAE maintained one of the largest armies in relation to its population anywhere in the world. Its armed forces totalled around 43,000, while its total population stood at just 1.2 million.[240] Furthermore, defence was the largest single item in the UAE budget.[241] During the 1980s, the Emirates were still in the process of drawing up a cohesive national defensive strategy. The UAE still did not have, for example, a national navy or air defence early warning system that covered the entire state. Abu Dhabi undertook most arms purchases on behalf of the UAE and then deducted the cost of the hardware from its contribution to the federal budget. However, Dubai also purchased weaponry independently of Abu Dhabi.

The most eagerly awaited decision of the mid-1980s for prospective supplier countries revolved around which country would be awarded the contract for new fighter aircraft. Once again, Britain and France were in competition over the order. The effective Congressional block on the sale of US equipment to the Gulf states at the time ruled out consideration of the F-15 or F-16. The French started out as favourites to secure the deal, aiming at a repeat order for 18 Mirage 2000s. The British bid rested on the sale of the Tornado, following the successful 1983 sale of the Hawk. In the event, the French bid prevailed, and Abu Dhabi ordered 36 Mirage 2000s. However, the unexpected prospect of the sale of the Tornado (following orders from Oman, Saudi Arabia, and Jordan) arose when Abu Dhabi refused to take delivery of the Mirage until additional equipment had been installed to make the aircraft compatible with US as well as French-manufactured missiles. As soon as this impasse emerged, a BAe sales team visited the UAE, following up a visit made by the Procurement Minister, Lord Trefgarne, in March 1987. The visit was supported by two RAF Tornadoes, which were 'comprehensively demonstrated to senior Abu Dhabi Air Force officers.'[242] Despite this, Abu Dhabi took delivery of the modified Mirage aircraft in 1990.[243]

While the UAE had taken a more equivocal stand over the Iran–Iraq War than most other Gulf states (low-key support for Iraq, coupled with continued trade with Iran), the unease which it generated motivated several of the Emirates' arms purchases. However, in retrospect, it seems fairly certain that much of the equipment was ordered for onward passage to Iraq. It is difficult to see otherwise what use the UAE would have had for so much weaponry, given its untried 40,000-strong army, whose commander-in-chief was, in the best czarist tradition, Sheikh Zayed himself. This would also help explain the bemusement of some defence attachés at UAE purchases in the mid-1980s, one suggesting that the 'UAE has probably got more armaments than it can usefully use'.[244]

However, it has been the sale of British repressive equipment rather than major arms which has caused most controversy here. In June 1987, the *Daily Mirror* revealed that the security firm Michael Huffey Construction had awarded a contract to construction company John Laing (company motto: 'We build for people') for two sets of gallows (one double, one single) for Abu Dhabi. Laing's passed the contract on to one of its subsidiaries, Victoria Joinery. Amnesty International took the case up, in an effort to bring an end to such a contract with a state that retained the death penalty for murder, adultery, armed robbery and drug-related offences. The government refused to intervene, FCO Minister, David Mellor, telling Amnesty that 'the manufacture of execution equipment in the UK is legal and its export is not subject to any form of control'.[245] However, Laing's agreed to discontinue supply, although one set of gallows had already been exported. It was not the last time that the export of torture or repressive equipment to the UAE was to stir controversy.

More substantially, in February 1988, the British company Bertlin & Partners began work on designs for the US$1 billion Taweelah naval base in Abu Dhabi. The base was to provide berths for 60 fast attack craft and troop carriers. When complete, the base, which would also include weapon stores, accommodation areas and training areas, would be the largest in the Gulf. In July 1989 the Sheikh paid a four-day state visit to Britain during which strenuous efforts were made to interest him in the purchase of at least one minesweeper and four fast patrol boats to be built by Vosper Thornycroft, as well as Westland naval support helicopters. This effort was partly motivated by the fact that in December 1988 Vosper had lost out on an order to supply minesweepers and patrol vessels to Kuwait. The Kuwaitis cancelled the order when the Monopolies and Mergers Commission reduced the Kuwaiti holding in BP. In addition, a Westland order had also been 'lost' to Aerospatiale. At the same time, GKN completed delivery of eight Saxon armoured personnel carriers ordered by the UAE for 'public security work'.

The Iraqi invasion of Kuwait had a profound effect on thinking in the UAE, as elsewhere in the Gulf. The Emirates embarked almost immediately on a crash programme to update their forces, with British companies figuring prominently in the plans. In late 1990, it was announced that a further 18 Hawk 100s were to be purchased, in a deal worth up to US$100 million.[246]

Another Gulf state where Britain initially dominated only to be displaced by the French, the UAE's relatively high level of defence spending in the 1980s (as a proportion of GDP), and the relative absence of a US hold on the market prior to the Gulf War (when the UAE became more interested in US arms at the same time as its prospects of being allowed to buy them increased), meant that the Emirates became one of the places where Anglo-French arms sales rivalry was most competitively played out. This was evidenced during Mrs Thatcher's 1981 visit, when an agreement to purchase the Hawk trainer rather than the Alpha was reached; over the purchase of Mirage rather than Tornado aircraft, and the last-minute British effort to wrest the contract away from France. The rivalry extended into the fields of tanks and armoured personnel carriers and even naval vessels. As the following chapter shows, this competition has now intensified as, in the post-Gulf War era, the UAE seeks to diversify its sources of supply, and also look more to the US, the ultimate guarantor of Kuwaiti and Gulf security.

Notes

1 PRO: FO 371/177820, 'Arms Control in the Middle East', FO Planning Committee paper, 30 December 1964. See also FO 371/186850, Minute by C. McLean, FO, 28 October 1965.
2 PRO: FO 371/175839, Minutes of Arms Working Party meeting AWP/M, 10 March 1964.

3 PRO: FO 371/175830, 'Arms for Israel', Briefing Paper by W. Morris, FO, 30 January 1964.
4 The UK had supplied 135 Centurions between 1959 and 1962.
5 PRO: FO 371/175830, Minute from Thorneycroft to Butler, 3 March 1964.
6 PRO: FO 371/175830, Minute from Butler to Thorneycroft, 10 March 1964.
7 PRO: FO 371/175850, 'Arms supplies to Israel', Minute by W. Morris, 24 March 1964.
8 PRO: FO 371/175831, Telegram from McGeorge Bundy to Sir Timothy Bligh, 4 May 1964 and Note from Robert McNamara to Thorneycroft via *ad interim* Chargé d'Affaires Elim O'Shaughnessy, 2 May 1964. Sloan and Komer had also planned to visit Paris, but decided not to because the French AMX-30 tank would not be available soon enough, and because of fears that the French might tell the Israelis of their mission.
9 This was, of course, unlikely. The Dimona nuclear weapons facility was nearing completion by this time. See Semour M. Hersh, *The Samson Option: Israel, America and the Bomb* (London, Faber & Faber, 1991).
10 PRO: FO 371/175831, 'Supply of Tanks to Israel', A. C. Goodison, 7 May 1964.
11 Supplementary Minute by R. S. Crawford, *ibid*.
12 PRO: FO 371/175831, 'Supply of Tanks to Israel – Record of a Conversation between Sir Geoffrey Harrison and Mr Komer of the White House staff and Mr Sloan of the US Department of Defence on 8 May, 1964'.
13 Komer and Sloan reported 'an embarrassment of riches' when they went looking for tanks in Bonn. However, they were determined to keep their efforts to secure tanks for Israel secret from all concerned, and were even surprised that knowledge of the mission had percolated around the FO. See PRO: FO 371/175831, Letter from Miss A. M. Warburton, Bonn, to A. C. Goodison, 23 May 1964. See also the summary of the meeting in DEFE 7/1092, 'Tanks for Israel', Minute by G. C. B. Dodds.
14 PRO: FO 371/175831, Telegram from Lord Harlech, Washington, to FO, 9 May 1964. This telegram also contains Komer's acknowledgement that while the West German Ministry of Defence was 'ready to supply tanks to Israel', the Foreign Ministry 'opposed' any transfer. A similar split marked British discussions, and the MoD was predictably less than enthusiastic about the FO's argument for restraint and only selling the Israelis 150 tanks when a market for over 300 existed. See PRO: FO 371/175831, Letter from G. C. B. Dodds, AUS(M), MoD, to M. S. Williams, FO, 5 June 1964, and Letter from M. S. Williams to G. C. B. Dodds, 23 June 1964.
15 PRO: FO 371/175831. The total cost of the order for 48 was about £900,000. The tanks came direct from BAOR stocks and were to be shipped via Antwerp, where 'Egyptian agents are few and loading can be very rapid'; letter from F. C. Herd to W. Morris, 18 June 1964.
16 PRO: FO 371/175832, Letter from Miss A. M. Warburton, Bonn, to A. C. Goodison, 20 June 1964.
17 PRO: FO 371/175832, Handwritten Minute by McLaren, 25 June 1964. 'They may therefore try to persuade the Germans to sell more than 220. If they don't or can't they will presumably still want more Centurions/Chieftains to make up their minimum requirement of about 350.' It is also to be noted that the longer range of the M-48 was better suited to Israeli military doctrine of the time. See PRO: FO 371/175832, Letter from John Beith, Tel Aviv, to W. Morris, FO, 6 July 1964.
18 PRO: FO 371/175832, Letter from P. R. H. Wright, Washington, to W. Morris, FO, 15 July 1964.
19 PRO: FO 371/175832, Memorandum 'Tanks for Israel', by A. C. Goodison, 3 September 1964.
20 PRO: FO 371/175832, Telegram, FO to Tel Aviv, 5 September 1964.

21 PRO: FO 371/175832, Memorandum 'Visit of Mr Shimon Peres', by P. Cradock, 8 September 1964.

22 PRO: FO 371/175832, Handwritten Note by A. C. Goodison, 10 September 1964. The cover story was that Peres was visiting the Farnborough Air Show and then paying 'routine courtesey calls in Whitehall'.

23 PRO: FO 371/175832, Telegram, FO to Tel Aviv, 10 September 1964.

24 PRO: FO 371/175833, Letter from A. C. Goodison to A. R. H. Kellas, Tel Aviv, 16 September 1964, and Limited Distribution Letter from A. C. Goodison to A. R. H. Kellas, Tel Aviv, 16 September 1964. Discussion of the tanks was kept out of the official minute of the meeting.

25 The elements were: 250 Centurions to be delivered before the end of 1967; 50,000 rounds of 105 mm ammunition; 20,000 rounds of twenty-pounder ammunition; 2 years' general and overhaul spares; 105 mm up-gunning kits for tanks; licence for partial manufacture of 105 mm gun; manufacturing licence for 105 mm ammunition; and feasibility studies for fitting the Centurions with 120 mm gun and diesel power pack. To prevent embarrassment if the order should become public, it was to be broken down into small subcontracts that could be presented as reasonable and moderate in scale: 'The purpose of this, which the Israelis accept, is that we should be in a position, if it seemed appropriate at the time, to assure the Arabs that any particular contract for tanks of which they got wind only covered a limited number.' PRO: FO 371/175833, Letter from Goodison to Kellas, 16 September 1964 and various other of HMG's representatives. H. N. Pullar, British Consulate General, Jerusalem, described the communication as 'very interesting' but had had it destroyed because it was 'too hot to hold'. Letter from H. N. Pullar to A. C. Goodison, 29 September 1964. See also the minute by W. Morris, 'Tanks for Israel', 7 September 1964.

26 See PRO: FO 371/175833, Memorandum 'Tanks for Israel – Informing other Governments', by P. Cradock, 2 September 1964, and minute by Sir G. Harrison, 1 October 1964, letter from A. C. Goodison to P. R. Metcalfe, CRO, 26 October 1964, letter from J. D. B. Shaw, CRO, to W. Morris, 3 November 1964, and letter from J. B. S. Pedler, Paris, to A. C. Goodison, 7 November 1964, letter from W. Morris to J. B. S. Pedler, 19 November 1964. Pedler had suggested that the French be informed, given that they would probably find out anyway. Morris's response was scathing: 'have the French ever been frank with us over their supplies to Israel? Eight years ago, when the Americans and ourselves were both playing the NEACC game according to the rules, we were well aware that the French were not informing us either within NEACC or outside it of anything like the total quantities of arms (particularly, if I remember accurately, of aircraft) which they were delivering to Israel.'

27 The Foreign Office Planning Committee paid lip service to the new government's proposed policy, producing a weighty paper that detailed just how difficult, unhelpful, unlikely and counterproductive Middle Eastern arms control would prove, except in a few very distinct areas, such as the supply of nuclear weapons. PRO: FO 371/177820, PLA 12/4, ref. PC(64)53, Planning Committee paper 'Arms Control in the Middle East', 30 December 1964. Quote from PRO: FO 371/180894, Minute by P. Craddock, 'Design Study for 120 mm Gun for Centurions for Israel', 21 June 1965.

28 PRO: FCO 17/579, Letter, Healey to Eshkol, 30 March 1965. See also Eshkol's reply of 20 April 1965. welcoming this 'general understanding'.

29 See PRO: FO 371/175832, Letter from A. M. Warburton, Bonn, to A. C. Goodison, FO, 1 December 1964.

30 PRO: FO 371/180894, Minute by W. Morris, 'Supply of arms to Israel', 11 February 1965, and telegram 320 from Sir F. Roberts, Bonn, to FO, 18 March 1965.

31 PRO: FO 371/180894, Telegram, FO to Damascus, 25 February 1965; Telegram, Beaumont, Rabat, to FO, 26 March 1965.

32 Letter from W. Morris to W. A. Warburton, Bonn, 11 May 1965. PRO: FO 371/180894, Letter ref. 11950/65 from N. C. C. Trench, Washington, to W. Morris, 15 March 1965. 'In return the Israelis assured the Americans that they would not be the first to produce or acquire nuclear weapons in the Middle East.'

33 See, for example, PRO: FO 371/186850, Telegram, Damascus to FO, 17 February 1966.

34 PRO: FO 371/180897, Letter from C. McLean to R. M. Hastie-Smith, DS.6, 12 February 1965.

35 PRO: FO 371/186850, Letter from M. Hadow, Tel Aviv, to W. Morris, 28 April 1966.

36 PRO: FO 371/186853, Telegram, FO and CRO to certain Missions, 8 July 1966, 'Tanks for Israel', and Telegram, FO to Tel Aviv, 8 July 1966.

37 PRO: FO 371/186853, Letter from D. A. Marston, Defence Supply Section, FO, to R. W. Bourne, Sales (General) Army Department, 21 February 1966. Nothing came of this – the Israelis bought M-113s from the US instead.

38 PRO: FO 371/186853, ER 1203/8, Various Enclosures, February 1966.

39 PRO: FO 371/186850, Minute by W. Morris, 'Israel: Arms Supplies', 23 November 1966.

40 PRO: PREM 13/2207, 'Note for the Record' of telephone conversation between George Brown and Harold Wilson, 19 May 1967.

41 This figure fell within the number of rounds for which the Israelis had already paid, complicating any decision to deny their request. PRO: FCO 17/582, 'Details of Ammunition required by Israelis', minute by W. Morris, 19 May 1967.

42 PRO: FCO 17/582, 'Tank Ammunition for Israel', W. Morris to F. Brenchley, 22 May 1967.

43 PRO: FCO 17/582, 'Tank Ammunition for Israel', Minute, W. Morris to F. Brenchley, 19 May 1967. If news of the pick-up leaked to the press, the line would be: 'It is not our practice to divulge details of sales of arms to other governments. The shipments being made are of material purchased under a contract dating from before this year and which is already Israeli property.'

44 Handwritten note of conversation between Brown and Wilson dated 23 May 1967, on PRO: FCO 17/582, 'Tank Ammunition for Israel', Morris to Brenchley, 22 May 1967. See also PRO: PREM 13/1617, 'Note of a Meeting between the Prime Minister, the Foreign Secretary and the Defence Secretary at No. 10 Downing Street at 10 a.m. on Tuesday, May 23, 1967'.

45 PRO: FCO 17/582, Letter from Aharon Remez to George Brown, 22 May 1967.

46 PRO: PREM 13/1618, 'Record of a Meeting between the Foreign Secretary and the Israeli Ambassador at the Foreign Ofice at 12.30 p.m. on Sunday, 28 May, 1967'. PRO: PREM 13/1618, 'Note of a Meeting between the Prime Minister and the Foreign Secretary in the Cabinet Room on Sunday, May 28, 1967, at 7.45 p.m.'.

47 PRO: CAB 130/323/150(67)/4, Minutes of Cabinet Meeting, 5 June 1967.

48 PRO: CAB 128/42/CC(67)/36, Minutes of Cabinet Meeting, 6 June 1967. See also Harold Wilson's comments in the House of Commons, Hansard, 6 June 1967, col. 806.

49 PRO: PREM 13/2207, Minute by C. M. MacLehose, FO, 7 June 1967.

50 PRO: CAB 128/42/CC(67)/37, Minutes of Cabinet Meeting, 8 June 1967.

51 PRO: FCO 17/582, Letter from Aharon Remez to George Thomson, 9 June 1967. 'Ammunition for Israel', Memorandum by George Thomson, 9 June 1967.

52 PRO: FCO 17/579, Letter from Aharon Remez to George Thomson, 11 July 1967.

53 PREM 13/2207, 'Centurion Tanks for Israel', Minute from George Brown to Harold Wilson, 2 August 1967.

54 PRO: CAB 148/30/OPD(67)/36, Minutes of OPD Meeting, 15 November 1967.

55 Ibid.

56 CAB 148/37/OPD(68)/38, 'Supply of Military Equipment to Israel', Memorandum by the Secretary of State for Foreign Affairs, 28 May 1968. The OPD agreed that the sale

could go ahead on 29 May 1968. PRO: CAB 148/35/OPD(68)11, Minutes of OPD Meeting, 29 May 1968.

57 PRO: CAB 148/38/OPD(68)/66, 'Sale of Chieftain Tanks to Israel', Note by the Secretary of State for Foreign and Commonwealth Affairs, 1 November 1968. This note also contains a detailed annexe comparing the superior performance of the Chieftain with that of the Soviet T55 and T62 operated in the region.

58 *Ibid.*

59 PRO: CAB 148/35/OPD(68)/20, Minutes of OPD Meeting, 7 November 1968.

60 PRO: CAB 148/38/OPD(68)/72, 'Supply of Tanks to Israel', Memorandum by Secretary of State for Defence', 11 November 1968. Michael Stewart produced a memorandum arguing against the sale, 'Sale of Chieftain Tanks to Israel', 12 November 1968.

61 PRO: CAB 148/35/OPD(68)/21, Minutes of OPD Meeting, 13 November 1968.

62 Jeremy Hanley, Minister of State, FCO. Hansard, 24 January 1996, cols 458–9.

63 PRO: FO371/163018. A. R. Walmsley, 'Arms Sales to Saudi Arabia', 28 March 1962.

64 John Stonehouse, *Death of an Idealist* (London, W. H. Allen, 1975), p. 50.

65 Interview with Frank Brenchley, London, 15 April 1998.

66 PRO: FO371/168886, Telegram, British Embassy, Jeddah, to FO, 8 July 1963.

67 PRO: FO371/168889, C. T. Crowe, British Embassy, Jeddah, to FO, 20 November 1963.

68 PRO: FO371/168889, 'What bothers me,' Crowe told the FO, 'is that Edwards and his friends and the Saudis will lead each other up the garden path into thinking they would like a new defence system based on British weapons which the Americans will not possibly stand for … One of the troubles is that Geoffrey Edwards is fanatically anti-American and most of the firms' representatives are pretty bad' (i.e. anti-American).

69 Interview with Sir Michael Weir, London, 13 March 1998. Interview with Frank Brenchley, London, 15 April 1998.

70 PRO: FO 371/168898, 'Lightnings for Saudi Arabia', Memorandum by Frank Brenchley, FO, 27 November 1963.

71 *Ibid.*

72 PRO: T312/1134, Lord Carrington, 'Canberras for Saudi Arabia', Memorandum, 7 February 1964.

73 PRO: PREM 11/5069, Memorandum, Thorneycroft to Carrington, 14 February 1964.

74 PRO: FO 371/174682, Brief appended to letter, British Embassy, Washington, to FO, 6 February 1964.

75 PRO: FO371/174682. Record of Conversation, Lord Caldecote and Lord Carrington, House of Lords, 12 February 1964.

76 This impression is confirmed by a memorandum of a meeting with Edwards and BAC's Mr Duguid with Sir Colin Crowe at the Jeddah embassy at that very time. Duguid asked Crowe for his opinion of Edwards. Crowe thought that Edwards 'operated in a rather disorderly kind of way' and Crowe 'would not recommend him as an agent for a regular line of business'. Duguid agreed, 'and said he did not find Mr Edwards' methods of business very agreeable, but from the way he went on to talk about Mr Edwards' contacts and the necessity for sweetening members of the Defence Committee, I had the impression that BAC wish to use Mr Edwards as the channel through which they would funnel whatever *douceurs* might be found necessary.' PRO: FO 371/174682, Memorandum from Sir Colin Crowe, 9 February 1964.

77 Lord Caldecote laid the blame for the government's coolness over BAC's prospects on the interpretation being offered by Crowe. Interview with Lord Caldecote, London, 12 March 1998.

78 PRO: FO 371/174682, Record of Conversation, Lord Caldecote and Lord Carrington, House of Lords, 12 March 1964.

79 PRO: FO371/74683, J. A. Snellgrove, FO, to A. W. Redpath, Commonwealth
    Relations Office, 28 August 1964. The obvious regional point of comparison was
    Nasser's Egypt. Precisely the same arguments were made in favour of selling British
    arms to Castro's Cuba in 1959. See Mark Phythian and Jonathan Jardine, 'Hunters in
    the backyard? The UK, the US and the question of arms for Castro's Cuba',
    Contemporary British History, 13:1 (1999), 32–61.
80 See PRO: FO 371/74683, 'Thunderbirds for Saudi Arabia', Memorandum of Meeting
    between Eilts and R. S. Crawford, Arabian Department, FO, 2 October 1964.
81 PRO: FO 371/74683, Denis Healey to Prince Sultan, 23 December 1964.
82 PRO: FO 371/179888, Telegram, Jeddah to FO, 23 March 1965.
83 PRO: FO 371/179888, Report by Stonehouse, 24 March 1965.
84 PRO: FO 371/179889, Jeddah to FO, 31 March 1965.
85 PRO: FO 371/179890, Washington to FO, 25 September 1965.
86 Interview with Frank Brenchley, London, 15 April 1998. Interview with Sir Michael
    Weir, London, 13 March 1998.
87 PRO: FO 371/179890, Washington to FO, 11 October 1965.
88 PRO: T 312/1134, Washington to FO, 11 October 1965.
89 PRO: FO 371/179/891, Jeddah to FO, 12 November 1965.
90 PRO: PREM 13/2362, Roy Jenkins to Harold Wilson, 24 November 1965.
91 PRO: T 312/1135, ECGD to Treasury, 18 November 1965.
92 PRO: T 312/1135, Telegram, Stonehouse to Jeddah, 19 November 1965.
93 PRO: T312/1135, 'Saudi Arabian Military Aircraft', Memorandum by D. F. Hubback,
    BoT, 22 November 1965.
94 *Ibid*.
95 PRO: CAB 148/027, Memorandum by Michael Stewart, 7 March 1966.
96 *Ibid*.
97 PRO: CAB 148/027, Memorandum by Denis Healey, 8 March 1966.
98 PRO: CAB 148/25, Minutes of OPD, 9 March 1966.
99 PRO: PREM 13/2362, Telegram, FO to Washington, 11 March 1966.
100 PRO: CAB 148/25, Minutes of OPD meeting, 17 March 1966.
101 PRO: FO 371/185494, 'Lightnings for Saudi Arabia', Note by the Air Force
    Department, 14 April 1966.
102 The Saudis were informed that launchers complete with *dummy* missiles could be
    supplied within one month, but Sultan was unimpressed.
103 PRO: FO 371/185494, Jeddah to FO, 23 April 1966.
104 PRO: FO 371/185494, Washington to FO, 25 April 1966.
105 PRO: FO 371/185494, Jeddah to FO, 29 April 1966.
106 PRO: FO 371/185496, Jeddah to FO, 1 August 1966.
107 See *Daily Telegraph*, 20 and 22 August 1966. As the FO noted, some of 'Donaldson's
    accusations are too close to the truth for his reports to be simply denied or dismissed
    as inaccurate.' PRO: PREM 13/2362, Guidance Note, FO to certain Missions, 2
    September 1966.
108 PRO: FCO 8/798, Record of Meeting between Ray Brown, HDS, and Prince Sultan,
    Paris, 24 February 1968.
109 PRO: FCO 8/781, 'Arms for Saudi Arabia', Memorandum by Denis Allen, FO, 23
    February 1968.
110 PRO: FCO 8/781, Report for January 1968 by Defence Attaché, Jeddah.
111 PRO: FCO 8/798, Briefing for Meeting with Prince Sultan, 27 February 1968.
112 Signed on 7 May 1973.
113 Cited in *Flight International*, 16 April 1977.
114 See, for example, *Guardian*, 23 October 1975, *Sunday Telegraph*, 26 October 1975. In
    the aftermath of the 1973 conflict, the RSAF had taken part in large-scale Syrian mili-

tary manoeuvres. At that time, the Saudi army garrison was still in Syria, where it had been stationed since the conflict.

115 Its value was initially put at around £500 million. See *Financial Times*, 16 September 1977.

116 The first foreign sale of the F-15 had been to Israel in 1975.

117 *Financial Times*, 10 February 1978.

118 This provided for the supply of armoured vehicles, mobile howitzers, machine guns and other infantry equipment, anti-aircraft guns and communications equipment. *International Herald Tribune*, 16 July 1979.

119 *Ibid.*

120 *Guardian*, 28 July 1979.

121 *Financial Times*, 25 April 1980.

122 The post of Saudi ambassador to London had been vacant since July 1979.

123 This visit had not then been officially announced, so there was no official announcement of the cancellation.

124 *Financial Times*, 20 January 1981.

125 The original phasing-out date had been 1982.

126 *Financial Times*, 8 June 1981.

127 *Ibid.*, 26 September 1981.

128 The final package comprised: five AWACS with three years' support and training; site survey for 22 communications centres; 1,177 Sidewinder missiles; 101 shipsets of F-15 conformal fuel tanks; and six Boeing KC-707 tankers, with an option on a further two.

129 As long ago as 1968 the British government believed that, in the words of Foreign Secretary Michael Stewart, 'the French ... policy of support for the Arabs has been largely designed to enable them to profit in this way.' PRO: CAB 148/38/OPD(68)/66, 'Sale of Chieftain Tanks to Israel', Note by the Secretary of State for Foreign and Commonwealth Affairs.

130 In addition to this activity, in December 1986 it was announced that Racal had won a £300 million-plus contract from Boeing to develop a tactical radio system for the Saudis as part of the Peace Shield deal. *Guardian*, 5 December 1986.

131 For example, in securing the Peace Shield deal, Boeing had agreed to reinvest 35 per cent of the value of contracts within a ten-year period in Saudi high-technology industry. By the time of Channon's visit, projects worth around US$350m had already been agreed. See *Financial Times*, 6 March 1987.

132 *J.D.W.*, 5 February 1994, p. 27.

133 *Ibid.*

134 *Independent*, 16 November 1988, *Sunday Times*, 28 January 1990, and *BAe Quarterly*, autumn 1989. The links with the FA had been formed in May 1989, when a five-year agreement was signed.

135 On this case, see Sampson, *The Arms Bazaar*, pp. 127–39.

136 *Observer*, 19 March 1989.

137 *Ibid.*

138 *Ibid.*

139 *Ibid.*

140 *Flight International*, 28 November 1989.

141 *J.D.W.*, 6 May 1995, p. 33.

142 *Financial Times*, 27 November 1989.

143 *Sunday Times*, 10 December 1989.

144 It also led to an immediate rise in the value of BAe shares.

145 The Tornadoes flew an estimated 1,500 offensive missions during the war. Initially, these were low-level attacks using the JP-233 crater bomb to destroy Iraqi runways.

146 The problem stemmed from the ingestion of sand into the engines. Prior to flights, RAF

personnel reportedly hosed them down in an effort to maintain them, although not always successfully. Furthermore, a fault on the aircraft's Foxhunter radar reportedly left crews tracking targets using stopwatches. See *Sunday Telegraph*, 25 November 1990.

147 *J.D.W.*, 1 September 1990.
148 *Sunday Times*, 30 September 1990.
149 *The Times*, 25 October 1991.
150 Hansard, 4 December 1995, col. 79w.
151 PRO: FCO 17/263, Telegram, Amman to FO, 2 January 1967.
152 PRO: FCO 17/263, 'Supporting Brief for Foreign Office Supplementary Estimates: Item £100,000 Supply of Aircraft to Jordan', undated.
153 PRO: FCO 17/263, Telegram, FO to Amman, 30 June 1967.
154 PRO: FCO 17/263, Telegram, Amman to FO, 12 July 1967.
155 They would also require US clearance because they were part-financed by US MDAP funds.
156 PRO: FCO 17/263, Minute from George Thomson to Denis Healey, 3 August 1967.
157 PRO: FCO 17/281, A. B. Urwick, British Embassy, Washington, to A. R. Moore, Eastern Deptartment, FO, 23 January 1968.
158 PRO: FCO 17/263, Denis Healey to George Thomson, 4 August 1967.
159 PRO: FCO 17/263, Minute from George Brown to George Thomson, 4 August 1967.
160 PRO: FCO 17/263, Telegram, FO to Amman, 4 August 1967.
161 PRO: FCO 17/264, Telegram, Washington to FO, 13 November 1967.
162 PRO: FCO 17/265, Memorandum, A. R. Moore to F. Brenchley, 9 February 1968.
163 PRO: FCO 17/281, Telegram, Washington to FO, 7 February 1968.
164 See PRO: FCO 17/281, Telegram, FO to Washington, 9 February 1968, and Telegram, Washington to FO, 13 February 1968.
165 PRO: FCO 17/265, Telegram, FO to Amman, 16 February 1968.
166 This latter shift was related to Jordan's refusal to approve the Camp David peace accords. The Hunter aircraft purchased in the 1950s were replaced by US F-5s, which were themselves replaced in the 1980s by the Mirage.
167 The Iranians had ordered 125 Shir Is, which had already been built, and 1,225 Shir IIs, which had not. As Jordan had identified a requirement for 200 tanks, the production run for the Shir I was extended by a further 75 vehicles.
168 *Guardian*, 1 October 1979; *Financial Times*, 2 October 1979.
169 *Financial Times*, 14 August 1985.
170 *Ibid.*
171 *Flight International*, 28 September 1985.
172 Hansard, 11 January 1994, col. 169. In the event, Jordan did not purchase equipment to these values. In an unprecedented disclosure, in 1993 the Government released full details of the equipment sold (60 separate projects), as the information had been required by the Scott inquiry. *Ibid.*, 3 November 1993, cols 295–6. See also 13 December 1993, cols 527–8.
173 The intention was that Jordan would be supplied with the same aircraft that the USAF chose when it came to evaluate the two aircraft later in the year.
174 *Financial Times*, 3 March 1988.
175 *Flight International*, 7 May 1988.
176 Panavia was 42.5 per cent German-owned.
177 *Observer*, 19 March 1989.
178 *Ibid.*
179 PAC, *Ministry of Defence: Costs and Receipts arising from the Gulf Conflict,* Fifty-fifth Report, 1992–93 Session, HC 729, p. 12.
180 *Observer*, 19 March 1989.

181 *Financial Times*, 23 March 1989.
182 Hansard, 23 March 1989, col. 693.
183 *Ibid.*, 23 March 1989, col. 1323. For a more detailed treatment of Rowland's role, see Tom Bower, *Tiny Rowland: A Rebel Tycoon* (London, Heinemann, 1993).
184 Hansard, 23 March 1989, col. 1329.
185 For a breakdown of the number of export licence applications for Jordan, and the number turned down, between 1985 and 1993, see Hansard, 5 May 1993, col. 106.
186 Scott Report, para. E2 February 19
187 *Ibid.*, para. E2 May 19
188 *Ibid.*, para E2.62.
189 PRO: WO 32/20760, Telegram, Kuwait to FO, 19 May 1966.
190 WO 32/20760, Telegram, Kuwait to FO, 19 May 1966.
191 WO 32/20760, Telegram, Kuwait to FO, 13 July 1966.
192 WO 32/20760, Telegram, Kuwait to FO, 27 August 1968.
193 WO 32/20760, Telegram, Washington to FO, 8 June 1968.
194 *Financial Times*, 16 February 1976.
195 *Ibid.*, 16 February 1976.
196 *Daily Telegraph*, 28 September 1981.
197 *J.D.W.*, 30 July 1988, and *Financial Times*, 11 July 1988.
198 Thereby making Kuwait the first country outside NATO and its immediate allies to acquire the aircraft.
199 Nevertheless, Congress had completely blocked the sale of 1,600 Mavericks to Saudi Arabia only a year earlier. See *J.D.W.*, 13 August 1988.
200 *Daily Telegraph*, 7 September 1988.
201 *J.D.W.*, 17 December 1988.
202 These consisted of 19 Skyhawks, 15 Mirage F-1s, six Hawks, eight Gazelle and one Puma helicopters. *Defence*, January 1991.
203 These were essentially spares and arms for the aircraft that had eluded the Iraqis: Exocets, HOT ATGWs, and engines.
204 Quoted in *The Times*, 30 April 1981.
205 See Michael Brzoska and Thomas Ohlson, *Arms Transfers to the Third World 1971–85* (Oxford, Oxford University Press, 1987), p. 347.
206 For example, France has supplied Exocet missiles and launchers, while the US has supplied AIM and TOW missiles, alongside a small number of helicopters and transport aircraft.
207 See Halloran and Hollingsworth, *Thatcher's Gold*, ch. 4.
208 *Guardian*, 24 April 1981.
209 *Sunday Times*, 26 April 1981. Of the British forces, 130 officers were seconded by the MoD. Around 500 were 'contract troops', i.e. mercenaries. See *The Times*, 30 April 1981. For a memoir see Alan Hoskins, *A Contract Officer in the Oman* (Tunbridge Wells, Costello, 1988).
210 *Guardian*, 24 April 1981. See also *The Times*, 30 April 1981: 'Even after the Second World War, British diplomats were still carried ashore in Muscat on cane chairs borne on the shoulders of liveried embassy personnel.'
211 Halloran and Hollingsworth, *Thatcher's Gold*, ch. 4.
212 *Ibid.*, p. 93.
213 *Ibid.*, p. 103.
214 For an overview see Fred Halliday, *Arabia without Sultans* (Harmondsworth, Penguin, 1974), Chs.9-11, and Tony Geraghty, *Who Dares Wins: The Story of the SAS 1950–1992* (London, Warner Books, 1993), pp. 166–205.
215 This latter deal was worth an estimated £45 million.
216 This order was worth £40 million, and had the distinction of being the first order won

by the company since its privatisation in November 1985.

217 Creasey had commanded the Omani armed forces (on secondment) between 1972 and 1975, during which time they fought the Yemeni guerrillas. He was later decorated with the Order of Oman, Second Class.

218 *Guardian*, 16 August 1984.

219 *Ibid.*

220 *Ibid.*

221 *Ibid.*

222 *Defence*, September 1985.

223 *Financial Times*, 20 February 1986.

224 The value was put at £2 million.

225 *Financial Times*, 21 January 1986.

226 *J.D.W.*, 25 January 1986.

227 Air Vice Marshal Bennet and Rear Admiral Balfour.

228 Quoted in *Flight International*, 13 May 1989.

229 *Ibid.*

230 Oman already purchased Exocet missiles and Puma helicopters from France.

231 *J.D.W.*, 17 February 1990.

232 *Ibid.*, 14 September 1991.

233 MoD news release, 2 September 1991.

234 *J.D.W.*, 11 August 1990.

235 PRO: WO 32/20760, Report, 'Visit to Bahrain by Director of Army Sales 5th–8th August 1968'.

236 Brzoska and Ohlson, *Arms Transfers to the Third World,* p. 349. Prior to the 1980s, the major British sales were of six Vosper Thornycroft P–1101 class patrol boats in 1974; 12 Rapier missile launchers and 50 Rapier missiles in 1975 and 1976; 36 Alvis Scorpion APCs in 1978; Lynx helicopters in 1979. In 1981, Rotork Marine sold two 12 m landing craft, and in 1983 Alvis secured a repeat order for 44 Scorpions.

237 *Guardian*, 24 March 1981, *Financial Times*, 23 April 1981. Only two days before the sale was announced, a joint RAF/BAe team returned from Abu Dhabi and Dubai following a Red Arrows display of the Hawk.

238 *Guardian*, 23 April 1981.

239 *Sunday Telegraph*, 16 January 1983.

240 However, these figures are, perhaps, somewhat misleading. The UAE armed forces were 60 per cent Omani, and also included Sudanese, Pakistani, Egyptian, Jordanian, and British personnel. See *Financial Times*, 7 January 1985.

241 For example, 1984's defence budget was Dh6.85 billion (US$1.86 billion) out of a total budget of Dh17 billion.

242 *J.D.W.*, 30 May 1987.

243 *Flight International*, 22 August 1990.

244 *Financial Times*, 14 April 1989.

245 Quoted in Amnesty International, *Repression Trade (UK) Limited: How the UK Makes Torture and Death its Business* (London, Amnesty International, 1992), p. 17.

246 *Flight International*, 23 November 1990.

6

Britain in the post-Gulf War arms market: the Major effort

Events in the post-Gulf War world show that there is still more interest in arms sales than in control. There are no rewards for restraint, but there is a heavy price to pay for loss of markets in terms of access, influence, status and employment. Nevertheless, the early months of 1991 seemed a particularly promising time for arms control initiatives. The end of the Cold War and its proxy wars in the South had reduced the importance of arms as an instrument of foreign policy. With the decline of the 'Soviet threat', arms proliferation itself came to be seen as one of the principal threats to international security. The East European implosion also bred concern over the uncontrolled spread of arms and their passage to the Middle East. In the immediate past lay the example of Iraq, and although the impact of that lesson could be expected to diminish over time, the protracted and ultimately impossible task of completely eliminating Iraq's nuclear, chemical and biological weapons capability facing the UN Special Commission (UNSCOM) would serve as a constant reminder of the folly of Western policy towards Iraq in the 1980s. Finally, the post-Gulf War situation in the Middle East seemed the most stable for some time, making it a propitious moment to attempt to make progress on arms control and confidence-building issues.

At the same time, other factors suggested that arms control would remain elusive. Most significantly, military technologies were becoming increasingly spread through the transnationalisation of military production, making complete control more problematic. The growth in the importance of dual-use technologies further suggested that complete control would be increasingly difficult to achieve. Whether or not the political will required for restraint existed in the West was also open to question, given that the likely post-Cold War recession in defence had been ameliorated only temporarily by the Gulf War. Once the immediate post-Gulf War orders were complete, the full effects of recession would begin to be felt, and national governments could be expected to look for ways to alleviate them. Moreover, the Gulf War had produced a high

demand for arms in that region, with the smaller Gulf states seeking to
arm defensively in order to minimise their vulnerability to invasion, Iran
rearming, Syria seeking missile technology to bridge the gap between itself
and Israel, and Israel seeking to purchase high-tech US weapons to maintain its qualitative edge. In the Gulf, a number of the smaller states now
acutely felt the need to replace ageing aircraft. As Joel Johnson of the US
Aerospace Industries Association gleefully noted: 'There is some elderly
equipment in the neighbourhood.'[1] Moreover, the lessons of the Iraqi
invasion of Kuwait for these Gulf kingdoms suggested that they would be
more willing to go through the potentially humiliating process of seeking
Congressional approval of US arms sales, and that such approval might be
more readily forthcoming. Neither of which developments would be good
news for the British arms export industry. In the post-Cold War era, the
days of tacit big-power agreement about how best to satisfy markets such
as these were a thing of the past.

Nevertheless, calls for the control of the international arms trade in
order to prevent 'another Iraq' began soon after the invasion of Kuwait,
and gained momentum in the aftermath of the 1991 war. The problem is
that they did not arise in isolation, but in the context of an energetic
scramble for contracts amongst the very leading Western suppliers nomi-
nally most committed to restraint. Given this situation, could the calls for
control, including several for the introduction of a register of conventional weapons, be seen as anything more than a response to a situation
where the states which had armed Iraq felt the need to be seen to be doing
something for essentially domestic political reasons?

The first steps on the road to Gulf rearmament began well before the
war itself, with the Bush administration offering US arms to both Kuwait
and Saudi Arabia.[2] Suggestions for control also began to proliferate, with
those states most culpable in the arming of Iraq to the fore. In November
1990 President Bush outlined an Enhanced Proliferation Control
Initiative,[3] and in February 1991 French Prime Minister Michel Rocard
indicated that France would be willing to lead moves towards arms
control in the Gulf.[4] However, by March 1991 a new arms race was under
way in the Gulf. This contradiction was being driven in part by the Lower
Gulf states, whose reaction to the invasion of Kuwait, combined with the
positive impression left by the battle-tested US military equipment,
weighed against any kind of regional arms control initiative. As the
Kuwaiti Secretary General of the GCC told journalists, 'We must have
more teeth and more bite,' adding that 'Cash on the barrel-head will
determine who gets arms.'[5]

The very act of holding the UN coalition together in the period leading
up to and during the conflict also militated against arms control initiatives. Egypt, whose debts arising from the purchase of US arms had been
written off to the tune of US$7 billion, now sought further arms such as

Hawk missiles, F-16 aircraft and M-60 tanks. By March 1991 the US had already announced the sale of 46 F-16s, 80 Maverick missiles and various other pieces of military equipment to Egypt.[6] These requests were closely monitored by Israel, which itself requested US$1 billion worth of US equipment.[7] At the same time, President Bush was telling a joint session of Congress that: 'We must act to control the proliferation of weapons of mass destruction and the missiles used to deliver them. It would be tragic if the nations of the Middle East and Persian Gulf were now, in the wake of war, to embark on a new arms race.'[8]

It was no accident that he chose to base his appeal on weapons of mass destruction, thereby legitimising US action in rearming the Gulf states. This stance was indicative of the pressures that the Bush administration was under. Domestically, the end of the Cold War jeopardised employment in the defence industry, which could be secured by contracts to arm the Gulf. In the build-up to the 1992 US presidential elections this was a major consideration, the more so as Bush began to trail in the polls. Arms sales would also cement US influence in the region, which could be lessened if the rearmament went ahead without the US to the fore. Ironically, restraint could only harm relations with the region. In March 1991, Prince Sultan, the Saudi Defence Minister, commented that: 'We want the US to be the main supplier but if there are problems, we will look elsewhere.'[9] It was in an effort to alleviate precisely these fears that Defense Secretary Dick Cheney told the House of Representatives Foreign Affairs Committee: 'Some caution is in order but our concern is to work with our friends and allies to be sure they are secure. I do not think an arms embargo is a good thing if it keeps the Egyptians or the Israelis or the Saudis undefended.'[10]

At the same time, leading Western governments were finalising their own proposals for conventional arms control. The first to emerge was a Canadian arms control initiative, unveiled in March 1991. This called for a world summit to establish an arms sales control regime by 1995. It was met by open US scepticism. However, following Bush's first overseas trip since the Gulf War, taking in Canada to meet Mulroney, Martinique to meet Mitterand, and Bermuda to meet Major, the White House announced that it had postponed action on new arms sales to the Middle East as part of the attempt to put together an international regime to control conventional arms sales. The following month, the Pentagon's co-ordinator for US arms sales to the GCC began a month-long trip to the Gulf states to discuss their requirements. Following this, the UAE submitted a request for 330 M-1A1 main battle tanks, 160 Bradley armoured vehicles, 18 helicopters and over 800 trucks.[11]

John Major's first significant contribution to the conventional arms control debate came during a meeting of the Council of Ministers in Luxembourg in April 1991, where he proposed a register of conventional

arms to monitor and control arms build-ups. In May 1991, President Bush
unveiled his five-point plan to curb weapons proliferation in the Middle
East, but it was clearly flawed, and notably did not adopt the call for the
introduction of a register made by Major. In unveiling the proposal, Bush
had gone so far as to state that Middle Eastern states should be free 'to
acquire the conventional capabilities they legitimately need to deter and
defend against military aggression.'[12]

It was against this background that President Mitterand's arms control
initiative was unveiled in mid-1991, in part a reflection of the deep embarrassment that the issue of arms sales to Iraq had caused in French political
circles. The inquest here was different from those conducted in the US
(links with Cardoen, Banco Nazionale del Lavoro, etc.) and Britain (the
supergun, Matrix Churchill, etc.) because it related to overt rather than
covert dealings. French weapons were used against French forces in the
Gulf; a French Roland missile shot down a British Tornado aircraft;
French Mirage aircraft had to be withdrawn from the conflict because
they were indistinguishable on radar screens from those sold to Iraq; some
of the equipment sold to Iraq was more advanced than the variants available to the French forces in the Gulf and, perhaps even worse, Iraq had
not actually paid for them. Hence Mitterand, perhaps more than any
other Western leader, needed to be seen to be doing something.

This initiative was followed up from 8–9 July 1991 by the Paris
meeting of the five permanent members of the UN Security Council (P5)
– the US, China, France, Britain and the USSR – 'to review issues related
to conventional arms transfers and to the non-proliferation of weapons of
mass destruction'.[13] During the same month, Britain announced that it
would no longer stand in the way of the EC lifting its embargo on arms
sales to Syria, having re-established diplomatic ties (severed in 1987 over
the Hindawi affair) in November 1990, as a reward for its role in the Gulf
conflict. However, it was a largely symbolic gesture, as Britain still operated its own national ban on arms sales to Syria, and the Netherlands,
which held the rotating presidency of the EC, was not proposing a lifting
of the EC arms ban.[14]

On 15–16 July 1991, the Group of Seven (G7) met in London.[15] The
British government's desire for the G7 to adopt John Major's arms register idea, 'to prevent the build-up of arms by countries that is
disproportionate to their defence needs',[16] ran into French resistance
based on apprehension over whether the G7 was the appropriate organisation to direct such controls.[17] In view of the French objection that the
summit did not have the authority to establish permanent machinery to
oversee arms control initiatives, the G7 moved away from a Japanese and
Canadian-led proposal for the creation of a G7 working group to monitor
implementation of its Declaration on Conventional Arms Transfers.

The final communiqué advocated the most far-reaching measures yet since the Gulf conflict, and underscored the emergence of the UN Arms Register concept as the leading proposal in the field of conventional arms transfer restraint. The only problem was that there was no consideration of how the measures advocated should be implemented. The communiqué called on states to apply the 'three principles of transparency, consultation and action' in the field of conventional arms. As regards transparency, this:

> should be extended to international transfers of conventional weapons and associated military technology. As a step in this direction we support the proposal for a universal register of arms transfers ... Such a register would alert the international community to any attempt by a state to build up holdings of conventional weapons beyond a reasonable level. Information should be provided by all states on a regular basis after transfers have taken place. We also urge greater openness about overall holdings of conventional weapons. We believe the provision of such data, and a procedure for seeking clarification, would be a valuable confidence and security building measure.[18]

Throughout August 1991, a working party of experts from 18 countries set to work on the terms of the embryonic UN Register of Conventional Arms. Lynda Chalker, Minister for Overseas Aid, echoed John Major in commenting that: 'We want to bring greater openness to the murky area of arms sales. If governments know that sales will be publicised, they will feel greater pressure to act responsibly. If it becomes clear that particular countries are acquiring weapons which go beyond the legitimate requirements of self-defence, then the alarm bells will ring and action will be taken.'[19]

Notwithstanding the supreme irony of the British government claiming that it wanted to bring light to bear on the arms trade (its own record on openness towards Parliament was lamentable), the government's priorities and Chalker's rhetoric were not exactly one and the same thing. At the same time that Chalker was speaking in support of conventional arms restraint, the Vickers Challenger II tank was preparing to undergo hot weather trials in Saudi Arabia, with Saudi delegations visiting Britain to view the vehicle. Furthermore, Britain was making a vigorous effort to sell the Challenger II throughout the region, alongside the Hawk aircraft and a range of other arms.

In October 1991, a further meeting of the P5 took place, this time in London, to discuss further international control of conventional arms.[20] An exchange of information on sales of conventional weapons to the Middle East was agreed, as was the principle that arms sales would be permitted only if they enhanced a country's legitimate self-defence or ability to take part in regional security pacts or UN-sponsored actions. Once again, however, there was no indication of how such assessments were to be made, of what objective criteria would be applied. Whereas the statements of the P5 leaders had, in the immediate aftermath of the Gulf conflict, implied recognition that they held responsibility for creating a system of conventional arms control (with the concept of transparency central to this), by the time of this meeting such recognition had come into conflict with their longer-standing commitment to Article 51 of the UN Charter, and the implicit notion that sovereign states have the right to acquire the means of self-defence.

George Bush's re-election bid-linked decision of September 1992 to authorise the sale of 150 F-16 fighter aircraft to Taiwan in any case killed off this phase of arms restraint diplomacy by ending Chinese participation.[21] By the end of 1992, the register of conventional arms initiative notwithstanding, the focus was once again firmly on sales, not control.

Rearming the Gulf: the US, the UK, France and the scramble for contracts

In June 1991, the US announced that it had agreed to sell 20 Apache helicopters to the UAE and six to Bahrain – the first sales of the Apache to Gulf states. Dick Cheney explained that this was not inconsistent with Bush's arms control initiative: 'With the Apache helicopter sale to the UAE, it is not inconsistent to say on the one hand we are interested in arms control, and on the other we want to make certain our friends can defend themselves.'[22]

On 1 November 1991, the Saudi government informed the US that it wanted to buy 72 more F-15s (in a deal worth US$5 billion). If Congress blocked the sale, McDonnell Douglas warned, it would have to shut down the F-15 production line before the end of 1993. The request carried a certain sense of *déjà vu*. In the mid-1980s, the congressional reaction to a Saudi request for F-15Es resulted in Saudi Arabia turning to the UK in the form of the Al Yamamah deals. Would Congress act differently in a post-Cold War, post-Gulf War setting, notwithstanding the notional international arms control agenda? Certainly, the actions of the Bush administration during the Gulf crisis of 1990/91 suggested a commitment to push these sales – it lifted the ceiling on Saudi Arabia owning just 60 F-15s, so that by early 1992 the US had sold the Saudis 98. While the Pentagon was unlikely to approve sales of the F-15E ground attack variant (probably the premier ground attack aircraft in the world) in this package, the company began an intensive lobbying effort which recalled the 1980s decision which had handed the Al Yamamah deal to Britain. A brochure warned: 'A Middle East ally wants 72 F-15s ... but will buy from Europe if refused.'[23]

At the same time, Britain was looking to secure the first stages of the Al Yamamah 2 agreement. It will be recalled that the first phase involved the sale of 72 Tornado, 30 Hawk and 30 PC9 aircraft, along with associated support and infrastructure. Although Al Yamamah 2 had been signed in 1988, by 1991 this wish list had still to be converted into actual contracts. David Gore-Booth, Assistant Under-Secretary at the FCO, described Saudi Arabia as 'easily Britain's most important partner in the Middle East, whether politically, commercially or militarily'. He explained that Britain did support the *principle* of arms restraint in the region, but added that: 'We have no intention of depriving our friends of the means to defend themselves.'[24] This approach was broadly in line with that of the Bush administration, and prompted *The Economist* to describe arms control as 'the sort of religion nobody can decently object to ... Like other religions, however, it is in danger of promising what it cannot deliver.'[25]

In October 1991, Prince Bandar, the Saudi ambassador to the US, confirmed that additional orders stemming from the Al Yamamah agreements, and worth £10 billion, would be placed with Britain by the end of the year.[26] In November, over 100 British companies exhibited at the Dubai Aerospace and Defence Exhibition, including BAe, GEC Marconi, Rolls-Royce, Vickers, Vosper Thornycroft and Westland. Sir Graham Day, BAe chairman, sought to apply the battle-tested tag to his hardware, commenting that: 'The Gulf war has been good for British Aerospace. Our equipment and support was ground-tested and not found wanting.'[27]

However, the Saudi Arabian interest in purchasing 72 F-15s,[28] which could well have represented an alternative to further Tornadoes, raised fresh anxiety at BAe over the Tornado component of Al Yamamah 2, without which its Tornado assembly line would be redundant. This anxiety was grounded in the fact that the Saudis' developed an interest in the Tornado only after their repeated requests for the F-15E had met with fierce Congressional resistance, blocking any sale. Now the Kingdom was publicising its efforts to get the aircraft it had long been denied. In addition, McDonnell Douglas was targeting Saudi Arabia to sell its F/A-18 to replace the ageing Northrop F-5, while Kuwait also showed great interest in acquiring a fleet of 35 F/A-18s, in addition to the 40 ordered prior to the Iraqi invasion.[29] In its case, it was obliged to place its largest orders with the US in return for the US role in repelling the Iraqi forces, and in case it was ever required to do so again – the sale would cement the military alliance on which Kuwaiti independence (or, at least, the rule of the al-Sabah family) rested. This obligation was to become more transparent as events unfolded.

In December 1991, just weeks after his initial declaration of interest, Prince Bandar announced that Saudi Arabia was withdrawing its request for 72 F-15Es, at least until the Congressional omens were more favourable. He did so in a letter to Senator Howard Metzenbaum, who had co-ordinated opposition to the sale. While President Bush still had to decide on how to proceed with an earlier request for 24 F-15Fs, the with-drawal of the later request, if permanent, meant that the F-15 production line, which employed around 7,000 people, would close in 1993, a devel-opment of heightened political importance in a presidential election year.[30]

Despite its high profile in calling for arms restraint, in June 1992 Bush confirmed that his administration would seek to sell Saudi Arabia US$1.8 billion worth of helicopters, missiles, rockets and small military vehicles.[31] Then, during a July campaign stop in Missouri (where the aircraft were assembled), Bush announced that the sale of the 72 F-15s to Saudi Arabia would go ahead. Although Bush had still to notify Congress, he intended to do so in advance of November, so as to be able to claim the credit for saving the 30,000 jobs that were held to be in jeopardy unless the sale went ahead. The Saudis were also keen for the deal to be concluded quickly in view of Bill Clinton's campaign rhetoric, promising to 'press for strong international limits on the dangerous and wasteful flow of conven-tional arms to troubled regions'.[32] The extent to which, by the summer of 1992, the momentum for arms control had been lost amid the clamour for contracts and George Bush's electoral concerns was reflected in a Saferworld Foundation report. This put the value of military equipment ordered by Middle Eastern states since the Iraqi invasion of Kuwait at between US$35 billion to US$45 billion.[33] While US orders accounted for around US$28.5 billion of this, British orders represented around US$4 billion of it. In addition, France and Germany, and – of more concern to the West – China, Russia, Czechoslovakia and North Korea had all received orders, with Saudi Arabia, Israel, Kuwait and Iran leading the way in imports.

Saudi Arabia and the al-Mas'ari affair

By December 1992, tension between the erstwhile UN allies over rearm-ing the Gulf was again evident. Britain responded to the continued threat posed to its arms sales interests by deploying the Defence Procurement Minister, and associate of the Saudi royal family, Jonathan Aitken. His Gulf tour focused on trying to sell the Challenger II and, in the wake of Vickers' failure to secure orders from Kuwait, concentrated on the UAE and the dependable Sultan of Oman. Oman had indicated that it had a requirement for around 60 tanks, while the UAE had an estimated requirement for 390. Although the Saudi army's tank order had promptly gone to the US, there also remained some hope that the Saudi National Guard would purchase the Challenger II, or even that the Saudis might seek to split their requirement so as not to be totally dependent on the US in this area. The government also began to see the potential of utilising a willing sales weapon denied to other countries – Prince Charles. During 1993, Charles called for his foreign visits to be more closely related to British export efforts, and demonstrated his potential on a tour of the Gulf, where, 'despite the flag-waving and flummery which enveloped the royal visit, there was a serious sub-plot. Prince Charles had come to bat for Britain.'[34]

Aitken's preparatory work paid dividends when Major flew to Saudi Arabia to meet King Fahd and discuss the stalled Al Yamamah 2 agreement. Before leaving, Major was able to announce that the delayed £5 billion order for 48 Tornadoes had been secured.[35] Negotiations on the Hawk, Black Hawk helicopter and naval vessels, however, continued.

Saudi concern over Iran's acquisition of Russian Kilo class submarines also led it into talks with the British government over the possible purchase of anti-submarine warfare versions of the EH-101 helicopter, produced jointly by Westland and Agusta of Italy. This looked to be one of the most promising export areas in the latter half of the 1990s, as Saudi Arabia was joined by the UAE, Kuwait and Oman in the desire to combat the threat posed by Iranian submarines. Concern over Iran's submarine capability also led Saudi Arabia to consider creating its own submarine force by acquiring four submarines. Having tried unsuccessfully to offload four ex-RN *Upholder* class submarines in 1993, Britain joined France and Sweden in offering proposals to fill this requirement.

However, British prospects of prevailing in the intense competition for Saudi contracts were jeopardised by the al-Mas'ari affair. This exposed something of the networks of influence which exist between government and the defence industry – the political–military–industrial complex, if you like. In US President Dwight D. Eisenhower's original conception, the 'conjunction of an immense military establishment and a large arms industry' would, if not guarded against, impose itself on the 'councils of government'.[36] In the Britain of the 1980s and 1990s, the most enthusiastic advocates of the military–industrial complex came from the political establishment. Their interests were synonymous with those of the arms export industry. Since the days of Mrs Thatcher, the state had become so heavily involved in the promotion of arms exports that it was, in practice, very difficult to consider the concept of a 'military–industrial complex' without reference to its political arm.

The activities of Mohammed al-Mas'ari, the London-based Saudi dissident leader of the Committee for the Defence of Legitimate Rights, united industry and government in the fear that the Saudis would retaliate by cancelling part of the Al Yamamah deal and by awarding up-coming contracts to anyone other than British companies if he was not silenced. This was a particular concern of Vickers, then having a hard enough time selling the Challenger II as it was. Al-Mas'ari's activities even led to calls from British industry that a forthcoming asylum Bill should include a

clause requiring that those who fell within its provisions must not undertake activities detrimental to the UK national interest. In a similar vein,
they also led Home Secretary Michael Howard to declare that the rights
of political refugees in the UK had to be measured against British
economic interests.

In a thinly veiled threat, the Saudi Interior Minister, Prince Nayef, had
warned that: 'We distinguish between who is an enemy and who is a
friend. We can find all our needs elsewhere in the world.'[37] With orders
for aircraft, main battle tanks and missiles pending, the British arms
export industry could not afford the government's toleration of al-
Mas'ari. Hence the British government took the unprecedented step of
ordering the expulsion of a political refugee to safeguard future arms
orders. As Archie Hamilton explained, Ministers 'had to weigh up the fact
that we were not going to get defence orders from the Saudis – and they
are our most important export customer for defence equipment – as long
as he remained in this country'.[38] Home Office Minister Ann Widdecombe
explained that: 'If people come here and use our hospitality in order to
attack extremely friendly governments with whom we have good diplomatic and very good trade relations, we have a very difficult balance to
strike. On this occasion, we have concluded that British interests do
require his removal.'[39] The expulsion papers were signed by Michael
Howard following an eve-of-Christmas meeting in Downing Street involving Howard, John Major, Michael Portillo, Ian Lang and Malcolm
Rifkind.[40] However, al-Mas'ari had broken no law. He had merely criticised an oppressive state with an appalling human rights record, which
groups like Amnesty International were also drawing attention to.[41]

Nevertheless, the government attempted to have al-Mas'ari deported to
the Caribbean island of Dominica. As a reward, Dominica would see
bilateral aid increased from £500,000 in 1994/95 to £2 million the following year, while the rest of the aid budget faced a 5.4 per cent cut.[42]
However, in March 1996 the courts ruled that the government had not
shown that al-Mas'ari would not be in danger in Dominica.[43] Judge David
Pearl, the Chief Immigration Adjudicator, criticised the government for
attempting to 'circumvent' obligations arising from the 1951 UN
Convention on Refugees.[44]

At the height of the al-Mas'ari affair, a memorandum from Sir Colin
Chandler, chief executive of Vickers, was leaked to the *Guardian*. This
showed that Chandler and Dick Evans of BAe had been discussing how
best to deal with al-Mas'ari and minimise the impact of his activities on
their arms sales interests in Saudi Arabia, and suggests that the government may well have acted on the promptings of British industrial as well
as Saudi figures. It also showed how wider foreign policy interests can
come to be subordinated to arms sales interests. According to Chandler,
the CIA was becoming interested in al-Mas'ari's activities, 'and, accord-

ing to Dick, are in some dialogue with their counterparts in this country. As you can imagine Evans said that he was in close contact with his "friend" in the United States on this subject.' Chandler suggested to Evans that one way of mending fences with the Saudis would be to pass on to them intelligence from the debriefing of Saddam Hussein's son-in-law, Hussein Kamal, who had fled to Amman (from where he would later return to Iraq and be killed). The UK ambassador to Saudi Arabia, Andrew Green (who, it emerged, was also at the time a non-executive director of Vickers[45]), subsequently contacted Chandler to tell him 'that British debriefing had been carried out in Amman and material had been passed to both King Fahd and the Saudi foreign minister. This had earned us many plaudits.'[46]

Al-Mas'ari's has not been the only case to expose the tension between the prerequisites of arms sales success and core liberal democratic values. Elsewhere too politicians have suggested that basic freedoms should be curbed to advance arms sales. For example, Douglas Hurd told the FAC inquiry into the Pergau Dam imbroglio that:

> Britain lives by its word, contracts and exports, not by speculative articles or sniping against those whose job it is to strengthen Britain in the market place … It is not for me … to tell the free press in this country what to write, or to tell democratic politicians what to say, but everybody needs to consider the consequences of his actions, in this case particularly the consequences for the livelihoods of others. I do not know of any exceptions that should be made to that rule.[47]

Arms and human rights in Saudi Arabia became entwined once more in 1997, when two British nurses were charged in connection with the murder of an Australian colleague. Fearing an anti-Saudi outcry, various UK companies with business interests in Saudi Arabia clubbed together to raise the 'blood money' (£776,000) required by the dead Australian's brother in order to spare one of the nurses, Deborah Parry, from being beheaded. Despite this generosity, the companies wished to remain anonymous, and BAe would neither confirm nor deny that it was one of them.[48]

Rearming Kuwait

Once the 1991 war was over, Kuwait had to completely rebuild its defences. The Kuwaiti army had lost most of its heavy weapons, destroyed, captured or disabled by the fleeing Kuwaitis. The navy lost most of its eight fast attack craft, while, after the dust had settled, the air force was able to save 15 Mirage F-1s, 19 Skyhawks and 6 Hawks. Almost all radar and surface-to-air missile defences were destroyed. The two air bases at al-Ahmadi and al-Jahra were also destroyed – ironically, largely as a result of Coalition bombing during the conflict. The first British contract to emerge from this rebuilding process was won by Land Rover, to supply over 400 vehicles at a value of over £8 million, with an option on a further 2,000.[49] In addition, Royal Ordnance secured the £50 million contract for the clearance of all battle areas, and for 'explosive ordnance' disposal.[50]

In September 1991, Kuwait signed a 10 year defence deal with the US. An Anglo-Kuwaiti defence agreement followed on 11 February 1992, by when a similar agreement with France was already being negotiated. It was signed in the wake of a visit to Kuwait by Secretary of State for Defence Tom King, where he also tried to sell the Challenger II, the GKN Warrior and Vosper Thornycroft naval vessels. Rather than emphasise the contribution this could make to Kuwait's defence, King highlighted how it could produce 'valuable orders for British industry'.[51] A memorandum of understanding followed in December. Vosper was also part of a consortium with construction companies Taylor Woodrow and Wimpey, selected to rebuild and upgrade the main naval base in a contract which on its own was worth over £200 million.The awarding of post-war contracts was proceeding in almost direct proportion to the role played by the supplier in Kuwait's liberation. Those Western states that had previously armed Kuwait *and* rushed to its defence (essentially, the US, France and Britain) had shown the necessary combination of commitment and capability and were duly rewarded, proportionately.

In September 1992, British hopes of securing export orders for the Vickers Challenger II suffered a setback when it was ruled out of the competition to supply 200 tanks to Sweden because the MoD refused to release one of nine prototypes for field trials. However, the MoD did release one of the prototypes for trials in Kuwait, Saudi Arabia, the UAE and Oman. At the same time, Defence Secretary Malcolm Rifkind visited Kuwait, to discuss British arms sales. Given Britain's role in the liberation of Kuwait, Rifkind could have been confident that the past arms sales relationship and the obligation arising from Britain's role in Kuwait's defence, together with the Kuwaiti need to continue to involve all the major military players in its liberation should a repeat performance ever be necessary, would result in significant British arms sales. Like his predecessor, Rifkind concentrated his energies on trying to interest the Kuwaitis in the Challenger II, then still awaiting its first export order, as well as naval vessels and Hawk aircraft, hoping to capitalise on the February 1992 UK–Kuwaiti Defence Co-operation understanding. Clearly conscious of the contradictions such activities revealed in British arms control rhetoric, Rifkind argued that Iraq still posed a threat to stability in the region, and went on to express concern at Iran's arms build-up by way of further justification.[52]

In October, Kuwait announced that it had chosen the US M-1A2

Abrams for its tank requirement, rather than the Challenger II.[53] Kuwait would order 236 in a deal worth £1 billion. Ghazi al-Rayes, the Kuwaiti ambassador to Britain, denied reports that the decision had been influenced by a letter from Dick Cheney demanding that the Kuwaitis award the contract to the US (along with the contract then being contested by the UK Warrior and US Bradley Fighting Vehicle) before the November presidential election, where Bush still trailed in the polls. This was said to contain 'an oblique threat that should America ever again need to go to the defence of Kuwait, it would make operational sense if they were both using the same equipment',[54] and was sent despite the apparent existence of an informal agreement amongst the Gulf War allies that post-war Kuwaiti orders would be divided amongst them thus: US – air force; Britain – army; France – navy.[55] A Pentagon spokesman did not contest the existence of the Cheney letter, but said it merely pointed out the Abrams's technical superiority.[56] Bush planned to visit the General Dynamics plant involved during his campaign once the decision was announced, so as to derive maximum political capital from the announcement.[57] Vickers accused the US administration of 'using political leverage' to secure the deal, with chairman Sir Colin Chandler complaining, 'We've not even discussed our price with them [the Kuwaitis].'[58] Vickers also contested the accuracy of accounts from US sources that the Challenger II had been outperformed in trials and when, for example, required to engage a target at 4,000 metres had seen all eight of its shots fall short.[59] Vickers later claimed that the evaluation of technical trials had not been completed when Kuwait announced its selection. For its part, the Pentagon claimed that in trials the Abrams scored 40 points more than the Challenger, adding for good measure that the Bradley Fighting Vehicle outscored the UK Warrior by 25 points (see below).[60] However, these claims and counter-claims need to be set against the fact that the two vehicles were competing across the region, with the UAE, Oman and Saudi Arabia still to decide on requirements.[61]

In the final analysis, the US won the contract because it had been and continued to be the guarantor of Kuwait's independence. Were a similar threat to emerge in the future, it would not be the 236 Abrams tanks that would defend Kuwait. Such a defence would require US involvement. From a Kuwaiti perspective, then, the deal served to further cement that alliance. This logic dictated that, despite the disappointment over the failure of the Challenger II, Britain would also be invited to supply military equipment to Kuwait. However, aside from the disputed performance of the Challenger, the success of the Abrams in Kuwait threatened the Challenger's export prospects elsewhere in the region, in that the sale of 236 to Kuwait would produce a lower unit cost for the Abrams should the UAE and Saudi Arabia select it.

In this atmosphere of tension amongst allies it proved very difficult to be seen to be critical towards or to question the wisdom of further arms sales, no matter who the recipient. In November the Labour defence spokesman, George Foulkes, fell victim to this sentiment. During Defence Questions in the House of Commons, Foulkes said that the Labour Party had a policy which 'excludes the sale of arms to military dictatorships'. When he challenged the government to give assurances that it shared this new direction in policy, he was greeted by laughter. Jonathan Aitken, Defence Procurement Minister, replied that: 'He has enunciated an extra-ordinary new Opposition policy: that we should sell arms equipment only to democracies.' Aitken reminded the House that only the previous month, Foulkes had urged the government to make a more vigorous effort to sell the Challenger II to Kuwait, 'which is not yet a democracy'.[62] The reality was that, aside from the US, few of the UK's best arms customers were even remotely democratic.

Despite the disappointment over the Challenger, by 1993 the government was estimating that during the previous two years it had secured a third of the Kuwaiti defence export market,[63] and there were further British arms sales successes in Kuwait during 1993. In August, it was announced that, in the wake of the acrimony and disappointment accompanying the tank failure, a British company, GKN, had secured a contract to supply 200 Desert Warrior armoured vehicles. Rifkind said he hoped it would be the first of a 'string of significant purchases' by Kuwait.[64] This was a reference to the ongoing negotiations over the purchase of air defence equipment from Short's, and of 100 Swiss-designed Piranha light tanks, also manufactured by GKN.[65] Under the terms of a memorandum of understanding signed by Rifkind in December 1992, the Warriors and any future UK equipment purchased would be bought through the MoD, which set up a programme office in London to manage the contracts. When the contract for the Warriors was finally signed in August 1993, it was for 254 Warriors and a 'substantial number' of Piranha vehicles, together estimated to be worth in excess of £500 million.[66] However, there was further bad news for Vickers, in the aftermath of the earlier Challenger II failure in Kuwait: the Kuwaitis had selected the US Delco turret for the Warriors rather than the Vickers turret option.

Throughout this period, Kuwait continued to sign defence agreements with members of the P5. As noted, it had already signed an agreement with the US in September 1991 and with Britain in February 1992 (one of four signed with Britain, dealing with manoeuvres and arms sales, during the course of the year). An agreement with France was signed in August 1992 (with a subsidiary agreement on arms transfers following in 1993). On 29 November 1993, Kuwait developed its security-through-friends policy further when it signed a 10 year defence agreement with Russia, providing for joint military manoeuvres. Payback came the following July, when a Russian military delegation visited Kuwait to finalise an arms agreement.[67] Subsequently, Kuwait ordered armoured personnel carriers and artillery rocket systems from Russia, at the same time as it was lobbying all P5 states not to weaken the sanctions imposed on Iraq.[68]

Having secured Russia's signature, it only remained for Kuwait to secure that of China to complete a full set of defence agreements with the P5, and to this end Kuwaiti Defence Minister Sheikh Ahmed announced that he would visit Beijing early in 1995 to sign a defence agreement with China.[69] It was duly signed on 24 March 1995. At this point, since its liberation Kuwait had bought arms exclusively from the other four P5 members; now China would join them in securing contracts. Kuwait had not looked much beyond the P5. It made no sense to – purchasing arms was a matter of politics rather than specification or capability. It was the political alliances created, rather than the weapons bought, which ultimately guaranteed its independence.

In November 1997, it was announced that Kuwait would buy a number of Chinese 155 mm self-propelled howitzers towards meeting its requirement for 75. This announcement was the culmination of considerable manoeuvring amongst the P5 suppliers. While it had initially been thought that China would be asked to supply between 24 and 36 such guns, US and UK pressure (offering the M-109A6 Paladin and the Vickers Shipbuilding AS90 respectively) saw the number being revised downwards. With the deal in jeopardy, China reportedly indicated that it would not support the extension of trade sanctions on Iraq in the UN Security Council unless it was awarded the contract. Indeed, in October it abstained in a vote on Iraqi sanctions.[70]

For its part, the US again reminded the Kuwaitis of the fact that they effectively retained their sovereignty at the pleasure of the US. As State Department spokesman Nicholas Burns put it: 'We saved Kuwait. We saved the royal family and we saved the economy and the structure of society as Kuwait knows it. We assume that Kuwait has not forgotten that.'[71] In the face of this pressure, and immediately following a visit by US Defense Secretary William Cohen, the Kuwaiti Defense Ministry announced that it would buy 48 Paladins. This led to protests from the Kuwaiti Parliamant that the Paladins were overpriced and, as a result of a design initiative aimed at helping the gun through Congress, did not have the same range as any of the competing artillery systems.[72] Hence Kuwait postponed the Paladin order while the Audit Bureau investigated the relative merits of all competing systems, including the Vickers AS90. In November 1998, during a visit to Kuwait, the Secretary of State for Defence George Robertson said he believed the competition was still open.

This represented a further case where considerable friction was being generated between the fledgling Kuwaiti Parliament and the ruling family over arms issues. While Kuwait in the late 1990s was not Iran in the late

1970s, there is much irony in a situation where the acquisition of mainly US arms – more than realistically could be absorbed – at a time when low oil prices were bringing ever closer the need to make hard choices domestically, was heightening internal divisions and tensions. There are few clearer indications that the principal benefactors of the post-1990 Gulf arms push were not the states buying the arms, but those selling them.

Towards the end of 1994, Kuwait ordered the Shorts Starburst missile defence system, a contract worth £50 million.[73] In May 1995 the Emir of Kuwait paid his first state visit to Britain, allowing John Major to offer an appropriately uncompromising stance on the retention of sanctions on Iraq: 'Saddam Hussein leads a dangerous and ruthless regime. Our aim must be to ensure that Iraq is not allowed to threaten its neighbours again,' adding for good measure that 'we will act again if [the Iraqis] threaten peace in the area.'[74]

Competition degenerated into controversy again in 1996. In January, Secretary of State for Defence Michael Portillo and French Defence Minister Charles Millon arrived in Kuwait within 24 hours of each other to sell their respective anti-ship missile packages, required to arm French-built fast attack craft, in a competition worth an estimated US$200 million. Portillo was selling the BAe Sea Skua, deployed during the Gulf War, where, amongst its successes, it sank Kuwaiti vessels captured by the Iraqis. Shortly afterwards, French President Jacques Chirac sent a letter to the Emir, reminding him that, under the terms of the French defence agreement with Kuwait, he understood that France would be granted all new contracts for naval requirements. However, political support rather than technical merit was the key factor, and in this respect Kuwait's leaning towards the Sea Skua reflected France's softer line in the UN Security Council on the easing of sanctions against Iraq, a source of special concern in Kuwait. By contrast, the hard-line on Iraqi sanctions adopted by the US and UK served to boost their arms sales prospects in the region.

Chirac's anxiety proved well founded, as Kuwait opted for the BAe Sea Skua rather than the reportedly less expensive French system. The Kuwaiti Parliament responded by demanding an investigation into the decision. One Kuwaiti MP alleged that the deal was secured by the payment of commission, while another called for the contract to be shown to Parliament, and the identity of the middleman and the size of the commission revealed.[75] Regardless, to secure the deal for 80 Sea Skuas BAe had to supply another 20 free of charge, and agree to meet a previously contested debt of US$11 million.[76]

Oman

In the aftermath of the Gulf War, Oman remained loyal to British arms. In February 1992 Vosper Thornycroft announced that it was signing a £150m contract for two 83 m missile corvettes, due to be delivered in 1994 and 1995.[77] In May, it was announced that Oman had placed a contract worth in excess of £40 million with BAe to upgrade its Rapier air defence system, supplied during the 1970s. Under the deal, the Omani Rapiers would be returned to the UK in batches, where BAe would carry out the upgrade.

On his way back from India, in January 1993, John Major made an 'unscheduled' stop in the Gulf to try to finalise a number of outstanding arms sales possibilities. The stop-off was reminiscent of much of Mrs Thatcher's 'batting for Britain' in the region, and a clear effort to emulate her arms sales diplomacy,[78] or at least assure Gulf leaders that her successor's commitment in this area was equal to hers. Prior to securing the Al Yamamah 2 Tornado deal, Major enjoyed Thatcheresque success in Muscat, where he secured a £150 million Omani order for 18 Challenger II tanks – the first export order (albeit a relatively small one) for the vehicle – together with four CRAAV armoured recovery vehicles.[79] Without export orders, the Challenger II production lines in Leeds and Newcastle would have been run down from 1995, with the British government's order for 140, worth around £500 million, due for completion by 1998. The US and France also needed to secure export orders to keep their tank production lines open. With the Middle East the only remaining significant export market for tanks, the ferocity of the competition and the acrimony surrounding it were inevitable.

In 1993, the Swan Hunter shipyard, in receivership, competed with the French yard CMN, which also had an empty order book, for a contract to supply Oman with at least two 45 m patrol craft. In the event the contract went to the French yard. In May 1994, Oman ordered 80 Piranha light armoured vehicles from GKN, with an option on a further 46, to be delivered between 1995 and 1997. The Piranha, made under licence from MOWAG of Switzerland, beat off competition from France, the US and Russia to secure the contract. However, in mid-1996 France did break into what had been an exclusively British market for armoured vehicles when it secured an order for 50 scout cars – a first step in the inevitable process of drawing France into providing for Oman's defence alongside the US and UK. In late 1997, Oman signed a £100 million contract for a further 20 Challenger II tanks, and during an October 1997 visit Defence Secretary George Robertson signed a contract to upgrade Oman's Jaguar aircraft, worth £40 million.

UAE

The Challenger II ultimately lost out in the UAE tank contest as well. The UAE placed an order in France for 390 Leclercs, in a deal worth around US$3.5 billion, to be delivered between 1994 and 1999. This deal represented the first export order for the Leclerc, and included 46 support vehicles, spares, training and a French commitment to reinvest 60 per cent of the contract's value in joint ventures. Significantly, it would be powered by a German engine, representing a major loosening of German policy on licensing arms exports to the region. Again, despite the rhetoric about preventing a regional arms race after the Gulf War, the French, US and British governments had all vigorously marketed their country's products, as they had in the competition to supply tanks to Saudi Arabia, Oman and, particularly, Kuwait. For its part, the Labour Party's defence spokesman called the UAE decision 'very, very bad news indeed'.[80]

In addition, the UAE was to be the site of what was dubbed 'the last great arms deal of the century' – the scramble to secure the contract for a requirement of up to 80 long-range strike aircraft, vigorously fought by all the leading suppliers, in particular the US (F-16), UK (Tornado and then Eurofighter, based on an option of leasing a squadron of Tornadoes until the Eurofighter became available) and France (Mirage 2000).

In July 1993 the UAE had concluded a defence agreement with the US, and in January 1995 the UAE and France became the latest P5 member/ arms supplier–Gulf state to conclude a defence agreement, signed in Abu Dhabi by the UAE Minister of Foreign Affairs, Sheikh Hamdan bin Zayed, and the French Defence Minister, François Léotard. The existence of such agreements was by now being viewed as a prerequisite of access to Gulf markets, and the logic which compelled the UAE to enter into such alliances with suppliers suggested there would be something for both countries in the final decision. Hence while in November 1997 President Clinton personally urged Sheikh Zayed to buy the F-16 to meet its fighter requirement, in December the UAE ordered 30 Mirage 2000-9 fighter aircraft, following a visit by President Chirac. Indicative of the extent of big power manoeuvring and competition over these contracts, the French Mirage deal had been held up for 10 months. The US reportedly pressured the UK government to withhold authorisation for the inclusion of the Black Shahine missile, with which the UAE wanted to equip the aircraft, notionally because of concern that its export would violate the terms of the MTCR.[81] That the UK took so long to approve the deal also suggests implicit linkage between its response and the future direction of US–UK market competition in the region. However, having satisfied French pride, the UAE then selected 80 F-16s from the US in a package worth US$7 billion. Given that the UAE had now recently bought 30 Mirage 2000-9s and the 80 F-16s, it seems highly likely that BAe will be able to secure a further order for the Hawk, thereby satisfying the three leading P5 suppliers to the region.

These requirements were driven not only by the threat posed by Iraq, but also by that posed by the region's premier military power – Iran – which was beginning to produce significant items indigenously, with help from China, North Korea and then Russia.[82] In November 1996 Iran also took delivery of its third Kilo class submarine. Rear Admiral Ali Shamkhani warned that Iran had the capability to position missiles from 'the north to the south of the Persian Gulf'.[83] The following year, Iran claimed it had the ability to close the strategically important Strait of Hormuz. This threat also explains why, at one point, there had been discussion about the UAE acquiring its own submarine fleet, although the British government's 1994 attempts to lease the UAE two *Upholder* class submarines, complete with crews, failed.

However, outstanding requirements generated by this threat did propel Defence Secretary Malcolm Rifkind to the UAE in January 1995, to try to interest the Emirates in Vosper Thornycroft frigates – even though Britain had still to conclude a defence agreement similar to that entered into by the US and France.

In 1995 the UAE also took a step closer to directly involving Russia in its defence plans when, in response to a build-up of Iranian troops on the Abu Musa and Sirri islands, it discussed purchasing three SA-10/12 air defence systems. These would, in effect, not cost the UAE anything, and could be deployed almost immediately, because Russia was keen to use them to repay a US$500 million loan from the UAE. Never enthusiastic about outside powers entering Gulf markets, the US fought a vigorous rearguard action to prevent Russian penetration of the market by stressing the benefits which would accrue from adopting the Patriot anti-missile system. This included a US threat not to fly in UAE air space if the UAE purchased the Russian system.[84] In July 1996, it was reported that the UAE had agreed to buy the Russian Smerch multiple-launch rocket system. Responding to the Iranian submarine threat, in July 1997 the UAE requested 24 Harpoon missiles (worth US$90 million) from the US, and looked set to order a number of 'small submarines', with Vosper Thornycroft in the running to fill the requirement.

Qatar

In 1994 Qatar prepared the way to purchase at least 12 Mirage 2000-5 fighter aircraft by reaching an agreement to sell 13 Mirage F-1s to Spain for US$132 million, with part payment to be made by Spain sending two new CASA CN-235 military transport aircraft to Qatar.[85] The following month, Qatar sealed the Mirage purchase, becoming only the second country – after Taiwan – to acquire it. The deal, signed in Doha by French Defence Minister François Léotard, was accompanied by the signing of a military co-operation agreement. That Qatar should have selected the Mirage was, of course, no surprise. France and Qatar have enjoyed the closest defence relations in the Gulf since the mid-1960s, with France supplying around 80 per cent of Qatar's major conventional arms requirements, including tanks, armoured vehicles, military helicopters and trainer aircraft, as well as the Mirage. When French Defence Minister Charles Millon visited Doha in March 1997, he not only announced that delivery of the Mirage was shortly due to begin, but also that France would gift the Emirate 10 AMX-30 main battle tanks, and signed a second military co-operation agreement committing France to depoly an undisclosed number of troops there.[86]

Aside from a 1992 order for four Barzan class fast attack craft from Vosper Thornycroft (to be delivered in 1996–98), [87] as of 1994, it was a market Britain had had little success in penetrating. However, British arms sales prospects were not harmed by the June 1995 palace *coup* which saw the Sandhurst-educated Sheikh Hamad (who was in any case the *de facto* ruler) overthrow his father and proclaim himself Emir. Britain rushed to be the first country to recognise the transfer of power.[88] These prospects were further enhanced by the signing, in April 1996, of a UK–Qatar defence agreement, making the UK the third Western power (after the US and France) to conclude such a deal.

In November 1996 payback came with the announcment that British companies had secured a £500 million order to supply Qatar with an assortment of arms, the news coming just days after the announcement by BAe of its £1 billion contract to sell 33 Hawk 100s to Australia.[89] The Qatari deal comprised Hawk aircraft, 40 GKN Piranha armoured vehicles, two Vosper-Thornycroft 46 m patrol vessels and Short Starburst missiles. The memorandum of understanding was signed in the capital, Doha, by Michael Portillo, Defence Secretary. As with Al Yamamah, the equipment would be paid for in crude oil.

This significant inroad into a French-dominated market contributed to the government's assessment that in 1996 it secured 25 per cent of the global arms market, generating contracts worth £5.1 billion and making the UK, by the government's own estimate, second only to the US (with 34 per cent) in the arms exporting league. Government figures estimated that this market share represented an increase from 19 per cent in 1995 and 16 per cent in 1994.[90]

The question of strategic depth

With those countries notionally most committed to arms sales restraint in the immediate aftermath of the Iraqi invasion of Kuwait actually fighting each other tooth and nail to secure lucrative Gulf markets for their weapons, the question arises as to how far their customers needed, or could even operate, the volume of hardware they had bought. With regard to Kuwait, the IISS's *Military Balance* records that at the time of the Iraqi invasion Kuwait possessed an impressive array of military equipment, largely purchased from leading Western suppliers, including 275 main battle tanks, 56 fighter aircraft and two squadrons of helicopters. If it did not have the strategic depth to operate them and prevent a 24 hour rout in 1990, the subsequent expulsion of non-Kuwaitis has sapped military strength still further. By 1998, Kuwait's armed forces stood at just 15,300, with an air force estimated at 2,500, giving it an impressive combat aircraft/personnel ratio (see Table 13).

In a similar way, in 1996 it was reported that Oman was employing RAF pilots to man its Hawk and Jaguar aircraft and military helicopters. In 1996 it still had only 24 pilots to operate 32 jet aircraft, and around 24 for the 30 helicopters.[91] In practice, of course, these states do not just depend on their own armed forces. Their military suppliers also deploy forces as a clear statement of intent, and to deter attack. UK and US military personnel are stationed in Bahrain, and British nationals play a large part in the estimated 3,700 foreign personnel (contract soldiers) in Oman. UNIKOM (the UN Iraq–Kuwait Observer Mission) coexists alongside UK and US forces and pre-positioned equipment in Kuwait. In Saudi Arabia, the heaviest foreign military presence, the Peninsular Shield Force, draws on US, UK and French military personnel and equipment. Pre-positioned (US) equipment is now in place across the region. Further afield, the UK provides 1,050, largely Gurkha, personnel in Brunei. This is itself recognition that, despite the volume of arms they have purchased, the Gulf states cannot defend themselves from attack from the north, raising a further question.

Buying arms or buying security through political influence?

Increasingly, then, with the strategic aim of securing pro-Western regimes in place in the Gulf having been met, there has been a trend towards Gulf states linking future arms orders with the signing of defence agreements. Essentially, these seek to guarantee that, should the means purchased from the West or P5 fail to secure the defence of the state as intended, those states from which they purchased the capacity will intervene to guarantee their sovereignty. However, it is not a great leap, once suppliers accede to

Table 13
Relative strategic depth: selected leading customers, 1998

Country	Population	Armed Forces – Active				Reserve	Paramilitary
		Total	Army	Navy	Air Force		
Bahrain	612,200	11,000	8,500	1,000	1,500	–	9,850[a]
Brunei	317,000	5,000	3,900	700	400	700	4,050
Kuwait	2,200,000[b]	15,300	11,000[c]	1,800[a]	2,500[a]	23,700	5,000
Oman	2,130,000[d]	43,500	25,000	4,200	4,100	–	4,400
Qatar	576,000[e]	11,800[a]	8,500	1,800[a]	1,500	–	–
Saudi Arabia	17,450,000[d]	105,500[a,f]	70,000	13,500[a]	18,000[g]	–	15,500+
UAE	2,580,000[h]	64,500[a]	59,000	1,500[a]	4,000	–	Not known

Notes [a] Estimated. [b] Of whom 35 per cent are Kuwaiti nationals. [c] Including 1,600 foreign personnel. [d] Of whom 27 per cent are expatriates. [e] Of whom 75 per cent are expatriates. [f] Plus 57,000 National Guard. [g] Plus 4,000 air defence. [h] Of whom 76 per cent are expatriates.
Source IISS: *The Military Balance 1998/99*, Oxford, Oxford University Press for the International Institute of Strategic Studies, 1998.

this principle, to a situation where Gulf states are not buying arms per se (that is, arms actually to defend themselves) but are buying security through political influence. The aim is not to buy the most appropriate arms, but to spend beyond the threshhold which guarantees supplier commitment to underwriting their security. In practice, of course, this means that a number of Gulf states will have a greater volume of advanced weaponry than they can ever hope to deploy operationally. While they did not need all these arms to guarantee their security, they did need to spend the money on importing them. As Kuwaiti Defence Minister Sheikh Ali al-Sabah put it: 'Protection is the friends you have, not the weapons you have.'[92]

A further expression of this reality can be found in an examination of the alliance meant to provide for mutual defence in the region – the GCC, comprising Saudi Arabia, Kuwait, the UAE, Oman, Qatar and Bahrain. The US has always, publicly at least, invested greater faith in the GCC than have its members. Notably, as Iraqi tanks rolled into Kuwait in August 1990, there was no military response whatsoever from the GCC. All has not been well since then, either. The focal point of the GCC's operation since 1991 has been the 20,000 Peninsula Shield Force based in Saudi Arabia, which is supposed to conduct annual exercises. However, during exercises in 1992, Omani forces reportedly refused to take orders from Saudi commanders. Qatar has refused to take any part in some of them at all, and even pulled out of the Peninsula Shield force entirely at one point when its border dispute with Saudi Arabia heated up. Such rivalries are one reason why the GCC failed to hold a naval exercise until 1994.[93] In short, the regional and tribal rivalries afflicting the Saudi-dominated GCC compound the existing hurdles to its effective operation caused by acute lack of strategic depth and the fact that interoperability has been a subsidiary concern when selecting military equipment.

Another expression of this reality can be seen in considering Kuwait's post-liberation behaviour. A Defence Co-operation Agreement signed with the US on 19 September 1991 is the cornerstone of Kuwaiti defence. It allows US access to Kuwaiti ports and facilities, and the pre-positioning of US military equipment, all of which provisions are more likely to guarantee Kuwait's security than the joint training also built into it. Joint military exercises have a significance arguably more symbolic than real. It is the defence agreement with the US, along with the agreements reached with the other four permanent members of the UN Security Council, and the stake which Kuwait has given each of them in the Kuwaiti defence market, that forms Kuwait's defence strategy. For Britain, as for France, arms sales and foreign policy are indistinguishable in the Middle East in a way which is not true of any other part of the world. The value of these alliances to Kuwait was further underlined in October 1994, when a swift response by the US, UK and France deterred Saddam from plans to invade Kuwait a second time – an intention confirmed by his defecting son-in-law Hussein Kamal shortly before his ill advised return home.[94] The bald fact remains that, no matter what conventional arms it buys (and it has difficulty absorbing those delivered since 1991), Kuwait cannot defend itself from either Iraq or Iran, and is dependent in a crisis on the deployment of outside force: effectively, US, UK and French, with Russian and Chinese diplomatic support in the UN Security Council.

All this was acknowledged in a defence review drawn up for the Kuwaitis by the US. It described Kuwaiti security as three-tiered: the first tier involved Kuwait strengthening its own armed forces; the second involved it strengthening defence links with regional allies; the third involved improving its defence relationship with the US, so that the US could assist in any future crisis.[95] From the perspective of European arms suppliers, however, it was also a plan which sought to extend US hegemony over the Kuwaiti arms market at their expense.

Similar defence agreements were signed across the region. Following on from the agreement with Kuwait, in October 1991 the US concluded a similar deal with Bahrain. This expanded a previous agreement to allow the US to preposition its equipment, and to allow it access to ports and airfields, as well as including a joint exercise programme. By the end of 1991 it had also signed an agreement with Oman. At the time, it was negotiating agreements with Qatar and the UAE. The agreement with Qatar was signed in June 1992, and in 1994 Qatar agreed to the pre-positioning of US equipment on its territory. In August 1994 the emirate also concluded a defence agreement with France, and conducted a joint exercise, Pearl Gathering II, the following year. In January 1995, France concluded a similar defence pact with the UAE. The terms of this defence agreement were not publicised, but it reportedly committed France to sending up to 85,000 troops, together with an aircraft carrier, support ships and 130 aircraft in the event of the UAE being invaded.[96] These agreements were also the passport to arms sales success. By contrast, the lack of such an agreement proved a barrier to UK companies. As *Jane's Defence Weekly* reported in January 1996, 'the UAE Government has made it clear that UK arms manufacturers would find it very difficult to secure any major contracts until a defence agreement has been concluded.'[97]

Belatedly, the British government got the message. Having already signed defence agreeements, implicitly linking access to the arms market with a commitment to intervene on behalf of these states militarily, with various Gulf states, in November 1996, FCO Minister Jeremy Hanley (a man who had previously taught Mark Thatcher accountancy) was despatched to Abu Dhabi, to be followed by Michael Portillo, who promised a deal once 'some legal issues' had been resolved (he in turn was followed by Prince Charles, who held a private reception on the destroyer HMS *Edinburgh*).

These legal issues revolved around the UAE's insistence that Britain should not just agree to bail out the UAE militarily should the need arise, but that, like France, its personnel would be subject to the jurisdiction of the UAE in doing so. Portillo insisted on a formula 'consistent with the tradition of armed forces being responsible to their own governments when they are in the service of those governments, even in another country'.[98] The compromise which was reached reportedly involved British troops being subject to local law when not on duty.[99] The agreement between the UK and UAE, finally signed on 28 November 1996, covered arms purchases, joint exercises and 'strengthening military co-operation'. As Portillo explained: 'The UK is committed to assisting the UAE in deterring threats and in the event of aggression taking place, to implementing joint military plans which are judged appropriate.' The unstated corollary was spelt out by an MoD official: 'Part of the reason for this treaty is to put British business in a good position for any future [arms] deals.'[100]

What are the implications of all this for British (and French) arms sales in the region? The pressure which the US brought to bear on the Gulf states – especially the smaller states – impacted on Britain and France in a number of ways. Firstly, the US role in Operation Desert Storm left the Gulf states so heavily obligated to the US that Britain and France would no longer be the primary suppliers of military equipment to any of the Gulf states in the medium term. This sense of obligation – coupled with the realisation that they might need to rely on the US in the future – overrode their irritation at the treatment they had received in the past from

Congress. Hence the days of Al Yamamah-sized packages for the UK are over, for the immediate future at least. Nevertheless, Gulf states are keen to involve Britain, France – and China and Russia in some cases – so as not to offend old allies, not to lose the advantages of diversity of supply which they sought in the 1970s and 1980s and, crucially, because of their political influence through the UN Security Council and other international forums. The logic of this suggests a continued role for Britain and France in selling arms to the Gulf states, but very much a secondary one where, rather than seek or be considered for the larger contracts, they will fulfil smaller, subsidiary requirements within larger programmes. However, from a purchaser perspective, these have to be made attractive enough to secure their military involvement in any future war of liberation. Such considerations are exemplified in Kuwait's post-occupation rearmament and security strategy. Since 1990, for Britain, France, and the US, arms sales policy and foreign policy in the Gulf region have been virtually indistinguishable.

Notes

1 Barbara Starr, 'Middle Eastern Promise', *J.D.W.*, 26 October 1991, p. 767.
2 In August 1990, the US Department of Defense announced a US$145.4 million contract with the Kuwaiti government-in-exile, to provide 40 F-18 aircraft and 300 Maverick missiles. In September, Saudi Arabia placed an order for US$20 billion worth of US equipment, including F-15 aircraft, Patriot missiles, up to 50 Apache helicopters, 400 Abrams M1-A1 tanks and 500 Bradley armoured vehicles. Naturally, all this was subject to the usual congressional approval. See *The Guardian*, 6 March 1991.
3 *Ibid.*, 13 May 1991.
4 *Ibid.*, 1 March 1991. France had supplied around 20 per cent of Iraq's arms before and after the war with Iran, and was still owed at least £1.5 billion. In April 1991, US Admiral Thomas A. Brooks, Director of US Naval Intelligence, told a closed session of Congress that French arms sales policy had been characterised by willingness 'to sell almost any conventional arms they build for their own forces on the export market. This has the effect of putting some of the best-designed, most lethal weapons in the world in the hands of virtually anyone who can afford them.' *Guardian*, 13 May 1991.
5 *Ibid.*, 6 March 1991.
6 *Daily Telegraph*, 13 March 1991.
7 This included hand-held battlefield navigation systems, M-109 artillery and the upgrading of F-15 aircraft.
8 Quoted in the *Guardian*, 13 May 1991.
9 *Daily Telegraph*, 13 March 1991.
10 *Observer*, 28 April 1991.
11 *Ibid.*
12 *Guardian*, 1 June 1991.
13 Communiqué issued Following the Meeting of the Five on Arms Transfers and Non-proliferation, 12 July 1991.
14 A Dutch Foreign Ministry official commented that: 'It would look very odd to lift the arms ban at such a sensitive time in the attempts being made to get a Middle East international peace conference off the ground.' *Guardian*, 11 July 1991.

15 See communiqué: London Economic Summit 1991: Declaration on Conventional Arms Transfers and NBC Non-proliferation, 16 July 1991.

16 *Guardian*, 16 July 1991.

17 Although the Chinese were not present, they were briefed on the arms control initiative in advance. *Independent*, 17 July 1991.

18 Communiqué, 16 July 1991.

19 *Guardian*, 7 August 1991.

20 Communiqué: Meeting of the Five on Arms Transfers and Non-proliferation, London, 17/18 October 1991.

21 Barbara Starr, 'F-16 sale justified by "discrepancy"', *J.D.W.*, 12 September 1992, p. 5. In part, Bush was reacting to the Chinese purchase of 24 Russian Sukhoi-27 fighter aircraft, and in so doing acting in a manner consistent with a 1982 memorandum written by Ronald Reagan, which stated that the US would restrict arms to Taiwan only 'so long as the balance of military power between China and Taiwan was preserved'. Cited in James Mann, *About Face: A History of America's Curious Relationship with China, From Nixon to Clinton* (New York, Knopf, 1990), p. 127.

22 *Financial Times*, 5 June 1991.

23 Barbara Starr, 'Further sales to Saudi debated', *J.D.W.*, 25 January 1992, p. 102.

24 Quoted in, *Financial Times*, 8 June 1991.

25 *Economist*, 8 June 1991, p. 16.

26 *Observer*, 27 October 1991.

27 *Ibid.*

28 Comprising 24 F-15Hs and 48 F-15 'multi-role' types.

29 *Financial Times*, 6 November 1991.

30 *Flight International*, 4 December 1991.

31 *Guardian*, 3 June 1992.

32 *Ibid.*, 25 July 1992.

33 Saferworld Foundation: *The Middle East Peace Process and the Arms Trade: A Fatal Contradiction?*, p. 5.

34 *Financial Times*, 22 November 1993.

35 The trip is briefly covered in Anthony Seldon, *Major: A Political Life* (London, Phoenix, 1998), p. 357. In September 1993, Major repeated the exercise, this time visiting Malaysia, where he did 'a bloody good job for industry, a bloody good job for Britain', according to Lord Prior, Chairman of GEC. See *Independent*, 23 September 1993.

36 Extracts from Eisenhower's farewell address cited in Gwyn Prins (ed.), *Defended to Death* (Harmondsworth, Penguin, 1983), p. 134.

37 *J.D.W.*, 8 May 1996, p. 19.

38 BBC Radio 4, *File on 4*, 13 February 1996.

39 *Guardian*, 5 January 1996.

40 *Independent*, 5 January 1996.

41 For example, a 1997 report on Saudi Arabia said that the criminal justice system was characterised by 'total disregard for the individual's right to a fair trial, which constitutes a basis for the enjoyment of other fundamental human rights', and found that torture, flogging, execution, amputation, and arbitrary arrest and detention on political grounds were normal practice. *Guardian*, 25 November 1997. See also the catalogue of abuses in the Amnesty International *Report 1998* (London, Amnesty, 1998), pp. 294–7.

42 *Independent*, 5 January 1996; *Guardian*, 6 January 1996.

43 Dominica seems to have been chosen because its Prime Minister, Edson James, was the next Commonwealth leader due to visit London after King Fahd and Prince Sultan had reportedly appealed to John Major to expel al Mas'ari. Edson arrived in London in

December 1995 in order to discuss the problems facing Dominica's banana industry, to be presented with an unscheduled additional meeting with Foreign Secretary Malcolm Rifkind on 18 December at which he agreed to take al-Mas'ari. See *Independent*, 5 January 1996. Edson later conceded that the offer of improved aid had secured his agreement. *Independent*, 23 February 1996.

44 *Ibid.*, 9 April 1996.
45 *Ibid.*, 6 January 1996.
46 'Confidential' memorandum, Sir Colin Chandler to J. D. Hastie, 6 September 1995. Published in *Guardian*, 6 January 1996.
47 FAC Report, Minutes of Evidence, 2 March 1994, p. 33.
48 *Financial Times*, 16 October 1997.
49 *The Times*, 27 March and 9 December 1991.
50 *J.D.W.*, 4 May 1991.
51 *Ibid.*, 22 February 1992, p. 274.
52 *Financial Times*, 23 September 1992.
53 *Ibid.*, 12 October 1992.
54 *Sunday Times*, 18 October 1992.
55 *Guardian*, 19 October 1992.
56 *Financial Times*, 14 October 1992.
57 *Independent*, 13 October 1992.
58 *Financial Times*, 13 October 1992.
59 *J.D.W.*, 12 September 1992, p. 5.
60 *Ibid.*, 24 October 1992, p. 22.
61 In September 1993, it was reported that the Challenger II was to undergo a series of modifications before being delivered to Oman, in the light of the trials it had undergone across the region. *J.D.W.*, 11 September 1993, p. 16.
62 Hansard, 24 November 1992, col. 730.
63 *Ibid.*, 18 May 1993, col. 140.
64 *Independent*, 10 August 1993.
65 *Daily Telegraph*, 10 August 1993.
66 *J.D.W.*, 14 August 1993, p. 5. The final Warrior vehicle was handed over in November 1997.
67 Kuwait had bought Russian (Soviet) military equipment previously, in 1975, 1982 and 1984. In addition, it had been the first of the future GCC states to establish diplomatic relations with the USSR, in 1963.
68 Christopher F. Foss, 'Kuwait's money buys more than artillery firepower', *J.D.W.*, 20 August 1994, p. 21.
69 *Ibid.*, 7 January 1995, p. 5.
70 *Ibid.*, 19 November 1997, p. 11.
71 *Ibid.*, 30 July 1997, p. 19.
72 *Ibid.*, 15 July 1998, p. 6.
73 This was awarded to Short Missile Systems – a joint venture company with Thomson-CSF of France.
74 *Daily Telegraph*, 24 May 1995.
75 *J.D.W.*, 12 November 1997, p. 29.
76 Ed Blanche, 'Kuwaiti MOD poised to drive Skua deal through', *J.D.W.*, 2 April 1997, p. 15.
77 In response to Iran's acquisition of Kilo class submarines, it later announced that it would fit the Thomson/BAe SEMA Active Towed Array Sonar system. *J.D.W.*, 8 September 1993, p. 18.
78 Jonathan Aitken even adopted this phraseology, telling the House of Commons: 'The Prime Minister ... batted for Britain splendidly.' Hansard, 9 February 1993, col. 811.

79 See *Guardian*, *Daily Telegraph* and *Financial Times*, 29 January 1993. The contract, which also included four Alvis Stormers, nine transporters and two driver training tanks, was eventually signed on 22 June 1993. See *Guardian*, 23 June 1993.
80 *Financial Times*, 16 February 1993.
81 *J.D.W.*, 7 October 1998, p. 6.
82 Although met with scepticism, in 1997 Iran even claimed to have produced its first jet combat aircraft. See *Jane's Defence Contracts*, October 1997, p. 6.
83 James Bruce, 'Concern in the Gulf as Iran's capability grows', *J.D.W.*, 27 November 1996, p. 18. See also James Bruce, 'Iran's military build-up in Gulf alarms GCC', *J.D.W.*, 4 December 1996.
84 *Ibid.*, 26 March 1997.
85 The Spanish aim was to maintain its F-1 force until the Eurofighter was available for service. See *J.D.W.*, 30 July 1994, p. 3.
86 *Ibid.*, 26 March 1997, p. 15.
87 *Ibid.*, 13 June 1992, p. 1009. See also Richard Scott, 'Qatar's new strikeforce', *Jane's Navy International*, July/August 1997, pp. 23–5.
88 *J.D.W.*, 1 May 1996, p. 4.
89 This contract was signed the following year. The final 21 aircraft were to be assembled in Australia. *J.D.W.*, 2 July 1997, p. 3.
90 *Daily Telegraph*, 31 January 1997.
91 James Bruce, '"Iron Magic" works to sharpen region's skills', *Jane's Military Exercise and Training Monitor*, January–March 1996, pp. 8–10.
92 *J.D.W.*, 28 March 1992, p. 531.
93 James Bruce, '"Iron Magic" Works to Sharpen Region's Skills'.
94 Phythian, *Arming Iraq*, p. 298.
95 Barbara Starr, 'Three-tier plan aims at stronger Kuwait', *J.D.W.*, 20 February 1993, p. 13.
96 J. A. C. Lewis, 'French activity has Middle East promise', *Jane's Military Exercise and Training Monitor*, October–December 1996, p. 11.
97 *J.D.W.*, 28 February 1996, p. 18.
98 *Guardian*, 19 November 1996.
99 *Ibid.*, 28 November 1996.
100 *J.D.W.*, 4 December 1996, p. 3.

7

Arms sales and the new Labour government: doves or hawks?

Labour got Britain into this sordid trade in a really big way by ordering the Defence Sales Office [sic] in 1966 'to ensure that this country does not fail to secure its *rightful* share of this valuable commercial market'. It would help make amends if Labour were to start us on the first few steps towards getting out of it. (Robin Cook, MP, June 1978[1])

There can be no greater test of a government which claims to have a foreign policy with an ethical dimension than the way it deals with the export of arms. (Menzies Campbell, MP, November 1998[2])

The election of a Labour government on 1 May 1997 with a commanding majority held out the prospect that the excesses of the arms sales policy of the previous Conservative administrations would be curbed. Public disquiet about aspects of arms sales policy arising from the serial arms and related scandals that afflicted the Major government (from allegations about commission paid on the Al Yamamah deal to the alleged involvement of Mark Thatcher, the 'supergun' affair, the Scott inquiry, the Pergau Dam controversy, the hearings into BMARC and the al-Mas'ari affair) had pushed arms towards the top of the political agenda. This expectation was fuelled by the interest of many Labour backbenchers in arms and defence issues. In 1995, Robin Cook had told the Labour Party Conference that a future Labour government would not license the export of arms to any country that would use them for internal oppression or external aggression. In Parliament, Cook had called for a public inquiry into Al Yamamah following allegations of Mark Thatcher's involvement. He had produced near-forensic performances, first as shadow trade and industry spokesman and then as shadow Foreign Secretary, in dissecting the duplicity and hypocrisy of the government over the arms-to-Iraq affair.

In addition, Cook was one of a number of senior Labour figures who had been critical of both Indonesia's forced annexation of East Timor and of continued British arms sales to Indonesia. For example, in an October 1996 press release he had said that:

The possibility that arms supplied by the UK may have been used to enforce the occupation of East Timor causes great concern. The Labour Party has always condemned Indonesia's occupation of East Timor and we are continuing to press the Government on the issue ... The next Labour Government will not issue export licenses for the sale of arms to regimes that might use them for internal repression or international aggression. Nor will we permit the sale of weapons in circumstances where this might intensify or prolong existing armed conflicts or where these weapons might be used to abuse human rights.[3]

In light of all this, Robin Cook's appointment as Foreign Secretary could be read as the logical culmination of a parliamentary career in which he had tenaciously pursued arms and related issues, and which could not fail to result in a more considered and open approach to the inherently difficult question of arms sales policy.

In the 1970s, as a young Labour MP, Cook had been part of the grouping that had produced the *Sense about Defence* report, arguing for cuts in both defence expenditure and arms exports.[4] Furthermore, he began to write for the *New Statesman* on defence and arms sales issues, from where he became a key critic of the Labour government's engagement in the arms trade. In a December 1976 article on British arms sales to Iran he criticised the way in which 'the West has slavishly courted this latter-day Caligula by pouring out a thorough cornucopia of arms before his throne'.[5] Why did the Shah want so much weaponry? 'In so far as there is a genuine rationale for the Shah's arms build-up it is internal ... In so far as there is a real possibility that any of his tanks and gunships will actually be used, it is most likely to be against domestic insurgence by either socialists or separatists. Both are ruthlessly suppressed ...'[6] In June 1978 he reported on how Chieftain tanks were used to suppress a demonstration in Tabriz which resulted in over 400 dead and 800 requiring hospital treatment. The lessons Cook drew from this confrontation were that 'the tactics of minimum force with which democracies repond to civil unrest are wholly irrelevant in regimes which are held in place by force' and that 'whatever the external threat by which their purchase was justified, arms imports are far more likely to be used by such regimes against their own people than their neighbours'.[7] As he went on to note, these observations were of 'crucial importance to Britain's arms exports, which now overwhelmingly supply the needs of some of the world's least likeable governments'.[8]

In 1978, as in 1997, the logic of these lessons could not ignore Britain's arms sales relationship with Indonesia. Cook, highly critical of the Labour government's decision to sell the Hawk, wrote that its sale was:

> particularly disturbing as the purchasing regime is not only repressive but actually at war on two fronts: in East Timor where perhaps a sixth of the population has been slaughtered in Indonesia's continuing efforts to

consolidate its invasion of 1975; and in West Papua where it confronts an indigenous liberation movement. At a recent meeting of the NEC Fred Mulley sought to defend the sale on the ingenious grounds that the Hawk is only a trainer aircraft ... No one need pretend that such a plane will not have a devastating potential against secessionist movements who have no air-cover of their own.[9]

Little wonder that those who had followed Cook's career so closely expected so much after May 1997.

Robin Cook as Foreign Secretary

> It [foreign policy] is ... like walking on to a conveyor belt. It started before you joined, it will continue after you have left, and the business of foreign policy is essentially an almost unceasing number of very small initiatives, ideas, developments, which add to the great stream of historical events that are working their passage in any event. (Malcolm Rifkind[10])

When he was appointed a junior Foreign Minister in the Attlee Government, Christopher Mayhew asked to see a document outlining the foreign policy he was being asked to implement. He was told that there was no such document and, furthermore, that 'it was really rather doubtful whether we had a foreign policy in the proper sense at all'.[11] Robin Cook's first weeks promised more than foreign policy as reaction to international circumstance. It offered vision – a vision in which ethics were writ large, and where arms sales policy was a key focus.

Cook's initial actions as Foreign Secretary did nothing to dispel these expectations. As well as lifting the Thatcher-imposed ban on unions at GCHQ, signalling a more positive approach to Europe, and announcing an international initiative to combat the sale of land mines, on 12 May 1997 he hosted a formal launch of his foreign policy 'mission statement', complete with video produced by David Puttnam.

The mission statement, he said, represented, 'an ethical content to foreign policy and recognizes that the national interest cannot be defined only by narrow realpolitik. Our foreign policy must have an ethical dimension and must support the demands of other people for the democratic rights on which we insist for ourselves.'[12] As Robin Cook himself subsequently noted, a 'more moral' foreign policy would allow the UK 'to demonstrate that we have confidence in our own values ... I personally believe that taking a pride in your identity as a nation is a very important national interest and, if you take pride in your identity as a nation, you also need to take pride in your values and that is best expressed by confidently making sure those values are projected in our foreign policy.'[13]

Points 1 and 4 of Cook's four-point mission for Britain implicitly related to the arms trade:

1. *Security*. We shall ensure the security of the UK and the dependent territories and peace for our people by promoting international stability,
fostering our defence alliances and promoting arms control actively . . .

4. *Mutual Respect*. We shall work through international forums and bilateral relationships to spread the values of human rights, civil liberties and
democracy which we demand for ourselves.

However, these aims existed in direct conflict with the second point:
'*Prosperity*. We shall make maximum use of our overseas posts to
promote trade abroad and boost jobs at home.' Herein lay the seeds of the
conflict that would haunt Cook's attempt to bring an ethical dimension to
the conduct of arms sales policy.

Within his first few days as Foreign Secretary Cook had written to his
Cabinet colleagues suggesting a review of arms export policy, an indication of the priority he initially attached to the issue. However, the tensions
apparent in the mission statement with regard to arms sales were evident
even before the 1997 general election and would determine the policy
outcome. In February 1997, while Cook had been marking the first
anniversary of the Scott Report by outlining principles that would govern
a more responsible approach to arms sales under a Labour administration, Tony Blair had been featured in BAe's internal newsletter, telling its
employees that a Labour government would be 'committed to creating the
conditions in which the [defence] industries can thrive and prosper.
Winning export orders is vital to the long-term success of Britain's defence
industry. A Labour government will work with the industry to win export
orders.'[14] Moreover, Cook's vision of a more restrictive approach to arms
sales did not necessarily sit comfortably alongside Blair's reassuring pre-
election vision of Britain's place in the world:

> Our Armed Forces are a vital part of Britain's standing in the world. They
> keep Britain where it should be, in the first division of the world's nations.
> This is not an issue simply of national pride. It has profound consequences
> for order and peace . . . Whenever the collective security of Europe or Nato
> is at risk, or there is an internal problem demanding a military response,
> Britain is at the forefront, respected and listened to. This is a precious
> national asset to be treasured.[15]

Moreover, Cook faced opposition to a more restrictive arms sales
policy from within the parliamentary party from those Labour MPs who
represented constituencies with significant defence interests, a number of
whom lobbied to restrict the impact of the change on the arms sales
agenda. Of course, New Labour's sensitivity to arms sales was an extension of its sensitivity to all matters relating to defence – an electoral black
hole throughout the 1980s. Blair had no desire to either alienate defence
industry employees and their families in the run-up to the 1997 election,

nor to provide the Conservative Party with any ammunition. After the election victory, his tendency to surround himself with figures like Lord Hollick – a director at BAe prior to becoming an adviser at the DTI, and a key figure in strengthening the Labour Party's links with the business sector – suggested there would not be any radical change of approach under Labour. Weighed against these interests and calculations, the groups that lobbied the FCO arguing for stricter controls – Amnesty International, Campaign Against Arms Trade, World Development Movement, etc., may have had access to FCO Ministers, but the contest to influence policy was never an even one. As Cook's PPS, Ken Purchase, explained, 'there are not two agendas, but there are differences in the agenda ... New Labour also has a very very significant agenda with British business that it has never never had before.' This meant that 'for the first time New Labour is seen to be the friend of industry ... if you are trying to win the confidence of business then you have to show that you understand the difficulties of actually making a living in industry.'[16] In other words, New Labour hens had come home to roost. Having courted British industry, a New Labour government had little option but to support its interests.

Nevertheless, on 21 May 1997, Cook announced a complete ban on the use, production, transfer and stockpiling of anti-personnel land mines, committing Britain to destroy its stockpiles by the year 2005. On 3 December 1997, the UK went on to sign the Ottawa Treaty which required signatories to destroy their stocks within four years (although the US, Russia and China were amongst those who did not sign). Much of the momentum in the UK on this issue arose from the fact that it had become one of the issues adopted by Diana, Princess of Wales, towards the end of her life, and hence there was unlikely to be any criticism of government action in this area. Banning land mines was a laudable initiative. Politically it was relatively uncontroversial.

Such unanimity, however, did not extend to the question of the new government's approach to the export of conventional arms. Indeed, when the FCO produced its draft arms sales review, it was not warmly received at Downing Street. According to Kampfner: 'John Holmes, Blair's principal private secretary and top civil servant, went through it with officials from Cook's private office for four hours, line by line, telling them to tone down various areas.'[17] When Cook and Blair met to go over it, changes were made.

Hence the criteria (see Appendix 1) were a product of compromise rather than the articulation of principle. The preambular paragraph is emblematic of this compromise, with its clear statement that: 'The government are committed to the maintenance of a strong defence industry which is a strategic part of our industrial base as well as of our defence effort.'

The section of the guidelines headed 'Human rights and internal repression' stated clearly that export licences would not be issued for military equipment where 'there is a clearly identifiable risk that the proposed export might be used for internal repression', something of a retreat from the position articulated in Cook's pre-election press release cited earlier. The significance of the shift was that the former position would have made the export of Hawk jets to Indonesia impossible, the latter did not. The difference between New Labour's approach and that of the Conservatives was presented as being that Labour's '*might* be used' was a more liberal indicator than the Conservatives' '*likely* to be used'.[18] However, the inclusion of the qualifier 'a clearly identifiable risk' also introduced the element of subjectivity essential to flexibility, offering considerable latitude in interpretation. Moreover, while in its mission statement the government had pledged to 'put human rights at the heart of our foreign policy' the arms sales criteria had included a much more limited commitment merely to 'take into account' respect for human rights in reaching licensing decisions, while at the same time according 'full weight' to the UK's national interest. Rather than being at the heart of this aspect of foreign policy, human rights were somewhere to one side. Furthermore, allowing the export of equipment for 'the protection of members of the security forces from violence' seemed to many a way of justifying exports to regimes which would fail on other grounds. Any sense of disappointment amongst those who understood the implications of the new policy formulation contained in the criteria was intended to be offset by the announcement the same day of a ban on the export of torture equipment.[19]

Despite the fact that the policy changes underpinning it were more apparent than real, Cook's high-profile launch irritated former Conservative Foreign Secretaries. Appearing before the FAC, Lord Hurd argued that 'there has always been an ethical dimension in recent years in British foreign policy which has not always been described in that slightly pretentious way ... What is slightly irritating ... is to pretend that a shift of two or three degrees is a shift of 180 degrees and that all his predecessors were immoral rogues.'[20] For his part, Lord Carrington offered a more Palmerstonian perspective: 'Ethical foreign policy – what does he think mine was? Corrupt? Foreign Secretaries don't need mission statements. Their only role is to look after British interests.'[21] Carrington felt that 'we always had an ethical foreign policy. I think that if you spell it out quite in the way that Robin Cook does, he is going to run into quite a lot of difficulty ... about British exports, about offending countries, about retaliation and all the rest of it. I think you have to be very careful about these things. I think it is much better to do these things without a great fanfare ...'[22]

The EU Code of Conduct

Towards the end of 1997, negotiators from the UK and France took a lead in securing EU-wide agreement on arms exports, working on a draft EU arms export code which could then be considered by a working group on which all member states were represented. Unveiled on 25 May 1998, the code was meant to supplant the EU common criteria for arms exports agreed in 1991 and 1992. Its core commitment was that member states would not issue an export licence when there was a 'clear risk' that equipment would be used for internal repression or foreign aggression. This was to be attained via an agreement that EU states would not seek to 'undercut' each other by offering to supply a state with arms where another EU state had refused to do so. Whenever a EU state turned down an export licence request, the information would be circulated to the other member states. Any of these which sought to enter into an 'essentially identical transaction' with the state in question within three years would be obliged to consult the state which had declined to supply and explain its reasoning. Robin Cook said this meant that: 'We will compete against each other on price and quality but we will not be competing on standards of human rights or democratic principles.'[23]

Inevitably, the need to secure all-member agreement resulted in compromise and, in some respects, a watered-down code. For example, the French had objected to a proposal that any state taking up an order after it had been declined by any other should have to explain its actions to all EU members. It had also opposed moves to tighten restrictions on sales to repressive governments. Hence French sensitivities were accommodated in the agreed Code of Conduct (see Appendix 2). What remainded contained sufficient loopholes for the defence industry to refrain from objecting. Rather, it was the anti-arms sales lobby which objected, together with prominent figures like Sir Michael Rose, the former SAS commander who headed UN forces in Bosnia in 1994–95. He pointed out that the code was not sufficiently strong to prevent another arms-to-Iraq-type scandal: 'Unless the code includes explicit and restrictive criteria governing exports, tough consultation mechanisms and provision for parliamentary accountability, it may simply legitimise business as usual.' Furthermore, he argued: 'There are compelling military reasons for tightly regulating arms sales to regions of tension and instability. Our own armed forces are endangered by irresponsible exports. The 'boomerang effect' has resulted in European troops facing military equipment supplied by their own governments in peacekeeping operations in Somalia, Rwanda and Bosnia. In the Gulf war the Allied forces faced a heavily-armed Iraqi military, supplied through the export of arms and equipment from the European Union in the 1980s.'[24]

In Parliament the opposition were also critical, although for different reasons. Michael Howard argued that: 'Britain, for example, would have to notify other EU countries of any order it refuses, so presenting them with these orders on a plate. If they then decide to supply the arms Britain has refused to sell, there is nothing anyone can do to stop them.'[25] Moreover, the code set a very high evidential threshhold for the circumstances under which states should not issue licences. Four of the eight criteria outlined such circumstances, the other four merely committed states to consider, take into account, or study given circumstances before issuing licences. Notwithstanding this, it is hard to see how continued arms sales to Indonesia were compatible with points 1, 2, 3 and 4.

The question of Indonesia: hawks or doves?

... Hawk aircraft have been observed on bombing runs in East Timor in most years since 1984.' (Robin Cook, May 1994[26])

Menzies Campbell. There is strong evidence that Hawk aircraft have already been used for the suppression of the people of East Timor.' (Menzies Campbell, 1997[27])

For many observers Indonesia represented the litmus test of Labour's commitment to link foreign policy with human rights. By the time Labour came to power, Britain was Indonesia's largest single supplier of arms. In 1996, British arms sales to Indonesia were worth £438 million – approximately 10 per cent of the record £5 billion British arms sales for that year, and represented over half UK total trade with Indonesia. Still, expectations were high. After a meeting with Cook at the FCO in July 1997, José Ramos-Horta came out convinced that arms exports would be blocked if there was evidence of their use for internal repression, commenting that 'I believe his arms policy review will meet our expectations.'[28] In June 1997 the Bishop of East Timor, and joint winner with Ramos-Horta of the 1997 Nobel Peace Prize, Bishop Carlos Belo, visited London. In a lecture he implored the British government: 'Do not sustain any longer a conflict, which, without these sales, could never have been pursued in the first place.'[29]

When Labour entered office, 16 Hawk aircraft for which the Major government had issued export licences (worth £160 million) had still to be delivered. As discussed in Chapter 4, contracts had also been signed in the run-up to the general election for Alvis to supply 50 Scorpion armoured vehicles valued at £100 million and for Tactica water cannon. If Cook refused to allow these exports to go ahead, the government would have been expected to compensate the companies involved. But the action would have far wider significance in the longer term, affecting perceptions of Britain's reliability as an exporter of arms. Whatever decision was reached was bound to be highly controversial. Hence the discussion leading up to the decision was lively, and marked by pronounced differences of opinion within the government.[30]

Could the government have revoked the licences already issued by the previous government? What was the substance of the legal opinion they sought on this question? The answer to the first question is yes. Paragraph 7 (1) of the 1994 EG(C)O states that: 'A licence granted by the Secretary of State ... may be varied or revoked by the Secretary of State at any time.' Furthermore, there were precedents, involving revocation in the context of the imposition of UN or EU arms embargoes, such as those imposed on Iraq in August 1990, on the former Yugoslavia in July 1991 and on Somalia in January 1992. Moreover, in April 1998, DTI Minister Barbara Roche revealed that between 2 May 1997 and 12 January 1998 the DTI had revoked 10 export licences covering goods on the Military List.[31]

On the second question, regarding the legal advice the government subsequently invoked parliamentary precedent to avoid publishing, it is this author's understanding that the advice was, in essence, that the government could do as it pleased.[32] This raises the question of compensation payments, and, again, it is this author's understanding that figures for compensation payments for BAe were discussed.[33] In cases where, for example, UN embargoes have in the past required the revocation of licences, the companies involved have been notified by the DTI and any claims for compensation have been directed to the DTI, which has considered each request on a case-by-case basis. There are no guidelines as such. This position is also consistent with legal advice given to the World Development Movement in June 1997. That too said, in essence, that under the terms of paragraph 7 (1) of the 1994 EG(C)O the government could revoke the licences.

However, as noted above, the outcome of the debate on the shape of the new arms sales criteria was that they were framed so as not to exclude the export of the Hawk and other major conventional arms to Indonesia, and thereby impair Britain's reputation for reliability of supply. There was to be no question of revoking the existing licences. Once that decision had been taken, the next issue was when to announce it. In the event, the government tried to minimise the fall-out by making the announcement on the same day as the new criteria governing arms exports and the ban on the export of torture equipment were announced.[34] Subsequently, FCO sources claimed that, in the light of the legal advice they had received, it was 'unrealistic and impractical' to revoke the licences.[35] As Robin Cook told Paul Barber of Tapol: 'I have to reiterate that the present Government was not responsible for the decisions on export licences made by the previous Administration. We concluded that, with the sheer volume of licences needing review, it would not be realistic or practical to revoke. We have therefore drawn a line under our predecessor's record.'[36]

Hence the government took the decision to allow the continued export of the Hawk aircraft, but to present it as the work of the previous government, continuing to arm Indonesia from beyond the political grave. This certainly amused David Owen, the last Labour Foreign Secretary, and one of those responsible for the initial sale of Hawks to Indonesia: 'It was a strange irony that their first real decision was actually to go against almost everything they had said for nearly twenty years of Opposition.'[37] Cook's defence was, of course, something of a red herring. He did not need to sift through all 20,000 outstanding licences to identify those which had generated most controversy. The previous government's industry in issuing so many licences for Indonesia became Cook's alibi. Nevertheless, the decision was a watershed and 136 (mainly Labour) MPs – around 20 per cent of all MPs – signed an early day motion attacking the decision.[38]

At the end of August 1997, Cook paid his first official visit to Indonesia. Before he got there Ali Alatas, the Indonesian Foreign Minister, warned that if Britain blocked arms exports: 'We would have to look at other sources and those, I can tell you, are very much available. It is, after all, a very competitive trade. The minute you cannot get it from one source, the other source is already knocking on our door and saying "Take ours".'[39] On arriving, Cook's first, symbolic, act was to telephone the Bishop of East Timor, Bishop Belo. He then met Alatas. Asked subsequently about their three-hour meeting, Cook said it had been 'frank' and that human rights had dominated the discussion.[40] However, during the meeting he also reportedly emphasised that the new guidelines were general and not aimed specifically at Indonesia, and that the UK wanted to maintain its defence relationship with Indonesia,[41] an apparently conflicting message which nicely encapsulated Cook's difficulties in 'trying to marry lofty goals with hard politics'.[42] In a clear signal to the Labour government, Indonesia had announced that it was ordering 12 Russian Sukoi-30 fighter aircraft in place of the US F-16s, which it had abandoned when the proposed deal became bogged down in Congressional criticism (although it ultimately shelved the plans). As the Minister of National Development Planning, Ginanjar Kartasasmita, observed: 'We are a sovereign country. We can buy arms wherever we wish to. So if one country says no, that's no problem. We'll simply buy them elsewhere.'[43] Asked how he responded to these threats, Cook said: 'We would not be surprised nor would we complain if they find water cannon elsewhere.'

Cook proposed sending a team of EU ambassadors to East Timor (although the EU had never formally recognised Indonesian sovereignty over the territory) and sending British police to advise their Indonesian counterparts on modern policing methods through a series of lectures, and offered computers and books to assist human rights and legal aid groups.[44] This firm stand in the face of tyranny formed the basis of Cook's observation that, after all, there was a 'third way' in foreign affairs, somewhere between 'kow-tow or row'. As he subsequently explained, the third way had an application in the realm of foreign policy in that it 'is not to accept the polarisation of blazing rows about human rights or else leave your values behind in Britain and go out simply to seek commercial contracts. You can pursue economic co-operation without being silenced on human rights.'[45]

Fearing that the subtle distinction might be lost on some delegates to September's Labour Party Conference in Brighton, Cook telephoned the *Guardian*'s political editor, Michael White, on its eve to inform him that, as the paper put it, 'in a show of symbolic determination', the government had 'blocked two arms contracts with Indonesia' worth up to £1 million. In reality, the contracts blocked – for sniper rifles and armoured Land-Rovers – were indeed symbolic in that the vast bulk of the trade continued, and fresh export licences for Indonesia continued to be approved. Moreover, just a week after Cook left Jakarta, the MoD was hosting an Indonesian delegation at the Farnborough Air Show. Nevertheless, the story provided Cook with precisely the sort of eve-of-conference alibi he felt he needed to offset likely criticism. As he told the *Guardian*, the decision 'certainly does demonstrate that we have put in place tougher criteria. Those criteria are biting and they're delivering the policy that we promised.'[46] Campaigners opposing the continued sale of military equipment to Indonesia were left to consider the paradox that a policy without teeth was apparently biting. But for the UK defence industry and the Indonesians the message was clear. A gesture had been made, integrity demonstrated. Ironically, while aiming to defuse likely conference criticism, the overriding message had also been aimed at reassuring manufacturers and retaining the confidence of the Indonesian military command. Even so, Downing Street was far from happy with Cook's intervention. According to Cook's biographer, Jonathan Powell told Cook's office he was 'extremely pissed off'. Blair's office was 'angry both at the decision itself and at the way Cook had announced it, circumventing the usual central command through Alastair Campbell'.[47]

After a year in office, New Labour's record on arms sales to Indonesia did not look impressive. It had granted 56 new export licences for Military List goods and rejected only seven applications. In this case the secrecy surrounding the arms trade was surely counterproductive. The government's unwillingness to break the figures down beyond identifying broad categories of equipment meant that precisely what was exported remains unclear. It cannot be clear, to MPs or to the public, from information of this quality that the government is rigidly applying its much-vaunted criteria. In addition, DESO's Jakarta office had seen its annual budget and staffing levels rise in 1997–98. The former had risen from £125,000 to £190,000, giving the Jakarta office a bigger budget than the FCO's Arms Control and Disarmament Unit.[48]

Moreover, by 1998, despite the existence of eye-witness testimony, which Robin Cook had found compelling while in opposition, Derek Fatchett was using the same defence of Hawk aircraft sales to Indonesia as his predecessors: 'We have studied all the information available about allegations of Hawk being used in East Timor. We are confident that UK-supplied Hawk aircraft have not been used in East Timor or, indeed, in a counter-insurgency role in Indonesia.'[49] Despite this seemingly confident assertion, it was made in the context of a situation where, as Fatchett conceded, 'no formal procedures exist for routinely monitoring the use that is made of British defence equipment, once exported'.[50] As Ann Clwyd, an indefatigable campaigner on these issues, noted, you 'cannot monitor the use of equipment sent out there so it is no use saying it's not our aircraft or tanks being used for repression.'[51] In reality, Ann Clwyd's scepticism was more justified than Derek Fatchett's confident defence of the Indonesian military. In July 1999, in the run-up to the East Timor independence referendum, the *Sydney Morning Herald* reported that one of three Hawk 100s based at Kupang in West Timor made two low passes over Dili, in what one diplomat termed '"macho posturing" to remind [the] East Timorese who was controlling the territory'.[52]

This use of the aircraft called into question Tony Blair's breezy assertion of just a week previously that 'none of these aircraft are used in repressive action'.[53] In response to questioning, FCO Minister of State Geoff Hoon explained that Robin Cook 'has already written to the Indonesian Foreign Minister to express our concern at press reports that UK-built Hawk aircraft have flown over East Timor. We have reminded the Indonesians that there are no circumstances in which UK supplied military equipment should be deployed there.'[54] In practice, having sold the equipment, the British government was impotent to prevent the Indonesian military from using it in whatever way they wished, although Cook still insisted that the Indonesians had assured him there would be no repetition of the fly-over.[55]

In addition to this sorry situation, the government also got into the messy position of claiming clean hands because British equipment used in a repressive manner in Indonesia after May 1997 had been licensed before May 1997, even though it permitted the continued delivery of such equipment after that date.[56]

Nosedive

In the event, the tension between Cook and Downing Street on the merits and scope of a restrictive approach to arms sales was settled conclusively in favour of Downing Street. During his first year in office Cook was perceived as having committed a series of gaffes or misjudgements, the cumulative effect of which was to erode his authority in government. To an extent, while he continued to occupy the office of Foreign Secretary, he did so increasingly on Blair's terms. In the first place, he had dumped his first wife, Margaret, at Heathrow Airport after being tipped off that the media had got hold of the story of his affair with his then secretary, Gaynor Regan. Then came the *débâcle* of the Queen's 1997 visit to India, followed by the media story of Cook's attempt to make Gaynor Regan his new diary secretary. His March 1998 visit to Israel also proved contro-versial. Even his handling of the Sandline affair, which for Cook contained near-parallels with the arms-to-Iraq affair, came in for criti-cism, and was contrasted in some quarters with Blair's preference for dismissing the whole affair because the government had been backing the 'good guys', and hence the ends justified the means. So far did his author-ity fall that he even felt obliged to deliver a speech to the Social Market Foundation in April 1998, extolling the virtues of the Blairite 'third way'.

One consequence of Cook's reduced authority, of course, was that arms sales came to assume a lower, almost non-existent, profile in the presentation of Labour's foreign policy. As one official put it, 'We try to do as much as we can without alerting Downing Street. Every time you draw attention to any of this you get a memo,'[57] a reflection of the fact that the ethical foreign policy intentions which Cook had carried into office had had to be put on a back burner. Cook no longer had the author-ity to challenge Tony Blair's priorities in foreign policy. In Anthony Howard's phrase, Cook became 'little more than a prisoner held in government custody at the prime minister's pleasure'.[58] When Blair took the opportunity of his annual Mansion House speech in 1997 to outline his 'five guiding light principles' of foreign policy, there was no reference to ethics or arms. When this was pointed out, two sentences were added which included the works 'arms' and 'ethical' in conjunction, but avoided even the most basic commitment: 'Human rights may sometimes seem an abstraction in the comfort of the West, but when they are ignored, human misery and political instability all too easily follow. The same is true if we ignore the ethical dimension of the trade in arms.'[59] In short, by 1998 the pre- and immediate post-election emphasis on arms sales had gone. The ethical dimension of foreign policy was to be defined more broadly, although even this changed definition came to be lost amidst UK support for the US bombing of Iraq and leading role in the war against Yugoslavia.

There is no doubting that the new arms sales criteria have resulted in the denial of licences in cases where previously they might have been granted. But such cases have been on the periphery, in terms both of the countries and the type of equipment involved. Under the criteria, denial is more likely with police and internal security equipment, and in countries

where there is little prospect of losing valuable orders for major weapons
– for example, Kenya. In March 1998, Derek Fatchett announced that:

> In accordance with the revised criteria for licensing arms exports, we do not
> issue arms export licences for Kenya where there is a clearly identifiable risk
> that the proposed export might be used for internal repression. During 1997
> we rejected licence applications (together worth over £1.5 million) to export
> certain types of riot control equipment, including baton rounds and tear gas,
> to the Kenyan police. Furthermore, we removed Kenya from the coverage of
> several Open Individual Export Licences for the supply of body armour,
> firearms and ammunition.[60]

In addition, during its first year in office, the Labour government rejected
licence applications for Military List goods for Armenia, Croatia, Iran,
Nigeria, Paraguay and Sudan.[61] Despite these peripheral cases, there has
been no appreciable slow-down in the number of licences issued for military equipment. Between 13 November 1997 and 2 February 1998 alone
(the white-heat period in the ethical foreign policy revolution) 4,069
licences were issued for Military List goods to 120 countries and territories.[62]

The Foreign Affairs Committee report

On 21 December 1998 the FAC published a wide-ranging and critical
report on the 'ethical' foreign policy. In a July 1997 interview, Cook had
said that: 'There is no question of shrinking from difficult questions raised
by large countries … no question of us picking on the little guys and
letting the big guys go.'[63] However, the report concluded that in practice
this is what had occurreed; human rights considerations had been applied
inconsistently. Where Britain had considerable trade or other interests, for
example in China and Indonesia, human rights had been downplayed. As
chairman Donald Anderson commented: 'The temptation is to be strong
[only] in weak countries. Indonesia was clearly a country where there
were substantial projects, including arms purchases, in prospect.'[64] The
commitment to human rights had been employed selectively, and there
were clear dangers in this:

> We recognise that there are inherent difficulties in maintaining a consistent
> approach to human rights abuses in respect of countries which have rela-
> tively small markets and unfavourable geostrategic location and of countries
> which are major trading partners or key allies. To put it bluntly, successive
> Governments have, for example, found it easier to denounce military repres-
> sion of indigenous people in Central America than to condemn lack of
> religious freedom in the Gulf.[65]

The report was particularly scathing about Robin Cook's decision to make Indonesia a target of 'constructive engagement' rather than endanger significant arms contracts. When Tony Lloyd was questioned on this, and in particular about a widely criticised photograph of Cook shaking hands with President Suharto included in the first annual report on human rights ('Is that included purely as a provocation?' asked David Heath[66]), Lloyd ingeniously explained that 'the fact that we show the Foreign Secretary in negotiations with the President of Indonesia showed the credibility and the intent of the Government's policy'.[67] Critics had already reached the same conclusion, but for different reasons. In a scathing passage, the FAC commented that: 'In the event the Indonesian people had less patience with their leadership than did the [British] Government: following prolonged and violent protests against his regime, President Suharto was forced to resign his office less than four weeks later.'[68]

Cook's arms sales criteria were also criticised. On reading them for the first time, what struck some observers was the similarity with the infamous Howe guidelines on the export of military and related equipment to Iran and Iraq. Both contained considerable scope for subjective judgement and flexibility. As the TISC concluded: 'Comparison of the new criteria with their predecessors suggests ... that the July 1997 criteria represent a rather less radical break with past policy than is sometimes represented to be the case. As before, Ministerial interpretation of the criteria in difficult cases is the touchstone of their real significance.'[69] In discussing his guidelines at the Scott inquiry, Lord Howe had been clear about the importance of flexibility, so as to allow an interpretation which permitted exports where this was deemed to be in the broader national interest, explaining that: 'You have to look at each case to decide whether, in fact, the damage being done to British national exporting interests, by this denial, is so large that there is some way of reconciling it with the Guidelines in general terms.'[70] This remained essentially the case under New Labour.

The disappointment evident in criticisms of the arms sales criteria reflected the fact that critics and government were essentially aiming for two different things. By instinct politicians and civil servants aim to produce criteria which, while consistent with prior pledges, at the same time offer sufficient latitude in interpretation to avoid every single decision they take being 'scored' against rigid criteria. Critics wanted criteria which were watertight, and against which each decision could be measured. The inclusion of ambiguous and subjective criteria clearly militated against this.

Overall, the FAC recommended that the tension between control and promotion to which the MoD was subjected should be counterbalanced by making the FCO the lead department in formulating and applying policy on arms exports. It was also critical of the 'Benetton' design of the first annual human rights report, recommending a more comparative, analytical report in future years.[71]

The annual report

The long-promised first annual report on arms exports, covering the period from Labour's election to the end of December 1997, was smuggled out in the form of a written answer on Thursday 25 March 1999. By coincidence, it happened to be the second day of the NATO bombing of Yugoslavia, hence the publication passed virtually unnoticed.

Because the information it contained was based on Military List categories, it is impossible to say precisely what was sold, or in what quantities. However, on the basis of the number of licences approved, the report further suggested that in power New Labour had made nothing more than a marginal impact on the course of UK arms exports. In particular, sales to states over which human rights concerns had been voiced continued, including such notorious cases as Indonesia (34 new standard individual export licences for Military List goods) and Turkey (101). For instance, Indonesia was licensed to receive aircraft spares, communications equipment, naval electronics, radar spares, body armour, an aircraft simulator and spares for aircraft engines. Turkey was licensed to receive equipment including shotguns, silencers, rifles, and aircraft and helicopter spares. Twenty-three new licences were issued for military goods to China, 71 for Malaysia, 124 for Singapore, 117 for South Korea, 31 for Saudi Arabia, 51 for Kuwait and 136 for the UAE. However, Saudi Arabia remains by far the UK's most important customer for arms, with almost half of all UK arms exports in 1997 destined for the kingdom. (Table 14.)

Table 14
Value of UK exports of military equipment, 1997

Rank	Country	Value (£ million)	% of total
1	Saudi Arabia	1,576.66	46.93
2	France	487.17	14.5
3	Germany	292.06	8.7
4	UAE	149.57	4.45
5	Kuwait	140.32	4.18
6	Brazil	126.32	3.76
7	Indonesia	112.49	3.35
8	Oman	110.23	3.28
9	Italy	59.20	1.76
10	US	54.21	1.61
11	Malaysia	34.54	1.03
Total value of top 11		3,142.77	93.55
Total value of all		3,359.59	100.00

Source Adapted from *Annual Report on Strategic Export Controls*, 25 March 1999, http://www.fco.gov.uk/news/

Attempts to elicit more detailed information suggest that the report represents a further confidence trick. For example, in trying to secure a more detailed breakdown of the equipment sent to Indonesia covered in the report, Ann Clwyd was told: 'The information requested relates to 10 Standard Individual Export Licences, and inquiries are being made under the Code of Practice on Access to Government Information. As confidential information is involved, the parties concerned are being asked if they consent to its disclosure, and this can take some time.'[72] Kim Howells could also have added that past experience suggests they will not.

Hence it is not unfair in considering the purpose and usefulness of the annual report to apply the model of information control used by Peter Gill in his work on oversight of the UK intelligence services.[73] From this standpoint, the annual report does not represent greater openness but a more subtle form of information control (defined as 'the processes used to make sure that certain people will or will not have access to certain information at certain times'[74]). It is more appropriate to consider its function as public relations rather than as providing genuine openness.

Concluding comments

The whole ethical experiment needs to be set in the broader context of the nature and direction of UK foreign and defence policy at the end of the twentieth century. One expression of this was George Robertson's Strategic Defence Review, which was 'designed to enhance New Labour as a party that had shed every particle of hostility to MoD ideology, rather than a party ready to reconsider Britain's place in a world which, between 1989 and 2009, is in the process of becoming unquestionably new'.[75] Arms sales are an important adjunct to this policy, and as such the Labour government has disappointed many who expected, on the basis of Labour performance and promise in opposition, a more vigorous conventional arms control policy. The reality, of course, is that the difference between Robin Cook *circa* 1977 and Robin Cook *circa* 1997 was not the product of a lonely Damascene journey that Cook took it upon himself to make. Rather, it is the outcome of the process of modernisation in the Labour Party which involved a repositioning around the centre-right of the political spectrum in order to secure election and to which, by the time of his April 1998 address to the Social Market Foundation at the latest, Cook had had to fully subscribe.

This disappointment also reflects the fact that Cook's grand, media-friendly, unveiling of his arms sales criteria somewhat masked the reality that the FCO was not the lead department in the arms sales process, and could not of itself determine the direction of arms export policy. In practice, having staked out such a bold position, it had to fight its corner against the countervailing forces of the DTI and MoD. Crucially, Cook also had to contend with Downing Street's broad support for an active arms sales policy, in part the price of New Labour's assiduous courting of British industry in the run-up to the 1997 general election. As Cook's authority declined through a series of blunders and misjudgements, so too did the prospect of his being able to carry the day in Cabinet.

In the final analysis, and despite Cook's protestations, the differences between New Labour and its predecessors in this regard are marginal when measured by results, so much so that the *Daily Telegraph* – without apparent irony – felt able to compare his approach to Indonesia with that of Mrs Thatcher towards apartheid-era South Africa, observing how:

> By refusing to join international boycotts, Mrs Thatcher won a degree of influence over the South African regime which she was able to translate into pressure for reform. Hers was a genuinely moral approach that placed practical change in South Africa above her own electoral and international popularity. By emulating it, Mr Cook has fallen foul of the student union tendency in his party, but he has advanced the cause of freedom in Indonesia.[76]

A by-product of all this is that Cook himself has come full circle. Having attacked the Callaghan government over its sale of arms to repressive regimes, and its sale of the Hawk to Indonesia, Cook finds himself at the helm of a policy which does both of these things, and for which he in turn is attacked in print by the likes of David Alton, and in places such as the *Daily Mail*.[77] Unintentionally, Cook has also provided us with a classic illustration of a pattern of foreign policy behaviour outlined by Zbigniew Brzezinski with reference to the US political system. For Cook, a desire to innovate after 18 years in the political wilderness, and tackle head-on issues which he had followed since at least the days of his occasional journalism for the *New Statesman*, contributed to his efforts conforming to this model. As Brzezinski wrote:

> Every Administration goes through a period of an ecstatic emancipation from the past, then a discovery of continuity, and finally a growing preoccupation with ... reelection. As a result, the learning curve in the area of foreign policy tends to be highly compressed. Each Administration tends to expend an enormous amount of energy coping with the unintended, untoward consequences of its initial, sometimes excessive, impulses to innovate, to redeem promises, and to harbor illusions. In time, preconceptions give way to reality ... and vision to pragmatism.[78]

The failure and shortcomings of Cook's efforts were graphically illustrated in August and September 1999. In the East Timor independence referendum 78.5 per cent of the 98.6 per cent turn-out voted for independence from Indonesia. In the bloody aftermath, as Indonesian military-backed and directed militias attempted to overturn the result by depopulating East Timor, the British response was constrained by the arms sales relationship with Jakarta. For the British government to cancel or suspend delivery of further British military equipment, in particular the nine Hawks still to be delivered, would have been to admit the error of the 1997 decision to allow their delivery. It would also expose as false the government's initial justification of this course of action – that it could not interfere with export licences once they had been granted.

However, belatedly, after the sustained massacre of the East Timorese, and after New Zealand and, more significantly, 48 hours after the US had frozen military ties with Jakarta, the New Labour government acted by 'suspending' the further export of all military equipment to Indonesia.[79] This action was followed by the announcement of a four-month EU embargo. The impression created by the length of time it had taken the UK – Indonesia's leading armourer – to respond was one of prevarication and reluctance to act, a clear consequence of the arms sales relationship. This was certainly an accurate reflection of the big picture, but somewhat unfair on Cook personally. As in earlier intra-governmental battles over arms exports, Cook had had to fight his corner – advocating termination of the contracts – against the MoD and DTI, and in so doing win the consent of Downing Street.[80] This contest was made public by Cook's PPS, Ken Purchase, who told BBC radio that:

> In the end, all of these things are a compromise. Robin did everything he possibly could to progress with policies which he felt were right. In the end you make an agreement with your colleagues. The DTI was very anxious to be a friend of business and industry. Business and industry mercilessly exploits [sic] that position.[81]

Symptomatic of this balance, it transpired that despite the ongoing atrocities in East Timor – directed by the very Indonesian military that UK training at the British taxpayer's expense was supposed to inculcate with respect for human rights[82] – the government had not acted to withdraw an invitation to an Indonesian military delegation to attend the upcoming arms exhibition in Surrey, but that the Indonesians themselves had taken the decision to pull out.[83] Fresh embarrassment arose with the discovery that the announcement of the suspension of arms deliveries had not come in time to stop three of the nine outstanding Hawks from being delivered. At the time of the announcement, these were in Bangkok, from where they were due to begin the final leg of their delivery.[84]

Although the government deserves credit for sheltering Xanana Gusmao in the British embassy in Jakarta during this period and for its role in committing troops to East Timor, ultimately, it was fatally compromised by the arms link. As Ann Clwyd pointed out: 'If the government had revoked these licences in 1997, they would never be in this mess. It is a problem entirely of their own making.'[85] As John Pilger wrote, 'East

Timor is the greatest, most enduring crime of the late twentieth century.'[86] It is a crime which successive British governments – Conservative, Labour, and New Labour – have all aided and abetted through their unswerving and unthinking supply of arms to the Jakarta regime.'

Notes

1 Robin Cook, 'The tragic cost of Britain's arms trade', *New Statesman*, 30 June 1978, p. 876.
2 Menzies Campbell, 'The international arms trade', *CDS Bulletin of Arms Control*, No. 33, March 1999, p. 1.
3 Press release, Robin Cook, MP, Shadow Foreign Secretary, 14 October 1996.
4 Labour Party Defence Study Group, *Sense about Defence* (London, Quartet, 1977).
5 Robin Cook, 'The Iranian connection', *New Statesman*, 10 December 1976, p. 828.
6 *Ibid.*, p. 829.
7 Robin Cook, 'The tragic cost of Britain's arms trade', p. 874.
8 *Ibid.*
9 *Ibid.*
10 *How to be Foreign Secretary*, BBC-2, 4 January 1998.
11 Cited by Hugo Young, *Guardian*, 30 July 1998.
12 Cited in John Kampfner, *Robin Cook* (London, Victor Gollancz, 1998), pp. 133–4.
13 'Taking the high road', *Analysis*, BBC Radio 4, 2 October 1997.
14 Cited in Kampfner, *Robin Cook*, p. 142.
15 Tony Blair, 'Labour's order of battle', *Daily Telegraph*, 3 February 1997.
16 Interview with Ken Purchase, Wolverhampton, 8 January 1999.
17 Kampfner, *Robin Cook*, p. 145.
18 Hansard, 31 July 1997, cols 482–4w.
19 *Ibid.*, 28 July 1997, cols 65–6w.
20 Foreign Affairs Committee, 'Foreign Policy and Human Rights', First Report, Session 1998–99, HC 100-II, Minutes of Evidence, 16 December 1997, para. 76.
21 *Daily Telegraph*, 23 January 1999.
22 *How to be Foreign Secretary*.
23 *Daily Telegraph*, 26 May 1998.
24 *Ibid.*, 16 February 1998.
25 *Ibid.*, 26 May 1998.
26 Hansard, 11 May 1994, col. 308.
27 *Daily Telegraph*, 29 July 1997.
28 *Times*, 11 July 1997.
29 *Independent*, 30 July 1997.
30 Interview – non-attributable.
31 Hansard, 8 April 1998, cols 345–7w.
32 Interview – non-attributable.
33 Interview – non-attributable.
34 Hansard, 28 July 1997, col. 27. Nevertheless, this preamble did not mention Indonesia by name. It stated that the 'present Government were not responsible for the decisions on export licences made by the previous Administration. We do not, however, consider that it would be realistic or practical to revoke licences that were valid and in force at the time of our election.'
35 *Daily Telegraph*, 29 July 1997.
36 Letter from Robin Cook to Paul Barber, 31 October 1997. Similarly, Foreign Office Minister Tony Lloyd told Ann Clwyd that 'the issue of revocation of licences is a diffi-

cult and complex subject. Following our election, we, nonetheless, gave careful consideration to possible options. This consideration included analysis of the legal aspects. We also took into account the fact that there are now some 20,000 licences issued under the previous Administration which may still be valid. We concluded that it simply was neither realistic nor practical to consider further the possibility of revocation.' Letter from Tony Lloyd to Ann Clwyd, 1 August 1997.

37 *How to be Foreign Secretary*.
38 'That this House believes that human rights should be at the forefront of decisions on arms exports; notes the appalling human rights record of the Indonesian Government; further notes that Indonesia has illegally occupied East Timor since 1975 in contravention of United Nations resolutions; further notes that United Kingdom-made military, security and police equipment has been used by the Indonesian authorities, in breach of assurances given by them, against civilians in Indonesia and East Timor; believes that any further equipment exported is likely to be similarly used; and calls upon Her Majesty's Government to stop the export of all military, police and security equipment to Indonesia, and to withdraw the invitations approved by the Conservative Government last year to the Commander in Chief of the Indonesian Armed Forces, and the Army and Navy Chiefs of Staff, to visit the Royal Naval and British Army Equipment Exhibition in Farnborough in September.'
39 *Daily Telegraph*, 29 August 1997.
40 *Ibid.*, 30 August 1997.
41 *Ibid.*, 29 August 1997. See also Hansard, 7 July 1997, col. 330w.
42 Robert Shrimsley in the *Daily Telegraph*, 2 September 1997.
43 *Ibid.*, 28 August 1997.
44 See Derek Fatchett's summary of this co-operation in Hansard, 14 May 1998, col. 204w.
45 Interview with Steve Richards, *New Statesman*, 1 May 1998, p. 23.
46 *Guardian*, 26 September 1997.
47 Kampfner, *Robin Cook*, p. 171. See also *Financial Times*, 3 October 1997.
48 IDC, 'Conflict Prevention and Post-conflict Reconstruction', para. 148.
49 Hansard, 12 May 1998, col. 108w.
50 *Ibid.*, 3 June 1998, col. 240w. See also 14 December 1998, col. 399. Furthermore, as Fatchett told Ann Clwyd, 'We cannot be comprehensive in assessing the use made of British defence equipment, given the difficulties of monitoring its deployment.' Letter from Derek Fatchett to Ann Clwyd, 5 May 1997.
51 *Daily Telegraph*, 18 May 1998.
52 Mark Dodd, 'UN green light for independence vote', *Sydney Morning Herald*, 16 July 1999.
53 Speaking on BBC-TV's *Question Time*, cited in the *Observer*, 8 August 1999.
54 Hansard, 20 July 1999, col. 951.
55 *Daily Mail*, 1 September 1999; Richard Norton-Taylor, 'In the swamp', *Guardian*, 2 September 1999.
56 Hansard, 14 December 1998, cols 398–9w.
57 Kampfner, *Robin Cook*, p. 213.
58 Anthony Howard, 'A star in the decendant?', *Sunday Times* Books section, 27 September 1998, p. 4.
59 Cited in Kampfner, *Robin Cook*, p. 216.
60 Hansard, 25 March 1998, col. 169w.
61 *Ibid.*, 15 June 1998, col. 99w.
62 *Ibid.*, 20 April 1998, col. 508w.
63 *Independent*, 18 July 1997.
64 *Times*, 22 December 1998.

65 FAC, 'Foreign Affairs and Human Rights', para. 120.
66 *Ibid.*, Minutes of Evidence, 5 May 1998, para. 456.
67 *Ibid.* Implicitly accepting that it had made a blunder in including the photograph, in the following year's report the FCO included a photograph of Derek Fatchett shaking hands with Xanana Gusmao.
68 *Ibid.*, para. 126.
69 TISC, 'Strategic Export Controls', Second Report, Session 1998–99, para. 28.
70 Scott Inquiry: day 54, 12 January 1994, Evidence of Lord Howe, p. 38.
71 FAC, 'Foreign Policy and Human Rights', paras 163 and 171.
72 Hansard, 10 June 1999, col. 364w.
73 Peter Gill, 'Reasserting control: recent changes in the oversight of the UK intelligence community', *Intelligence and National Security*, 11:2 (1996), 313–31.
74 Richard W. Wilsnack, cited in Gill, 'Reasserting control', p. 314.
75 Hugo Young, *Guardian*, 30 July 1998.
76 *Daily Telegraph*, leader comment, 30 August 1997.
77 For example, see David Alton, 'New Labour, new arms deals?', *Catholic Herald*, 19 February 1999; Paul Eastham, 'Critics gunning for Cook over arms to Indonesia', and Anthony Sampson, 'Ethics? Pull the other one, Mr Cook', both *Daily Mail*, 1 September 1999.
78 Zbigniew Brzezinski, *Power and Principle: Memoirs of the National Security Advisor, 1977–1981* (New York, Farrar Straus & Giroux, 1985), p. 544.
79 *Independent*, 12 September 1999.
80 See, for example, the accounts in the *Independent* and the *Guardian*, 13 September 1999.
81 Cited in the *Independent*, 17 September 1999.
82 See David Usborne, 'Revealed: proof that Indonesian army directed Timor slaughter', *Independent*, 20 September 1999. See also the comments of Mary Robinson, UN High Commissioner for Human Rights, in the *Straits Times*, 15 September 1999.
83 At the height of the carnage Baroness Symons, Defence Procurement Minister, defended the decision thus: 'The assurances we have had are sufficient to say you have the right under the UN charter ... to come and look at the equipment that you may be able to get for that self-defence and we have the right to decide whether or not to grant you the licence.' *Guardian*, 1 September 1999. See also *Tribune*, 17 September 1999.
84 *Sunday Times*, 19 September 1999.
85 *Ibid.*
86 John Pilger, 'We helped them descend into hell', *New Statesman and Society*, 13 September 1999, p. 11.

8

Conclusion

Proposals

The exercise of a degree of control and restraint in the international arms trade is not a hopelessly utopian expectation. The end of the Cold War has created the political space necessary for states to co-operate over control. The Cold War game of rewarding Third World clients with arms has ended. The fact that the permament members of the UN Security Council are themselves responsible for around 90 per cent of the global arms trade itself provides strong grounds for believing that a degree of control and restraint is achievable if the political will to pursue that end can be generated.

However, given the vested interests of state and industry in Britain continuing to play as prominent a role as possible in the international arms trade, it is unrealistic to expect unilateral abandonment of support for it. Given this, the most realistic question may well be to ask how the government should address the shortcomings of the past, and adopt a more responsible, and hence restrictive, approach to arms sales issues. I would argue that a more progressive and responsible arms sales policy should address the following ten areas.

Internal repression

Given that arms cannot be controlled once they have been delivered – despite the contention that they could representing a prominent plank of Conservative defences of policy in the 1980s and 1990s – no weapons *capable* of being used for internal repression should be exported. Government support for the exploration of alternative production options for companies dependent on the production of such equipment should be prioritised here. There are two things to add in support of this proposal. Firstly, a ban on the export of repressive technology – like Tactica water cannon – is the next logical step from the 1997 ban on the export of instruments of torture. Secondly, the very requirement suggests an absence of legitimacy on the part of the regime requesting the equipment, which should raise serious questions about British involvement.[1]

UN Security Council resolutions

No arms should be exported to states currently in breach of UN Security Council resolutions. As a consequence, no arms should have been sold to Indonesia until the question of East Timor's future had been satisfactorily resolved.

Warring states

No arms should be sent – either offensive or defensive, lethal or non-lethal – to states at war, or to states from where there is a significant risk of their diversion to warring states. A history of proven diversion by a state should preclude future exports. Suppliers need to demonstrate that there is a political price to pay for diversion.

Parliamentary oversight and transparency

While recognising that there exists a legitimate requirement for commercial confidentiality prior to the signing of contracts, it is essential for Parliament to be more centrally involved in decisions on arms sales issues. While there have been welcome moves towards greater transparency in terms of the type and quality of information made available to Parliament since May 1997 (albeit with continued exceptions), these moves need to go further, so that the public may be more fully informed. To facilitate this a parliamentary committee with the power to call witnesses should be constituted to explore issues surrounding the arms trade. It should publish periodic reports which should be debated in the House. Given the overriding public interest in these matters, a committee formulated along the lines of the parliamentary Intelligence and Security Committee would be inadequate, and any such proposal should be rejected. Transparency and oversight are essential corollaries of an ethical dimension in foreign policy, as there must be a way of testing its application, based on adequate information that allows informed judgements.

In its December 1998 report on 'Foreign Policy and Human Rights', the FAC considered this issue. It considered parliamentary discussion of export licence applications prior to approval to be unrealistic, as it would delay processing, putting British exporters at a disadvantage *vis-à-vis* their competitors. At the same time, the knowledge that their requests would be debated in public – as in the US Congress – would for some states act as a disincentive to seek arms from the UK in the first place. This is the point where a line needs to be drawn to maintain a legitimate requirement for commercial confidentiality. The FAC did say, however, that it 'would support the development of a Parliamentary mechanism whereby export licences may be scrutinised retrospectively and detailed recommendations made. The Government's proposed annual report on strategic export controls ought to provide a basis for such an exercise.'[2]

This principle of Parliament's right – indeed, duty – to scrutinise the arms export process needs to be considered against the background of similar moves across Europe. Rather than the introduction of parliamentary scrutiny in the UK representing a radical development, it would merely bring the UK into line with a growing number of its European partners, and add to the national pressure that exists in other EU states for the introduction of similar checks. For example, in Belgium a 1991 law on the import and export of arms obliges the government to submit an annual report to parliament on the application of the law. The report must indicate the value of arms exported across different regions and by category. However, the report remains confidential and is not made public. Since 1990 the Italian government has been required to produce an annual report on arms sales, containing information on the value of military equipment exported to individual countries. This is a public document. In Sweden, since 1985 the government has produced an annual report on arms transfers, including the total value of exports to each country, and information on licensed and co-production. More significantly, Sweden requires prior notification of arms export proposals to a parliamentary committee – the Export Control Council. The council can object to specific exports and, while its advice is not binding, the Swedish government has never granted an export licence where the council objected. Elsewhere, in Spain there have been important moves towards greater transparency.

However, the idea of prior notification is not one about which Robin Cook has been particularly enthusiastic. As he told the FAC:

> My immediate response is to be doubtful whether that is a practical proposition. First of all, do remember that at this stage this is a highly commercial contract at a sensitive stage, it is not yet signed. Also recall that there are other countries who are competitors in seeking contracts. Therefore, for both those reasons one does not necessarily want to expose them to wide press coverage and publicity. Thirdly, it may well be the case that in private we can halt a contract proceeding in ways that are not offensive to the host government but which would be politically much more difficult if it was done in the full glare of publicity.[3]

Furthermore, it is a principle which was, not surprisingly, rejected by the DTI in its July 1998 White Paper, which was also less sympathetic to *post-facto* discussion of individual exports, on a predictable amalgam of trading grounds:

The Government does not consider that there should be parliamentary scrutiny of individual applications either before or after the decision on whether to grant a licence has been taken. Parliamentary scrutiny before licence decisions are taken would inevitably slow down significantly the process of decision-making on those licence applications. Furthermore, any process involving publication of individual applications, whether before or after decisions have been taken would mean identifying companies and the nature of their planned or actual export business which would be likely to harm their competitive position. Overseas Governments would also have a legitimate concern about the details of their purchases of defence-related equipment being made known to, for example, neighbouring countries. There would be a danger that they would seek in future to buy equipment from countries which would not disclose details of individual contracts.[4]

It would be difficult to find clearer confirmation that transparency and success in the arms trade are considered uncongenial bedfellows. Although Sir Richard Scott ventured that 'to be exposed to captious criticism and informed criticism is one of the prices to be paid for an open democratic governmental system',[5] there seem to be those in the defence industry and DTI who believe it is too high a price to pay when it comes to arms exports. The lessons drawn from the experience of the majority of Britain's leading arms customers at the hands of the US Congress, and the consequences for both the US and the British arms export industries, have helped define the DTI's approach to such issues. However, as has been argued elsewhere, the continued invocation of the necessity of such a high degree of secrecy goes beyond the requirements of commercial confidentiality, and in effect amounts to 'a confidence trick ... being played on Parliament and the public'.[6] Opposition to any form of scrutiny which goes beyond the annual report fails to balance the democratic right of the public and Parliament to be informed, and engage in meaningful debate, about arms sales policy and thereby determine the 'national interest' with regard to this trade.

Nevertheless, the DMA pronounced itself 'delighted' that the DTI had rejected prior and post-licensing scrutiny (a view echoed by the CBI), reminding any waverers that: 'Greater Parliamentary scrutiny on export control matters and increased public accountability must not create opportunities for unrepresentative pressure groups unduly to influence policy or decisions. It is important to maintain a pragmatic, realistic and rational approach to defence exports and to avoid being swept along by the idealistic and emotive arguments of a vocal minority.'[7]

Such a rearguard action should be expected from the DTI, but should be rejected, as it was by the TISC report on the White Paper, which, while rejecting prior scrutiny, argued that what is required is 'a system of parliamentary scrutiny which combines the greatest possible access to the details of decisions taken – licences granted, refused and delayed – with safeguards to protect commercial confidentiality in the interests of individual exporters and customers' legitimate demands for confidentiality'.[8]

In what ways could scrutiny of export licence applications help to inform future policy on the sale of arms and repressive technology (a question posed, amongst others, by the DMA)? Giving evidence to the TISC, Fiona Weir of Amnesty International UK offered a good example: 'In Tiananmen Square, traffic control equipment was used to photograph and help capture dissenters. A similar such system has now been installed in Tibet in Lhasa, an area with no traffic congestion. NGOs such as Amnesty International might have alerted you to the possible use of equipment which might otherwise have seemed inocuous.'[9] Does this mean that prior scrutiny is required, so that when the export application for Tibet was being considered such concerns could be raised? Not necessarily. Given the existence of the committee, the original export to China would have come under scrutiny there, and a warning about its application given to the FCO. If the FCO would be unwilling to advise against issuing an export licence given this information, then they would be unlikely to do so under a system of prior scrutiny either.

End-use monitoring

Develop reliable mechanisms to allow monitoring of the end use of major arms exported. The Scott Report fills several pages with selected examples of the diversion of British arms to Iraq. There are also various examples relating to Iran during the 1980s. The end use of military and related goods exported to Indonesia has been of on-going concern. Yet, as Tapol told the TISC, 'the onus is on the victims of human rights violations to obtain evidence of the misuse of equipment, often at great risk to themselves'.[10] With Indonesia in particular, no news was good news in a situation which amounted to avoidance bordering on self-deception. Successive governments adopted positions with regard to Indonesia that Albert Speer would have recognised. During the Third Reich, Speer 'talked himself into believing that his work was strictly that of an architect and administrator, and that it was not his role to agonize over "political" matters',[11] but he was able to maintain this position only by not asking questions or making enquiries. When advised by his friend Karl Hanke not to visit Auschwitz, he did not ask why: 'I did not query him, I did not query Himmler, I did not query Hitler, I did not speak with personal friends, I did not investigate – for I did not want to know what was happening there ... from fear of discovering something which might have made me turn away from my course. I had closed my eyes.'[12]

Various politicians, officials and companies have been candid enough to admit that in some cases end-user certificates are not worth the paper they are drafted on. As Lucas Varity told the TISC, an end-user certificate is just 'a piece of paper supplied by the customer stating the intended end use of a product. It guarantees nothing ...'[13] Alan Clark told the Scott inquiry that in the 1980s 'false end-user information had almost the status of a commercial practice in the Middle East'.[14]

Shortly after Labour came to office, in June 1997, John Spellar stated that: 'We are committed to strengthening the monitoring of the end use of defence exports to prevent diversion to third countries and to ensure that exported equipment is used only on the conditions under which the export licence has been granted. Work is in hand to take forward this commitment.'[15] George Robertson assured MPs that Labour policy was designed to ensure that 'when the best products of the British defence industry are exported, they are not misused', and that Labour would 'not turn a blind eye to the end use of that equipment'.[16] Subsequently, the government's July 1998 White Paper *Strategic Export Controls* recognised a need to 'strengthen monitoring of the end-use of defence exports to prevent diversion to third countries'. However, the DTI has still got no further than 'reviewing the options'.[17] As late as June 1999 the government's response to questions on end-monitoring of arms exports to Indonesia was no different from that of its Conservative predecessor.[18] In short, it is difficult to see this as a New Labour priority.[19]

Effective monitoring procedures are another natural corollary of a foreign policy that seeks to include an ethical dimension and seeks to ensure that arms exports adhere to published criteria. Without effective monitoring, how can informed decisions on future licences be made? In effect, the FCO has an obligation to provide it. Monitoring reports on end use should form one of the areas of oversight performed by the proposed parliamentary committee. Any identified use in internal repression or international aggression would disbar the recipient from receiving any further British arms and stop the flow of spare parts for those already exported. As outlined above, and notwithstanding recent government statements, the Secretary of State for Trade and Industry has complete discretion under the EG(C)O to do so. The real objection lies in the fact that such action is unlikely to be cost-free, in that it will invite reprisals against civil trade with Britain. Nevertheless, it remains a vital gap to plug. In the recent past, having no formal procedures for monitoring military equipment after delivery was politically convenient – for example, with regard to Jordan and Indonesia. Such applications of *Realpolitik* cannot be consistent with a foreign policy incorporating a genuinely ethical dimension, which must be based on consistency and transparency in application.

In practice, the principle of the inviolability of existing contracts has served to reward repressive or aggressive regimes. The government should end the pretence that this is a legal obligation, recognise that it is a principle born out of political convenience, and be prepared to cancel existing contracts if the circumstances demand it. Ideally, the government should work towards international harmonisation of end-use requirements to prevent individuals seeking to operate through those countries which are least demanding in such terms, as they do at present.

Multilateral co-operation

Work to strengthen multilateral co-operation as in the EU Code of Conduct and work with interested parties in the US Congress to investigate the viability of extending a similar code in the US.[20]

Brokerage

Other important loopholes, a number of which characterised claims about illegal exports of arms to Iran and Iraq in the 1980s, remain. For example, there is the issue of brokerage – the practice of UK companies organising the export of equipment from third countries, often to destinations they would be prohibited from supplying direct from the UK. A spate of allegations in the late 1990s concerning the role of UK companies in supplying arms to African countries have highlighted the persistence of this practice, for example the activities of the Isle of Man-registered company Mil-Tec (with a correspondence address in Hove, links with a travel agency in north London, and directors who operate from the Channel Island of Sark) with regard to Rwanda, and Sandline, which organised the transfer of arms from Bulgaria to Sierra Leone. With regard to Rwanda, in May 1994 the UN imposed an embargo on arms sales but both before and after Mil-Tec was delivering arms flown in from Israel and Albania (having sourced the arms in Bulgaria and the former Yugoslavia) via Goma in neighbouring Zaire, with Zairois end-user certificates.[21] Mil-Tec officials were never prosecuted, as the government had failed to extend the UN embargo to Crown dependencies such as the Channel Islands and Isle of Man, but at the same time the arms did not originate in or flow through the UK. The 1998 White Paper *Strategic Export Controls* proposed the introduction of controls on trafficking and brokering, but the difficulty of enforcing any such legislation mean it would require a high degree of multilateral commitment and co-operation.[22]

There is nothing new in the practice of brokerage in order to sidestep national embargoes. For example, in November 1966 the Minister of Power, Richard Marsh, wrote to Prime Minister Harold Wilson, voicing his concern about the activities of brokers in general, and of one – Major Robert Turp – in particular.[23] Wilson took up the issue, asking whether it would be possible to make it illegal for British citizens to sell weapons abroad without government authorisation. Both the Attorney General, Sir

Elwyn Jones, and the Foreign Office legal advisers agreed that it was
possible, without breach of international law, to make it an offence for
UK nationals to sell arms via third countries except under licence.[24] In
1999 the IDC recommended that the government should introduce a
register of arms brokers and press for the extension of the principle across
the EU.[25]

Transnational production

A related issue is that of licensed or transnational production through the
purchase of overseas subsidiaries, whereby a UK company can legitimately export equipment to a country against which the UK operates
restrictions or an embargo so long as the equipment is exported from a
third-country subsidiary. For long regarded as legitimate business practice, this process is now being subject to scrutiny in the wake of a number
of controversial cases. For example, in January 1998 Heckler & Koch, a
Nottingham-based subsidiary of BAe, was reported as having secured a
US$18 million contract for the licensed production of 200,000 infantry
rifles in Turkey by the state armaments manufacturer MKEK.
Subsequently, it was reported that MKEK would be exporting 500
Heckler & Koch machine guns to Indonesia. In another example, at the
beginning of 1999, a manager of Pains Wessex was filmed explaining how
the DTI and DESO were not concerned about the export of licensed
equipment to sensitive destinations: 'Just as long as we're not shipping in
the UK, they don't give a toss.'[26] The difficulties here are similar to those
faced in combating the brokering of arms by UK nationals through third
countries, and the remedy – working through multilateral bodies to
achieve international support – is the same.

Training

The bases on which military training and education are provided should
be reviewed. Training has long been regarded as a vital element in preserv-
ing Britain's good relations with various militaries across the world,
retaining influence in their procurement choices and providing a valued
complementary service alongside the sale of arms. This has largely taken
place in the UK and at the expense of the British taxpayer. As John Reid
explained:

> Military and related police assistance is provided in support of a range of
> foreign and defence policy aims. It can be an important factor in the devel-
> opment of the United Kingdom's relations with countries in all parts of the
> world, and can make a significant contribution to regional stability by
> promoting military effectiveness, which helps to deter aggression. This assis-
> tance is a key element of defence diplomacy. All requests for military

assistance are considered in the light of the Government's wider foreign policy.[27]

However, the Cook criteria do not address and thereby seek to apply any form of conditionality to this. While the FCO and MoD undoubtedly work to internal guidelines, these have never been made publicly available. The nearest they have come to being disclosed is John Reid's November 1997 written answer:

Requests for training are considered in the light of the Government's ethical foreign policy. Training would not be provided where we considered that it would risk contributing to human rights violations or aggression. Other criteria used to determine which requests for military training by overseas security forces should be granted include: the availability of resources to carry out the training; security considerations; and the defence and foreign policy benefits of providing the training. The defence policy benefits taken into account include in particular whether the provision of military assistance would: bring direct benefit to the United Kingdom by (for example by providing access to training areas); represent an investment to avoid later expense (for example by averting a conflict in an area where there would be a high likelihood of British forces being committed); help to build military interoperability with key potential partners; maintain existing close defence links; support defence sales.[28]

Commissions

Address the corrupting impact of the commission process, something which the New Labour government is no more willing to do than the previous Conservative administrations, under whose watch some of the most serious concern in this respect arose.[29]

Arms sales and the politics of delusion

As we have seen, exporting arms requires governments to reconcile two conflicting demands which go to the very core of their function: those concerning trade and security. Arms sales politics also require governments to choose between the functionally incompatible forces of principle and pragmatism, between ethics and the satisfaction of domestic constituencies. In these constituencies the benefits of arms sales are considered not in terms of levels of government subsidy or the facilitation of a global role, but on narrower sectoral and individual bases. Meanwhile, adherence to a vision of a global role has meant that, with few exceptions, Labour and Conservative governments have followed arms sales policies of remarkable similarity. While Labour governments entered office in 1964, 1974, and 1997 committed to restrictive policies towards specific states (South Africa, Chile and Indonesia respectively), their performance has fallen short and the armourers have continued to thrive. In practice, the varied benefits held to accrue from arms exports have secured them a primacy at the expense of human rights and associated lobbies and, on occasion, the security of the UK, its forces, and its allies. The entire UK administrative structure relating to arms exports offers an illustration of the way in which this primacy has been institutionalised, while the evidence of recent years shows that the benefits have been pursued at a cost. Increasingly, the sacred cow that arms sales produce economic benefits is being called into question, and cost–benefit analyses of such high-profile involvement in the international arms trade suggest that it is not in the national interest. Elite definitions of the national interest ignore such arguments.

Many of the key features in the evolution of UK arms sales can be found in the example of the sale of Lightning aircraft to Saudi Arabia. Initially, in the post-World War II period, arms sales were seen as a way of securing and extending influence abroad, and of generating much-needed foreign exchange earnings and securing jobs at home. At the time, the only real competitor was the US and, in practice, a 'gentlemen's agreement' – extended to France for a while under the NEACC – meant that competition could be resolved amicably. It was politically useful for the US to forgo certain sales in favour of the UK, safe in the knowledge that the political aim underpinning them – of securing pro-Western hegemony in arenas of Cold War competition and confrontation – would still be realised. At times the US political system made sales impossible and the UK was available to act as a willing surrogate. An active, co-operative arms sales policy was one of the factors that made Britain a junior partner in maintaining global order (Robin to the US Batman) and helped maintain influence within a framework of gradual decline. Hence sales were beneficial at both the political and the economic levels and required minimal governmental involvement.

However, as the arms market became increasingly competitive in the 1960s, with a growing number of suppliers chasing more valuable markets, so companies began to demand greater effort on the part of the government in support of their efforts. BAC was one of the early proponents of the view that the UK government was deficient here by comparison with the French and US governments. Such was also the broad conclusion of both the Plowden Committee and the Stokes Report. Hence in 1966 Denis Healey, in order that Britain could retain its 'rightful share' of the arms market, announced the appointment of a head of defence sales – initially Ray Brown. The emergence of the DSO and then DESO followed. Government became more heavily involved in the promotional work required to secure export orders. At the same time, as credit became the weapon with which arms sales contests were fought, the ECGD was obliged to offer increasingly flexible terms, heightening the risk of default. Rigorous marketing, often in open competition with the French and in qualified co-operation with the US, became the order of the day. So too did the competitive payment of commissions (or 'bribes' as they were more freely referred to when UK nationals succumbed to the culture of corruption it engendered). At the same time, it is possible to put a date on the time when arms sales co-operation with the US ended, and with it the working assumption of the 'special relationship'. It was the day in January 1968 when Lyndon Johnson received Harold Wilson's reply to his appeal not to scrap the F-111 deal and pull out of the Gulf, leaving the US to assume its self-appointed responsibility for global order alone.

By the 1980s, credit terms had given way to alternative forms of payment – counter-trade – detracting further from the face value of a contract, as did the trend towards investment through offset agreements. Today, 100 per cent offset obligations are not unheard of. For example, both the 1993 and the 1996 Hawk deals with Indonesia incurred a 100 per cent offset obligation.[30] The rise in these trends coincided with increased customer preference for direct government-to-government deal-ings, drawing government departments and DESO more heavily still into such deals. Until the 1960s arms sales diplomacy had not been carried out at even junior ministerial level (John Stonehouse blazed a trail here), but by the 1980s the Prime Minister was the leading, and indispensable, arms salesman.

The Major government paid some of the political price of Mrs Thatcher's arms sales successes in the 1980s. The Scott inquiry, Pergau Dam investigation, issues surrounding Al Yamamah, and periodic ques-tioning of the arming of Indonesia, all contributed to the 'sleaze factor' which afflicted the government – as, latterly, did the brazen actions of Jonathan Aitken. So prevalent was the atmosphere of sleaze that by March 1994, an opinion poll showed that 29 per cent of respondents thought that the government 'is corrupt and/or abuses its power'.[31]

By the end of 1992, in the aftermath of the 'supergun' imbroglio, the trial of three executives of the machine tool manufacturer Matrix Churchill, charged with illegally exporting arms-making technology to Iraq, had collapsed. In the wake of the failure of the government's claim of public interest immunity in the case, a flood of documents were released which revealed how, from the mid-1980s, the Thatcher govern-ment had connived at breaches of its own guidelines, notionally intended to stem the flow of arms and related technology to warring Iran and Iraq. The trial exposed how elements of the government knew full well what Matrix Churchill was exporting, where it was going to and the likely mili-tary end use but allowed an ill-advised prosecution to go ahead anyway. The outcry over this revelation was such that the Major government was obliged to move quickly in order to limit the damage. Its response was to establish the Scott inquiry.

The inquiry's public hearings shed further unwelcome light on the role of the government in the international arms trade. It took Scott over three years to produce a 2,000 page report which was critical of the way in which the Matrix Churchill and similar prosecutions had been prepared and conducted, critical of the manner in which the regulatory machinery in Whitehall had allowed machine tools to be exported to Iraq when it was effectively known that they were going to be used to make weapons, and critical of the way in which the government virtually turned a blind eye when British arms were passed on to Iraq by neighbouring states like Jordan and Saudi Arabia. Early in the Thatcher era, Britain fought a war in the South Atlantic where it was faced by arms made in the UK. At the end of the Thatcher era, as a consequence of the government's actions, British forces once again faced that prospect.

As a result of all this, the bases of the 1980s successes came to be increasingly called into question, as is evidenced not just by the Scott inquiry, but also by the two TISC investigations into arms to Iraq and Iran and the FAC investigation into the Pergau Dam arms link, all of which were critical of the government's conduct of this aspect of foreign policy. To an extent, the successful but controversial approach to arms sales adopted during the Thatcher years was possible only because of the unusually high level of secrecy that attaches to questions surrounding British arms and which is justified in terms of commercial confidentiality and national security – a convenient cloak that in practice concealed the lengths governments were prepared to go to in order to secure arms contracts.

However, even under the Thatcher governments, important changes in the UK arms export industry were taking place. Given the continuing internationalisation of production, 'batting for Britain' increasingly came to involve batting for collaborative projects from which Britain would take only a share of the export revenue. By the time of Mrs Thatcher's exit the UK was involved in collaborative military projects with 10 states, and was in the process of developing links with a further three.[32] Increasingly, securing large orders from the developing world – especially in South East Asia – required some commitment to licensed or co-production, commitment which obviously eats into future market potential and hastens the arrival of new competitors. Furthermore, by the end of the decade, the circumstances that had made the 1980s such a propitious time for the Thatcher arms export drive had begun to change.

After a heightening of tension in the late 1970s and early 1980s, the Cold War had ended by 1990. The aura of reliability surrounding British arms was somewhat dented by the removal of Mrs Thatcher and the second cooling of the 'special relationship'. One source close to the Saudi royal family went so far as to argue that 'the Saudis will buy where the political strength is. Saudi interest in buying British died with Mrs Thatcher's resignation.'[33] The Iraqi invasion of Kuwait served as a cautionary tale and the post-Gulf War configuration of the Middle East opened the way to increased US penetration of Britain's most important regional market. The UN Register of Conventional Arms raised the spectre of a degree of transparency in the market, while a series of parliamentary investigations (although hardly far-reaching) suggested increased legislature interest and renewed determination to police excesses – a trend boosted by the revelations arising from the Scott inquiry. With the exception of South East Asia, arms markets were becoming increasingly saturated, while Middle Eastern kingdoms could neither afford, nor in many cases operate, all the weapons they had ordered.

More important, for them the lesson of 1990 and 1991 was that their security could best be guaranteed by the US. Hence they felt unable to resist the more aggressive US marketing effort, as it sought additional markets to compensate for the post-Cold War fall in domestic demand, sometimes at the expense of British arms. Even though the UK will continue to play a significant role in supplying the needs of Gulf security, it will not do so in Al Yamamah proportions. Finally, in the post-Cold War era it became increasingly hard to rationalise the turning of a blind eye to human rights abuses by purchasers of arms, while heightened emphasis on corruption or 'sleaze' in the post-Cold War era ensured that it would be difficult to re-employ some of the more controversial methods previously involved in securing arms deals. All of which suggests that while Mrs Thatcher batted energetically for the British arms industry in the 1980s, and John Major enjoyed some success in imitating her approach, the subsequent resurgence in British arms exports, notwithstanding the Blair government's enthusiastic support, is unlikely to continue beyond the immediate term.

Throughout this period, as government involvement in arms sales became ever greater – taking a qualitative leap from the 1980s, when the aid budget was enthusiastically prostituted in pursuit of arms sales – and so the costs of securing arms deals rose, the profitability of arms exports should have been called into question. It was not, for two reasons. Firstly, successive British governments sought to play a global role, despite the country's reduced domestic circumstances. Arms sales offered a visible global role, maintained a broad network of military contacts and, it was assumed, bestowed influence and with it some leverage. Arms exports also contributed to the maintenance of the defence industrial base that made such a global military role possible in the first place. In short, arms sales helped realise a view of Britain's rightful place in the world that successive leaders, with few possible exceptions (Edward Heath would be one), have held.

Secondly, the enlarged arms sales bureaucracy (stretching across a number of government departments – DTI, MoD, DESO, Cabinet Office, even the FCO) and the leading arms companies and their employees (voters) – the last significant surviving expression of British manufacturing industry – combined to form a dominant interest group, readily deploying the old arguments regarding the economic benefits of arms exporting, even when the extensive government investment required to sustain such a large market share had undermined them. Government, however, has been all too willing to accept these arguments, because, in practice, the continued subsidising of the arms trade facilitates the continuation of the global role it has been unwilling to relinquish. The logic of this conjunction is that, given Britain's clear desire to play a leading role in NATO and in EU military groupings in the future, and given the trends in the arms market which make Britain's prospects rather less rosy than the upbeat assessment which DESO in 1999 offered the Defence Select Committee suggests[34] (the new configuration of post-Gulf War Middle Eastern politics and resultant US domination of the market, the impact of the financial crisis in South East Asia, the medium-term impact of the emergence of new suppliers, the implications of the consolidation of the US defence industry, etc.), ever greater governmental support will be required to maintain a diminishing share of the market. Hence the costs of Britain's continued involvement in the arms trade are likely to increase just as the performance declines from its 1990s peak.

The power of this conjunction was graphically illustrated by the ignominious fate of Robin Cook's plan to control arms sales more rigorously through the introduction of an 'ethical dimension' to British foreign policy. This has failed. Instead, British arms sales policy has contributed to human rights abuses, repression and suffering abroad, and has meant that between 1982 and 1991 British forces fought wars in which they were twice faced with an adversary the UK had helped arm. It has also required the faithful purchase of weapons on grounds other than technical merit because, as is well known, the 'weaker the domestic market becomes, especially through bringing into service imported systems, the less attractive the rejected British systems will be'.[35] Its essentially corrupt nature has infected the British system, as is evidenced by cases ranging from Frank Nurdin and Gordon Foxley to the allegations against Jonathan Aitken. It is a trade which has been antithetical to open government, and over which Parliament has been denied any meaningful say, so as to avoid replicating conditions in the US, where transparency led to criticism in Congress which cost the arms industry dear, and the beneficiary was the UK. It has also been corrosive of the country's political values, as evidenced in the Conservative government's response to the case of Mohammed al-Mas'ari.

There is also the extent to which the UK's record has created something of a delusion concerning just what, at the end of the twentieth century, represents the country's 'rightful' share of the market. As this study has shown, in reality, for all this involvement, for all the DSO/DESO's efforts, British arms have not always been sold simply on the strength of their quality – 'the excellence of the British arms industry', as John Major put it. Flexibility over methods of payment, the embrace of counter-trade and barter deals, the payment of excessive commission, constructive dispersal of the aid budget in support of arms, and so on, have all been important. But, as suggested in a number of the preceding studies, so too, in key deals, has something over which the British government has had no control – namely, the absence of US competition, either through US refusal to supply, or willingness to supply only 'with strings'. This was most significantly the case with regard to Al Yamamah, of course, but was also true of the 1996 Hawk deal with Indonesia, secured in the context of US denial of the F-16, and the mid-1980s arms package for which Jordan has been unable to pay. As far back as the mid-1960s, Britain won its pathbreaking contract to supply Lightning aircraft to Saudi Arabia only because US Defense Secretary Robert McNamara effectively prevented US companies – the Saudis' preferred suppliers – from meeting any requests for aircraft. Partly so that it could afford the F-111 aircraft and hence make a full contribution to Western security, the US was willing to stand aside in other markets to secure arms sales for the UK. To take another example, the 1993 sale of six second-hand Type 21 frigates to the Pakistani navy in a deal worth around £8.5 million occurred only because Pakistan needed to replace the eight leased US frigates which were recalled following Washington's imposition of a ban on economic and military aid to Pakistan over its attempts to develop nuclear weapons.[36] In connection with this, in July 1994, Pakistan went on to purchase three second-hand Lynx helicopters from Britain, to be deployed on three of the frigates.

In the Gulf, since 1991, other 'victories' have involved securing subsidiary sections of major military restructuring contracts while the US now dominates the market. In their similar ways, the examples of Kuwait and the UAE illustrate the future course of arms purchases in the region and suggest that the British share of the market will decline, and that Britain will see its brief pre-eminence as supplier to Saudi Arabia steadily eroded.

A further delusion concerns the extent to which arms bring influence over purchasing states. In practice, the record presented here shows that arms sales relations are a constraining factor, because the supplier's reaction to events involving a purchaser is taken as a gauge of the supplier's reliability – that most valued quality from the point of view of the purchaser. Logically, the greater a supplier's stake in a particular arms sales relationship the greater the risk that attaches to adverse reaction, and hence the less likely it is to occur. Rather than bringing influence, arms sales have made Britain dependent apologists for insecure governments.

It is also worth highlighting the contradiction in attitudes to arms sales and the arms business, touched on by William Waldegrave in his evidence to the Scott inquiry. As he put it: 'There is in this country a certain ambivalence ... People want the jobs but they do not always want to think about them. Whenever Mrs Thatcher or Mr Major comes back, having batted for Britain and won a great deal, everyone says "Hooray!" They are heroes on the front page.'[37] But this is a contradiction which extends beyond public distaste to the very politicians who secure the deals and trumpet them while in office. Where are the accounts of their arms sales triumphs in the memoirs of the likes of Roy Jenkins, Denis Healey, James Callaghan, David Owen, Margaret Thatcher or John Major? This is no more than a reflection of the fact that the arms trade is perceived as being a dirty and corrupt business, and that Britain's most enthusiastic clients are corrupt and/or undemocratic, often with problematic human rights records – which Britain has been constrained from speaking out against or acting over because of its stake in the arms sales relationship.

Hence the notion that British arms sales over the past 30 years or so have represented a success story is something of a delusion. Arms sales were meant to be a means of securing Britain's otherwise declining influence, but all too often they have served to diminish its authority internationally and corrode values at home. As Foreign Office Minister Tony Lloyd told Conservative MP Gerald Howarth during an early exchange on New Labour's arms sales policy:

> The Government might find it easier to take lectures from Conservative Members ... if they had not been part of a Government with an incredibly sleazy record on arms sales. He well recalls the way that that Government prostituted the aid budget to obtain arms sales at the time of the Pergau dam scandal, and how that Government wriggled and tried to hide the truth about arms sales to Iraq. They were prepared not only to put at risk the lives of British people in the services but were so economically incompetent that we are still owed money by the Iraqis for those deals. If he wants to talk about arms sales, he should start by apologising to the House for his role in that shameful Government ... his party in government ran defence sales in such a way that they brought great shame to Britain. They made Britain's name abroad one of disrepute.[38]

Unfortunately, the position remains largely the same today.

Notes

1 A point made by Alan Clark. Interview, London, 3 February 1999.
2 FAC, *Foreign Policy and Human Rights*, Report, para. 149.
3 FAC, *Foreign Affairs and Human Rights*, Minutes of Evidence, 6 January 1998, para. 212.
4 DTI, 'Strategic Export Controls', July 1998, para. 2.1.7.

5 Scott Inquiry, Day 54, 12 January 1994. Evidence of Lord Howe, p. 253.

6 Miller and Phythian, 'Secrecy, Accountability and British Arms Exports: Issues for the post-Scott Era', p. 122.

7 TISC, *Strategic Export Controls*, Memorandum submitted by the DMA.

8 TISC, *Strategic Export Controls*, Second Report, Session 1998–99, para. 42.

9 TISC, *Strategic Export Controls*, Minutes of Evidence 10 November 1998, para. 9.

10 TISC, *Strategic Export Controls*, Appendix 5: Memorandum submitted by Tapol: Comments on the White Paper on Strategic Export Controls, para. 20.

11 Sissela Bok, *Secrets: On the Ethics of Concealment and Revelation* (Oxford, Oxford University Press, 1982). Quote from 1986 paperback edition, p. 67.

12 Albert Speer, *Inside the Third Reich*, cited in Bok, *Secrets*, p. 67.

13 TISC, Report, para. 54.

14 Scott Inquiry: Day 50, Evidence of Alan Clark, p. 25. He added that: 'I would never attach any significance to assurances from customers such as these, or indeed practically anyone. They are not worth the paper they are written on.' *Ibid.*, p. 31.

15 Hansard, 10 July 1997, col. 603w.

16 *Ibid.*, 6 April 1998, col. 7.

17 DTI, 'Strategic Export Controls', July 1998, para. 5.2.1.

18 'No formal mechanisms exist at present for systematically monitoring the use of British defence equipment once it has been exported. We have made clear to the Indonesian authorities that British-supplied equipment should not be used against civilians to prevent the exercise of their rights of free expression, assembly and association, or in violation of other international human rights standards.' Hansard, 8 June 1999, col. 236w.

19 In August 1999, the IDC recommended the establishment of an EU-level body to monitor arms transfers, commenting that: 'It is vital that export licences be granted or refused on the basis of adequate intelligence. If there is a reasonable risk of diversion then the export licence should be refused.' IDC, 'Conflict Prevention and Post-conflict Reconstruction', para. 162.

20 See the memorandum submitted by Senator John Kerry to the FAC inquiry into *Foreign Policy and Human Rights*, Appendix 18.

21 The story was broken in *The Times*, 18 November 1996.

22 See, TISC, *Strategic Export Controls*, Second Report, Session 1998-99, para. 35. Amnesty International and other NGOs have suggested a register of arms brokers as a first step.

23 PRO: DEFE 13/546, Memorandum, Richard Marsh to Harold Wilson, 16 November 1966.

24 PRO: DEFE 13/546, Sir Elwyn Jones to Harold Wilson, 1 February 1967.

25 IDC, 'Conflict Prevention and Post-conflict Reconstruction', para. 159.

26 Channel 4, *Mark Thomas Comedy Product*, 20 January 1999.

27 Hansard, 27 February 1998, col. 374.

28 *Ibid.*, 12 November 1997. Although Robin Cook was later to disavow the term 'ethical foreign policy', here is an example of it being used by the government in answering parliamentary questions.

29 See IDC, 'Conflict Prevention', and David Pallister, 'The Dirty Game', *Guardian*, 6 August 1999.

30 Hansard, 27 October 1997, col. 663w.

31 ICM/*Guardian* poll, *Guardian*, 17 March 1994.

32 *Statement on the Defence Estimates 1990* (London, HMSO, 1990), vol. I, p. 35. The 10 were: Australia, Belgium, Canada, Denmark, France, (West) Germany, Italy, the Netherlands, Norway and the United States. The three were: Greece, Spain and Turkey.

33 *Guardian*, 19 October 1992.

34 See the memoranda by DESO and Minutes of Evidence in Defence Select Committee, *The Appointment of the New Head of Defence Export Services*, Second Report, Session 1998–99.
35 H. St J. B. Armitage, CBE, 'Trends in the Conventional Arms Market: The Middle East', *RUSI Journal*, February 1994, p. 59.
36 *Guardian*, 28 July 1993.
37 *Ibid.*, 6 January 1996.
38 See Hansard, 8 July 1997, cols 763–5.

Appendix 1
Robin Cook's 28 July 1997 statement
on arms export criteria

The Government are committed to the maintenance of a strong defence industry which is a strategic part of our industrial base as well as of our defence effort. Defence exports can also contribute to international stability by strengthening bilateral and collective defence relationships in accordance with the right of self-defence recognised by the UN charter, but arms transfers must be managed responsibly, in particular so as to avoid their use for internal repression and international aggression.

It will be important to avoid a situation in which our policy of seeking to prevent certain regimes from acquiring certain equipment is undermined by foreign competitors supplying them. We will therefore work for the introduction of a European code of conduct, setting high common standards to govern arms exports from all EU member states.

Licences to export strategic goods are issued by the President of the Board of Trade and the export control organisation of the Department of Trade and Industry is the licensing authority. All relevant individual licence applications are circulated by the DTI to other Government Departments with an interest, as determined by it in line with its policy responsibilities. These include the Foreign and Commonwealth Office, the Ministry of Defence and the Department for International Development.

The present Government were not responsible for the decisions on export licences made by the previous Administration. We do not, however, consider that it would be realistic or practical to revoke licences that were valid and in force at the time of our election.

The criteria set out below will be used when considering all future individual applications for licences to export goods entered in part III of schedule 1 to the Export of Goods (Control) Order 1994 and existing licence applications on which a decision has not yet been made. The criteria will also be applied when considering advance approvals for promotion prior to formal application for an export licence and licence applications for the export of dual-use goods when there are grounds for believing that the end user of such goods will be the armed forces or the internal security forces of the recipient country.

The criteria will constitute broad guidance. They will not be applied mechanistically and judgement will always be required. Individual applications will be considered case by case.

Criteria used in considering conventional arms export licence applications

1. An export licence will not be issued if the arguments for doing so are outweighed by the need to comply with the UK's international obligations and commitments, or by concern that the goods might be used for internal repression or international aggression, or by the risks to regional stability, or other considerations as described in these criteria.

The United Kingdom's international obligations

2. An export licence should be refused if approval would be inconsistent with:
   (a) the UK's international obligations and commitments to enforce United Nations Organisation for Security and Co-operation in Europe and European Union arms embargoes, together with any national embargoes or other commitments regarding the application of strategic export controls;
   (b) the UK's international obligations under the nuclear non-proliferation treaty, the biological weapons convention and the chemical weapons convention;
   (c) the UK's commitments to the international export control regimes—the Australia group, the missile technology control regime, the nuclear suppliers' group and the Wassenaar arrangement;
   (d) the EU common criteria for arms exports, the guidelines for conventional arms transfers agreed by the permanent five members of the UN Security Council, and the OSCE principles governing conventional arms transfers;
   (e) the UK's commitment not to export all forms of anti-personnel land mines and their components.

The United Kingdom's national interests

3. Full weight should be given to the UK's national interests when considering applications for licences, including:
   (a) the potential effect on the UK's defence and security interests and those of allies and EU partners;
   (b) the potential effect on the UK's economic, financial and commercial interests, including our long-term interests in having stable, democratic trading partners;
   (c) the potential effect on the UK's relations with the recipient country;
   (d) the potential effect on any collaborative defence production or procurement project with allies or EU partners;
   (e) the protection of the UK's essential strategic industrial base.

Human rights and internal repression

4. The Government:
   (a) will take into account respect for human rights and fundamental freedoms in the recipient country;
   (b) will not issue an export licence if there is a clearly identifiable risk that the proposed export might be used for internal repression.

5. For these purposes equipment which might be used for internal repression will include:
   (a) Equipment where there is clear evidence of the recent use of similar equipment for internal repression by the proposed end user, or where there is reason to believe that the equipment will be diverted from its stated end use or end user and used for internal repression;

(b) Equipment which has obvious application for internal repression, in cases where the recipient country has a significant and continuing record of such repression, unless the end use of the equipment is judged to be legitimate, such as protection of members of security forces from violence.

6. The nature of the equipment proposed for export will also be carefully considered. Certain goods have more obvious potential for use in internal repression that others, such as armoured personnel carriers specifically designed for internal security. In other cases, there may be *prima facie* reasons for believing that a particular equipment might be used in such roles in certain circumstances. Any proposed export which is to be used by the recipient country for internal security purposes should be considered particularly carefully.

7. Internal repression includes extra judicial killings, arbitrary arrest, torture, suppression or major violation of human rights and fundamental freedoms. In some cases, the use of force by a Government within its own borders does not constitute internal repression. The use of such force by Governments is legitimate in some cases, for example to preserve law and order against terrorists or other criminals. However, force may be used only in accordance with international human rights standards.

International aggression

8. The Government will not issue an export licence if there is a clearly identifiable risk that the intended recipient would use the proposed export aggressively against another country, or to assert by force a territorial claim. However, a purely theoretical possibility that the items concerned might be used in the future against another state will not of itself lead to a licence being refused.

9. When considering the risk that the country for which arms are destined might use them for international aggression, the Government will take into account:

(a) the existence or likelihood of armed conflict between the recipient and another country;

(b) a claim against the territory of a neighbouring country which the recipient has in the past tried or threatened to pursue by means of force;

(c) whether the equipment wold be likely to be used other than for the legitimate national security and defence of the recipient.

Regional stability

10. The need not to affect adversely regional stability in any significant way will also be considered. The balance of forces between neighbouring states, their relative expenditure on defence, and the need not to introduce into the region new capabilities which would be likely to lead to increased tension, will all be taken into account.

Other criteria

11. In assessing the impact of the proposed export on the importing country and the risk that exported goods might be diverted to an undesirable end user, the following will be considered:

(a) the legitimate defence and domestic security interests of the recipient country, including any involvement in UN or other peacekeeping activity;

(b) the technical capability of the recipient country to use the equipment;

(c) whether the purchase would seriously undermine the economy of the recipient country, taking into account its public finances, balance of

payments, external debt, economic and social development and any
International Monetary Fund/World Bank-sponsored economic reform
programme;

(d) the risk of the arms being re-exported or diverted to an undesirable end
user, including terrorist organisations—anti-terrorist equipment would
need particularly careful consideration in this context.

12. The following factors will also be taken into account:

(a) the risk of use of the goods concerned against UK forces;

(b) the need to protect UK military classified information and capabilities;

(c) the potential for the equipment to be a force multiplier in the region;

(d) the risk of reverse engineering or technology transfer.

13. In the application of all the above criteria, account should also be taken of,
for example, reporting from diplomatic posts, relevant reports by international
bodies, intelligence, and information from open sources and non-governmental
organisations.

Reporting to Parliament

To ensure full transparency and accountability to Parliament, the Government
will report annually on the state of strategic export controls and their application,
thereby providing for parliamentary consideration of the application of the criteria. The Government will also inform Parliament of any changes to the criteria.

Source Hansard, 28.7.97., cols 26–29w.

Appendix 2
The European Code of Conduct
on arms sales

The code of conduct agreed by EU foreign ministers lays down eight criteria that member states should observe when deciding whether to grant export licences.

Criterion One

Respect for the international commitments of EU member states, in particular the sanctions decreed by the UN Security Council and those decreed by the Community, agreements on non-proliferation and other subjects, as well as other international obligations

An export licence should be refused if approval would be inconsistent with:
a the international obligations of member states and their commitments to enforce UN, OSCE and EU arms embargoes;
b the international obligations of member states under the Nuclear Non-Proliferation Treaty, the Biological and Toxin Weapons Convention and the Chemical Weapons Convention;
c their commitments in the frameworks of the Australia Group, the Missile Technology Control Regime, the Nuclear Suppliers Group and the Wassenaar Arrangement;
d their commitment not to export any form of anti-personnel landmine.

Criterion Two

The respect of human rights in the country of final destination

Having assessed the recipient country's attitude towards relevant principles established by international human rights instruments, Member States will:
a not issue an export licence if there is a clear risk that the proposed export might be used for internal repression;
b exercise special caution and vigilance in issuing licences, on a case-by-case basis and taking account of the nature of the equipment, to countries where serious violations of human rights have been established by the competent bodies of the UN, the Council of Europe or by the EU.

For these purposes, equipment which might be used for internal repression will include, inter alia, equipment where there is evidence of the use of this or similar equipment for internal repression by the proposed end-user, or where there is reason to believe that the equipment will be diverted from its stated end-use or end-user and used for internal repression. In line with operative paragraph 1 of this Code, the nature of the equipment will be considered carefully, particularly if it is intended for internal security purposes. Internal repression includes, inter alia, torture and other cruel, inhuman and degrading treatment or punishment, summary or arbitrary executions, disappearances, arbitrary detentions and other major violations of human rights and fundamental freedoms as set out in relevant international human rights instruments, including the Universal Declaration on Human Rights and the International Covenant on Civil and Political Rights.

Criterion Three

The internal situation in the country of final destination, as a function of the existence of tensions or armed conflicts

Member States will not allow exports which would provoke or prolong armed conflicts or aggravate existing tensions or conflicts in the country of final destination.

Criterion Four

Preservation of regional peace, security and stability

Member States will not issue an export licence if there is a clear risk that the intended recipient would use the proposed export aggressively against another country or to assert by force a territorial claim.

When considering these risks, EU Member States will take into account inter alia:

a   the existence or likelihood of armed conflict between the recipient and another country;
b   a claim against the territory of a neighbouring country which the recipient has in the past tried or threatened to pursue by means of force;
c   whether the equipment would be likely to be used other than for the legitimate national security and defence of the recipient;
d   the need not to affect adversely regional stability in any significant way.

Criterion Five

The national security of the member states and of territories whose external relations are the responsibility of a Member State, as well as that of friendly and allied countries

Member States will take into account:

a   the potential effect of the proposed export on their defence and security interests and those of friends, allies and other member states, while recognising that this factor cannot affect consideration of the criteria on respect of human rights and on regional peace, security and stability;

b the risk of use of the goods concerned against their forces or those of friends, allies or other member states;

c the risk of reverse engineering or unintended technology transfer.

Criterion Six

The behaviour of the buyer country with regard to the international community, as regards in particular to its attitude to terrorism, the nature of its alliances and respect for international law

Member States will take into account inter alia the record of the buyer country with regard to:

a its support or encouragement of terrorism and international organised crime;

b its compliance with its international commitments, in particular on the non-use of force, including under international humanitarian law applicable to international and non-international conflicts;

c its commitment to non-proliferation and other areas of arms control and disarmament, in particular the signature, ratification and implementation of relevant arms control and disarmament conventions referred to in sub-paragraph b) of Criterion One.

Criterion Seven

The existence of a risk that the equipment will be diverted within the buyer country or re-exported under undesirable conditions

In assessing the impact of the proposed export on the importing country and the risk that exported goods might be diverted to an undesirable end-user, the following will be considered:

a the legitimate defence and domestic security interests of the recipient country, including any involvement in UN or other peace-keeping activity;

b the technical capability of the recipient country to use the equipment;

c the capability of the recipient country to exert effective export controls;

d the risk of the arms being re-exported or diverted to terrorist organisations (anti-terrorist equipment would need particularly careful consideration in this context).

Criterion Eight

The compatibility of the arms exports with the technical and economic capacity of the recipient country, taking into account the desirability that states should achieve their legitimate needs of security and defence with the least diversion for armaments of human and economic resources

Member States will take into account, in the light of information from relevant sources such as UNDP, World Bank, IMF and OECD reports, whether the proposed export would seriously hamper the sustainable development of the recipient country. They will consider in this context the recipient country's relative levels of military and social expenditure, taking into account also any EU or bilateral aid.

Operative provisions

1 Each EU Member State will assess export licence applications for military equipment made to it on a case-by-case basis against the provisions of the Code of Conduct.

2 This Code will not infringe on the right of Member States to operate more restrictive national policies.

3 EU Member States will circulate through diplomatic channels details of licences refused in accordance with the Code of Conduct for military equipment together with an explanation of why the licence has been refused. The details to be notified are set out in the form of a draft pro-forma at Annex A. Before any Member State grants a licence which has been denied by another Member State or States for an essentially identical transaction within the last three years, it will first consult the Member State or States which issued the denial(s). If following consultations, the Member State nevertheless decides to grant a licence, it will notify the Member State or States issuing the denial(s), giving a detailed explanation of its reasoning.

   The decision to transfer or deny the transfer of any item of military equipment will remain at the national discretion of each Member State. A denial of a licence is understood to take place when the member state has refused to authorise the actual sale or physical export of the item of military equipment concerned, where a sale would otherwise have come about, or the conclusion of the relevant contract. For these purposes, a notifiable denial may, in accordance with national procedures, include denial of permission to start negotiations or a negative response to a formal initial enquiry about a specific order.

4 EU Member States will keep such denials and consultations confidential and not to use them for commercial advantage.

5 EU Member States will work for the early adoption of a common list of military equipment covered by the Code, based on similar national and international lists. Until then, the Code will operate on the basis of national control lists incorporating where appropriate elements from relevant international lists.

6 The criteria in this Code and the consultation procedure provided for by paragraph 2 of the operative provisions will also apply to dual-use goods as specified in Annex 1 of Council Decision 94/942/CFSP as amended, where there are grounds for believing that the end-user of such goods will be the armed forces or internal security forces or similar entities in the recipient country.

7 In order to maximise the efficiency of this Code, EU Member States will work within the framework of the CFSP to reinforce their cooperation and to promote their convergence in the field of conventional arms exports.

8 Each EU Member State will circulate to other EU Partners in confidence an annual report on its defence exports and on its implementation of the Code. These reports will be discussed at an annual meeting held within the framework of the CFSP. The meeting will also review the operation of the Code, identify any improvements which need to be made and submit to the Council a consolidated report, based on contributions from Member States.

9 EU Member States will, as appropriate, assess jointly through the CFSP framework the situation of potential or actual recipients of arms exports from EU Member States, in the light of the principles and criteria of the Code of Conduct.

10 It is recognised that Member States, where appropriate, may also take into account the effect of proposed exports on their economic, social, commercial and industrial interests, but that these factors will not affect the application of the above criteria.

11 EU Member States will use their best endeavours to encourage other arms exporting states to subscribe to the principles of this Code of Conduct.

12 This Code of Conduct and the operative provisions will replace any previous elaboration of the 1991 and 1992 Common Criteria.

As adopted on 8–9 June 1998. Source: *http://projects.sipri.se/expcon/eucode.htm*

Index

Note: page numbers in **bold** refer to main entries.